The Sexual Self

The Sexual Self

The Construction of Sexual Scripts

Michael Kimmel, Editor

VANDERBILT UNIVERSITY PRESS | NASHVILLE

11 10 09 08 07   1 2 3 4 5

This book is printed on acid-free paper
made from 50% post consumer recycled paper.
Manufactured in the United States of America
Designed by Wendy McAnally

Library of Congress Cataloging-in-Publication Data

The sexual self : the construction of sexual scripts /
Michael Kimmel, editor.
p. cm.
Includes bibliographical references.
ISBN 978-0-8265-1558-2 (cloth : alk. paper)
ISBN 978-0-8265-1559-9 (pbk. : alk. paper)
1. Gagnon, John H. 2. Sex—Social aspects. 3. Sex (Psychology)
4. Communication in sex. 5. Identity (Psychology) 6. Sex role.
7. Sexology. I. Kimmel, Michael S.
HQ21.S4738 2007
306.01—dc22
        2006038359

Contents

Part III: Sexual Behavior

Part IV: Sexual Politics

Michael Kimmel

John Gagnon and the Sexual Self

I

In his breakthrough book *The Structure of Scientific Revolutions*, the physicist and philosopher of science Thomas Kuhn described the opening stages of the process by which a scientific paradigm—by which he meant the entire edifice of assumptions, observations, and instruments that ground all empirical research—begins to shift. The first rumblings of such a shift usually come from some marginal outsiders—the ones usually too young or too innocent to have been corrupted or seduced by the trappings of glory that accompany centrality in the social community that supports the current paradigm. They are usually ignored or condemned by the scientific authorities of the time—largely because those authorities have staked their entire careers on building and sustaining the paradigm in the first place. Some visionaries slink off and some are wrong, but some "stay the course" (some are wrong anyway), and a few attract an audience and are believed right.

The trouble with the paradigm and its supporters is that these dissident scientists begin to notice what Kuhn felicitously calls "anomalous results." They see that these anomalous results just don't fit within the paradigm; indeed, these findings can only be explained by discarding the reigning paradigm and replacing it with a new one.

I have often thought of John Gagnon in those terms. He had been brought to the Kinsey Institute to work on its ongoing study of sex offenders. Trained by Kinsey collaborators Paul Gebhard and Wardell Pomeroy, he co-authored the fourth volume of the great Kinsey studies of sexual behavior. During his six years at the Institute, however, Gagnon grew less and less comfortable with Kinsey's model of understanding sexual behavior as just another type of mammalian behavior—nothing more and nothing less.

In 1965, when his former graduate school colleague William Simon came to the

Institute, Gagnon's little remaining comfort with Kinsey's ideas about sexuality dissipated. Gagnon and Simon kept bumping up against empirical findings that just didn't fit in Kinsey's understanding of sexual behavior as the simple aggregation and categorization of the number of orgasms one achieved through any of a variety of possible methods. Even though the Kinsey data were nearly all organized by social and cultural factors, it remained at its base too biologically driven. The old explanations were ultimately too behaviorist—too rooted in a biological paradigm. Sex seemed so much more than that—and also, ironically, so much less.

Finally, unable to reconcile their emergent view of sexuality as a social phenomenon with Kinsey's model, Gagnon and Simon began to break away from it. In the end, their vision of social constructionism supplanted Kinsey's crude behaviorism, turned Kinsey on his head and their model became the dominant paradigm of social scientific inquiries into human sexuality.

When I say that sex was so much more than Kinsey understood, I mean that Kinsey failed to see that sexual behavior is fundamentally social. I've often thought that his books are really doubly mistitled: they were hardly about "human males" or "human females"—that is, the universal expression of mammalian activities—but rather about the specific activities of a specific group of gendered people in a specific location. The volumes should have been called *Sexual Behavior Among American Men* and *Sexual Behavior Among American Women*. And, among those American men and women, the purpose, meaning, and experience of sex varied widely. To be sure, for many of us, it is experienced some of the time as scratching that biological itch. For many of us, it's a surprisingly pleasurable method to reproduce. But sex is also about homosocial competition among and between men or women, cross-gender conquest, self-validation, status anxiety, and peer expectations. It is also the expression of something deeper and emotional—perhaps even transcendent and spiritual. Human sexual behavior cannot be so easily mapped like that of other animals. Not all orgasms are created equal; the pleasures of domestic sex within a long-term monogamous relationship are fundamentally different from the breath-catching thrill of lust. Stripping the biological facts from their social moorings may result in useful taxonomies, but it tells us less about sexual behavior than one might think.

Recall what Lionel Trilling wrote about the Kinsey volumes (1948; 1957, 232):

> The preponderant weight of its argument is that a fact is a physical fact, to be considered only in its physical aspect and apart from any idea or ideal that might make it a social fact, as having no ascertainable personal or cultural meaning and no possible consequences—as being, indeed, not available to social interpretation at all. In short, the Report by its primitive conception of the nature of fact quite negates the importance and even the existence of sexuality as a social fact.

What's ultimately interesting to us about sex is less those moments of animal exercise and more about what we think it *means*. (Pretty much anyone can have an orgasm—any male, anyway, as Kinsey found—but to have a "good" orgasm—now *that* requires culture.) What matters to us is not behavior but experience.

But when I say that it was so much less, I mean that Gagnon and Simon also rea-

soned that sex is not all that different from any other social activity. Indeed, while Kinsey
sought to "normalize" sex by making it just one more zoological behavior, Gagnon and
Simon sought to normalize it by making it mundane and social. In fact, they argued, its
simultaneous elevation to the realm of the mysterious and taboo and denigration to the
realm of sinful lust had virtually nothing to do with the intrinsic behaviors themselves
and everything to do with the ways we felt about them.

Gagnon and Simon married the study of sexual behavior to the dominant themes
they had taken from the epochal era of Chicago sociology—the notion of the career
and the notion of the self. This effort to understand both the multiple meanings of sex
and sex's centrality in the construction of identity set Gagnon and Simon's work apart
as revolutionary; indeed, their breakthrough book *Sexual Conduct* (1973) heralded the
new paradigm from which all subsequent readings of sexuality in the social sciences and
humanities have sprung. Without Gagnon and Simon, there could not have been a Judith Butler.

II

Gagnon's career began modestly and inauspiciously enough for him to title an elegant
1990 autobiographical essay "An unlikely story." He thought it "unlikely" because he was
about as far from "to the academic manor" born as one could possibly get. He was born
to working class parents belonging to different ethnic groups (mother, second generation Irish American; father, first generation French Canadian) at the opening of the
Dust Bowl depression years, and when his family moved to southern California in the
1940s, they were treated as itinerant Okies by the state police who were keeping out the
precursors of the Mediterranean fruit fly and other undesirables. His early life sounds
more Tom Joad than Talcott Parsons (whose father was a minister, a professor, and ultimately the president of a small college; see Ritzer 1991, 100). His early years in California were spent in a one-room canvas-roofed tent followed by a one-room apartment,
and he was headed for a job in a local aircraft plant or at best a couple of years of city
college. However, a chance meeting with a University of Chicago alumnus plucked him
from his peers and shipped him off to Illinois. Under the leadership of Robert Maynard
Hutchins, the university had embarked on a program both to diversify its student base
and admit promising and gifted kids who would otherwise never get near its gates.

The University of Chicago was like Shangri-La to Gagnon—less because of the brilliance of its faculty, and more because of its library. Here was the perfect escape for a
boy who was outside his milieu; marginality has pretty much defined Gagnon's intellectual life. He lost himself in literature, reading voraciously, widely, and pretty indiscriminately. (Gagnon remains my favorite colleague with whom to discuss literature and art.)
One of his work-study campus jobs was returning books to their shelves, and he recalled
reading one for every two he shelved on those lazy autumn days.

Like virtually all of us who care to admit it, Gagnon drifted to sociology after brief
stops in pre-med and psychology. (Who enters college thinking they'll become a sociologist? How many even know what one is?) It was there, in the Chicago sociology department of the early 1950s, that his intellectual course was set.

The older grand tradition of Chicago-school sociology (of Mead, Park, and Blumer)
had largely fallen out of favor at the faculty level, gradually being supplanted by the

quantitative and empirical approaches of younger social "scientists." The only "true" member of the Chicago School in the department when Gagnon was there was Everett Hughes; even Erving Goffman and Howard Becker, who were graduate students at the time, were too far along to be of much influence. However, the questions raised by the first Chicago School were still in the intellectual air. Understanding the social self remained a central sociological project, as was the construction of identity and its maintenance. While the idea of the *individual* was born in classical theories of political economy, in the works of Locke and Smith, it was in sociology that this *self* was first understood to have a symbolic and cultural life as well. The project of the self—of an identity that one "works on" for one's entire life—is itself the cornerstone of modernity. If the twentieth century was the century of the self—of the individual as disconnected autonomous actor—who, then, was he or she?

Inspired in part by the older tradition of Chicago urban sociology and criminology—a tradition kept alive by Everett Hughes and his students—Gagnon became interested in the extension of the term "career" to all arenas of social life, especially the non-occupational world. This was particularly the case with deviance, the arena in which Gagnon became interested in working. The career model offered a normative structure to the non-normative and seemingly unstructured conduct. There were governing rules, hierarchies that structured mobility, standards of evaluation. "The careers of a banker and a gangster could be analyzed in exactly the same way," Gagnon told an interviewer. "Learning how to do a job, acquiring skills and insider knowledge, learning how to deal with all of the other social actors in a particular social milieu" (see the postscript of this book).

Readers will no doubt be familiar with the ways that concept was employed so brilliantly to discuss mental patients and marijuana users, by Goffman and Becker respectively. Becker's magisterial work on art and artists (1981) suggested both the promise and the perils of the approach, as it completely demystified art into a set of relationships among social actors embarked on careers, but also tended to flatten or discount the often visceral sensation of experiencing a work of art itself.[1]

Gagnon credits the cultural critic Kenneth Burke as his other major influence. Burke was an intellectual gadfly—a public intellectual who wrote about art and literature, reviewed books, and wrote essays about symbolic action, stressing the mutually reinforcing ways that social action was a form of communication and communication a form of social action (Burke is credited by sociolinguists as a forerunner of "speech acts" theorists).

One of the many jobs Gagnon held to support himself as a student was working in the Cook County Jail for just over three years. (He had also worked on assembly lines at Continental Can and as a machinist at the aircraft engine divisions of Studebaker and the Ford Motor Company.) Although the memories are hazy, Gagnon recalls that he had "evolved into someone who was believed to know something about drugs, delinquency, crime and prisons" (1990, 220).

All of which made him the perfect candidate when Wardell Pomeroy, one of Kinsey's original collaborators, came through Chicago looking for a social scientist/criminologist to help with the research and writing of the fourth volume of the Kinsey study, *Sex Offenders.* So it was off to Bloomington, Indiana.

Gagnon arrived at the Kinsey Institute in 1959, three years after Kinsey himself
had died, but a place where the research on sexuality was in full gear. He became a senior research sociologist there and joined its board of trustees. (His portrait hangs in
the entrance, alongside that of the other collaborators.) Although the volume *Sex Offenders* (1965) was eventually published, it never received the acclaim of the two earlier
volumes, in part because of its own intrinsic methodological and especially conceptual
flaws, and in part because readers simply refused to believe that sex offenders represented end points on a continuum of sexual behaviors that would include their own
sexual activities. It was far easier and more convenient to label sex offenders as a species
apart and leave our own tendencies out of it.

In 1964, Bill Simon passed through Bloomington. Though the two men had not
been close when they were graduate students at Chicago years earlier, they now hit it off
marvelously; Gagnon hired Simon and brought him to Bloomington the next year. Like
Marx and Engels, or Astaire and Rogers, it was the collaborative synthesis that produced
their best work; while each was talented in their own individual ways, their collaboration brought forth a third entity that redefined a field.

III

While at the Kinsey Institute, from 1965 to 1968 (and in a long-distance collaboration
that lasted until 1973), Gagnon and Simon applied many of their Chicago-bred insights
to the study of sexuality. In a sense, their arguments are simple; their implications, vast.
Sex—sexual behavior, that is—is profoundly social. And sex—sexual identity, the identity constructed through sex—is among the central building blocks of our identities.

Sex, they argue, is more than the product of instinctual drives: it is the enactments
of complex sets of cultural meanings. We are less creatures of instinct than actors following "sexual scripts"—the normative cultural contexts that give sex its meaning, and enable us to distinguish appropriate partners and to know what to do with them once we
select them.

This argument set conventional wisdom on its head, and, of course, contradicted the
assumptions that had guided Kinsey's work. Most of us believe that our sexualities are
driven by biological urges—that our bodies "know" what they want. Men are especially
vulnerable to this fiction; women are far more aware of how they "learn" to have and like
sex. Indeed, men often believe that their penises have decisive personalities of their own
that drive men towards various people and behaviors. Reversing the masculinist cliché
that held that "penises have a mind of their own," Gagnon and Simon argued that, as
Gagnon commented to me recently, "the mind had a penis or clitoris of its own."

The notion of scripting made sexuality at once more mundane and more exotic.
That sex was normal meant not that it was "natural" but that it was normative. Gagnon
and Simon's notion of sexual scripts used the dramatistic metaphor coined by Burke
(and extended by Goffman) to great effect. Scripts provided a cognitive map to the domain of the sexual—through scripts we learned how to have sex, what was sexy and
what was not, even how to experience pleasure. Orgasms, it turned out, were socially
constructed!

And sex was not a realm apart, a special domain immune to social norms; in fact, sex wasn't very different from anything else we did. Here is how Gagnon put it in his 1977 textbook *Human Sexualities:*

> In any given society, at any given moment, people become sexual in the same way as they become everything else. Without much reflection, they pick up directions from their social environment. They acquire and assemble meanings, skills, and values from the people around them. Their critical choices are often made by going along and drifting. People learn when they are quite young a few of the things that they are expected to be, and continue slowly to accumulate a belief in who they are and ought to be through the rest of childhood, adolescence and adulthood. Sexual conduct is learned in the same way and through the same processes: it is acquired and assembled in human interaction, judged and performed in specific cultural and historical worlds. (2)

Normative and routine, perhaps, but sex *was* important. Gagnon and Simon argued that the project of the self in the twentieth century increasingly revolved around sexuality. Sexual activity was one of the ways we constructed our selves, and sexual identity became increasingly important in those constructions throughout the twentieth century. This argument, though, slyly turned Freud on his head. True, like Freud, Gagnon and Simon saw sex and sexuality as a core constituent of the self. But Gagnon and Simon were unmoved by the notion of sexual drives as libidinous impulses existing prior to society, and uninterested in a notion of sexual repression and sublimation as the foundations of culture and civility. Kenneth Burke's ideas helped Gagnon and Simon reverse Freud: Freud having argued that there was a sexual component to all manner of non-sexual activities—Freud discerned libidinous motives in art, music, political movements, and literature—Gagnon and Simon argued that one could find political, economic, cultural, and even moral motives in sexual conduct itself. One could do sex for social mobility, economic gain, or spiritual transcendence.

Gagnon and Simon distinguished three different levels of sexual scripts. These were the "cultural scenarios" that provide larger frameworks and roles through which sex is experienced; the "interpersonal scripts" that represent the routine patterns of social interaction that guide behaviors in specific settings; and the "intrapsychic scripts"—their nod to Freud and Mead—that suggest that social action is always conducted with an ongoing internal dialog about internalized cultural expectations.[2]

These small accretions of insight gradually took shape into *Sexual Conduct* and gave birth to the twin notions of the social construction of sexual behavior and sexual identity. *Sexual Conduct* is one of those rare books in social science that ages well; to read it today is to savor the complexities of the argument in light of their validation by subsequent historical development. Its intent, Gagnon wrote in 1990, was "to bring the field of sexuality under the control of a sociological orientation . . . to lay a sociological claim to an aspect of social life that seemed determined by biology or psychology" (231).

By choosing to focus on sex—even making the argument, before Foucault or others stumbled onto it—was as momentous professionally as it was intellectually. It ensured that Gagnon would remain somewhat of a sociological pariah, perpetually semi-marginalized in the profession. Sociologists, it turned out, avoided talking about sex because they were as moralistic and prudish as the society they studied. A sociologist of sex occupies the same status position in sociology as a sex worker in the larger society: a reminder of the seamy unpleasantness of the bodies to which our minds happen to be connected. Occupational mobility seemed far more optimistic—and far less messy.

Simon and Gagnon left the Institute for Sex Research in 1968—Simon first to Chicago at the Institute for Juvenile Research and a few years later to the University of Houston, and Gagnon to the State University of New York at Stony Brook, where he remained (with a number of years as a visiting scholar elsewhere) until his retirement in 1998.

Gagnon and Simon's work inspired a new generation of scholars—many of whom have contributed essays to this volume—who saw social constructionism as especially evocative. One group of gay and lesbian social scientists found it liberating to understand sexual behavior and sexual identity as contingent and social, as opposed to constant and physical. Groundbreaking work in the sociology of homosexuality followed.

Another set of scholars immediately set to work understanding the ways in which the social influences and shapes the sexual—the ways in which religion, politics, and cultural assumptions of all sorts provide the raw materials from which we construct sexuality. Some were interested in behaviors, others in identities.

Fewer scholars, alas, saw the proto-feminist arguments in Gagnon and Simon's work. Had their essays been written by a woman, perhaps, this notion that sexual behavior is socially constructed and is therefore fluid and constantly changing might have served as a potential blueprint for reconstruction by those who were trying to understand rape, violence, and pornography as something other than an inevitable expression of some putatively male biology.

But eventually society has a way of catching up with those who break new ground and fashion new paradigms. At the end of "An unlikely story," Gagnon asks, "Will I do anything else interesting?" His answer, slyly taken from Hemingway, is that "it would be pretty to think so."

Pretty, indeed. One of the unanticipated consequences of the AIDS pandemic was a new frankness about sexual behavior. It was startling to hear the mayor of New York City discuss anal sex on television. Confined largely and initially to the gay male population and IV drug users, the possible spread of the epidemic into the heterosexual population was the cause of significant public health concern.

And, it provided an opening for researchers. A 1986 report by the National Academy of Sciences posed the questions and revealed the anxiety. "Infected bisexual men and IV drug users of both sexes can transmit the virus to the broader heterosexual population," the report concluded, "where it can continue to spread, particularly among the most sexually active individuals" (Institute of Medicine 1986, 9).

But just how would HIV be transmitted to the heterosexual population? Would it be through those self-identified heterosexual and otherwise monogamous married men who stopped off for anonymous sex with other men in the public restrooms off the New Jersey Turnpike or the waiting rooms of Grand Central Station and then commuted back home to their leafy suburban families? Would it be from promiscuous men and women who had no ideas about the sexual histories of the partners? Perhaps it would be from those self-identified straight men who had sex with other men for money?

These questions could not be answered by recourse to sexual *identity*, because all of those groups identified as heterosexual. Suddenly, there was again a need for a systematic study of American sexual *behavior*—a study that could adequately map the human ecology of sexual activity as well as our routine sexual practices.

Once again, Gagnon found himself at the University of Chicago, now teamed up with two colleagues: Edward Laumann, a sociologist who had made a reputation studying social networks, and Robert Michael, an economist, dean of the Graduate School of Business and then-director of the National Opinion Research Center, perhaps the most prestigious survey research institute in the world. (The trio added Stuart Michaels, an exceptional graduate student in sociology, as a co-author.)[3] The vast intellectual resources and unsurpassed intellectual and scientific credibility of the university made this team the obvious choice to conduct such a study, much as the innocuous heartland empiricism of Indiana University had provided such a haven for Kinsey a half-century earlier.

Their joint project, the National Health and Social Life Survey, produced a series of landmark books, beginning with the simultaneous publication of two volumes in 1994—a scientific work, *The Social Organization of Sexuality*, complete with all methodological apparatuses, and a popular work, *Sex in America*, for more mainstream audiences. (Gagnon and his colleagues wanted to avoid the bowdlerization of their work, as had happened to Kinsey earlier, by working with a skilled science journalist.) Together, these volumes represent the largest and most ambitious study of American sexual behavior ever undertaken in our history.

That the work ever appeared is itself a story of the politicization of social science. The study was initially to be supported by a federal contract coordinated by the National Institute of Child Health and Human Development (NICHD). Then right-wing anti-sex research zealots got wind of it. Jesse Helms, the conservative senator from North Carolina, went after it like a religious Rambo in a brothel. Wildly inflating cost estimates, an organized religious radio-inspired phone call barrage to the Office of Management and Budget, spurious political accusations and a series of deliriously unfounded personal attacks by Helms and others on Gagnon, and the funding was pulled. Gagnon thus, perhaps, became one of the few members of the American Sociological Association ever denounced by name on the floor of the United States Senate (Laumann, Michael, and Gagnon 1994, 36).[4]

Their funding evaporated, as it had for Kinsey before them. The research team went to private foundations, hats in hands. A more modest but still extensive study was cobbled together, anchored by funding from the Robert Wood Johnson Foundation and buttressed by funds from the Kaiser, Ford, Rockefeller, Mellon, and MacArthur foundations and AMFAR (the American Foundation for AIDS Research).

It is ironic, but telling, that the findings of this comprehensive study pleased virtually no one. The findings were far too conservative for the sexual left. The incidence of homosexuality was less than half what Kinsey estimated, for example, and most people were relatively modest in their sexual tastes, engaging in occasional monogamous marital sex. Sexually speaking, Americans were less *Sex and the City* and more *Little House on the Prairie*.

On the other hand, the anti-sexual right was not appeased. That little prairie dwelling contained far too many women who liked sex, as well as unapologetic gay men and lesbians, and they found the steadfast refusal of the researchers to make value judgments about sexual behavior particularly irksome.

As a result, the study was criticized for its methodology by those who thought the rates and incidences of non-marital and non-heterosexual sexual activity should have been much higher, and for its politics by those who would have liked those same rates to have been significantly lower. To make both sides unhappy is a difficult task, and one that probably indicates just how accurate were the data.

IV

But a staid, contented, and sexually faithful America isn't the stuff of tabloid headlines, and the media fanfare that initially greeted the books—cover stories in every major newspaper and national news magazine—dissipated. The work, and the subsequent volumes that have since appeared, have taken their place a bit more quietly on shelves of serious social scientists, to be referred to for the most accurate, if more monochromatic, data on American sexual behavior ever undertaken.

The real sexual revolution turned out not to be Kinsey's revolution—a revolution comprised of randy sexual acrobatics of all sorts with many partners (that is, a revolution of sexual *behavior*)—but, rather, Gagnon and Simon's revolution—a transformation of the social meanings of sex and of the proliferation of sexual identities, rather than behaviors. A revolution, in short, that took place more in our heads than between the sheets.

At the end of the 2004 Hollywood movie about Kinsey's life, there is a remarkable and deeply moving scene that was intended to suggest the lasting impact of Kinsey's work and legacy, especially in bringing sex out of the closet and making it visible. But it also underscores Gagnon and Simon's break with Kinsey, and especially the significance of their ideas that sexuality is a core component of identity. In the scene, Kinsey, played by Liam Neeson, is interviewing an unnamed woman who had repressed her lesbian desires behind a shame-filled effort at heterosexual marriage. Played elegantly and simply by Lynn Redgrave, the character describes to Kinsey her decades-long pain and repression. Kinsey shakes his head, resignedly, and comments how little has changed.

Redgrave looks a bit perplexed. She's happy now, and everything is okay, she tells him.

"Well, what happened?" he asks.

"You did," she says, as tears well up in her eyes. After the publication of the Kinsey Report, she realized she was not the only one who felt as she did, and she found the courage to confess her affection to another woman, who, in turned out, felt the same way as she. And they've been happily together for several years. "You saved my life," Redgrave says.

Gagnon and Simon's work on the centrality of sex in the construction of identity and the significance of the social in the experience of sex probably didn't save any lives, but their work did make those lives more comprehensible. Will sociology ever come around to regarding John Gagnon and William Simon among the founders of a new sociology of the self—a sexual self? It would be pretty to think so.

The Plan of This Book

The authors of the essays and articles in this volume span three generations of scholars, writers, and activists. First, the book includes two collaborative works by two colleagues and contemporaries of Gagnon's: Ed Laumann and Anke Ehrhardt. Both have known John and worked with him for decades, and it is fitting that their contributions are also collaborations with younger scholars.

The next group is those who were influenced initially by the early work of Gagnon and Simon, and built their often distinguished careers in part by extending, challenging, and wrestling with the ideas of social constructionism, sexual scripts, and the centrality of sexuality in the construction of the self. For us—I include myself in this group—the initial encounter with Gagnon and Simon's ideas was startling, perhaps even pushing us off the trajectory we had anticipated, opening up new vistas and, more importantly, new ways to look at them.

This group includes Stevi Jackson, Ken Plummer, Peter Nardi, Jeff Escoffier, Pepper Schwartz, Barry Adam, Gil Herdt, and Leonore Tiefer. (This generation also includes Gayle Rubin and Carole Vance, who were not able to contribute to this volume due to health and family issues.) It's interesting sociologically that such a list includes feminist women—that is, women who write not about sexual orientation but about the politics of sexuality—and gay men. Although one of the more radical breakthrough chapters of *Sexual Conduct* concerned lesbians, the first group of this generation of scholars and writers to pick up on the liberatory ideas in scripting theory was gay men—the politically active gay social scientists whose work emerged in the decade immediately following Stonewall. It's also worth noting, both sociologically and politically, that this group of gay male sociologists generally became well-established before their lesbian colleagues.

It is within the third generation where some of the most innovative work is now being done—younger scholars in their 30s, several just finishing their degrees and others a bit further along in their careers. This group was influenced not only by Gagnon and Simon (and often the second generation scholars as well), but also by postmodernist theories of sexuality and scripting. The second generation remains largely wedded to scripts and relatively diffident in the face of postmodernism (the Burkean element of Gagnon's work anticipates postmodernism while the empirical social scientist resists it); this new generation is as versed in the works of Michel Foucault and Judith Butler as the second generation is in the work of Freud, Weber, and both Meads (Margaret and George Herbert). This group includes Rebecca Plante, Arlene Stein, Steve Epstein, Shari Dworkin, Lucia O'Sullivan, Rita Melendez, and David Whittier.

These divisions are more than generational; they are also, in some ways, substantive. The second generation's work largely established the empirical validity of the social constructionist model and the utility of a scripts framework proposed by the first generation. Taken together, it is the work of this generation of social scientists that established sexuality studies as a legitimate subfield of sociology and allied social sciences. Today, the major professional organizations, such as the American Sociological Association, have sections for students of sexualities. (The ASA's section gives an annual prize for distinguished scholarship named after Gagnon and Simon.) The third generation's work integrates social science research on the social construction of sexual identity and the scripting of sexual behavior with postmodernist theorizing—particularly drawing from feminist theory and queer theory. It also stretches it, extends it, and, in some cases, even challenges it.

This book is organized into several sections, each mirroring the central concerns of Gagnon's work. These sections are neither discrete categories nor mutually exclusive, and while the placement of essays and authors is not arbitrary, many of the essays speak to concerns in other sections as well. This is, of course, as it should be: work that is so decidedly interdisciplinary and wide-ranging is bound to cross any arbitrarily set categorical boundaries.

The first section, "Sexualities and selves," establishes the centrality of sexuality in the construction of the self. Before Gagnon and Simon's work, sexuality was considered peripheral to the self, located more in the sociology of deviance than in identity formation. Neither Freud, with his insistence on the repression of sexual impulses, nor Kinsey, with his exclusive behaviorist focus on behavior, saw sexuality and identity as so closely and intimately linked. Here we find a mixture of the modernist concerns with identity itself and the postmodern playfulness with the fluid and contingent nature of those identities.

The second section, "Sexual scripts," takes as its starting point the centrality of sexuality in identity formation, and explores the ways in which different groups—gay men, heterosexuals, intimate couples—develop coherent sexual relationships based on scripts. Even, it turns out, in unwanted sexual experiences, there are important elements of different sexual scripts between women and men that lead to miscommunication and even sexual assault.

The third section, "Sexual behavior," observes the implementation of those scripts in our sexual behaviors: how do gender and sexual orientation construct not only our scripts but our actual sexual activities? Laumann and his colleagues provide a panoramic view of American sexual culture, while the two other essays are more focused on sexual behaviors among gay men.

The fourth section, "Sexual politics," moves beyond identity and interaction into the implications of scripting theory for current sexual politics. Whether it's the medicalization of sexuality or the connection of behaviors to social movement or even knowledge itself, the implications are vast and significant.

Finally, the book concludes with Gagnon and Simon reflecting on their work in pair of succinct but revealing interviews conducted originally for a German journal in 1998. Theirs was, indeed, an unending conversation.

Acknowledgments

I am grateful to Jeffrey Escoffier's foreword to Gagnon's book, *An Interpretation of Desire*, which was particularly helpful in preparing this essay.

Notes

1. See Becker 1981 and my review of it in *American Journal of Sociology* (1983).
2. While they focused most of their attention on the latter two, it was the first that initially captivated me, and it dominated the work that Gagnon and I did on the gender of sexuality—that much of sexual activity was in the service of demonstrating gender conformity, and that homosexual behavior was understood to be the consequences of gender nonconformity.
3. That the study was carried out entirely by four white men seemed to irritate none of the researchers; nor had a parallel line-up worried Kinsey and his colleagues Pomeroy, Gebhard, and Martin.
4. The erotophobic right wing has never known what to make of Gagnon's work. Helms denounced both Gagnon (for his support of "homosexuality and sexual decadence") and the study (for its efforts to "legitimize homosexual lifestyles") but a recent issue of *American Enterprise*, the in-house magazine of the right-wing think tank, celebrates Gagnon and Simon's break with Kinsey as a significant achievement.

References

Becker, H. 1981. *Art worlds*. Chicago: University of Chicago Press.

Gagnon, J. H. 1977. *Human sexualities*. Glenview, IL: Scott Foresman.

———. 1990. An unlikely story. *Authors of their own lives: Intellectual autobiographies of twenty American sociologists*, ed. B. Berger, 213–34. Berkeley: University of California Press.

Institute of Medicine. 1986. *Confronting AIDS: Directions for public health, health care and research*. Washington, DC: National Academy of Sciences Press.

Laumann, E. O., R. T. Michael, and J. H. Gagnon. 1994. A political history of the National Sex Survey of Adults. *Family Planning Perspectives* 26, no. 1 (January): 36.

Ritzer, G. 1991. *Contemporary Sociological Theory*. New York: McGraw-Hill.

PART I

SEXUALITIES AND SELVES

Stevi Jackson

1

The Sexual Self
in Late Modernity

I first encountered the work of John Gagnon and his collaborator Bill Simon in 1972 when, as a graduate student, I was looking for a way of theorizing and researching the gendered self as a sociologist and as a feminist. There was not a lot to go on: the psychological literature on sex roles was mechanistic and insufficiently social, and while I read a great deal of Freud, psychoanalysis had little appeal—like most feminists at that time, I found it literally incredible. As I read around in circles, unable to find anything that gave me purchase on the problem, Laurie Taylor (my supervisor at the time) placed in my hands an article by Gagnon and Simon. I never looked back. Their arguments, later elaborated more fully in *Sexual Conduct,* made immediate sense and prompted me to focus on sexuality, which has remained one of my central interests ever since. Without that first encounter, my academic career might have followed a very different path, and I therefore owe an enormous intellectual debt to John Gagnon and Bill Simon: I found their ideas inspirational in the 1970s and I find myself continually returning to them three decades later.

My reading of Gagnon and Simon was influenced by my familiarity with the American interactionist tradition, particularly the work of G. H. Mead. Drawing on this, I argue in this chapter for the continued salience of a broadly interactionist conceptualization of the sexual self, suggesting that it offers a viable alternative to psychoanalytic analyses. Moreover, in locating the sexual self within the wider social relations through which it is constituted, it enables us to think about the ways in which sexuality has become a contested site of reflexive self-construction in late modernity.

Sexual selves in social context

So what was it about Gagnon and Simon's argument that I found so compelling, and why does it remain relevant in these late or postmodern times? Most obviously, it was the first thoroughly social constructionist approach to sexuality, predating the now more familiar variants of social constructionism deriving from poststructuralism and post-modernism.[1] At the time *Sexual Conduct* was written, ideas associated with social constructionism were widespread within interactionist and phenomenological sociology. While others, such as Berger and Luckman (1967) did discuss the social constitution of sexuality, Gagnon and Simon were the first to develop a radical contestation of and alternative to drive reduction models.[2]

Gagnon and Simon did more than simply asserting the pre-eminence of the social over the innate: in questioning the concept of repression, they allowed for a positive conceptualization of the social—as producing sexuality rather than negatively molding or modifying inborn drives. In this respect, their argument presaged Foucault's critique of repressive hypothesis but also directly addressed the social construction of desire and of the sexual self.[3] From a feminist perspective, this had distinct advantages: female sexuality could not be seen as a repressed version of male sexuality, and neither male sexuality nor heterosexuality could be taken as norms of human sexual being.

We have still not won the battle against biological determinism. While for most critical thinkers in academia it has become axiomatic that gender and sexuality are social rather than natural phenomena, elsewhere the idea that they are ordained by nature still has considerable purchase on commonsense reasoning. Indeed, biological determinism has gained ground through evolutionary psychology; theories of female, male, and gay brains; and the increasing medicalization of sexuality. Part of the appeal of biological perspectives is that they "make sense" in terms of individuals' view of themselves: it is one of the paradoxes of our late modern times that everyone insists they are unique individuals who make choices, yet most experience their gender and sexual preferences as fixed and pre-determined. To challenge this effectively requires not only critiques of biological essentialism, but also an approach that connects with everyday experience. This is precisely what Gagnon and Simon provide.

Here, an interactionist approach has the edge over psychoanalysis: it makes sense in terms of the ways our sexuality is interwoven with the everyday social fabric of our past and present lives. Psychoanalysis, with its emphasis on the unknowable unconscious, says little about everyday sexuality. Gagnon and Simon's approach also allows for agency and change in the sexual self: it is not set on an irreversible course by the traumas of infancy, but is constantly modified throughout life. Its changeability is not a consequence of unpredictable eruptions of the unconscious but is envisaged as an ongoing reflexive process, in which there is a two-way relationship between our past and our present. Rather than the past determining the present, "the present significantly reshapes the past as we reconstruct our biographies to bring them into greater congruence with our current identities, roles, situations and available vocabularies" (Gagnon and Simon 1974, 13). Thus, in place of the unconscious as the foundation of the psyche, we have the intrapsychic, "a socially based form of mental life" (Gagnon 2004, 276), in keeping with Mead's conception of the reflexive social self. And this is a self "in process" as the poststructuralists say (e.g., Weedon 1987), constantly constructed and reconstructed in interaction with others. The sexual self is viewed as actively "doing sex," not only in terms of sexual acts, but as making and modifying sexual meaning, since intrapsychic scripting is inevitably interdependent with both the interactional and wider sociocultural scripting of the sexual.

Sexual conduct and the sexual self are fully social, embedded in wider patterns of sociality. One of the most important critical insights of Gagnon and Simon was and is their emphasis on the everydayness of sexuality, forcing us to reflect on the importance accorded to sexuality in late modern societies, to question the idea of the sexual as a high intensity drive, and to be aware that sexual conduct can be guided by non-sexual motives—that it occurs in the context of ordinary lives and is shaped by wider social institutions. This view of sex is radical in that it runs counter to much common-sense thinking. Sex is usually seen as special, outside and apart from routine sociality, uniquely exciting and transforming, raising us out of mundane quotidian banality—or alternatively as a dangerous force with the power to undermine "civilization" and reduce us to barbarism. I share Gagnon and Simon's opposition to "traditions that stressed the power of the sexual for purposes of social change or appealing to sexuality as a source of political and personal redemption" (Gagnon 2004, 280). I have always been suspicious of inflated claims made about sexuality, whether in the form of psychoanalytic arguments that trace of all subjectivity back to sexuality, feminist theories that reduce women's oppression to an effect of male sexual appropriation, or libertarian hopes of social subversion through sexual transgression. I continue to ask: what *is* so special about sex? (see Jackson and Scott 2004a).

This question clearly echoes Gayle Rubin's "fallacy of misplaced scale" whereby "sexual acts are burdened with an excess of signification" (1984, 278–79). This fallacy should be challenged not only in relation to disproportionately negative reactions to sexual transgression, but also in relation to disproportionately celebratory endorsements of it. Only if we question the idea of sex as in itself either bad *or* good (Jackson and Scott 2004b) can we explore why the sexual has become so important to the late modern "project of the self" (Giddens 1991; 1992); why, despite postmodern attempts to destabilize it, sexual identity remains central to our sense of who we are; and why, judging by the booming market in sexual self-help books, there appears to be a widespread preoccupation with the pursuit of sexual self-improvement (see Jackson and Scott 1997; 2004a).[4] Moreover, in getting sexuality back into proportion, we can also better understand how our sexual selves are constructed. I will argue, in keeping with Gagnon and Simon's perspective, that rather than sexuality being the foundation of human subjectivity, it is but one facet of the self.

The way in which Gagnon and Simon initially theorized the construction of sexual selfhood had immediate relevance for me as a feminist. Rather than viewing sexuality and gender as inextricably interrelated, with sexual/affective desires and identifications determining gender, they argued that the sexual self was developed on the basis of the prior construction of a gendered self. While the precise ways in which they initially described these processes (within the developmental vocabulary of the socialization paradigm) may now seem outmoded, their central insight on the relationship between gender and sexuality is not. Once again refusing to abstract the sexual from its wider social context, Gagnon and Simon avoided conflating gender and sexuality and provided a means of making an analytical distinction between them while exploring their empirical interrelationship. This is another highly significant aspect of their perspective, not only differentiating their position from psychoanalysis but also from Foucauldian perspectives. Foucault's sex/sexuality formulation makes no distinction between "sex" as sexual division and "sex" as acts and desires. The "heterogeneous ensemble" constituted as sex through the apparatus of sexuality includes "the body, the sexual organs, pleasures, kinship relations, interpersonal relations" (1980, 210).

From Gagnon and Simon's perspective, how gender and sexuality are interrelated becomes a matter for exploration rather than being decided in advance. As I have argued at length elsewhere, the intersections between gender and sexuality are complex: the relationship is two-way, and the ways they intersect at different levels of the social (the institutional, the cultural/ideological, the interactional and the subjective) do not necessarily map directly onto each other and these interconnections change over time (2005). Moreover, sexuality and gender may be interrelated but they are rather different and not directly comparable social phenomena. Gender, whatever else it is taken to encompass, denotes a social division. Sexuality refers to a sphere of social life and, in the broad sense in which I am using it, to all erotically significant aspects of life—for example, desires, practices, relationships, and identities. The concept of "sexuality" thus refers to a rather amorphous and shifting field since what makes an act, a desire, or a relationship sexual are the meanings invested in it (see Gagnon and Simon 1974). It could be objected that gender is a matter of social definition too—and so, in a sense, it is—but as a fundamental social division it is a ubiquitous feature of social life. Although other aspects of it (the ways in which it is embodied and practiced) may be more variable, the division itself has a certain incorrigible facticity that is difficult to evade. What is more comparable with gender in this sense is the binary divide between heterosexuality and homosexuality. We might, therefore, produce greater conceptual congruence by pluralizing sexuality— speaking of "sexualities" rather than "sexuality." But this move, while recognizing sexual diversity, directs attention away from the broader scope of sexuality (singular) as a field of study and sphere of life, and limits explorations of the gender-sexuality linkage to the ways in which gender is related to sexual "identities." Sexual selfhood entails more than our identities or "orientation"; it is not reducible to the gender of those we desire. In order to elucidate this further, I first need to say more about the conception of the self I am working with.

The social self

For the last two decades, most feminist and critical theorist have spoken of "subjectivity" rather than "the self." The human subject has been conceptualized as decentered and/or fractured. whether as a product of (psychoanalytically understood) splits and losses or as a result of her positioning within the ebb and flow of competing discourses. Such accounts challenge humanist and modernist, ideas of an essential unitary self, drawing our attention to the contradictions of subjectivity. On the other hand, the recent resurgence in theorizing the self has emphasized the process of "self making" (Skeggs 2004) or the self as "project" (Giddens 1991; 1992). This self is seen as historically specific, a product of increasing individualism over the last few centuries, something consciously, reflexively fashioned as a coherent life. Self and subjectivity thus emerge as rather different objects of study, and can be represented as co-existing with each other—a consciously constructed self papering over the cracks of a fragmented subjectivity lurking beneath its carefully crafted surface.

As conceptualized by G. H. Mead, however, the self encapsulates much of what is usually termed subjectivity, and thus bridges the divide between a self-consciously fabricated self and a less coherent, more fluid self. Mead's self is envisaged as process rather than structure and is hence neither unitary nor fixed, but it is not as decentered and fragmentary as the postmodern subject. On the other hand, it does not necessarily entail the heightened self-consciousness and coherence of the late modern reflexive project of the self. Rather, Mead's notion of reflexivity entails what it is to *be* social and to participate *in* the social. Reflexivity here is the capacity to engage in conversations with ourselves and to see ourselves as subject and object in order to situate ourselves in relation to others. Without it, we would not be able to interact or cooperate with others, and thus any sociality would be impossible. The reflexive self as Mead conceived it does not, in and of itself, imply a well-constructed narrative of self, though it makes this possible.

Mead's work must be understood in context. First, he framed his project in opposition to behaviorism, against the idea that human behavior is externally determined. Thus, he stressed the importance of interpretative processes in guiding human actions. Second, Mead's work was located within a tradition of American pragmatist thought which, as Holstein and Gubrium (2000) note, effected a decisive break with the Enlightenment conception of a transcendental self that stood outside the social, replacing it with a self very much embedded in everyday sociality. We are now more familiar with postmodernist critiques of the Enlightenment subject as "a stable, reliable, integrative entity" (Flax 1990, 8) as against a posited fragmentary, decentered subjectivity. Mead's theory of self provides an alternative to postmodern subjectivity—an alternative that is more fully social.

The postmodern subject might be seen as constituted in the social, but it is not of the social, participating in it and acting on it. As Dorothy Smith argues, this is a subject whose being neither affects nor is affected by the social contexts in which everyday life goes on. Subjectivity is entirely the effect of language and discourse, conceived as independent of the local production of meaning and of "people's intentions to mean" (Smith 1999, 89–99). Moreover, as Lois McNay points out, this view of subjectivity cannot explain "how individuals are endowed with the capabilities for independent reflection and action" (2000, 3). From a psychoanalytic rather than social perspective, Jane Flax also takes issue with the idea of a fragmented, decentered self. We could not function, she maintains, without a "basic cohesion" within ourselves, which she locates in a core self that provides "a sense of continuity or 'going on being'" (1990, 218–19). While a sense of "going on being"—of oneself as having a past, present and potential future—would certainly seem necessary to be able to act in the world at all, this does not have to be seen as a core self or as, in Flax's terms, "deep subjectivity." A better metaphor for the self as ongoing might be a complex, many-stranded cord running through our lives, but one which does not necessarily stay the same since the threads that comprise it can be frayed or strengthened and are continually being spliced or woven in with other threads, remade over time. So, while we have a sense of our self as continuing, that self is never unchanging. I would suggest that our "going on being" derives from *social* experience, constructed and reconstructed through everyday social practices, rather than being lodged deep in the psyche.

In interactionist thinking, reflexivity (or "reflexiveness," as Mead called it)[5] is fundamental to our social being and to our active participation in social life. This idea of a reflexive self is sometimes misunderstood as presupposing a pre-social or pre-discursive "I" that does the work of reflexivity. However, in Mead's work there is no assumption of an essential, inner "I": the "I" is only ever the fleeting mobilization of a socially constituted self. Both the "I" and the "me," in dialogic interplay, are part of a social process—an ongoing reflexive constitution and reconstitution of the self. The self comes into being and continues to be only in relation to the social "other." It is in and of the social, acting on the social, and it is essential to ongoing practical activity and to ordering our relations with others.

Viewing the self as always already social yet also subject to change across time and with social context potentially enables us to locate individual subjectivities and biographies within specific historical, social, and cultural contexts. We can therefore link the self to the actualities of social existence. Doing so requires us to go beyond Mead, to take account not only of the different social conditions under which selves are made, but varied forms of reflexivity available for self-making in different times, places, and contexts. It is at this point that we can begin to consider how Mead's account of the reflexive self might be related to the forms of selfhood deemed typical of late modernity. I suggest that in order to do so we need to think in terms of varied levels or layers of reflexivity.

Mead's self is not the historically specific modernist self associated with a hyper-reflexive self-concern. His reflexivity is the basis for the self to function socially at all and for process and change within the self. It need not imply a high degree of self-awareness—merely that sufficient to interact with others. To stand outside oneself—to engage in self-judgment or self-description—requires another layer of reflexivity: a self-conscious standing back from the self in an effort to come to make claims about the sort of person one is. This is the beginning of accounting for the self, or "telling the self." It is here that the fluid self in process becomes more ordered—where we seek to bring coherence to the self to "fix" it, if only momentarily or strategically ("I am this sort of person . . ." "I did this because . . ."). It is less "in the moment" and habitual than simple reflexivity, but may still be provisional, contextual, and relatively fleeting.

The idea of a reflexive project of the self (Giddens 1991), associated with late modernity, requires another level of reflexivity entailing far more self-conscious "work" on the self. As well as being a product of the increasing individualism of modernity, this has been linked, following Foucault (1978), with the rise of a confessional culture, the emergence and institutionalization of the "psy" professions (Rose 1989), and with the seepage of therapeutic discourses into popular culture. Thus we can analyze our inner selves, seek self-knowledge, and pursue self improvement. And, since the therapeutic and confessional are interrelated, we can engage in a more complex "telling of the self" (Skeggs 2004) or storying of our lives (Plummer 1995). It becomes possible to construct and embrace an identity and to locate it within a narrative of self—"this is who I am; this is why." But the ability to tell our own stories and author(ize) our own lives is not equally open to all and certainly not on the same terms. Stories are located in the wider social context in which they are recounted and received, and this in turn depends on the social contexts in which our selves are forged and the forms of reflexivity available to us and deployed by us—and this is as much the case for our sexual selves as any other facet of the self.

Becoming and being sexual selves

The interactionist account of gendered and sexual subjectivity stands in stark opposition to psychoanalysis.[6] Psychoanalytic approaches see gender and sexuality as too closely entwined to be separated: both are subsumed under the single term "sex." In particular, the (gendered) objects of our desires are seen as crucially determining the sex (gender) we become: thus to be one sex is to desire the other. Moreover, since we become "sexed subjects" at an early stage in our lives (albeit, after Lacan, as a precarious accomplishment), both sexual identification and "object choice" are determined as soon as we move from infancy to childhood. Against this, Gagnon and Simon uncoupled gender and sexuality, accorded temporal priority to gender, and insisted that children cannot become sexual selves without access to the sexual scripts through which acts, relationships, and feelings (emotions and sensations) become sexually meaningful. To be clear on this, they are not saying children are either sexual or asexual in any essential sense: only that sexual selfhood depends on being able to make sense of oneself as sexual. And, while children today may have far more resources available for sexual self-making than they did when *Sexual Conduct* was written, adults still attempt to police that availability. From this perspective, then, a gendered sense of self precedes awareness ourselves as sexual (see Jackson 1978; 1999).

I would follow Kessler and McKenna in arguing for the primacy of gender attribution in the everyday "doing" of gender and in the individuals' life-course. Gender attribution is the first act of social categorization a child undergoes: as soon as it is born (or, in this era of scanning technology, even earlier), it is identified as either a girl or a boy. It is only when a child becomes "she" or "he" rather than "it" that it can be seen as fully human—hence the immense over-reaction when that identity is not immediately evident (Kessler 1998). But for gender to be "evident" requires at least three distinct social processes: first, the baby's genitals are read as a sign of its sex; second, the baby is reduced to its sex ("it's a girl"); and third, this reductive act effectively brings the child into being as gendered, as a little girl. This naming, as Butler puts it, begins the process of "girling the girl" (1993). Unlike Butler, however, I would see the process by which girls continue to be girled as interactional ones.

This self begins to be formed early in life as the child learns to distinguish between self and other, to "take the attitude of the other," and to locate herself in relation to the others in her immediate circle and ultimately to social others in general (Mead's "generalized other"). All this occurs in gendered terms, for these others are gendered and the child, in interacting with them, becomes able to locate herself within a gendered social field. While the self is premised upon differentiation between self and others, this is quite a different view of the self-other relation from that posited by postmodern and Lacanian psychoanalytic theories—not only is the self active in the process of coordinating action with others, but the other is not conceptualized as oppositional to the self (see Stanley and Wise 1993), but as relational in the sense that selfhood is forged and mobilized through being able to locate oneself within the social world of others. Moreover, while others are gendered, they do not need to occupy specific places in an oedipal drama. There is, therefore, no need to assume, as psychoanalysis does, that the *processes* of self-formation differ for boys and girls—simply that they acquire differently gendered selves through participating in gendered social interaction. Thus, gendered selfhood emerges as variable—there is no single way of being a little boy or a little girl.

Gender difference itself, however, remains significant: a child cannot locate herself in a gendered social order without a sense of herself as gendered—without being able to make sense of self and others as embodied, gendered beings. Awareness of ourselves as gendered is part of "going on being"—a thread that runs through our lives linking past present and future. Once the basic reflexive capacities of self-formation have been set in motion, the self continues, throughout life, to evolve and change through social interaction by virtue of its constant reflexivity. In growing from childhood to adulthood, sexuality is braided into our selves and becomes closely entwined with gender.

Obviously we "do not become sexual all at once" (Gagnon and Simon 1974, 27). Children are not only developing gendered selves but also assimilating much from their social environment that is of potential sexual relevance. It is only the specifically erotic component of sexual scripts that adults attempt to conceal from children: other aspects of adult maps of sexuality impinge on children's self-understanding.[7] The sense children make of their own bodies, for example, is ordered by meanings deriving from adult sexual scripts and their conventions of modesty, decorum, and morality. Crucially, children acquire a great deal of commonsense knowledge about the institution and practice of heterosexuality—about heterosexual love and marriage, about families, mothers and fathers—way before they are aware of the sexual activities these entail. They are also aware that there are secrets adults keep from them—that there are aspects of adult life from which they are excluded. But the ways in which this partial access to everyday adult knowledge is made available is rather like a jigsaw puzzle with important pieces missing.

To illustrate, I will draw on my recent involvement in a research project on adults' and children's understandings of risk, including sexual risk.[8] Children aged 9 to 11, in the last years of primary school,[9] had already received some sex education and had also been thoroughly inculcated with fear of "strangers." When asked what they thought strangers might do to them, however, even the most sexually aware of them were unable to identify sexual risk—the youngest child able to do so explicitly was aged 12. Even those who had picked up such terms as "paedophile" and "child-molester" from adults or the media[10] did not appear to understand what this meant, and while some understood this to mean a strange person and by implication a potentially dangerous stranger, they did not join the pieces of the jigsaw together. Rather than recognizing the basis of adult motivations for warning them against strangers, they talked about being kidnapped for ransom or forced into a life of crime (usually drug-related). Older children, those in secondary school, did identify sexual risk. Some of them reflected back on their earlier lack of awareness of these dangers, able now to reinterpret them as sexual and to make sense of their earlier ignorance in terms of the jigsaw pieces then missing but now in place.

Once children do begin to fit the pieces together, to construct a provisional picture of the sexual world (provisional because this construction will always be subject to change), their sense-making is governed by their gendered self—their embodied gendered being. This affects not only new knowledge and experience, but also retrospective reinterpretation as they begin, in Gagnon and Simon's terms, to bring that past into greater congruity with their present understandings of themselves and their social world. It is for this reason that, for example, adult gay men and lesbians are able to tell a story of self in which they "always knew" they were lesbian or gay or that they always were but only later came to "realize" that this was the case—often on the basis of feeling "different" as children and, particularly, feeling they weren't quite normally (normatively) gendered. These accounts are not, as Vera Whisman says, simply reflections of their experience but are "told to fit those experiences into a coherent, conventionalized story" (1996, 181). Of course, those who grow up to be heterosexual may also have felt themselves "different" as children—but would not tell the same story. Heterosexuals are not called upon to account for their sexuality. They therefore do not feel it necessary to construct narratives explaining "how I became a heterosexual" or "how I knew I was heterosexual"; it is simply taken for granted. Since heterosexuality is the privileged norm, interrogating it is not integral to heterosexuals' emergent sexual selfhood.

Gender, however, remains central to young heterosexuals' sense of themselves as socially competent sexual actors. And, conversely, heterosexual sexual competence helps validate their sense of gendered selfhood. This is particularly important as young people struggle to leave the dependent status of childhood behind and make claims to autonomy and adulthood, since sexual and social maturity are gendered—and asymmetrical. For example, as Janet Holland and her colleagues found in investigating the experience of first heterosex, having sex is still understood as making a boy a man, but it does not make a girl a woman (1996). Yet a young man can have the option of opting out of sexual activity without imperiling his masculinity (unless, of course, his heterosexuality per se is called into question), since there are other ways of validating manhood, such as through physical prowess, toughness, and courage. Investigating the construction of masculinity in a tough neighborhood of Glasgow, Daniel Wight (1996) found that some young men showed disdain for any involvement with women, including sex: in the local argot, sex was for "jessies." Generally, though, what confirms masculinity is being (hetero)sexually *active;* what confirms femininity is being sexually *attractive* to men.

Young heterosexual women's sexual and gendered selfhood, however, is becoming more complex as they negotiate contradictory expectations. Their horizons are no longer limited to heterosexual domesticity, yet they still inhabit a highly heterosexualized social and cultural world where success in sexual relationships matters in terms of social esteem and self-worth. Here, new sexual scripts are on offer, replacing the older goals of romance and marriage with aspirations towards sexual autonomy and experimentation. Magazines marketed to young women positively exhort them to take control of their own sexual pleasure, to "discover" the potential of their bodies, and to become proficient in new sexual skills. Yet the double standard of morality, although considerably eroded, has not disappeared altogether—and neither has sexual violence and coercion. The contemporary sexual landscape would seem to require a high degree of self-reflexivity and indeed self-surveillance from young women as they attempt to avoid the pitfalls of deficiency (not being sexual enough) and excess (being too sexual). As a result, young women's desires, and their ability to manage a sexual project of the self, remain more constrained and more problematic than those of young men even when they stay within the bounds of normative heterosexuality (Holland et al. 1998; Tolman 2002).

Sexual self-awareness in our late modern world

Whether male or female and however they define their sexuality, young people approaching sexual adulthood in late modern Western societies are constructing their sexual selves at a time of rapid social change and in an uncertain sexual climate. Within everyday and media representations a liberal story of progress towards greater sexual freedom, tolerance, and diversity predominates. Yet our sexual world is far more complex and far less predictable than this comfortable narrative implies. It is not simply that the moral right is fighting against such change (with more political clout in the USA than in the UK), but that these changing sexual times have thrown up a host of tensions, contradictions, and associated anxieties (see Jackson and Scott 2004a). Ours is a world saturated with sexual imagery, yet one where adults still try to preserve children's "innocence"; where pre-marital and often casual sex is a feature of normal young adulthood, yet where sex education is hedged about with all manner of cautions and prohibitions. This is a world in which gay and lesbian chic can be fashionable while gays and lesbians are being bullied and assaulted in school playgrounds, at work, and on the streets. Our sexual climate is one where "openness" is valued and where ordinary people's intimate sexual secrets are revealed in detail on television and radio and in the "problem pages" of magazines and newspapers, yet where most young people remain unable to discuss sexuality freely with their parents.

Our confessional culture does, however, provide copious resources for fashioning a sexual self—for drawing on others' sexual stories in order to tell ones own. Late modernity also offers new avenues for sexual self-telling, whether through participating in "reality TV" or marketing our sexual selves through computer dating. Within these stories, endless possibilities for sexual self-knowledge and self-improvement, and for sexual choice and fulfillment, jostle with diverse risks and anxieties, from fears of violence, disease, and pregnancy to anxieties about not being "fit" enough to compete in the sexual marketplace or not being proficient enough in one's sexual performance. And, to answer these anxieties, there are the numerous products of a confessional culture that is also a therapeutically ordered one—self-help books offering cures for "sexual dysfunction" and techniques for improving performance, all in turn adding to the climate of excessive concern with the sexual and fuelling the anxieties it creates.

The cultural resources we draw on in the process of making sense of ourselves are, of course, historically specific. Thus particular modes of self-construction become available at different historical moments in specific social locations. Not only do socially located individual biographies and particular cultural understandings of the sexual provide materials for self-composition, but the social and cultural worlds each of us inhabits may affect the mode of composition itself, the forms of reflexivity available to us, and the ways in which we are able to account for or to tell the self. If theorists of modernity and late modernity are correct, over the last few centuries Western societies have become more and more concerned with exploring the self's interiority—with telling the self and surveillance of the self. This historical shift has coincided with and made possible a focus on sexuality as a central part of the self, a route to self-fulfillment, a touchstone of mental health, and more (see Heath 1982; Jackson and Scott 1997). Thus, heightened reflexive self-awareness has converged with the growth in the significance of sexuality, creating the conditions for a highly self-conscious sense of sexual subjectivity and opportunities for endless sexual self-telling.

A critical postscript

I have argued that an interactionist view of self provides a means of conceptualizing how we come to be embodied gendered and sexual individuals who nonetheless have the capacity to renegotiate gender divisions and resist dominant constructions of sexuality.

It can help to explain why gender is so central to our sense of self without there being a single way of being male or female and why it is so fundamental to the development of a sexual self without positing a deterministic link between gender and sexuality. It provides a basis for analyzing how the reflexivity entailed in the construction of our gendered and sexual selves can be mobilized into particular forms of self-understanding and self-telling in late modernity.

I do, however, have some reservations. These shortcomings (which are also, by the way, characteristic of much poststructuralist theorizing) concern inattention to what we might call social structural or institutional constraints.[11] From a purist interactionist perspective there is no social structure—sociality is entirely the product of intersubjective meaning and social action. As Herbert Blumer (1969) famously argued, people do not act in terms of social structures but in terms of the situation they find themselves in and their definition of that situation. But, I am not a purist. The situations we find ourselves in are shaped by material social circumstances and our location within gendered, classed, racialized, and sexual hierarchies; our definitions of those situations and, in particular, whether our definition "works" for us depends on our social and cultural resources. If we take seriously the idea that our sexual lives are simply one facet of our broader social lives, then we must recognize that our sexual selves are shaped within profoundly unequal local, national, and global social orders. Those who inhabit an affluent world characterized by sexual choice and freedom should not forget that in other places lives may be constrained by poverty and lack of choice – sexual or otherwise (Hennessey 2000; Plummer 2004). In saying this, I am not seeing agency as an exclusive possession of the privileged: the capacity for agency is basic to being a human, social animal (a humanist, foundational claim, I know, but one I am prepared to stand by). The point is that agency is both enabled and constrained by particular social circumstances—and nowhere is that clearer than in the conditions of self-narration that prevail in late modern societies.

Notes

1. "Social constructionism" is a rather clumsy term, perhaps because there is no single perspective laying claim to it but rather a cluster of differing approaches deriving from varied theoretical roots. In addition to phenomenological and interactionist sociology, poststructuralism, and postmodernism, by some definitions Marxism can be seen as a form of social constructionism, as can some versions of psychoanalysis. All these perspectives have been engaged with and developed by feminist, lesbian, gay, and queer theorists. For an earlier discussion of how they have informed feminist debates on sexuality, see Jackson 1996.

2. Berger and Luckman, though drawing on pragmatist and interactionist work, located themselves within the phenomenological tradition; Gagnon (2004) sees the American pragmatist tradition (a forerunner to symbolic interactionism) as a major influence, and I would see *Sexual Conduct* as closer to interactionism than phenomenology.

3. Foucault was never particularly interested in the question of where sexual desires come from—only in how bodies and pleasures had been ordered into "sex" by the apparatus of sexuality. Only in his late work did he become concerned with "technologies of the self," and the self here does not encompass the self as subjectivity—rather the self as object of its own aesthetic and moral governance.

4. This paragraph, and much of what follows, is peppered with references to my collaborative

work with Sue Scott, who shares my commitment to the interactionist tradition and whose contribution to my thinking on these issues is immense.

5. Mead actually uses the words "reflexive" and "reflexiveness" only occasionally: the emphasis on self-reflexivity comes to us through Herbert Blumer's exegesis of Mead. However, Mead's notion of "reflexiveness," "the turning back of the experience of the individual upon himself [*sic*]" (1934, 134), along with the idea that the self is both subject and object to itself, is fundamental to his conception of mind, self, and society.

6. One aspect of this I have been unable to deal with here is emotion. Interactionism is often accused of being overly cold and cognitive in contrast to psychoanalysis. Self-feeling and emotions can, however, be addressed within this perspective (see Jackson 1993).

7. In my early work, I referred to this as "protosexual learning" (see Jackson 1978; partially reprinted in Jackson 1999).

8. This research was carried out in collaboration with Sue Scott, Kathryn Backett-Milburn, and Jeni Harden.

9. The research was undertaken in Scotland, where children move from primary to secondary school at age 12.

10. In the UK, as in the U.S., "paedophiles" feature prominently in the media as among the most prominent "folk devils" of our time. A major media witch-hunt against suspected paedophiles took place just after we had completed our interviews with the children. It is possible that more children would have been aware of this term had we interviewed at this time, but even so, I am not convinced that they would have joined their fragments of knowledge together into a coherent idea of specifically sexual risk.

11. These doubts are partially, though not fully, answered by the addition of sociocultural scripting to interpersonal and intrapsychic scripting and by Gagnon's later attention to the sociocultural order and institutional setting of sexuality (Laumann, Gagnon et al. 2000; Gagnon 2004), though I still feel that insufficient emphasis is placed on structural inequalities.

References

Beck, U., and E. Beck-Gernsheim. 2002. *Individualization: Institutionalized individualism and its social and political consequences.* London: Sage.

Berger, P. L., and T. Luckman. 1967. *The social construction of reality: A treatise in the sociology of knowledge.* London: Allen Lane.

Blumer, H. *Symbolic interactionism: Perspective and methods.* Englewood Cliffs, NJ: Prentice Hall.

Butler, J. 1993. *Bodies that matter.* New York: Routledge.

Flax, J. 1990. *Thinking fragments: Psychoanalysis, feminism and postmodernism in the contemporary west.* Berkeley: University of California Press.

Foucault, M. 1978. *The history of sexuality*, vol. 1. New York: Random House.

———. 1980. The confession of the flesh. In *Power/Knowledge*, ed. C. Gordon. Brighton: Harvester.

Gagnon, J. H. 2004. *An interpretation of desire: Essays in the study of sexuality.* Chicago: University of Chicago Press.

Gagnon, J. H., and W. Simon, eds. 1974. *Sexual conduct: The social sources of human sexuality.* London: Hutchinson.

Giddens, A. 1991. *Modernity and self-identity: Self and society in the late modern age.* Cambridge, UK: Polity.

———. 1992. *The transformation of intimacy: Sexuality, love and eroticism in modern societies.* Cambridge, UK: Polity.

Heath, S. 1982. *The sexual fix.* London: Macmillan.

Hennessey, R. 2000. *Profit and pleasure: Sexual identities in late capitalism.* New York: Routledge.

Holland, J., C. Ramazanoğlu, S. Sharpe, and R. Thomson 1996. In the same boat? The gendered (in)experience of first heterosex. In Richardson, 143-60.

Holstein, J., and J. Gubrium. 2000. *The self we live by: Narrative identity in a postmodern world.* Oxford: Oxford University Press.

Jackson, S. 1978. *The social construction of female sexuality.* London: Women's Research and Resources Centre.

———. 1993. Even sociologists fall in love: An exploration in the sociology of emotions. *Sociology* 27, no. 2: 201–20.

———. 1996. Heterosexuality and feminist theory. In Richardson, 21-39.

———. 1999. *Heterosexuality in Question.* London: Sage.

———. 2006. Heterosexuality, sexuality and gender: rethinking the intersections. In *Intersections between feminist and queer theory*, ed. D. Richardson, J. McLaughlin, and M. E. Casey, 38-58. London: Palgrave.

Jackson, S., and S. Scott. 1997. Gut reactions to matters of the heart: reflections on rationality, irrationality and sexuality. *Sociological Review* 45, no. 4: 551–75.

———. 2004a. Sexual antinomies in late modernity. *Sexualities* 7, no. 2: 233–48.

———. 2004b. The personal *is* still political: heterosexuality, feminism and monogamy. *Feminism and Psychology* 14, no. 1: 151–57.

Kessler, S. 1998 *Lessons from the intersexed.* New Brunswick: Rutgers University Press.

Kessler, S., and W. McKenna. 1978. *Gender: An ethnomethodological approach.* Chicago: University of Chicago Press.

Laumann, E. O., J. H. Gagnon, R. T. Michael, and S. Michaels. 2000. *The social organization of sexuality: Sexual practices in the United States.* Chicago: University of Chicago Press.

McNay, L. 2000. *Gender and agency: Reconfiguring the subject in feminist and social theory.* Cambridge, UK: Polity.

Mead, G. H. 1934. *Mind, self, and society: From the standpoint of a social behaviorist.* Chicago: University of Chicago Press.

Plummer, K. 1995. *Telling sexual stories: Power, change and social worlds.* London: Routledge.

———. 2004. Not a love story. Plenary address at the *Pleasure and danger revisited* conference, University of Wales at Cardiff.

Richardson, D., ed. 1996. *Theorising heterosexuality: Telling it straight.* Buckingham: Open University Press.

Rubin, G. 1984. Thinking sex: notes for a radical theory of the politics of sexuality. In *Pleasure and danger*, ed. C. Vance, 267-319. London: Routledge.

Rose, N. 1989. *Governing the soul: The shaping of the private self.* London: Routledge.

Skeggs, B. 2004. *Class, self, culture.* London: Routledge.

Smith, D. 1999. *Writing the social: Critique, theory, and investigations.* Toronto: University of Toronto Press.

Stanley, L., and S. Wise. 1993. *Breaking out again: Feminist ontology and epistemology.* London: Routledge.

Weedon, C. 1987. *Feminist practice and poststructuralist theory.* Oxford: Blackwell.

Whisman, V. 1996. *Queer by choice: Lesbians, gay men, and the politics of identity.* New York: Routledge.

Wight, D. 1996. Beyond the predatory male: The diversity of young Glaswegian men's discourses to describe heterosexuality. In *Sexualizing the social: Power and the organization of sexuality*, ed. L. Adkins and V. Merchant, 145–70. London: Macmillan.

Ken Plummer

2

Queers, Bodies, and Postmodern Sexualities

A Note on Revisiting the "Sexual" in Symbolic Interactionism

The choice is not between throwing away rules previously developed and sticking obstinately by them. The intelligent alternative is to revise, adapt, expand and alter them. The problem is one of continuous, vital readaptation.
John Dewey, Human Nature and Conduct

As is now very well known, at the heart of much sociological thinking on sexuality lies the work of what might be called the "social constructionist turn" and responses to it. In contrast to thinking about sexuality as biological and "natural," with the prime goal of reproduction, constructionists have aimed to show the myriad ways in which human sexualities are always organized through economic, religious, political, familial, and social conditions. From the 1970s onwards, "constructionists," a group with diverse positions, have nonetheless argued that any analysis that does not at least recognize this must be seriously flawed.

Sexuality, for humans, is not simply a free floating "desire" but is always grounded in wider material and cultural forces. There is no essential "sexuality" with a strictly biological base that is cut off from the social. From the social acts of rape to the social processes surrounding reproduction, sexuality for humans has no reality *sui generis*. Any concern with "it" must always harbor wider social issues, for human sexualities have to be socially produced (no human can ever just "do it"), socially organized, socially maintained, and socially transformed. Overlapping with and omnipresent in all of social life, human sexualities are always conducted at an angle: they are never "just sex." And yet the major traditions of studying sexuality in general—through clinical analysis, sociobiology (and evolutionary psychology), social survey research, cognitive psychology, medical research, and "sexology" more generally—generally remain obstinate in seeing the world in this social way.[1] Although constructionism—in its various guises—may

An earlier version of this chapter appeared in *Qualitative Sociology* 26. no. 4 (Winter 2003): 515–30. With kind permission of Springer Science and Business Media.

have become a dominant "way of seeing" in the social sciences, its impact elsewhere re-mains slight.

Looking back to the sixties and seventies:
One foot forward . . .

My original forays into constructionist thought started in 1967 as part of the back-ground to my PhD thesis. Simultaneously becoming aware of the legal and political de-bates about changing the law surrounding homosexuality, "coming out" as a young gay man, and hanging around London's gay scene to conduct a somewhat primitive ethnog-raphy for my thesis—it was indeed a turning point in my life. My initial research goal was to "socialize" a world that had hitherto been almost wholly seen as a clinical aberra-tion. I wanted to understand the social nature of an experience formerly designated as a biological and psychological one, and I wanted to analyze it in a period when homo-sexuality was becoming partly decriminalized in the United Kingdom. (I was also in-volved at that time in the Albany Trust and the Homosexual Law Reform Society—two leading reformist organizations aimed at changing the law).[2] My core reading for that period—although I did not fully appreciate it at the time—was a series of early construc-tionist texts: Peter Berger and Thomas Luckmann's *The Social Construction of Reality,* Howie Becker's *Outsiders,* David Matza's *Becoming Deviant,* Herbert Blumer's *Symbolic Interactionism,* and Norman Denzin's *The Research Act,* as well as Mary McIntosh's "Ho-mosexual role" and a series of papers by Gagnon and Simon (notably "Psychosexual development") which were later to become the book *Sexual Conduct.* Slowly, I began to develop what I then started to call a "symbolic interactionist account of sexuality"—more general than just the topic of homosexuality with which I started. This position was written up as a paper for the British Sociological Association Annual Conference in 1974,[3] and later revised for the late Mike Brake's collection of essays on *Human Sexual Relations* in 1981.[4] At the same time, the Gay Liberation Front came along and the ex-hilaration of this suggested to me how sexualities were changing before my very eyes. I was one of about ten who sat in a room at the London School of Economics hearing how GLF had happened in the United States a year earlier and who started to make plans for it to happen in the United Kingdom.

Although I am not by inclination a very activist being, this meeting nevertheless changed my life. It was my epiphany. I could see that there was no need to stay in a closet (although I was already partially "out"). I found that the very experiences of being gay changed dramatically once I was fully out and on the streets. Interestingly, one of the first things that happened to me was to be thrown out of a gay bar for being too political: the conservative institutions of the gay world of the fifties and sixties saw the new radi-calism as a major threat and did not like it. The new radical gays were sensed as their enemies. Whatever "homosexuality" was in the past, it was never to be the same again, and this exciting sense of change fueled my thinking that sexuality—and gayness—were not simply "givens": they were wide open to social changes and were indeed the very "social constructions" that Becker, Berger, and others has been writing about. And so, both politically and theoretically, I came to see the world in constructionist terms.

The PhD moved more and more away from being an ethnography and turned into a series of theoretical statements about the social organization of sexuality and sexual differences. I suppose it was the first of its kind. It took symbolic interactionism and allied positions and applied them first to sexuality, then to sexual diversity, and finally to case studies of gay life. Eventually it became the foundation of my first book, *Sexual Stigma*. Despite the serious limitations of things we did not know then, I would still support the general line that I argued in this early work. There was the critique of essentialism and the language of perversion; the importance of emergent and contested sexual meanings; a sense of the "constructed" nature of human sexualities; an awareness of the significance of variation and diversity in sexual life; and a growing sensitivity to the role of metaphor in thinking about the erotic. But it was written in an era that was pre-AIDS, when the Foucauldian deluge had not yet happened,[5] when the "feminist sexuality" debates were still being shaped[6] but not yet fully formed, and when Thatcherism and Reaganism were just on the horizon. Postmodernism and all its accroutrements—from globalization to cybersex—were waiting in the wings. My symbolic interactionist account of sexual conduct now borders on being nearly thirty years old!

Nearly three decades on, then, a lot of changes have happened—theoretically, politically, and sexually. In retrospect, it is clear that there were problems with my early formulations. What was most conspicuously missing from the early writing (though it is not surprising) was a concern for the nascent feminist theorizing that was also taking place at that time. Indeed, my major encounters with feminist theory did not really take shape until the early 1980s, with a key text for me at the time being Andrea Dworkin's *Pornography: Men Possessing Women*. Extreme as that book may be for many people, I needed a book like that to jolt me into thinking about wider issues than the contextual and the gay (and it was soon followed by the *Pleasure and Danger* debate).[7] Yet, at the same time, much of the constructionist position has now become a commonplace for sociologists and many other social analysts (though sadly not, I hasten to add, for many sexologists or medical people for whom the biological world remains exclusive and prime).

Constructionism itself can mean many things to many people. A number of recent writers—especially in social psychology—often talk as though it is new.[8] For me, the version I have always gravitated towards is indeed the one that flows from the theory of symbolic interactionism, which takes us back a century or so to pragmatism. Yet, retrospectively, there are actually very few theorists of "the constructionism of sexualities" who speak in interactionist terms—most simply do not acknowledge this branch of theory, or they have roots elsewhere (in history, cultural anthropology, feminism, materialist Marxism, or activism). It is true that Gagnon and Simon may be seen as its key protagonists, but they actually rarely referred to themselves as symbolic interactionists.[9] Others—for example, Jeffrey Victor, Pepper Schwartz, Barry Dank, Richard Troiden, and Martin Weinberg—have made brief linkages. Many others have let it inform their work without acknowledging the roots. But, all in all, it would seem that the symbolic interactionist version of sexuality is a minority position within constructionism.

And, in a sense, what does this matter? It matters to me because of the continuing development of the theory itself. It has not remained shrouded in its foundations but has gone on generating lively debates that may well continue to refashion the way we think about sexualities. A number of happy circumstances—a new journal, a new organization, new leaders, new students, and new ideas!—brought about a certain revitalization of the theory during the 1980s and 1990s, such that one reviewer of interactionist fortunes could talk of the "sad demise, mysterious disappearance, and glorious triumph of symbolic interactionism" (Fine 1993).[10] Several others have recently claimed that interactionism is indeed the understated foundation of all sociology! (Maines 2002; Atkinson and Housley 2003).

We need not go this far, but it can be sensed that from interactionism has indeed come a series of lively new concerns. Among many other concerns, there has been the development of a sociology of emotions and a sociology of bodies. There has been a turn to cultural studies, with much work now focusing upon narratives, storytelling, and semiotics, as well as on mediated communication. Some have reasserted the importance of structures and histories, and most agree on the importance of power. An awareness of racism, sexism, and heteronormativity has become more prominent. There have been challenging new directions in qualitative research and interpretative research strategies. There has been an interest in the field of inequalities. There has been a hearty debate about the links between symbolic interactionism and postmodernism[11] as well as major attempts to rework and reintegrate many of its theoretical concerns. All of these have implications for the continuing study of sexualities. In what follows, I wish to suggest how just a few of these issues can take the study of sexualities forward.

Worrying about postmodernism: On going (a bit) queer

Nobody writing in the 1990s could seriously have avoided the issues posed by postmodernism for very long, and indeed the theme of postmodernism has been a recurrent issue in interactionist writings over the past fifteen years or so. Some, like Norman Denzin, a longtime interactionist and leader in the field,[12] have been taking a strong adversarial line that the contemporary social world is indeed postmodern; that the theories and methods used to study it should be postmodern; and that interactionist ideas should be ruptured through an engagement with the works of Derrida, Lyotard, Baudrillard, and others. Postmodernism can take us beyond the limits of interactionist analyses. Others—and I would count myself amongst these—argue against the worst excesses of some postmodern analyses while suggesting that there is indeed an elective affinity between much symbolic interactionism (with its foundations in pragmatism) and postmodernism. I tend to agree with David Maines who has argued that while symbolic interactionism "finds an easy affinity with much of postmodernism," it "has no need for it" (1996, 323).[13] In short, because of the strong interpretative centre of both theories, there is an affinity. Both accounts of the world highlight localism, ambiguity, differences, instability, signs and symbols, and a certain playfulness. They tend to withdraw from accounts of the world that overgeneralize, seek totalism and closure, stress homogeneity, and unearth heavy structures. But interactionism—unlike much postmodernism— does not wish to lose its grip on the "obdurate empirical world" and its search for a truth that will at least hold for the time being.

When this debate is applied to sexualities, the interactionist/postmodernist offers up a much more modest account of sexualities than many in the sexological world would have us believe. It throws into doubt any Grand Narratives of Sexuality—from Freud to

Sexology—that have haunted much of the modern world's analysis of sexuality. It can see that the modern discourse of "autonomous sexuality as a separate sphere of existence" (Halperin 1993, 418) is deeply flawed. Indeed, all the theoretical talk over "queer" over the past fifteen years has in part been talk about a postmodernization of sex in signaling a breakdown of clear and stable categories and a loss of faith in any compelling grand narrative of sexuality. Queer theory is really poststructuralism (and postmodernism) applied to sexualities and genders.[14]

The late William Simon's too-neglected study of *Postmodern Sexualities* has charted some of this critique and change. According to him, we are now increasingly living our lives in ways that are "different from any that humanity has previously known" with pluralization, individuation, and multiplying choices making social life very different from any previous era. Spaces start to emerge for new kinds of sexualities; "sex" is no longer the source of the truth; human sexualities become destabilised, decentred and de-essentialized. The sexual life is no longer seen as harboring an essential unitary core locatable within a clear framework (like the "nuclear family," or even "the gay lifestyle") with an essential truth waiting to be discovered: there are only fragments. It is, as Simon says, "accompanied by the problematic at every stage" (20).

I am very sympathetic to this view but there have to be cautions too. The postmodern world is really only the world of a few at the present time. For as Steven Seidman, himself both a postmodernist and a "queer theorist,"[15] has argued, "Modernity is not abruptly coming to an end. In most parts of the globe, modernization remains the chief social goal . . . it may be in crisis, but it continues to shape the contours of our lives" (1994, 1). So, while there is a newer space for the more problematic thinking generated by such developments as "queer theory," there should still be plenty of room for traditional kinds of analyses. When I read some of the wilder textual analyses of the queer theorists or hear of the fragmenting sexual identities championed by the postmodernists, I do sometimes wonder just whose worlds I am entering? They rightly raise very challenging ideas, and I am often excited when I read them, but I also have a gnawing feeling that they are very much removed from the ordinary everyday lived experiences of sexuality that most people encounter across the world in their daily lives. To see this, we do also need a more conventional interactionist grounded ethnographic work alongside the queer studies.[16]

Worrying about research: On taking new routes

Behind much interactionist writing has been a pragmatic concern with methodology. Most recently this can be found in the analysis of "New directions in qualitative research" (Holstein and Gubrium 1997) and of the influential *Handbook of Qualitative Research* by Denzin and Lincoln (third edition, 2005). There has been a challenging new turn in methodology that brings a more experimental feel to research along with new ways of gathering and presenting data. An important issue is to sense ourselves in and around our research, jolting the reader in almost Brechtian ways to rethink what the data is actually about and what is being presented. A much greater self-reflexivity is generally being encouraged.

Such exhortations may well benefit the study of sexualities, because it seems that, despite a great deal of research and theory, remarkably little of it confronts head on (so to speak) the nature of sexualities, sexual meanings, and sexual lives. Apart from a few constructionist ethnographies and studies, the interactionist study of sexualities has not actually been very innovative or empirical. The classic *Tearoom Trade* (Humphreys 1970), for all its flaws, is a major exception, and in its wake did come a series of linked studies that showed how gay men had sex in public places—cruising the truckers, sex on the highway, the silent community, (see Delph, 1978). Others have told us a great deal about communities, cultures, and identities (from *Identity and Community in the Gay World* to *Sex and Sensibility*). But in such studies the sexual often disappears: we have identities, interaction patterns, and managed selves, but the body and its orgasmic moments are hardly a presence. There are odd flashes of innovation, but in the main, we could speak of a "vanishing sexuality"—a certain absence of the sexual in much contemporary constructionist/interactionist research on the sexual. Mainstream sexual research focuses on the sexual but gives it no meaning while much constructionist thought overwhelms the sexual with meanings and gives little focus to the sexed body and its desires.

Thus, it has seemed to me for some time (although I am not brave—or interesting enough—to do it) that we are in need of some research that is auto/ethnographic: the study of the sexual self of the sexual researcher in the mode of "On first being a john"— still almost unique and too neglected (Stewart 1972). How such work can proceed is partly exemplified in the (non-sexual) auto/ethnographies of Carolyn Ellis's *Final Negotations* and Susan Krieger's *Social Science and the Self: Personal Essays on an Art Form*. The work of Carol Rambo Ronai on strip dancing provides a clearer exemplar,where she discusses her multiple feelings as she strips. Here she engages in self-reflection, and provides what she calls a "layered account" that allows different aspects of the researcher's self to "roam around the text."[17] The complexity of being sexual is partially brought to the fore.

It seems to me that sociology could learn some lessons here from queer theory.[18] Queer is seen as partially deconstructing our own discourses and creating a greater openness in the way we think through our categories. Queer theory is, to quote Michael Warner, a stark attack on "normal business in the academy" (1993, 25). It adopts a "scavenger methodology that uses different methods to collect and produce information on subjects who have been deliberately or accidentally excluded from traditional studies of human behavior." In its most general form, it is a refusal of orthodox method. Again, I repeat, I am a very cautious queer theorist—I worry that it sometimes goes incomprehensibly too far and removes itself from interactionist concerns with grounded everyday life. But some queer theorists' ethnographic reconstructions around texts prove very telling. D. A. Miller's odd study *Place for Us* of the musical and gay life proves to be annoyingly insightful about a lurking homophobia in the gay love affair with musicals and piano bars, while Judith Halberstam's *Female Masculinities* jolts the reader into thinking about the diversities of womanly experience.

Halberstam's study argues for a "certain disloyalty to conventional disciplinary methods" as she "raids" literary textual methods, film theory, ethnographic field research, historical survey, archival records, and taxonomy to produce her original account of emerging forms of "female masculinity" (1998, 9–13).[19] This is the mode of "deconstruction," and in this world, the very idea that types of people called homosexuals or gays or lesbians can be called up for interview becomes a key problem in itself.

Instead, the researcher should become more and more open to start sensing new worlds of possibilities. Many of these social worlds are not immediately transparent, while others are amorphously nascent and forming. Here, then, is a rag bag of ethnographic descriptions: of aristocratic European cross-dressing women of the 1920s, butch lesbians, dykes, drag kings, tomboys, black "butch in the hood" rappers, trans-butches, gender inverts, stone butches, the female-to-male transexual (FTM), raging bull dykes, and the tribade! She is quite happy also to show through films as diverse as *Alien* and *the Killing of Sister George* at least six prototypes of the female masculine: tomboys, predators, fantasy butches, transvestites, barely butches, and postmodern butches. All this research brings to the surface social worlds only dimly articulated hitherto—with, of course, the suggestion that there are more, many more, even more deeply hidden.

Side by side with this new turn to a queer ethnography, there also comes a concern with amongst both queer theorists and interactionists with writing strategies. As the editor of a journal, *Sexualities,* I have become more and more aware of the conventionality of academic writing and how this often does not do justice to interesting material. Nor do many contributors seem very aware of the very formal conditions which shape textuality. In a major summary of this growing concern, anthropologist James Clifford comments about the writing of one major social science form—ethnography—but I think it can be applied to most presentations of "academic sexuality."

> Writing is determined in at least six ways: (1) contextually (it draws from and creates meaningful social milieux); (2) rhetorically (it uses and is used by expressive conventions); (3) institutionally (one writes within, and against, specific traditions, disciplines, audiences); (4) generically (an ethnography is usually distinguishable from a novel or a travel account); (5) politically (the authority to present cultural realities is uniquely shared and at times contested); (6) historically (all the above conventions and constraints are changing). These determinations govern the inscription of coherent ethnographic fictions. (1986, 6)

The simplest way of grasping this is to take any finished "text" on sexuality (like a research report or a book, but even a film or a web site), hold it in your hands, look at it, and ponder: *Just how did this writing come to get there with those "sexual" words in that form. What were the social conditions that enabled this text about sexuality to be organized in this way?*[20]

Worrying about theory: On not being too grand

Interactionism insists on being a humble theory, not claiming too much and not dealing with major abstractions and false dualisms. Indeed, the real task of an interactionist is simply to look at social life as people "do things together":[21] its core interests lie in the doing of ethnographies and in an intimate familiarity with ongoing social (sexual) worlds. It is a hands-on "down-to-earth" empirical approach, even though there have always been those who have spoken more theoretically about it. (Both the early pragmatists and Herbert Blumer wrote major defensive essays[22] where there was no empirical data at all.) In general, the tradition is one steeped in the exploration and inspection of data.

Yet the theory has tended to remain lodged in false binaries and dualisms: biology versus the social, determinism versus choice, essence versus construct. Pedagogically, overstated "splits" and "dualisms" may often be needed to clarify debates: a one-sided accentuation of a position can often shift arguments along and can be a useful teaching device. But the lived, empirical world is never that simple. "Reality" has to be more messy than this. And indeed, a symbolic interactionism that wants to make these false splits is unfaithful to its roots. For the founders—Mead, James, Dewey, and others—all wanted to avoid these false philosophical dualistic antinomies and show how the dilemmas they posed were worked through practically in everyday circumstances. Not for them biology versus the social, determinism versus choice, essence versus construct. False dualisms were shunned. Hence, the biological and the social interact; chance, choice, and determination interact; childhood learning and adult life interact; symbols and the material worlds interact. Even words like "perversion" and "normality" interact in everyday worlds.

And in this interactive process, of course, new forms emerge. For interactionists, the task is to step into the flow of practical life and to break down the spurious and false abstractions of the philosophical world. The problem is not to take a side with one position on these debates; rather the task is to see how supposed antimonies work their way through practically in everyday affairs.

To take an example: one of the dualistic splits that I overstated in earlier work[23] (and I fear I may have done it again at the start of this article!) was that between "essences" or "emergents" along with the importance of process. I would now worry that the emphasis on process may get taken too far. Of course, symbolic interactionism has always properly highlighted the fluidity, emergence, and processual aspects of social life. Their analytic focus is always on becoming, emergence, and change. But interactionism has never said that there are no stable patterns of routine interactions or that selves do not become routinized, lodged, committed, or stabilized. Indeed, process and pattern commingle together, and the task of interactionists is to chart this stable process. Thus, the precarious everyday flux of life is open to constant stabilizing and essentializing, and this has important implications.

Thus, for instance, sexual radicals—like Kate Borenstein and Susie Bright (and maybe theorists like Judith Butler or Kath Weston)—usually claim that our sexualities and our genders are open to wide, wild, and wobbly transgressions. They sense identities as malleable and variable; of sexuality as transforming performances, and the like. I have some sympathies with this group, but it has to be said that while the sexual/gender fringe may indeed be a little like this (but only may be and only a little), empirically I have found it very rare indeed to come across people who live their lives in such fleeting, fragmentary, and unstable ways. Radical theorizing apart, it is quite the contrary: sexualities and genders tend to be organized very deeply indeed. Gender pervades almost every aspect of our lives, and seems to have a very deep structure. It cannot be lightly changed, performed, or wished away very quickly. Likewise, patterns of sexual desire also seem subject to deep routinization. This is not of course to say that gender or desire cannot be changed over lives or over cultures, or that they do not vary over time and space—all the constructionist writings point to the fact that they can and they do. Those who argue that there are universal women and men, universal homosexuals, or universal transvestites striding around history and across cultures simply miss the importance of precarious and contingent social organisation. But with the exception of some radically sexual transgressors, changes do not happen that easily or quickly—and the unstable, identity-less, utterly fractured sexual and gender identity seems to be largely a myth created by social science!

On worrying about the body:
On facing the lustily erotic

Symbolic interactionism may have traveled some way in rethinking the sexual over the past thirty years, but it may also have gone too far. A now commonly recognized weakness with much of the new thinking of sexualities from the 1970s onwards was its lack of concern with the body. There has been an exaggeration of the symbolic at the expense of the corporeal being. Of course this was much needed in the 1970s: sexuality is most certainly a hugely symbolic, social affair—a point that flew in the face of much sociological thought then. But, it is also (and not contradictorily) a lusty, bodily, fleshy affair, and it is a stunning omission from many earlier formulations that the living and breathing, sweating and pumping, sensuous and feeling world of the emotional, fleshy body is hardly to be found. This has posed a problem: there is little humping and pumping, sweatiness or sexiness in much sociological work. Instead, we have discourses, identities, cultures, patriarchies, queer theories, transgender politics: you name it. Anything but the lustily erotic. Until recently, the body and emotions have been largely absent. This is a serious error, as Dowsett says:

> We must no longer refuse the sedition of ordinary human bodies-in-sex . . . Were
> we to follow this path, we might find a new sexuality exists . . .we may see sexuality in modes of sociality that confound conventional structural categories. We
> may begin to take seriously the sex experiences and activities of other peoples,
> place and times. We may even cease that pastoral project, stop seeking to clean up
> sexuality in some liberal pluralist project of purification, and instead begin to enjoy
> a little more of creative potential in its sweat, bump and grind. (Dowsett 2000, 44;
> Dowsett 1996)

It is no longer possible to ignore this body, as it has started to play more and more of a central role in social thought. It is true that in the past the body has been "an absent presence in sociology" (Shilling 1993, 9) with its own "secret history" (Turner 1996), but since the 1980s there has been a major development of a "sociology of bodies" which transcends binary thinking and grounds social life, subjectivities, discourses and bodies together. For some sociologists, the body has indeed become the core feature of social life on which all social processes seem to be founded. "The body" has increasingly moved centre stage.[24] Still, it remains something of an irony that the two contemporary sociological literatures on sexualities and bodies somehow rarely manage to connect. It is true that the gendered body has been much discussed, but the sexualized or eroticized body has generally been of less concern to those who study the body. Indeed, when it is discussed, it is usually the sexualized text or representation and not the corporeal body. And at the same time, as we have seen, those sociologists who have studied sexuality have generally focused more on it as a script, a discourse, a power strategy, or an identity and only rarely as a body, body project, or embodiments. But the body, surely, is both a central site of concern for both the symbolism and the practices of sex. We can see the body as both an erotically charged symbol harboring a host of meanings and a series of material practices of embodiments. We can think firstly of just how much sex comes to be represented and how it touches nerves through, for instance, pornography—the persistent litmus of social conflict around sexualities—but we can think also of commingled skins, of being inside another's body or having another's body inside you: to be penetrated, to be invaded, to be engulfed, to be taken. What too of a sociology of embodiments around the erotic activities surrounding the mouth, the vagina, the anus, the breast, the toe? It is apparent that the body needs bringing back into sexuality studies.

We might start to speak of the embodiment of sexual practices: of doing body work around sex. "Sexualities" involve social acts through which we "gaze" at bodies, desire bodies, taste (even eat) bodies, smell bodies, fashion and adorn bodies, touch bodies, hear bodies, penetrate bodies, and orgasm bodies. These bodies can be our own or those of others. "Doing sex" means "doing erotic body work." Sex body projects entail, at the very least, presenting and representing bodies (as sexy, non-sexy—on the street, in the gym, in the porno movie); interpreting bodies and body parts ("the gaze" and the "turn ons" and "turn offs"—sexual excitements of different kinds, from voyeurism to stripping); manipulating bodies (through the use of fashion, cosmetics, or prosthetics); penetrating bodies (all kinds of intercourses from body parts like fingers and penises to "sex toy objects"); transforming bodies (stages of erotic embodiment and movements towards orgasms); commodifying bodies (in sex work, live sex acts, stripping, pornography and the like (Chapkis 1997)); ejecting and ejaculating bodies as all kinds of bodily fluids—semen, blood, sweat, saliva—even urine and fecal matter—start to commingle; possessing bodies (as we come to own or dominate others bodies); exploiting bodies (as we come to abuse or terrorize them); and transgressing bodies (as we go the extremes in the use of our erotic bodies).

From this, we could also start to talk about the new body technologies of sexuality. These new technologies include at one extreme how erotic bodies are (and have been for some time) managed through medical interventionism. I think here not only of the long histories of birth control, but of the more recent medical interventions such as Viagra that work to engorge the body with eroticism; with transgender realignment surgery, which helps refashion the genitalia; with the new methods of assisted conception (artificial insemination (AI), in vitro fertilization (IVF), embryo transfer (ET), gamete intra-fallopian transfer (GIFT)) that further separate out acts of sex, reproduction, gestation, and childrearing; and with the multi-billion dollar industry of the cosmetic industry, where the breasts, the face, and the rest of the body becomes transformed through medical procedures, often for a sexual end. These are but instances of technology at work to shift the sexualizing body (see Melluci 1996; Marshall 2002; Holmes 2002). They also start to suggest an iceberg tip of such transformations. The body is being reconstituted for postmodern times and we are entering the age of the post-human and the cyborg (e.g., Gray Hables 2000). This also means new modes of (dis)embodied sexualities such as may be found in the worlds of the seemingly rapidly growing cybersex. Through telephone sex, online porn, sex chat rooms, webcam erotics, virtual realities, etc., new disembodied sexual worlds may be in the making. Masturbation, solitariness, and isolation may be one hallmark of such a world, but accessibility to sexual imagery on a global scale and a permanent supply of partners is another.

Symbolic interactionist worlds and the future of sex research

Human sexualities have been studied and theorized about for over a century, and as with all such studies they have congealed into various "social worlds" (Clarke 1998; Strauss 1993). One world (for instance, "the medical models of sexuality") will have its own history, language, journals, and conferences, and it may indeed have little contact with another (such as "queer theory") with its own history, language, journals, and conferences. Thus, to juxtapose some of the writings from *GLQ* alongside the *Archives of Sexual Behavior* would be to enter different planets (ironically, Warner's book is called *Fear of a Queer Planet*). The social worlds of studying sexualities can and often do overlap, but in the main they function more or less autonomously. While there are already some interesting histories of researching and theorizing the sexual,[25] an account of their social worlds and the tensions therein must be awaited.

But one of these social worlds has been that of the symbolic interactionist. Itself part of a larger set of theory worlds, throughout the twentieth century symbolic interactionism has been a persistent, if not always manifest, influence on social thought in general. Its concern with meanings, process, interaction, and a grounded familiarity with everyday life makes it a prime tool for approaching all aspects of social life as they emerge and transform. This is no less true for its study of the erotic and the sexual. Although there have been remarkably few self-confessed interactionist students of sexualities, I have suggested throughout this article that nevertheless the influence of interactionism has been considerable. It may be a small social world when compared with the medical worlds of sex research, but it has had some impact within sociological circles at least.

Yet, like any theory, it is constantly subject to revision in changing times. It has, for instance, had to engage with debates around the body, with new trends in queer theory, with new styles of ethnographic work, and with the fashions of postmodernism. There are other issues which I have not had space to deal with here—like the need to connect theories of sexual action to sexual order, and the promise of interactionist analyses of sexuality in looking at power—but my goals in this brief paper have not been exhaustive. I have merely wished to signpost the continuing vitality of one major theoretical approach to the study of sexualities functioning in its own social world. There is plenty more work to be done.

Acknowledgment

The author wishes to thank Janice Irvine for her suggestion that the article needed writing and for her advice on the content.

Notes

1. A brief look at two of the leading journals in the field, *Archives of Sexual Behavior* and *The Journal of Sex Research,* would soon reinforce this (although more so for the former than the latter). *Archives of Sexual Behavior* is almost exclusively clinical and biological, whereas *The Journal of Sex Research* is certainly more eclectic and does contain both theoretical and socially linked articles. Its main focus, however, is what we might call the "psychological survey" study. This is an approach that draws out correlates of sexual functioning through survey samples. It is very common in most of the "sexological" journals. This is in stark contrast with the "queer" journals like *GLQ* where social theory dominates.

2. I did my PhD part time at the London School of Economics between 1968 and 1973, initially with David Downes but primarily with Paul Rock as my supervisor. Paul Rock is a leading UK symbolic interactionist and author of *The Making of Symbolic Interactionism* (1997). My external examiner was John Gagnon, who was visiting Cambridge in the academic year 1972–73.

3. Presented at the University of Aberdeen, April 1974.

4. I had worked with Brake on a small study of male prostitution during the early 1970s while he was a colleague at Enfield College (now Middlesex University).

5. Michael Foucault's *The History of Sexuality,* Vol. 1 was not published in the U. S. until 1978 (and in the UK in 1979). It is mentioned in the article only briefly. Its significance for sexuality studies only became truly apparent during the 1980s, largely after Foucault's death.

6. Vance's *Pleasure and Danger* is seen as the *locus classicus* of this debate.

7. It was in "The social uses of sexuality" that this first really became apparent.

8. Ken Gergen's work is also not very familiar with the sociological traditions of constructionism but it is a very wide-ranging analysis.

9. In their later works, it is possible to see Gagnon gravitating towards Durkheim and Simon towards psychoanalysis. They certainly came from the Chicago tradition and they went to Symbolic Interactionist conferences, but they did not seem to have a passion to label themselves this way. See their comments on their work in *Sexualities.*

10. I have also provided a review of the state of modern symbolic interactionist theory in Plummer 2003. Many key references are cited therein, and there is also a bibliographic guide to the field.

11. A standard source for these complaints is chapter 3 of B. N. Meltzer, J. W. Petras, and L. T. Reynolds's *Symbolic Interactionism* (1975), reprinted in Plummer 1991.

12. He has long been the editor of the annual yearbook *Studies in Symbolic Interaction,* and has written a number of influential texts — not least *Symbolic Interactionism and Cultural Studies.*

13. In a recent study, he also suggests that SI may be the understated basis of all U.S. sociology.

14. Often a distinction is made between queer theory, queer politics, and queer culture. Here we are talking mainly about queer theory (see Stein and Plummer, 1994).

15. Queer theory may be regarded as a theory of sexuality closely allied to postmodern theory. See Seidman's *Queer Theory/Sociology* (1996).

16. I also feel that the use of the word "queer" is a younger person's game. Knowing the history of the word, and how it was used in my childhood playgrounds, I still cannot easily use it.

17. Some recent social science anthologies make a virtue of these new modes. Ellis and Flaherty's *Investigating Subjectivity,* for instance, has ethnographic research presented in the forms of drama, personal narrative with multiple voices, and as poetry.

18. I have made some preliminary moves into this analysis with Mahoney and Kong (2001), where we attempt to "queer the interview."

19. She borrows from Eve Kasofsky Sedgwick's "nonce taxonomy": "The making and unmaking

and remaking and redissolution of hundreds of old and new categorical meanings concerning all the kinds it takes to make up a world" (Sedgwick 1990, 23).

20. I take this much further in my chapter on writing in Plummer 2001.

21. In a recent interview I conducted with Howard S. Becker (2003), he claims to not recognize much of what passes as interactionism these days and returns to his old theme of *Doing Things Together* (1986).

22. Classically, Blumer's major book of essays is full of abstractions and polarized debates!

23. Notably, Plummer 1982 and reprinted in Stein et al 2002.

24. Indeed, by 1998 the British Sociological Association could organize its annual conference around the theme of "making sense of the body," and just a year earlier the journal *Body and Society* had been launched.

25. Robinson's *The Modernization of Sex* is now a classic and details the work of Kinsey, Masters and Johnson, and Ellis in terms of both their content and their social impact. More recently, Weston's *longslowburn*, Irvine's *Disorders of Desire*, and Eriksen's *Kiss and Tell* have provided major critical reviews (though again strongly tied to the US traditions). Other works have brought together some of the key "sexual documents" of our time (including Jeffreys 1987; Porter and Hall 1995; and Bland and Doan 1998). We do have starts, then, in looking at the histories and social worlds of sex research and theory, and it is clear that there is both massive data and secondary sources for such a project.

References

Atkinson, P., and W. Housley. 2003. *Interactionism: An essay in sociological amnesia*. London: Sage.

Becker, H. S. 1986. *Doing things together: Selected papers*. Evanston: Northwestern.

Blumer, H. 1969. *Symbolic interactionism: Perspective and method*. Englewood Cliffs, NJ: Prentice Hall.

Brake, M., ed. 1981. *Human sexual relations: Towards a redefinition of sexual politics*. Middlesex: Penguin.

Chapkis, W. 1997. *Live sex acts: Women performing erotic labor*. New York: Routledge.

Clarke, A. 1998. *Disciplining reproduction: Modernity, American life sciences, and the problem of sex*. Berkeley: University of California Press.

Delph, E. W. 1978. *The silent community*. London: Sage.

Denzin, N. K., and Y. S. Lincoln, eds. 2005. *The Sage handbook of qualitative research*. 3rd ed. London: Sage.

Dowsett, G. 1996. *Practicing desire: Homosexual sex in the era of AIDS*. Stanford: Stanford University Press.

———. 2000. Bodyplay. In *Framing the sexual subject: The politics of gender, sexuality, and power*, ed. R. Parker, R. M. Barbosa, and P. Aggleton, 29–45. Berkeley: University of California Press.

Dworkin, A. 1981. *Pornography: Men possessing women*. London: Women's Press.

Ellis, C., and M. G. Flaherty. 1992. *Investigating subjectivity: Research on lived experience*. London: Sage.

Eriksen, J. 1998. *Kiss and tell: Surveying sex in the twentieth century*. Cambridge: Harvard University Press.

Fine, G. A. 1993 The sad demise, mysterious disappearance, and glorious triumph of symbolic interactionism. *Annual Review of Sociology* 19:61–87.

Gagnon, J. H. and W. Simon. 2005. *Sexual conduct: The social sources of human sexuality*. 2nd ed. Chicago: Aldine.

Gergen, K. J. 1999. *An invitation to social construction*. London: Sage.

Gray Hables, C. 2000. *The cyborg citizen: Politics in the posthuman age*. London: Routledge.

Halberstam, J. 1998. *Female masculinity*. Durham: Duke University Press.

Halperin, D. 1993. Is there a history of sexuality? In *The lesbian and gay studies reader*, ed. H. Abelove, M. Barale, and D. Halperin. London: Routledge.

Holmes, M. 2002. Rethinking the meaning and management of intersexuality. *Sexualities* 5, no. 2: 159–80.

Holstein, J., and J. Gubrium. 1997. New directions in qualitative research. Paper presented at the meeting of the American Sociological Association. Toronto.

Humphreys, L. 1970. *Tearoom trade: Impersonal sex in public places*. Chicago: Aldine.

Irvine, J. 2005. *Disorders of desire: Sexuality and gender in modern American sexology*. Rev. ed. Philadelphia: Temple University Press.

Mahoney, D., K. Travis, and K. Plummer. 2001. Queering the interview. In *The handbook of interviewing*, ed. J. Gubrium and J. Holstein. London: Sage.

Maines, D. R. On postmodernism, pragmatism and plasterers: some thoughts and questions. *Symbolic Interaction* 19, no. 4: 323–40.

———. 2002. *The faultline of consciousness: A view of interactionism in sociology*. New York: Aldine de Gruyter.

Marshall, B. 2002. Hard science: Gendered constructions of sexual dysfunction in the Viagra Age. *Sexualities* 5, no. 2: 131–58.

Melucci, A. 1992. *The Playing Self: Person and Meaning in the Planetary Society*. Cambridge: Cambridge University Press.

Miller, D. A. 1998. *Place for us: Essay on the Broadway musical*. Cambridge: Harvard University Press.

Nardi, P. M., and B. E. Schneider, eds. 1998. *Social perspectives in lesbian and gay studies: A reader*. London: Routledge.

Plummer, K. 1975. *Sexual stigma: An interactionist account*. London: Routledge.

———. 1982. Symbolic interactionism and sexual conduct: An emergent perspective. In *Human Sexual Relations*, ed. M. Brake. Middlesex: Penguin.

———. 1984. The social uses of sexuality: Symbolic interaction, power and rape. In *Perspectives on Rape and Sexual Assault*, ed. J. Hopkins, 37–55. London: Harper and Row.

———, ed. 1990. *Symbolic interactionism: Two volumes of readings*. Aldershot: Edward Elgar.

———. 1995. *Telling sexual stories: Power, change and social worlds*. London: Routledge.

———. 1996. Symbols of change. Introduction to Simon 1996.

———. 1998. The past, present, and futures of the sociology of same sex relations. In Nardi and Schneider, 605–14.

———. 2000. Symbolic interactionism in the twentieth century: The rise of empirical social theory. In *The Blackwell companion to social theory*, ed. B. Turner, 223–51. Oxford: Blackwell.

———. 2000b. *Documents of life 2: An invitation to a critical humanism*. London: Sage.

———. 2001. The square of intimate citizenship. *Citizenship Studies*. November.

———. 2002. *Sexualities: Critical assessments*. Four volumes. London: Routledge.

———. 2003. Continuity and change in Howard S. Becker's work: An interview with Howard S. Becker. *Sociological Perspectives* 46, no. 1: 21–39.

Robinson, P. 1976. *The modernization of sex: Havelock Ellis, Alfred Kinsey, William Masters, and Virginia Johnson*. London: Elek.

Rock, P. 1997. *The making of symbolic interactionism*. London: Macmillan.

Ronai, C. R. 1992. The reflexive self through narrative: A night in the life of an erotic dancer/researcher. In Ellis and Flaherty, 102–25. London: Sage.

Shilling, C. 1993. *The body and social theory*. London: Sage.

[30]   Seidman, S., ed. 1994. The postmodern turn. Cambridge: Cambridge University Press.

————. 1996. *Queer Theory/Sociology*. Oxford: Blackwell.

Sedgwick, E. K. 1990. *Epistemology of the closet*. Berkeley: University of California Press.

Simon, W. 1996. *Postmodern sexualities*. London: Routledge.

Strauss, A. 1993. *Continual permutations of action*. New York: Aldine de Gruyter.

Stewart, G. L. 1972. On first being a john. *Urban Life and Culture* 1:255–74.

Turner, B. 1996. *The body and society*. 2nd ed. Oxford: Blackwell.

Vance, C., ed. 1984. *Pleasure and danger: Exploring female sexuality*. London: Routledge.

Warner, M., ed. 1993. *Fear of a queer planet: Queer politics and social theory*. Minneapolis: University of Minnesota Press.

Weston, K. 1998. *Longslowburn: Sexuality and social science*. New York: Routledge.

Rebecca F. Plante

3

In Search of Sexual Subjectivities

Exploring the Sociological Construction of Sexual Selves

Q. *So how did you learn anything [about sex]?*
A. *School, friends . . . I had a problem when I was like 10 years old, 12 years old, and I had a stricture in my urethra, and I couldn't tell my parents, 'cause . . . I could have, but I didn't 'cause I was a little kid. I went to the library and I just read everything I could, and then I pretty much diagnosed it myself. I waited till I was 18 to tell my parents.*

MIKE, 22, PSYCHOLOGY MAJOR

When Mike was 10, he began developing a sexual self, though he did not know it at the time. All he knew was that it hurt when he urinated, and he could not tell anyone about it, not even his parents. He had no way of knowing then that a urethral stricture would combine with influences from his friends, family, and girlfriends to create his adult sexual self.

This is an essay about sexual subjectivities, selves, and stories. My purpose is to begin to explore the contours of the sexual self (at the intrapsychic level of scripting) for individuals not normally called upon to explain who they are: young adults who are mostly heterosexual, Caucasian, American, and middle class. How do they construct themselves as sexual beings, complete with sexual stories and subjectivities? How are selves and stories scripted? Drawing on 45 interviews and six months of participant observation with university peer sex educators (PSEs), I explore how sexual selves are socially constructed. This work is inspired by Gagnon and Simon's sexual script theory (1973) and Plummer's work on sexual stories (1995), along with the rich but relatively unsexual symbolic interactionist theoretical tradition (e.g., Goffman 1956; Blumer 1969).

Why explore subjectivities, stories, and selves in a group of PSEs? The shortest answer is that they provide an intriguing example. Most were heterosexually oriented, are Caucasian, and grew up middle-class, though some were African American, same-sex oriented, or working-class. But for the most part, they were not culturally "programmed" to engage in a storytelling process and delve deeply into the construction of the sexual self (e.g., heterosexuals do not typically fashion "coming out" stories about sexual orientation). Yet those who trained to become PSEs were not predictable or simplistic; they grappled with contradictory and complex sexual selves. There is not enough research specifically on the ways in which heterosexually oriented people develop sexual selves in social contexts. This is a significant oversight that some have begun to address, but the work is not yet complete (e.g., Allen 2003; Tolman 2002; Holland, Ramazanoğlu, Sharpe, and Thomson 1994).

Sexual subjectivity, sexual selves, and sexual stories

Alfred Kinsey ushered in the era of sexology defined by the continuum—the Kinsey Scale, an attempt to classify individuals on the basis of "relative amounts of hetero-sexual and homosexual experience or response" (1948). Though the continuum was a novel way to conceptualize sexualities at that time, and has remained a heuristic in some sexuality research (see Davis, Yarber, Bauserman, Schreer, and Davis 1997), it does not fully capture the more contemporary idea that "sexuality" is bigger than conduct and arousal. The Kinsey Scale has perhaps misled us into thinking that we can (and should) locate ourselves somewhere on a charted sexual course—the straight line implied by the continuum.

If sexuality is bigger than just conduct and arousal, then what else might it include? Perhaps *sexual subjectivity,* defined as a person's sense of herself as a sexual being, com-bined with a feeling of agency and the ability to identify one's own desires (Tolman 2003; Schalet, Hunt, and Joe-Laidler 2003; Pauly Morgan 1994). *Sexual identity* should surely be included, defined as "all the ways in which people operate in a socially-defined sexual sphere, see themselves as sexual beings, and achieve a greater or lesser degree of consis-tency in their sexual relational experiences" (Epstein 1991, 827). Subjectivity and identity are implicated, along with sociocultural variables, in the development of a *sexual self:*

> The sexual self is a fluid, complex entity consisting of various forms of self-relevant knowledge . . . beliefs and perceptions that a woman holds about the sexual aspects of herself. . . . It involves physical and biological capacities, cognitive and emotional development, and evolving needs and desires. It is a product if the private and the public, the personal and the political, the individual and her context (Daniluk 1998, 15).

Gagnon and Simon (1973) posited that the most individual and unique conceptuali-zation of sexual self can be found in the intrapsychic level of sexual scripts. Intrapsychic scripting involves internal, mental rehearsals of sexual(ized) scenarios, drawing on fan-tasies, memories, arousals, preferred modes of engaging one's sexuality (e.g., via playing with power or integrating intimacy). At the intrapsychic level, we see "the less directly observable dimension of . . . that which elicits and sustains sexual arousal" (Simon 1996, 48). Epstein posed the question of how desires "become organized in ways that people perceive as constraining, driving, and largely outside of one's capacity to shape" (1991, 825). Here is the precise conundrum of the intrapsychic. Because it is internal, mental— fantasized even—it is difficult to directly measure, study, or assess.

Nack studied stigma management and self-concept among 28 women diagnosed with herpes and/or human papilloma virus. She wrote that the term sexual self means something fundamentally different from gender identity or sexual identity. Invoking the term sexual self is meant to conjure up the innately intimate parts of individuals' self-concepts that encompass how they think of themselves with regards to their experienced and imagined sensuality. Components of a sexual self may include the following: level of sexual experience, emotional memories of sexual pleasure (or lack thereof), perception of one's body as desirable, and perception of one's body parts as healthy. (2000, 96)

Her inclusion of pleasure, the body, and perceptions is crucial. This conceptualization of sexual self seems especially relevant for teens and young adults, encompassing some specific operationalizable elements of sexual scripting. Using Nack's definition, we could imagine how to actually study the intrapsychic "memories of sexual pleasure" or "perception of one's body as desirable."

Sexual stories

Here are the beginnings of a story of The Story. It can be taken as emblematic of many. It hints at many themes found in many sexual stories. There is a self-consciousness at work here which scans the past life for clues to one's sexual being. There is a sense of an identity . . . there is a searching though the public world . . . significant others and role models . . . harking back to a motivational story to be found in childhood . . . a solitude, a secrecy, and a silence . . . the stories of many (Plummer 1995, 33).

"The Story" is the narrative of the many. It is the way in which Western citizens make sense of the need to make sense, to develop and sustain a continuous self. There are rape stories, gay and lesbian "coming out" stories, and recovery/self help stories, according to Plummer. The stories of the young adults in my analysis are less organized around the possibly ossified themes found in adults' sexual stories, though there are surface similarities. This may be attributable to what Foucault calls "the pedagogical institution," which "has imposed a ponderous silence on the sex of children and adolescents . . . [The pedagogical institution] has established various forms of discourse on the subject; it has coded contents and qualified speakers" (1988, 28).

The "ponderous silence" simultaneously quashes young adults' attempts at interpretation while also defining their initial attempts to develop a coherent narrative about the development of sexuality. Researchers have argued that differences in the sexual-emotional world of children and adolescents can predict the development of stable selves (van Zessen 1995, cited in Vanwesenbeeck, van Zessen, Ingham, Jaramazovic, and Stevens 1999). A climate of warmth, contact, clarity, respect, and predictability could be associated with more careful and caring attitudes in adult relationships. "The opposite—affective neglect, abuse, loneliness, isolation, and unclear 'rules'—preceded objectifying, sometimes compulsive, sex lives, as well as more incompetent behaviour and relationship management" (Vanwesenbeeck et al. 1999, 37). What versions of stories are produced in these different social-psychological contexts? How do these dynamics become reflected in sexual selves and subjectivities? Analysis of sexual stories would provide a glimpse into both the individuality of sex *and* the collective nature of the cultural scripts that underlie individual stories.

Methods

This analysis is drawn from 45 interviews with mostly white, mostly middle-class college students or alumni aged 19 to 26.[1] Data were collected in 1994, and respondents were born between 1968 and 1975. All had trained as peer sexuality educators at the "University of Academia." Semi-structured interviews moved from general, hopefully unthreatening memories of childhood (e.g., "What's the first thing you ever heard about sex?") to adolescent curiosities and teenaged relationships (e.g., "Did you and your friends talk about sex?" "Tell me about your first crush . . .") to college experiences. In discussing college, we covered initial learning about sexuality in the campus setting via relationships, classes, and general environment, eventually addressing the decision to train as a PSE and learn to provide sexuality and sexual health programming on campus. Interviews lasted between 55 minutes and 90 minutes.

I also spent about six months observing the weekly peer sexuality education training class, and PSE workshops in classrooms, dormitories, and sororities. I attended the regular meetings of some students who decided to become sexuality activists and formed their own group. In addition, I interacted with many of my respondents on a more informal basis, sharing coffee, meals, and library work sessions. These informal interactions fully complemented the interviews in painting a fuller picture of their everyday lives.

Respondent demographics

Respondents' backgrounds were very similar. All but two were raised in the South, and the majority of the Southerners grew up in small towns in the state where Academia is located. Most had Southern-born and bred parents ranging in age from 38 to 59. Yet there did not seem to be any connection between parents' age cohort and their attitudes about sexuality, which were exemplified by the kind of education the parents had provided and their reactions to the news that their children had become peer sex educators.

Most parents emphasized organized religion, predominantly Protestant (Southern Baptist and Methodist were cited the most). Few considered themselves religious though several said they were "spiritual." Parents' occupations and educational backgrounds differed quite a bit, but most respondents said that they were middle-class. One woman clarified that this was "makin' it, not savin' it—check to check." One man was the first person in his family to go to college—he had eight siblings, and his father had only completed third grade. Several respondents had parents with advanced degrees, and most parents worked in management or business. Politically, respondents characterized themselves as either Democrat or "nonpartisan." Views ranged from "ultra-liberal, card-carrying," to fiscally conservative but moderate about everything else. Several of the women considered themselves feminists and said they would "proudly divulge" this. The majority of respondents were Caucasian and self-identified as heterosexual; five were African American and four identified as gay, lesbian, or bisexual.[2]

Developing sexualities

Connecting childhood to the sexual self

Everyone was able to remember something from early childhood or adolescence related to sexual curiosity and how that curiosity was handled. Their recollections may have been facilitated by an activity done during one PSE training class. In an attempt to understand how sexuality attitudes and values develop, each presented a *lifeline,* a chronological history detailing their relationships and prior experiences with sexuality. Many remarked that the lifeline assignment represented the first time they had ever really thought about their sexualities as a continuous, life-course variable (instead of as a discrete variable). This was especially true for heterosexually oriented respondents. It was as if they had been walking around with disparate elements of sexual (hi)stories that did not coalesce into "The Story" until they employed the heuristic of the "chronological history."

When one woman first got sex information from her mother, it was in the form of books distributed by their church. Unlike most parents, this respondent's mother allowed her daughter to ask follow-up questions:

> Then we talked about things; mainly my mom was just really open, and I would just ask her questions. A lot of it I figured out on my own from school. I'd come home and say, "Mom, what's fuck mean?" or something, and she'd tell me. . . . But that was basically it. It wasn't just blatantly laid out on the table, but then again, it wasn't one of those things we never talked about either.

Most parents engaged in much more indirect communication. This was described as being "given The Book" or coming home one day to find a pamphlet on puberty on the bed. Even those who were handed "The Book" with the admonishment, "If you have any questions, come talk to me," reported somehow "knowing that this was just talk, that my mom would be really uncomfortable with any questions."

One man's parents' had a more conservative, closed approach:

> Sex is something that you do not bring up in any aspect, to any person in my family. My grandparents, my father. . . . Because my family was very religious, it was something that was always repressed. I think of my grandparents just having sex four times, because they have four children!

Another man, initially educated at the church where his father was the preacher, got additional information at home:

> My brother had his mischievousness (that's how I'll call it) in our house, and my father was really indignant. He was like, "Wait, I talked to him; maybe I talked to him a little bit too late . . ." He was like, "Well, I'm not going to make that same mistake again." So I think that really provoked the conversation.

This father was one of only two who ever addressed sexuality with his children; every other respondent who received any sexuality information at home received it from a mother or stepmother.

One woman's parents had a much more open approach. They took her and two older brothers to a church-organized seminar that was "pretty progressive." One memorable evening, she and a brother watched TV while their parents hosted a bridge game in the next room. Her brother "set her up" by telling her to go ask their father what impotence was (the topic had arisen on the show):

> So this other woman said, "I think it means you can't walk," but I knew it didn't mean that because the person who was impotent already was in a wheelchair . . . I was like, "Noooo . . ." and my dad kind of said, "We'll talk about this later," and he came and woke me up. He said, "It's when a man's penis doesn't work and he can't have sex."

The remarkable thing about this was that her father was direct and clear, and that the information came from her father and not her mother (he was the second of two fathers to directly address sex with his child).

About half the respondents had early exposures to sexuality that included pornography:

> This family moved in down the street from me . . . and they were pretty cool and I hung out down there a lot. They had all kind of dirty books and stuff. I was about six or seven years old. I'd go down there and read dirty books and smoke cigarettes, do all kind of bad stuff.

This male respondent said that the "dirty books" were more explicit than *Playboy* or *Penthouse*: "It was like, a lot of [sex]. Hardcore stuff." His association of sex with "dirty" things was not merely rhetorical. He had considerable ambivalence about his partnered sex life, which primarily involved short-term, late-night sex-only rendezvous with women. His parents reinforced his perceptions:

> They call me up all the time and warn me not to get diseases and stuff, like I don't know about it. A month ago, they found a condom in some old clothes of mine. . . . It was dried up, but they called me up to tell me I shouldn't do that because they're not foolproof, and they're not 100% safe, and you can catch things if you sleep with dirty people.

His father provided a mantra (of sorts) to use when contemplating sexual activities— "This weekend, he just told me there's no piece of ass in the world worth herpes." He agreed with his father but had organized his sexuality around demonstrations of hetero-sexuality via a lot of uncommitted sex with multiple partners.

Two women found *Playboy* magazines in their fathers' dressers when they were about eight years old. One later found her dad's copy of *The Joy of Sex*. They never discussed these discoveries with either parent. But the images depicted in the pornography had a salient impact on one woman:

I was like, "Oh my gosh, is that what I'm going to look like?" I was freaking out . . .
I should have thought about that more. I think that was a real bad influence. . . .
You know, the women with the big hair and they all had names like, Candy, and
stuff like that. They all wore high heels, slip-on shoes and dainty things. I don't
think that was . . . good for me at all. I think that had a lot to do with, you know,
like, a lot of the feminist things I think.

It occurred to her at that time that these were not entirely accurate representations of
women, but she said, "I liked the magazine, and I couldn't find anything more interesting. So I would rather take that than [nothing]." As a 20-year-old, however, she was
unwilling to look at or use pornography, admitting that it made her feel badly about herself, especially her body. She worried that she would be seen as prudish or rigid, and she
was uncomfortable dating men who chose to use pornography.

Other contexts

Two of the respondents mentioned above described a social component to their early
discoveries of sexuality. The man became an eavesdropper, listening to the sex talk of the
older boys at the house where he had discovered "dirty books." The woman began steal-
ing her brother's and father's *Playboy* magazines and showing them to her friends. Other
respondents described the process of sharing their information about sexuality. "Me and
a friend of mine discovered this [encyclopedia] together. We, like, sat and read it, the
whole thing," another man said, admitting that all of his friends seemed equally in the
dark about sexuality. Unfortunately, school was not a place for illumination; only three
respondents recalled having received any formal sexuality education.[3] In grade six or
seven, the boys and girls were separated for at least part of the sexuality module, which
took place in a health course. The focus was reproductive anatomy with a smattering of
superficial contraception information.

One woman described the first time she learned anything concrete about sexuality.
Her best friend was the oldest of nine—so her mother had had to explain where babies
came from. She in turn explained it to the respondent, who recalled being somewhat
stunned to hear the information. The details of the day stayed in her mind—the jungle
gym on which she and her friend sat, the sneakers they were wearing, and other details:

She told me everything. Her mom had to tell her. I didn't have any younger brothers or sisters to question it really. My parents never told me anything.

Q. Did your mother tell you about menstruation?
A. My mother hasn't told me about that yet! I pretty much learned from my
friends.

Her vivid recollection of that day highlights one key aspect of her sexuality—learning
that sex is linked to secrets, so much so that her parents never said a word about it. Her
adult sexual self was organized around the fear that her parents would discover that she
had had sex with one boyfriend in high school and another in college. She felt very self-
conscious about her own sexuality and acknowledged that her desire to become a PSE
was linked to the desire to become more comfortable.

There were other contexts that appeared to have had negative effects on sexual development. One respondent said that she could not remember a time when she was ignorant about sex:

> I think my childhood was tainted by my family. When I used to stay with my cousin, his parents . . . they used to have sex on the couch, in the bedroom with the door open—they didn't care. They walked around the house naked . . . they would have sex in the bed while me and [my cousin] were in the bed sleeping. Although I wasn't really asleep—I was trying to be asleep!

She worried that her sense of sexuality—her subjectivity—had been negatively skewed. She developed the perception that the point of intimate relationships was to have intercourse, and sex would solve any and all relationship problems. This belief led her to one relationship where she had intercourse without ever wanting to, and another in which there were three "physical fights" before she ended it.

About six respondents had early childhood or pre-pubertal exposure to sexuality via some form of sexual trauma—both stranger and acquaintance rape, incest, sexual assault, or medical issues (including sexually transmitted infections). Several admitted that they trained to become peer sexuality educators as a way to "heal" themselves. These traumas were fundamental to respondents' developing sexual selves. Similarly to questioning one's sexual orientation, respondents were forced to examine their otherwise taken-for-granted notions, required to develop a sexual story to make sense of how the traumas affected them. I expand on this following a more general discussion of respondents' intimate relationships.

Relationships: Interpreting sexuality

> I was very innocent, I was very innocent. I wouldn't even hold hands till like seventh grade. The first time I really kissed a guy was on my first date, and he was 16 and I was 15, and he kissed me goodnight. That was my first kiss—I was old!

This woman's experience illustrates a paradoxical but common experience. These respondents shared the common experience of having trained to become sex educators, leading some to assume that they were unusually or especially interested in sex. What else would explain their ability to demonstrate proper condom use with a banana or cucumber and use explicit language with complete strangers? The perception was that PSEs were therefore different—more sexual, perhaps—compared to students who did not become trained educators. Paradoxically, the majority of respondents were relatively circumspect about their sexual relationships and explorations. They were not especially sexually active. Some were virgins in most respects—including penile-vaginal intercourse—while others had had only one or two sexual partners. In interviews, no one said that the desire to become a PSE was related to being "really interested" in sex.

Wary and cautious: Experiences

Everyone had had at least one self-defined "serious" relationship before becoming a peer sexuality educator. About half were involved with someone at the time of our interview.

Many did not have penile-vaginal intercourse (PVI) until their late teens, between 17 and 20. Three of the women had never engaged in PVI; a fourth woman said she had been a lesbian since she was young and had never had sexual contact with a male. Most "first times" were in long-term love relationships. Three were engaged or had been previously, complete with engagement rings and wedding plans.

Most respondents were relatively sexually inexperienced, having engaged in only a handful of relationships that included penile-vaginal intercourse (e.g., fewer than four). Many compared themselves to peers, noting that their friends' behavior provided an impetus for their own (relative) chastity. One woman described that context:

> My friends were doing things like screwing their teachers, screwing their friends' fathers. I had a very promiscuous set of friends. I would have been promiscuous too, had I been able to get laid! In high school, I had only two people, and it was a really big deal to me. I was in love with them.

Another contrasted college with the environment in which she grew up:

> My best friend goes to Furman University. . . . The circle of her friends that she hangs with, they're all like virgins. One just got married and both of them were virgins. I wondered what was wrong with [where I grew up], because everybody was having sex way before I did, and I had sex at 13. And they were all having sex way before me. Or so they said . . . [I] thought they knew more than I did, because everybody seemed to be doing it.

This woman later clarified that her first intercourse experience was coerced, and that she was very reluctant to have sex in subsequent relationships.

One 20-year-old woman had been in a relationship since age 16 (her first); her boyfriend also attended Academia. They had never had penile-vaginal intercourse:

> Q. Tell me about your decision, together, not to be sexually active in terms of intercourse.
> A. Well, when I found out my mother had [an abortion]. I mean, she told me almost right off the bat. I started dating Jeff, and like, three months later she told me this, you know. I mean, to me, I wasn't even thinking about having sex anyway. I was very slow, 'cause I hadn't ever really been with anyone, you know? So I was very slow in kind of [*voice dropping*] picking up the pace, or whatever. . . .

The sexual story she had created was organized around two major themes—being completely different from her parents (especially her mother) and preserving her ability to become a politician one day in the future (she spoke of having no "skeletons in the closet"). Her divorced parents openly assumed that their daughter was sexually active with her boyfriend; one had purchased bunk beds so they could share her bedroom, the other had bought them matching pajamas.

Her ambivalence was obvious in the way she described their sex life:

And then it got to the point, we would be like, "Well, maybe this summer" or like, "Okay, we'll do it before I go off to college." This was when my dad was letting us sleep downstairs and stuff, and he was kind of like, "Well, y'all aren't having sex yet, right?" . . . I mean, you know, totally, like my parents know that they, like, we have two lines on our phone and they'll call first if they want to come downstairs. Or like, make a lot of noise, or knock on the door, you know, so it's not like they think we're in there playing Parcheesi or whatever. But at that point, we had already had the whole trust thing. I was like, "Well, before I go off to school, we will . . ." and we didn't. Then, like this summer, I was out in England. I was in Oxford for six weeks, and he came out the last week to see me, and I was like, "Well wouldn't that be romantic, to have sex in England . . . ."

She did not experience herself as being motivated by sexual desire. Instead she was motivated by twin fears. First, she was afraid of getting pregnant and could not convince herself that contraception would really work. Second, she was afraid of ending up like her mother, whom she saw as a sexual manipulator who had gotten pregnant to trick her father into marriage. Her mother's abortion revelation made her angry and she had resolved to remain a virgin for as long as possible.

Meanwhile her boyfriend had no such desire to remain a virgin, and struggled to accommodate her growing disinterest in any kind of sexual activity:

I mean, but I never, I mean, and now . . . I mean, he wants—I mean, he wants to, but I mean, it's not a big deal for either of us at all. It's more frustrating for us now because we both have roommates. . . . Like, sexually, that's the most frustrating thing right now. One of my roommates walked in on us, and so, now, like, we have this whole thing like, you just respect. . . . So you know, now, I'm like real hesitant to even, like, when my roommate in my room is gone, you know. . . .

It made her uncomfortable when anyone assumed that she was sexually active, and though she appreciated having a boyfriend, she was not very interested in sex. Her sense of agency was instead connected to gaining and maintaining people's trust in her, which she believed she could maintain by maintaining her chastity.

Trauma and sexual selves

I was raped my senior year [of high school], so I just shied away from relationships and getting close. Then I met this guy with this purely, purely physical relationship. He was very possessive, very obsessive. When I left for college, he would go and just sit in the cul-de-sac outside my house. Just sit in front of my house for hour upon hour, and then call me up, crying, "I miss you, I miss you." So that was a really bad experience too. I haven't had that many boyfriends.

In this case, after her acquaintance rape, this respondent attempted to reclaim (or perhaps discover) her sexuality by having a "purely physical" relationship, only to be victimized again in that relationship. His stalking and manipulation frightened her, and she began to withdraw from relationships and friendships. Once she had been at college for a semester or so, she relaxed a little. The rape and the stalking left her with a poor sense of boundaries, and she was assaulted again; a friend raped her at a party after she had passed out. She later discovered that she had ended up with a sexually transmitted infection from the assault.[4]We cannot overestimate the significance of these kinds of traumas on developing sexual selves and subjectivities. There are multiple consequences to learning about sexuality via rape, incest, and assaults. Gavey (2005) would suggest that "normalizing discourses of heterosex" that can imply that sex is something that is "done" to women. My respondent's very real feeling of having been the *victim* of men's predatory behavior was not disrupted by more socially correct attempts to rewrite sexual violence as something one instead *survives* (and thus is not victimized by it).

Another PSE described her initiation into sexuality:

> My great aunt, she lived down the street from the aunt I stayed with. She adopted these two boys. When I joined the PSE program and we were sitting in class one day, I had these flashbacks about them taking me off, away from everyone else in the house, and making me pull down my pants, and touching me. I only have like two faint memories, but I guess that means I was molested when I was a child. So I should tell you that . . . I think that has something to do with my crazy views on life.

In describing the molestation as precursive to her "crazy views on life," it seemed that this respondent was trying to make light of what the boys had done, trying to minimize their violation of her. But when we discussed the repercussions, it became clear that this event had been foundational in the development of her sexual self. She said that she would never fully know how it had affected her. She had wondered, "How would I be if that had never happened?" Would she have been raped by a friend during her first year in college? She said, "Would I have been so intimidated and just afraid of sex then, until the point where I couldn't enjoy it with my last boyfriend?"

Training to become a peer sex educator inspired this respondent to tell her mother about what had happened:

> I told my mom, last fall. She was really upset, first of all, because she'd just found out that I'd had sex. She called me, "I can't believe this! You had sex?" "Let me tell you something, that's my business." She called back . . . we got talking, and I just told her everything. I told her that those two cousins molested me when I was [younger]. I told her that I was raped when I got up here [to college], when I transferred here that's why I hated it so much and didn't come back for winter quarter. I told her that, yes, my last boyfriend and I were sexually active, and he was my first. I told her everything. You know what's weird? When I told her that, found out the same thing happened to her. The same thing happened to her.

There are interwoven strands of a "Bigger Story" in this quote. The respondent's sexuality had been deeply affected by the molestation and rape, yet she had not revealed the incidents to her mother when they occurred. Her mother had also been raped in college, yet did not reveal it to her daughter until the "shared" story was revealed. The respondent's mother had always stressed that sex was something to be taken very seriously, something that should occur only in a loving (heterosexual) marriage. Maybe her insistence about this was connected to her own experience of rape. Each had apparently been shaped by sexual violence and trauma. Is *this* the Bigger Story of women's sexualities? Is it the Bigger Story of women's absent, awkward or ambivalent sexual subjectivities?

Another respondent was coerced into sex by someone she had known for four days. She was 13 and he was 14. She said, "I was all of 85 pounds; he was 5'9", 165 [pounds]— he was big. I just thought if I said no he would do it anyway. I didn't know I could say no and it would be okay." After that, she was very apprehensive about sex, because she knew she "wasn't ready." She said, "I don't think I was saving myself till marriage, but I just knew that I wasn't ready for that. I wasn't gonna do anything until I was ready. I was just like, 'I *am not* having sex.'"

One respondent was sexually abused by her stepfather at about eight and as a teen-ager, she was raped by an older acquaintance. Her relationships throughout late adolescence and high school ranged from anonymous "flings" to asymmetrical, longer-term relationships (where she or her partner was less invested or interested). The asymmetry gave her a measure of control that she always sought, even if she was the more invested partner. Having been unable to control her sexuality as a child, she developed a sexual self marked by a need to control the outcome of her relationships. Her sexual story and subjectivity were defined by the sexual abuses, rendering her aloof and distant to men who desired her while being accommodating and generous to men who had little interest in her.

Although everyone had some kind of personal or professional motivations for becoming a PSE, those who had survived sexual traumas were far more invested in their personal goals than the other PSEs:

> Q: When you started the program, did you have personal goals, in addition to more—?
> A: Yeah, because . . . by sharing and talking about my experiences, it really helps me grow and heal. So yeah, I wanted to help in my own mental health.

Contrast this with a more typical response:

> A lot of it has to do with my major. The main part of my major—the part I'm most interested in is the sexuality issues—and if I could, that's the direction I would head in, but I'm not limiting myself.

Sexual traumas inspire a different narrative and sense of self for the survivor—they represent wounds to be healed, events to be described and shared, stories to be told.

The story, the subject, and the self: A case example

Heterosexual male respondents did not describe any instances of surviving sexual violence, but one respondent, Mike, experienced a different kind of trauma.[5] At age 10, he discovered painful strictures in his vas deferens and urethra. He learned what it was by reading at the library and finally told his parents when he was eighteen (although he had discussed it with his doctor several years earlier). This experience got him interested in sexuality education: "This isn't right—a kid shouldn't have to feel uncomfortable talking about stuff in front of his parents." It also had significant effects on the development of his sexuality.

Mike was 22 at the time of our interview, a senior in college, and studying psychology. He had been born in the Midwest, in the suburb of a large city. When Mike was nine, the family moved to the state where Academia was located. His parents were middle-class, white-collar employees; his father owned a business. Mike's family was Catholic but he was not, and he considered himself a "socialist atheist." His parents never spoke to him about sex, so he borrowed "The Book" they had discreetly offered his older sister. "I was too young to really read it. I just kind of looked at the cartoon pictures," he said. There was no real follow-up, and instead, Mike learned early that adults were wary of addressing sexual topics:

Q. What did you do in response to reading the book? Did you go and ask them questions?
A. No, I showed my friends. And we laughed about it, and we hassled the babysitter with it. We took the book and said, "Well what is this?" to the babysitter . . . she made us put it away.
Q. Did your parents [ever] sit you down?
A. No.
Q. So you never got that?
A. Uh-unh. That's why I feel deprived. [*laughs*]

Mike laughed but it became clear that the unambiguous communication—"don't ask the adults about sex because we won't tell"—had long term consequences.

When he diagnosed himself with a urethral stricture at age 12 (a conclusion later supported by his doctor), he was scared: "When it first happened I thought I had cancer and I was just gonna die and not tell anybody." Mike's reluctance to tell his parents seemed well-founded when the stricture was later revealed to his father:

As a matter of fact, when I first went to a specialist when I was 18, he said, "Yeah, the stricture's usually from gonorrhea." He said that right in front of my dad and my dad told me he was ashamed of me after that. That kind of blew my relationship with him.

The doctor's pronouncement about the cause of the stricture was as insensitive as Mike's father's reaction. There are actually several causes of strictures. According to a urology website, "the common causes of stricture are trauma to the urethra and gonorrheal infection. However, in many cases, no cause can be identified" (www.urologyhealth.org). Congenital strictures do happen; though they are rare, that seems to have been the explanation for Mike's condition, first observed at age 10. In fact, Mike said, "The doctor that I saw most recently said it's probably just congenital." Seeing his father's disgust and shame, Mike never again spoke to his parents about sexuality, and they never even knew that he had become a peer sexuality educator.

The urethral strictures contributed to Mike's feelings of fear, insecurity, and sexual reticence. Though he was attractive, intelligent, thoughtful, and athletic, Mike was reluctant to become sexually involved with any of his high school girlfriends. Since his library research had revealed that a common cause of strictures was gonorrhea, he worried that he had somehow contracted gonorrhea as a child. Though he was never tested for the (treatable) disease, throughout puberty and his teenage years he had no other information, so he turned down sexual overtures from his girlfriends. Mike was also consumed with fear that inhibited his desires and disconnected him from his body; he was 19 before he had PVI:

Q. You didn't actually become sexually active until you were 19. But you had girl-friends . . . so by sexually active you mean intercourse, right?

A. No, really nothing until I was . . . well, when I was about 18, I had a girlfriend in college and we had oral sex and mutual masturbation. Actually, it was mostly mutual masturbation in high school and then I had oral sex my first semester in college.

Q. Was it painful? Did it affect your ability to get an erection?

A. I don't know. It's hard to tell because I never really needed an erection, you know. I don't think so. . . . If I would've just said something about it [when I was younger].

Mike's sexual self revolved around his pre-pubertal experience of himself as damaged and in pain. His private experiences, shared with no one, differed from his public presentation of self. In private, Mike tamped down his sexuality and his fantasies, masturbating infrequently and avoiding thoughts of partnered sexual activities. In public, he was a budding sex expert, telling his classmates "how to prevent premature ejaculation" via "the squeeze techniques and stuff." His female friends started using this technique, involving a squeeze or pinch at the tip or base of the penis to reverse ejaculatory inevitability.

Privately Mike's life was different. The strictures represented a continuing source of shame and discomfort.

Q. Did your girlfriends know?

A. Nobody knew. I didn't tell them. As a matter of fact, I told my parents. My parents told my family, which I asked them not to. I told my sister. And then I told a girlfriend that I went out with for about six months, but this was after I had the surgery. I don't know, maybe a year after I had the surgery. And I have a girlfriend now . . . and she knows about it. I told her from the start.

Mike's sexual self was profoundly shaped by the shame and stigma that accompanied his erroneous fear that the strictures were caused by a (treatable) sexually transmitted infection. In contrast to the women Nack (2000) interviewed, Mike had not really developed a sexual self independently of the strictures. Nack's respondents had engaged in partnered sex and had begun to develop a sense of self before becoming infected with herpes, chlamydia, and the like. Deep down, Mike knew that it was impossible for his strictures to have been caused by gonorrhea, but the social stigma of such infections overwhelmed logic.

Other disjunctures continued after he had become a PSE. His girlfriend Mary was a

19-year-old freshman from a small town. Mike was her first serious boyfriend, though she had first engaged in penile-vaginal intercourse with a high school boyfriend and immediately regretted it. Mike and Mary's relationship was troubled because Mary was very disinterested in sex. According to him, about once a month Mary would "allow" him to have sex with her, provided he had taken a day or so to romance her with gifts, special outings, dinner, and a movie. When he did have sex with her, he tried to be as "efficient" as possible and climax quickly "for her sake." He spent a lot of time reassuring her that he really did love her and had no intention of breaking up with her or dating anyone else. Occasionally she would become angry with him for not returning her calls quickly enough and would refuse to speak to him. In the six months that I knew Mike, they "took a break" at least three times, though he was not allowed to date others. The relationship "tortured" him, but he said that he loved her and did not want to end it.

There was a glaring disjuncture between this aspect of his personal life and his PSE programming. Mike was the *only* PSE who routinely spoke about sexual pleasure, though he experienced almost none with his girlfriend. Yet in his final interview, he explained:

> I think I was sex-positive more than some of the other people [PSEs]. I at least tried to say something about the beauty of sex, and that true safe sex can only enhance that beauty. Because you feel better about the sex and you feel better about your own safety and the safety of your partner, stuff like that.

Mike was unusual in this respect. He was the only PSE to mention pleasure in the 40 or so programs I observed during my fieldwork. I saw more than 30 condom demonstrations, a handful of "Sexual Jeopardy" contests, and at least 15 "who can roll the condom onto the cucumber fastest?" audience participation games, and I *never* heard anyone else mention pleasure as the main goal of (partnered) sex.

Mike did try to disseminate his point of view. Early in my fieldwork, a splinter group of PSEs formed their own organization, the "Sexual Health Information Network" (SHIN), independent from the paraprofessional role they were expected to play in the PSE program.[6] The group wanted to do "guerrilla" sex education, radical and political, beyond the constraints they had as PSEs. Under the auspices of SHIN, Mike suggested doing a program on sexual pleasure and techniques. But the members of SHIN were unsure about how to facilitate a program on pleasure. One woman, uncomfortable presenting herself as an "expert" on pleasure, suggested that program participants do a "kiss and tell" where they shared their favorite techniques. Mike wanted to show excerpts from pornographic movies, figuring that the films would explicitly depict what the group wanted to discuss. The program was never more formally planned and it never came to fruition. Given how few times any PSE ever mentioned pleasure during a standard program, it was not surprising that Mike's idea went nowhere (Plante 1999).

Mike is an excellent case of a heterosexually oriented man who was forced to develop a broad understanding of his sexual self. His desire to educate others about the pleasures of sex contrasted sharply with his life story—a narrative of pain, shame, fear, bodily disconnections, and uncomfortable partnered sex.

The complexity of selves and subjectivities

The more time I spent with my respondents, the more I got to know them. Conversations over coffee or dinner revealed that, for many of them, their everyday sexual lives and experiences were very different from what they presented in their sex education programs. One PSE specialized in the "Sex and Self Esteem" programs but was rarely any sexual with her partner, seemingly unaware of how her partner's self-esteem was affected by this. He felt rejected and sad, while he experienced his desire for sex as "being overbearing or aggressive." A heterosexual male PSE had never had a relationship, remained a virgin, and had barely ever kissed. Yet he talked about sexual health and healthy relationships, hiding his inexperience and bitter misogyny from his audiences and his supervisors.

One woman had never had a gynecological exam, although she was 20 years old. (Health professionals recommend an exam by age 18 if a woman is not sexually active with a partner, earlier if one is sexually active. When she talked about women's health during her programs, only I knew that her words had a hollow ring.) One PSE, whose programming messages were personal responsibility, condom use, and open communication, kept his pregnant ex-girlfriend a secret from everyone, including his current girlfriend. The three women who were virgins poorly and awkwardly demonstrated proper condom use on cucumbers, never having put condoms on actual penises.

Without realizing it, one gay-oriented respondent perfectly exemplified the struggle of becoming a sexual subject. He described his approach before becoming a PSE, before getting "the facts" about safer sex:

> I knew the basics—no anal or vaginal intercourse without a condom, bodily fluid things, blood. I pretty much protected myself from anal intercourse. Every now and then I would have slipped up. It was usually like [when] I was in a monogamous relationship with someone.

After his training, however, there was a slight shift in his perception of sexuality. The tensions are clear in the following quotes, all made within a seven-minute period:

> We can all slip up, and there's no reason to risk it. I wasn't really that safe about oral sex until this class. I always thought that . . . if I were performing oral sex I wouldn't do it till they would come or anything. It would be a brief thing. And if we were to have anal sex, we would use a condom. That would be a definite. I figured if people can get it through oral sex, then the cases would be . . . everybody would have it. That proves it is a low risk.

> Every now and then I might slip up. Then I realized, "Just try not to do it, and if you do, just do your best."

> We're under so much stress, we try so hard, but every now and then we're going to slip up a little bit, and you just have to do the best you can. There's no more you can do, unless you abstain, and who's going to do that?

This respondent's interpretation of safer sex is not solely attributable to his gender or sexual orientation. It reflects the tensions inherent in contemporary safer sex and sex education discourses, where knowledge is thought to empower individuals to forget that sex can feel really good even in the *absence* of latex, planning, or responsibility. But his comments are not just about the shortcomings of safer sex education—they also reveal the core of subjectivities and selves.

Conclusion

Vanwesenbeeck et al. (1999) conclude that every aspect of (hetero)sexuality, from discussing and using contraception and prophylaxis to setting limits, clarifying desires, and developing empathy for a partner, is related to what they call *interactional competence*. A complex combination of psychodynamic, interpersonal, subcultural, and cultural influences affects the development of this competence. Seeing one's self as the sum of these parts, if not greater than the sum, is perhaps the primary accomplishment of sexual subjectivity—the sense a person has of herself as a sexual being, combined with a sense of agency and the ability to identify one's own desires. Feelings about one's sexual self, agency, and desires are certainly located in the intrapsychic level of sexual scripting, given more definition and nuances in the interpersonal level, and refined and ossified in the form of sexual stories. But what kinds of sexual selves are made possible given the context of cultural and interpersonal scripts? And what forms of subjectivity are realistic or possible?

The disjunctures and discontinuities in these respondents' stories became obvious in light of their training as peer sex educators. These narratives reveal that there is more to young adults' developing heterosexualities than just worries about pregnancy, reputations, or reciprocity. Discourses of pleasure and desire were missing from nearly all these accounts, replaced or overwhelmed by the effects of insecurity, inexperience, traumas, and fears. Are these respondents—mostly heterosexual, Caucasian, and middle-class—unusual? What role did peer sexuality education training and programming play for these individuals? Did they examine, question, or reflect on their sexualities because of their paraprofessional roles as peer educators? But this paper is not an evaluation of peer sex education. It is an exploration of how sexual selves and subjectivities are formed within social contexts. For these respondents, being a PSE was one of only several interstitial contexts; it was not the key context for anyone.

The menu of possibilities for sexual conduct and sexual selfhood is indeed socioculturally constructed. We know the basics of cultural sexual scripting, the hegemonic *who, what, why, where, when,* and *how.* But we do not know enough about the "what if"—what if these possibilities were less socially constrained? What if we had more analytical mapping of the sexual selves of individuals? Would we see a more elegant and consistent process of reassessment and revision? The individuals featured in this essay are older now—done with college (and for some, graduate school)—on to jobs and careers, and perhaps also to marriages, relationships, and children. I wonder what the intervening years have done to enhance, change, or solidify their sexual stories. Have they moved through their narratives to the realization that sex is a seemingly endless source of pleasure and fascination? It is this fascination that should inspire us to delve further into the attempt to understand its contours, its meanings, and its narratives.

Notes

1. The research was approved by the university's institutional review board for research with human subjects.
2. I focus here on the heterosexually oriented respondents.
3. Note that these respondents completed junior high and high school before AIDS education and sex education became mandatory and/or comprehensive in many school districts. Most had completed high school in the South.
4. I am inclined to observe that her rapist could not possibly have been a "friend," but certainly she had considered him a friend before the rape. She refused to continue the friendship but elected not to report the crime.
5. The name is a pseudonym.
6. This group was entirely student formed and run, in contrast to the PSE program, which was run by professional staff at the campus health services (thus PSEs were expected to behave as paraprofessionals).

References

Allen, L. 2003. Power talk: Young people negotiating (hetero)sex. *Women's Studies International Forum* 26:235–44.

Blumer, H. 1969. *Symbolic interactionism: Perspective and method.* Englewood Cliffs, NJ: Prentice Hall.

Davis, C. M., W. Yarber, R. Bauserman, G. Schreer, and S. L. Davis. 1997. *Handbook of sexuality-related measures.* Thousand Oaks, CA: Sage Publications.

Epstein, S. 1991. Sexuality and identity: The contribution of object relations theory to a constructionist sociology. *Theory and Society* 20:825–73.

Foucault, M. 1988. *The history of sexuality*, vol. 1. Trans. R. Hurley. New York: Vintage Books.

Gagnon, J. H. and W. Simon. 1973. *Sexual conduct: The social sources of human sexuality.* Chicago: Aldine Publishing.

Gavey, N. 2005. *Just sex? The cultural scaffolding of rape.* London: Routledge.

Goffman, E. 1956. *The presentation of self in everyday life.* New York: Doubleday.

Holland, J., C. Ramazanoğlu, S. Sharpe, and R. Thomson. 1994. Power and desire: The embodiment of female sexuality. *Feminist Review* 46:21–38.

Nack, A. 2000. Damaged goods: Women managing the stigma of STDs. *Deviant Behavior: An Interdisciplinary Journal* 21:95–121.

Pauly Morgan, K. 1994. Sex, sex education, and the paradoxes of liberalism. *Philosophy of Education 1994.* www.ed.uiuc.edu/EPS.

Plante, R. 1999. Policies and resistance in a university peer sexuality program. In *A dangerous knowing: Sexual pedagogies and the master narrative,* ed. J. T. Sears and D. Epstein, 270–82. London: Cassell.

Plummer, K. 1995. *Telling sexual stories: Power, change and social worlds.* London: Routledge.

Schalet, A., G. Hunt, and K. Joe-Laidler. 2003. Respectability and autonomy: The articulation and meaning of sexuality among girls in the gang. *Journal of Contemporary Ethnography* 32:108–43.

Simon, W. 1996. *Postmodern sexualities.* London: Routledge.

Tolman, D. L. 2002. *Dilemmas of desire: Teenage girls talk about sexuality.* Cambridge: Harvard University Press.

Vanwesenbeeck, I., G. van Zessen, R. Ingham, E. Jaramazovic, and D. Stevens. 1999. Factors and processes in heterosexual competence and risk: An integrated review of the evidence. *Psychology and Health* 14, no. 1: 25–50.

Peter M. Nardi

4

Friendship, Sex, and Masculinity

This entrance of the entire undivided ego into the relationship may be the more plausible in friendship than in love, for the reason that, in the case of friendship, the one-sided concentration upon a single element is lacking, which is present in the other case on account of the sensuous factor in love.

GEORG SIMMEL (1906, 457)

Two men strolling around the town square, arm and arm, talk about the latest political news and football scores. What do you make of this scene? Your answer might reveal some truths about the society you grew up in, along with the meanings it attached to friendship, sexuality, and masculinity.

Place that image in different cultural contexts: two men on their *passagiatta* in the *piazza* might conjure up an image of heterosexual Italian men spiritedly discussing the latest strike or soccer match. Two men leaving a neighborhood bar in West Hollywood could break the stereotype of gay men talking about sports, yet the scene barely would raise an eyebrow. If they were known to be relatives renewing their ties, how would this display then be interpreted? And what if it were known that one of the men is straight and the other is gay? Research on hate crimes indicates that two men walking with arms entwined in a public space in many cultures increases their risk for violence or verbal insults. Attributing friendship ties to men's public displays of touch does not inoculate them from danger. Friendship between men in our American culture is often an ambiguous relationship with inconsistent definitions of acceptable behavior, intimacy, and emotional feelings.

Friendship interactions take on meaning depending on the social situation. Let's consider the meanings of men's friendships in different contexts, how they may vary depending on sexual orientation, and the ways in which people work at creating intimacy and support in the face of cultural resistance and intimations of sexuality. To paraphrase Gagnon and Simon's (1973) notion of sexual scripts, there are many ways to become a friend, to be friendly, to act as a friend, and to feel friendly. Like sexual scripts, we should consider "friendship scripts" and the way these are socially produced, organized, and maintained in different social contexts.

Historical context

Throughout history, male-dominated images have characterized the ideal of friendship; women were often seen as incapable of "true friendship." Men's friendships have been portrayed as "souls mingling and blending with each other so completely that they efface the seam that joined them," as Michel de Montaigne wrote in his sixteenth century essay, *Of Friendship*. Stories, poems, and essays exalted men's heroic friendships, such as the one between Jonathan and David in the Old Testament or Achilleus and Patroklos in Homer's *The Iliad*. Upon hearing about Patroklos' death, Achilleus poured black ashes over his head and face and tore at his hair. He lamented that recent accomplishments bring little pleasure "since my dear companion has perished, Patroklos, whom I loved beyond all other companions, as well as my own life."

These heroic friendships provoked an intensity of intimacy between men that, up to the mid- to late-nineteenth century, were often indistinguishable from the language and images of love relationships (see Bray 2003). These friendships could be erotic but not necessarily sexual since a certain degree of affectionate desire was allowed. However, as same-sex relationships began to be redefined in pathological terms in the scientific and legal literature of the late nineteenth century, labels of perversion (as well as the newly created medical word "homosexual") were applied to same-sex romantic friendships (Rotundo 1993).

The concept of friendship between men once included a range of erotic, sexual, and platonic possibilities. As issues related to homosexuality, masculinity, and sexuality in the post-Freudian era became part of the public discourse, men's friendships in particular became more limited in scope. Romantic friendships, especially for men, were less visible and not a topic typically to be discussed in poems and literature. True friendship, in the early twentieth century and continuing to this day, emerged as something only women were more capable of experiencing. The ideal form of friendship is now usually described with more "female" language: intimacy, trust, caring, disclosing, and nurturing (see Friedman 1993).

Contemporary friendships

Most academic research on friendship supports the idea that men's friendships, in general, exhibit instrumental, "side-by-side" interactions, while women's friendship demonstrate expressive, "face-to-face" styles of intimacy (Wright 1982). Women are much more likely to spend time with friends, share feelings, confide, and disclose intimate details of their lives, while men look for friends to participate in activities, share views on sports and other interests, and talk about work. Men's friendships are less emotional, self-disclosing, and physically affectionate than women's. Men also tend not to focus on the friendship relationship itself as a topic of conversation. Compared to women, men engage in less intimate touch, sit further apart from their male friends, and spend less time with friends (Fehr 1996).

In addition, men have fewer numbers of supportive relationships and receive less help from them when compared with women; women provide more emotional support compared to men. Men rate the meaningfulness of and satisfaction with their same-sex friendships lower than women do, while men view their cross-sex friendships as closer and more intimate than their same-sex ones, compared to women who see their same-sex ones as closer (Fehr 1996).

However, studies are uncovering the greater diversity within categories of gender, linked to such characteristics as race, class, and sexual orientation. It's not simply some psychological or biological force limiting men's interactions with friends and providing women with more intense emotional contacts with their friends. Men often report close and intimate friendships, and some women describe their friendships only in terms of doing shared activities. As Allan (1989) suggests, social structural explanations are salient when studying friendship patterns. Context provides ways for how people engage with others and create meanings for friendship. The situations and power dynamics of the workplace, men's roles in the neighborhood and kinship network, and their social class, sexual orientation, and ethnic/racial characteristics impact how friendships are constructed, defined, and maintained. These social elements intersect to create contexts in which many men are limited in the ways they can express intimacy with other men in friendship, while for other men, these social dynamics allow them to break out of the constraints imposed by the culture.

Not all men interact with friends in the same stereotypical "side-by-side" way. For example, studies on social class show that financial circumstances affect people's interests and abilities to engage in activities with friends. The kind of work people do, where they live, who is in their network, and how their daily lives are organized restrict or contribute to friendship formation (Fischer 1982). Working-class friendships tend to develop primarily in the workplace; friends are rarely invited into the home. Middle-class friendship styles stress reciprocity and emphasize the relationship over the setting. Class-related resources become salient, therefore, in the enactment of reciprocity, a key element in the formation and maintenance of friendships.

Ethnic, cultural, and racial differences also impact how men develop and maintain friendships (Franklin 1992). For example, in some Mediterranean societies, public displays of friendship tend to be strongly gender-segregated. Despite our own diverse American society, friendships typically form along racial lines. In a study of working-class black men in Chicago, Duneier (1992) showed how they developed friendships based on surrogate kinships through regular gatherings in a local cafeteria where the men gained a strong sense of respectability in their routine interactions.

Differences in men's friendships can also be attributed to sexual orientation. For most gay men, friendships are inextricably part of their narrative histories and coming out stories. Their friendships take on political power as they challenge the constraints imposed by the culture's social institutions of family, marriage, and sexuality. Friendships can feed social movements when they provide the power and identity that are often minimized in gay men's lives by the dominant culture. Friends become the source for learning about gay identity and cultures, entering gay communities, organizing into resistance groups, and maintaining personal identities within an otherwise non-supportive social environment (Chauncey 1994). In my survey of gay men (Nardi 1999), "face-to-face" activities, such as getting together just to talk or calling friends to chat about relationships, were as important and occurred more frequently than the "typical male" friendship patterns of getting together primarily to do something or calling someone only to arrange an activity.

Studying men's friendships reveals insights about a culture's concepts of masculinity, sexuality, and relationships. Rather than look at friendship formation as something explainable solely in terms of gender roles, personality theories, species-specific genetic differences between men and women, consider how various locations in the economic, occupational, and other power spheres can lead to different kinds of interpersonal interactions and masculinities. Getting married or having children, for example, greatly changes the nature of one's friendships and the time available for maintaining them (Cohen 1992).

People meet people in specific social contexts, such as work, school, neighborhood, and recreational organizations. Often, access to these places is controlled by certain requirements, like age, education, race, class, gender, and sexual orientation. Furthermore, the dominant institutions reflect varying definitions of masculinity and meanings about sexuality, thereby structuring the ways men can comfortably interact with one another. So what may appear to be a "problem" with men's friendships can be viewed instead as a function of the constraints imposed by the social institutions and their definitions of gender. How men bond in all-male military settings as opposed to more open diverse environments (as found in universities, for example) may reflect these institutions' constructions of what is considered masculine and appropriate sexual behavior.

Friendship is an essential component of people's lives. It is with friends that we get to test boundaries, find identity, and learn to express intimacy and commitment. Friendships between men, and between men and women, however, are affected by the norms and values of the culture, especially those centered on gender and sexuality. For some, such as gay men, friendship can be a powerful means of solidifying identity, building communities, and exploring sexual behaviors. For other men, close friendships can be a process of overcoming the limits of a heterosexist culture and a journey in search of the intimacy and reciprocity once characteristic of the heroic friendships of the past.

Sexuality and friendship

In her classic study of friendship, Rubin (1985, 179) wrote that "best friends are drawn together in much the same way as lovers. . . . people often talk as if something happened to them in the same way they 'happened' to fall in love and marry." The erotic component of friendship is typically not discussed, studied, or highlighted. It is often said that heterosexual men and women cannot just be friends—the sexual thing gets in the way. Conversely, it is said that heterosexual male and female friends cannot become lovers—the friendship thing gets in the way. We also hear that two heterosexual men have some difficulty becoming close and intimate friends—the heterosexism and homophobia things get in the way. Many gay men say that it's difficult to have sex with someone they are friends with because the sex might ruin the friendship. And what do we make of friendships between gay and straight men? Does the sexual thing or the masculine friendship thing get in the way then? With all the possible combinations of men doing friendships, it becomes clear that any one set of rules cannot apply to all. Yet all these barriers suggest a strong set of social structural factors and cultural scripts guiding people's meanings about sexuality and friendships.

Heterosexual men's cross-sex friendships

The popular 1989 movie *When Harry Met Sally* was premised on the beliefs that heterosexual men and women can't become friends due to sexual tensions, and that, once friends, they would find it even more difficult in becoming lovers. Yet, Harry and Sally went on to demonstrate otherwise. But these stories are typically the exception: studies indicate that cross-gender friendships often involve the continual monitoring of sexual attraction which can result in less intimate friendships between heterosexual men and women (O'Meara 1989). The culture provides guidelines and implicit rules about these relationships and how close men and women can be, especially in the context of marital status, age, and workplace norms. O'Meara finds that cross-sex friendship "is an ambiguous relationship in American culture in the sense that it has a deviant status reflected in a lack of instructive role models and appropriate terminology to capture its unique qualities, lacks coherent cultural scripts for guiding everyday interaction, and is influenced by gender-based schematic processing" (530).

Studies show that heterosexual men are more likely than women to see the sexual dimensions of cross-sex friendships (Rawlins 1992), while women view the intimacy and sexuality as troublesome to the friendship (Bell 1981). These friendships are often initiated because of the sexual attraction by the men. Sexual interest may serve as a motivation for developing the cross-sex friendships, but rarely as the reason for maintaining them. Part of this is due to the cultural script which tends to define a friendship between a man and a woman that has a sexual component as a dating or romantic one leading to an eventual commitment. For most heterosexual men, when the sex ends, the friendship ends (Bell 1981). Yet, for others, the sexual tone is what keeps the friendships going, or as Swain (1992, 167) put it, "cross-sex friendships are both enriched and plagued by fluctuating and unclear sexual boundaries." Pahl (2000, 90) similarly argued that "*Eros* may be the trigger that helps some men and women to discover true friendship."

However, the social environment can provide situations for initiating and maintaining cross-sex friendships while minimizing the sexual dimension. The rules governing workplace interactions limit sexual overtures (in theory) and thereby create a potential for nonsexual friendships. Certainly, the dynamics of marital life limit the number of ways men and women can be friends without sex intervening. Yet, strict cultural norms continue to be present, especially among married people who are limited in having individual cross-sex friendships outside the couple. While it may be okay for a husband to tell his wife that he is going out with the guys tonight, consider the impact and meanings that might develop if he said he was going out with the girls (or a girl) instead! On the other hand, consider an emerging norm among many male and female high school and college students that apparently allows for sex between friends without commitments. Called "hooking up," young people report social expectations about sex with each other while not allowing it to interfere with the friendship (see Lambert, Kahn, and Apple 2003).

Gay men's gay friendships

Foucault (1983) said in an interview that "friendship is reciprocal, and sexual relations are not reciprocal. . . . if you have friendship, it is difficult to have sexual relations." When negotiating and discussing sexuality, power and control imbalances can emerge to challenge the equality, reciprocity, and balance implicit in a culture's definitions of a friend-ship. And when focusing on gay men's friendship and sexual relationships with other gay men, these interactions can reflect a breaking of the hegemonic definitions of mascu-linity, while simultaneously reinforcing the dominant norms of gendered masculinity.

Although gay men's friendships with other gay men don't regularly begin with sex, sex is a starting point for many of their friendships. In one study (Nardi and Sherrod 1994), over 60% of gay men reported having sex with some of their gay male *casual* friends, around 75% responded with some of their *close* gay male friends, and just over half with their one *best* gay friend (about 17% said their best friend was an ex-partner). With a few exceptions, the gay men did not report having sex with the majority of their friends, although the majority of gay men have had sex with friends. For most, the sex-ual experiences were in the past, rather than with current friends (Nardi 1992).

Despite some contemporary cultural norms which also push gay men to define on-going sexual relationships as romantic and committed ones, many gay men are able to engage in nonromantic sexual relationships. Some manage to have sex on an occasional basis with their current social friends while others develop a "fuck buddy" relationship whose sole purpose is to be friends only sexually but not socially (Nardi 1999). How-ever, most gay men report that the transition to a nonsexual friendship is what typically happens and usually follows the oft-used phrase, "let's just be friends." If these friend-ships develop into close, family-like relationships, as many of them do, an "incest taboo" might evolve which precludes sexual interactions with their friends.

Friendships between gay men highlight the complexities of the impact of culture on social relationships and the resistance to heteronormative meanings about masculinity. Most gay men grow up in a society pushing them to conform to acceptable standards of what it means to be masculine. Ironically, the method is often to engage in activities and in spaces occupied by other men. The goals of the socializing institutions focus on instilling the gender norms without encouraging sexual attractions and behavior. Note the intense legal and social rules of such places as same-sex schools, the military, and sports teams, all of which attempt to control sexuality while also trying to build close male bonding.

This dialectic is replicated in many ways in the social and sexual lives of gay men as they negotiate the scripted ways of interacting with other men, while forging friend-ships and experimenting sexually. As Weeks et al. (2001, 58) phrased it, "Non-hetero-sexual friendships must therefore develop simultaneously as a focus for survival and self-actualisation in a hostile world, and as a framework for love, sex, reciprocity, and commitment in building alternative forms of life." The rules of gay subcultures may ac-commodate sexuality and friendship, but those participating also live within a social context which has developed limited ways men can interact with other men. Resolving the conflict between the hegemonic order (perceived and/or actual) and the alternate ways of expressing masculinities is at the heart of the "coming out" process for most gay men. And it's often through networks of friends building communities of identity and social movements—"the political relevance of friendship" in Hannah Arendt's (1968) words—that gay men attempt to rewrite the sexual and gendered scripts of the culture. In so doing, they can create more complex relationships that both enact the normative and display the contested definitions of masculinity, resulting in what R. W. Connell (1992) describes as a "very straight gay."

Gay and straight men's friendships

When heterosexual men become friends, any sexual aspects or intimations of romance usually remain unspoken. If friendship formation is similar to the way people develop romantic relationship—that is, by attraction to values, personalities, and maybe physical attributes—then what about possible sexual tensions between two straight men becoming friends? There is virtually no research on this topic, not surprising given the cultural restrictions in our culture about expressing emotion and intimacy between men. When I ask heterosexual men if they are attracted to their closest male friends, they get uncomfortable and change the words to "admire," "like," maybe see them as "attractive," but never "attracted to." The role of sexuality in straight men's friendships remains mysterious, not like the highly discussed concerns about the role of sexuality in cross-sex friendships. We await the research that delves deeper into the way heterosexual men view the process of friendship formation with each other and the role attraction, sexuality, and erotic emotion might or might not play.

However, a friendship between a gay man and a heterosexual man introduces questions about intimacy, sexuality, and masculinity. Popular media, especially after the 2003 debut of the cable TV show *Queer Eye for the Straight Guy*, implied that a "trend" of gay-straight male friendships was emerging in urban centers just as heterosexual men were creating a new type of male, called the "metrosexual." This type of sensitive straight male maintains his heterosexual identity but adopts an aesthetic sense focused on appearance and lifestyle.

In a magazine article, Sohn (2003) discusses conversations with some gay men who welcomed a break from the gay scene by befriending what one person called "fag stags" (with reference to the stereotyped "fag hag" of straight women and gay men). They did not come on to them sexually because they wanted to maintain the friendship and not let sexual attraction interfere. Some of the straight men also had to convince their male friends and a romantic girl friend that they were not some "closet case" just because they had gay friends. Issues of sexuality, attraction, and masculine identity regularly emerged in the discussions.

What little academic research on the topic verifies some of these popular images. Using various friendship scenarios, Muraco (2005) found that heterosexual respondents evaluated friendships differently depending on the sex and sexual orientation of the friend. Heterosexual men tended to view the appropriateness of straight friends' behaviors more favorably than gay friends' behavior. They also applied culturally dominant beliefs about sex and sexual orientation to friendship behaviors, such as highly valuing their gay male friends who acted more conventionally masculine. In addition, through interviews with respondents, Muraco found that they identified certain behaviors with their gay friends (such as an overnight stay) as appropriate only under specified conditions (a clear understanding that their friendship is platonic), what she called "conditional appropriateness" (597).

Muraco also noticed that both the straight men and women respondents continuously invoked identity issues as a means of distancing themselves from a gay or lesbian friend, reminding the researcher that they were heterosexual when discussing their friendships with gays and lesbians. In his study of gay-straight friendships, Fee (2000) found that straight men viewed their friendships with gay men as less instrumental, closer, more open, and less rigid than their friendships with other straight men (see also Price 1998). They tended to emphasize the sexual differences between themselves and their gay male friends.

On the other hand, the gay men often sought to find similarities they had with their heterosexual male friends, thereby reinforcing the value of hegemonic definitions of masculinity. At the same time, some gay men would talk about their attraction to their straight friends, in a few cases stating that the friendship was partly built on some erotic feelings (Fee 2000). While contesting the dominant norms that constrain men from being attracted to men, gay-straight friendships illustrate simultaneously how for some gay men—by sexualizing the feelings about the relationships (even if not sexually enacted)—they verify the stereotypical image of masculinity. Like straight men dealing with women friends, some gay men have to work around the sexual in order for the friendship to continue.

A city of friends

In 1860, Walt Whitman wrote:

> I dream'd in a dream, I saw a city invincible to the attacks
>   of the whole of the rest of the earth;
> I dream'd that was the new City of Friends. . . .

Often debated are the sexual intimacies that Whitman and other men may have had with their same-sex friends, but the imagery remains vivid. With these words, Whitman illustrates the essence of the late nineteenth century's meanings of romantic friendships and the power of the concept of men's heroic friendships. In gay men's friendships with gay men and straight men, the historic traits of comrades characterized by valor, bravery, and devotion become linked to the more contemporary ones of sharing, reciprocity, intimacy, and vulnerability. Men's friendships can redefine masculinity, create identity and community, and provide the groundwork for political movements. Heading into the twenty-first century, we find ourselves with numerous opportunities to go beyond the limitations imposed by society's normative scripts for masculinity, sexuality, and interpersonal relationships. Nearly 150 years after Whitman, we have the tools, and perhaps the desires, to build that invincible city of friends.

References

Allan, G. 1989. *Friendship: Developing a sociological perspective.* Boulder: Westview.

Arendt, H. 1968. *Men in dark times.* New York: Harcourt.

Bray, A. 2003. *The friend.* Chicago: University of Chicago Press.

Chauncey, G. 1994. *Gay New York.* New York: Basic Books.

Cohen, T. 1992. Men's families, men's friends: a structural analysis of constraints on men's social ties. In Nardi 1992a, 115–31.

Connell, R. W. 1992. A very straight gay: Masculinity, homosexual experience, and the dynamics of gender. *American Sociological Review* 57: 735–51.

Duneier, M. 1992. *Slim's table.* Chicago: University of Chicago Press.

Fee, D. 2000. "One of the guys": instrumentality and intimacy in gay men's friendships with straight men. In *Gay masculinities,* ed. P. M. Nardi, 44–65. Thousand Oaks, CA: Sage.

Fehr, B. 1996. *Friendship processes.* Thousand Oaks, CA: Sage.

Fischer, C. S. 1982. *To dwell among friends: Personal networks in town and city.* Chicago: University of Chicago Press.

Foucault, M. 1983. On the genealogy of ethics: an overview of work in progress. An interview in *Ethics: Subjectivity and truth. The essential works of Michel Foucault,* Vol. 1, edited by P. Rabinow (1997). New York: New Press.

Franklin, C. W. 1992. "Hey, Home—Yo, Bro": friendship among black men. In Nardi 1992a, 201–14.

Friedman, M. 1993. *What are friends for? Feminist perspectives on personal relationships and moral theory.* Ithaca: Cornell University Press.

Gagnon, J. H., and W. Simon, eds. 1973. *Sexual conduct: The social sources of human sexuality.* Chicago: Aldine.

Lambert, T., A. Kahn, and K. Apple. 2003. Pluralistic ignorance and hooking up. *Journal of Sex Research* 40:129–33.

Muraco, A. 2005. Heterosexual evaluations of hypothetical friendship behavior based on sex and sexual orientation. *Journal of Social and Personal Relationships* 22, no. 5: 587–605.

Nardi, P. M., ed. 1992a. *Men's friendships.* Newbury Park, CA: Sage.

———. 1992b. Sex, friendship, and gender roles among gay men. In Nardi 1992a, 173–85.

———. 1999. *Gay men's friendships: Invincible communities.* Chicago: University of Chicago Press.

Nardi, P. M. and D. Sherrod. 1994. Friendship in the lives of gay men and lesbians. *Journal of Social and Personal Relationships* 11:185–99.

O'Meara, J. D. 1989. Cross-sex friendship: Four basic challenges of an ignored relationship. *Sex Roles* 7/8:525–43.

Pahl, R. 2000. *On friendship.* Cambridge, UK: Polity.

Price, J. 1998. *Navigating differences: Friendships between gay and straight men.* Binghamton, NY: Harrington Park Press.

Rawlins, W. 1992. *Friendship matters: Communication, dialectics, and the life course.* New York: Aldine de Gruyter.

Rotundo, E. A. 1993. *American manhood: Transformations in masculinity from the revolution to the modern era.* New York: Basic Books.

Rubin, L. 1985. *Just friends: The role of friendship in our lives.* New York: Harper and Row.

Simmel, G. 1906. The sociology of secrecy and of secret societies. *American Journal of Sociology* 11:441–98.

Sohn, A. 2003. Mano a mano. *New York Magazine,* October 20. newyorkmetro.com.

Weeks, J., B. Heaphy, and C. Donovan. *Same sex intimacies: Families of choice and other life experiments.* London: Routledge.

Wright, P. 1982. Men's friendships, women's friendships and the alleged inferiority of the latter. *Sex Roles* 8:1–20.

PART II

SEXUAL SCRIPTS

Jeffrey Escoffier

5

Scripting the Sex

Fantasy, Narrative, and Sexual Scripts in Pornographic Films

In Billy Wilder's great film *Sunset Boulevard,* the writer-hero played by William Holden complains that most people don't realize that someone "writes a picture; they think the actors make it up as they go along." If that seems like something of an exaggeration for movies, it is probably *exactly* what most viewers of pornography believe about the "sexual action" in triple-X films. It strikes many viewers as somewhat unlikely that anyone actually "plots," "directs," or "choreographs" the sex in a porn movie—no doubt, most of those who watch porn videos believe that all any porn scene requires is two "hot" performers going at one another. In fact, the ability of pornographic films to create credible sexual fantasy worlds depends upon "scripts" and scripted performances, both figuratively and literally.

What role do the "sexual scripts" that shape everyday sexual conduct play in the production of these commercial sexual fantasies? What role do overarching narratives and stories play in the construction of sexual fantasies? John Gagnon identified two stages in the transformation of fantasies into everyday sexual scripts. The first stage consists of a mélange of "erotic mental fragments," images and "emotions" that are subsequently encoded in a second stage into the "organized cognitive scripts" that guide an individual's sexual conduct (2003, 138–39). The production of porn movies requires these two stages to take place simultaneously—the movies activate the fragments and emotions of sexual fantasies, and require for their completion the pragmatic use of the cognitive scripts formulated by performers, directors, and script writers in order to realize both the sexual performances and the filmed version of the fantasies. However, these sexual performances and scenes of sexual action are often embedded in larger narrative structures and film genres. What role do these overarching narratives play in the shaping of sexual action that is portrayed?

In this essay, I will examine the interplay between the everyday sexual scripts of the sort employed by individuals in their sex lives and the film scripts (which can exist either as completely written scripts or as loosely sketched outlines) used in the production of porn movies. I will discuss how the sexual fantasy world created in porn films draws upon the everyday sexual scripts of performers, scriptwriters, and directors. One of the things that link adult film scripts to the sexual scripts of everyday sexual conduct is the significance in pornographic movies of erections and orgasms to a "realistic" and credible representation of sexual behavior. It requires the male performer, in particular, to activate his own sexual fantasy scripts in order to achieve an orgasm that can be visibly displayed (the money shot) (Williams 1989, 100–119). These reality effects (erections and orgasms) make performing in pornographic films something more than only "acting as though one was being sexual" (though there *is* a great deal of that in adult movies). While the argument I make in this essay relies upon an analysis of gay male pornography, much of it applies to straight pornography as well—in fact, the "reality" aspects of male performance and the signifying role of erections and orgasms are important in both gay and straight porn.

"Scripts," in Gagnon and Simon's theoretical perspective, are a metaphor for understanding how people conduct themselves within social life. In order for people to engage successfully in any aspect of social life, something resembling scripting must take place on at least three distinct levels: cultural scenarios, interpersonal scripts, and intrapsychic scripts. Cultural scenarios guide an individual's behavior as a participant of collective social life—providing prescriptions for various social, gender, or occupational roles; class and racial identities; sexual beliefs; popular cultural ideals and symbols; and broad social values and norms. Interpersonal scripts are those improvised by social participants to guide everyday patterns of interactions. These scripts are suggested by each individual's presentation of self and focused interactional strategies, and draw upon cultural scenarios for normative and symbolic materials. Fantasies, desires, expectations, and ambitions are articulated through an individual's intrapsychic scripts. In these scripts, the private world of wishes and desires is linked to social meanings and actions.

Thus in Gagnon and Simon's view, everyday sexual scripts incorporate informal guidelines, rules, and social norms governing sexual conduct. These scripts bring together both symbolic and nonverbal elements in an organized and time-bound sequence of conduct. Such scripts take into account the participants, their personal and social qualities, their implied motives, and various behavioral cues. Scripts help organize a sequence of verbal and nonverbal activities that produce sexual experiences for its participants.

Porn movies, like all movies, involve scripts, camera movement, composition, editing, sound-recording, and music. These elements shape the sexual fantasy materials for the film's viewers. For the most part, these elements are coordinated by the film's director. Though the performers, the film's editor, and even other members of the production team help to shape the sexual action of a film, the final product is refracted through the sexual scripts and fantasy materials of the director. Ironically, porn movies exemplify, even more than conventional (non-porn) feature films, the significance of the director and *mise-en-scene*—the central tenets of *Cahiers du Cinema*'s classic auteur theory (Astruc 1985; Bazin 1985; Hillier 1985).

The sexual action in porn movies is often explicitly scripted. It is scripted in a number of different ways—sometimes the sex to be performed is actually described in a written script with dialogue and nonsexual action, and at other times, the sex is implied by the setting and casting, or directed by the director in person. Video scripts take different forms, but they are all examples of a more general category of scripted behavior—the sexual scripts that John Gagnon and William Simon have explored both jointly and individually, in a series of publications since 1972 (Gagnon and Simon 1973; Simon and Gagnon 1986; Gagnon 2003). Thus, to explore the connection between everyday sexual scripts and porn film scripts requires an exploration of the social production of sexual fantasies.

The laws of desire:
Fantasy, sexual scripts, and performance

The pornographic film creates a fantasy world—which for many people is usually constructed from fragments of narratives, from loose sets of related situations, or by full fledged stories—in which a utopian sexuality exists without the everyday encumbrances of social convention, endurance, or availability. The cinematic realization of a sexual fantasy world is envisioned by the scriptwriter or director—and, as a fantasy, it consists almost *always* of some sort of story or at the very minimum implies a story/script. Whether or not the fantasy world that is created succeeds or fails with its viewers depends upon whether or not the film's actors (with the help of editing or special effects) give credible sexual performances.

Sexual performers must rely on their ability to activate and use their own sexual scripts—the cultural scenarios, social interactions, and, of course, especially their intrapsychic scripts—to perform in the sexual scenes. In particular, male performers must achieve erections, engage in sexual activities that produce and show erections, and ultimately achieve an orgasm—"the money shot," the result that performers need to produce in order to be paid, and also the filmed act that makes a sexual scene credible and marketable (Williams 1989). Sexual scripts are necessary to the performers in order to successfully create the fantasy world of a hardcore movie.

The effectiveness of video pornography depends upon the viewer's *belief* that the sex is plausibly "real" in some way; a pornographic film or video is both a "documentary" and a fantasy, of successful arousal and orgasm as enacted by the performers. The viewer's sexual arousal requires a suspension of belief in pornography's fictional character. A "documentary illusion" exists in the photographic pornographic genres, which promise to enact certain sexual fantasies and certify them through the "authenticity" of erections (although some significance may be lost with the increased use of Viagra and other drugs) and orgasms (Escoffier 2003). The psychological as well as the ideological power of pornography is achieved through this certification of sexual fantasy by its "documented" sexual conclusions, visibly displayed orgasms (Patton 1988, 72–77; Williams 1989, 93–119; Barthes 1986).

The successful production of fantasy is *not* primarily dependent on the physical desirability per se of the performer, but on the performance *and* the setting of the performance together—that is, the *mise-en-scene*: the physical set-up (the set), décor, costumes, props, the lighting, positions of the camera, and the movements and actions of performers themselves. Arousal, according to Elizabeth Cowie, "is stimulated by the scenario of presentation, by the *mise-en-scene* and the implied narrative" (133). Pornography, like fantasy, follows the "laws of desire"—it is created by the construction of an imaginary script elaborated from our wishes, frustrations, pleasures, denials, conflicts, daydreams, and memories of past events, erotic and non-erotic—and is never solely stimulated by an "object of desire" itself, but by an entire setting, scene, or narrative that the spectator can imaginatively enter. The successful sexual performance in a fantasy or in a porn movie protects the spectator's excitement from being ruined by anxiety, guilt, or boredom, and allows adult movie producers to simulate reality without the risks that we all face in real life situations—unless, of course, we have the power to manipulate reality, especially real people. It is the fantasy scenario that stimulates a subject's desire; it is not the fulfillment or satisfaction of the desire. "Through fantasy," Slavoj Žižek has pointed out, "we learn how to desire."

> Desire is not something given in advance, but something that has to be construc-
> ted—and it is precisely the role of fantasy to give coordinates of the subject's desire,
> to specify the object, to locate the position the subject assumes in it. (1991, 6)

And for many people, erotic excitement is heightened when the fantasy's outcome is un-certain—when it includes an element of risk, danger, mystery, or transgression (Stoller 1985, vii–viii).

The virtual porn script, as the blueprint for a cinematic fantasy world, consists of a number of identifiable components: the set-up—that is, the physical setting (locker room, kitchen, barracks, bedroom) or the situation (the loss of a diary, runaway boy-friend) that frames the physical and social space necessary to realize the fantasy; the objects of desire (the desirable bodies of performers); the idealized sexual action in which the physical or social obstacles (performance anxieties, physical exhaustion, satiation) to unrestrained sexual activity are eliminated; and the reality effects (real erections and/or orgasms) that authenticate the sexual fantasy.

For most spectators of porn, masturbation is the primary activity that accompa-nies watching an adult movie and it helps to establish both the pace and timing of a sexual scene and its narrative of sexual action—kissing, oral action, anal action of vari-ous kinds, penetration, and finally orgasm. "Pornography's narrative form, in each of its many genres," Andrew Ross has noted, "is closely tailored to the demands of its tra-ditional male market, broadly based around the activity of masturbation" (1989, 195). Masturbatory fantasies also frequently suggest a scene's implied narrative. For instance, a scene's set-up may imply a narrative that activates certain fantasies. Jerry Douglas ob-serves that

> [t]he set-up has its roots in a masturbatory—in the director's masturbatory fantasy,
> that he assumes is shared by his viewers. I remember quite vividly, one of the first
> men I ever interviewed in this industry was Matt Sterling. We talked about one of
> his most famous loops, which is "Mr. Egan and the Paperboy." It's legend; it's one
> of the landmark loops. . . . I said, "Where did the idea for this come from?" And he
> said, "Oh, I don't know. I just always thought that every time my paperboy came
> around to collect for the weekly subscription, I always thought, 'What if this turned
> into a sex scene?' And I'm sure I'm not the only one who's ever thought that." (2001)

Though we construct our fantasies as a loose narrative, we rarely retell our fantasies as narratives, as Andrew Ross points out:

> The plot of realist films is often recounted to others in the same way as we reconstruct dreams out loud to friends, but pornography is like fantasies in this respect: no one would dream of recounting the narrative form of either. Pornography, for the most part, provides a stimulus, base, or foundation for individual fantasies to built upon and elaborated. It merely provides the conditions—stock, generic, eroticizable components such as poses, clothing, and sounds—under which the pleasure of fantasizing, a pleasure unto itself, can be pursued. (196–97)

The narrative dimension of a porn film does not necessarily have to be presented as a story, but a story must be *implied* in order to set up and activate the fantasy scenario. Thus in porn, the narrative—whether explicit or implied—motivates the set-up and establishes cues and other signs for the activation of desire.

The spectator's fantasy video script is elaborated through an intrapsychic dialectic that oscillates between desire and identification—the movement between the arousal stimulated by the set-up and for the desirable objects (the active role) and imagined substitution of oneself in place of the objects of desire (the passive role). It is the continued imagining of an unattained but "possible" sexual satisfaction that nurtures desire. The pleasure of sexual fantasy and pornography is sought for itself, not as a means to physical sexual gratification.

The spectator's fantasy script is created as he (or in some cases, she) watches the porn video by fast-forwarding through the "boring" parts, pausing on the exciting moment or running the favorite scene in slow motion in order to savor the action. The spectator uses the remote control to edit the commercial sexual fantasy into one that is more immediately arousing.

Thus, in porn films, sexual scripts operate on many different levels most importantly, each of the participants' conduct on the set is guided by their own scripts. In addition, the film itself is the product of a formal (or not so formal) film script, but it also shaped by the director's choreography (and direction of the performers) of the sexual action implied or explicitly included in the script; by each performer's enactment of the sexual action (in the film script as choreographed by the director) and the scripts dictated by their own sexual fantasies; and, last but not least, by the film's editor who (with or without the director) assembles the final print of the film.

The production frame: Making a pornographic film

The porn production frame organizes the sexual activities of the performers hired to appear in a pornographic movie (Goffman 1974, 123–55). Within the production frame, performers are supplied with two other kinds of sexual scripts. One is the script per se, which may be a fully written text with instructions about the sexual activity to be filmed or it may be merely an outline that the director uses as the basis for choreographing the sexual activities of the performers. The second production "script" is the *mise-en-scene*, which is the overall visual style of the production and the sexual activity that is to take place before the camera (Gibbs 2002, 5–27). Ultimately, the *mise-en-scene* establishes the overarching visual/fantasy vocabulary of the movie—the erotic gestalt of the porn movie.

The porn film production framework also contributes to the scripted behavior in several other significant ways. It establishes the social and physical conditions for sexual performances to be filmed: it creates a bounded space that is defined as a set (creating access to a setting where certain type of sexual activities are expected to take place) where sexual performances will be filmed, it supplies sexual partners (via casting) who expect to perform sexual acts before a camera with other performers, and it employs a production crew—the producer, director, cinematographer, lighting expert, make-up person, editor, and composer—who will help to produce (direct, film, edit, supply music, and prepare the performers) the final product. (Simon and Gagnon 1986, 109–10)

Like any other form of sexual conduct, pornographic film performances rely upon the scripting capabilities of individual performers, directors and film editors to create a cinematographically convincing fantasy world through its "construction" of credible sexual performances. Video scripts and vernacular sexual "scripts" function somewhat differently. Video scripts and their *mise-en-scene* organize sexual performances and set the stage in order to create a credible fantasy world on film, whereas in real-life sexual activities, "scripts" are usually improvised to some degree from the participants' personal fantasies, social roles, cultural codes, and symbols, in addition to the socially-available interactional strategies that are used to orchestrate a sexual encounter.

Many porn scripts are mere outlines—a sheet of paper with the situational premise, cast, and a sequence of action. The screenplay may include detailed descriptions of the sex to be performed (as do those of Jerry Douglas), but it may also leave the choreographing of the sex to the director, who is sometimes also the author of the screenplay (for example, Wash West). The movie's screenplay sets the stage, introduces characters, provides dialogue, and sketches the sex scenes. But the written—or sometimes, unwritten—script draws upon the scriptwriter's and/or the director's personal fantasies (what Gagnon and Simon have called "intrapsychic scripts") and extensively upon cultural symbols, roles, and social types (cultural scenarios)—as well as the interactional skills and private fantasies of the performers (their repertoire of sexual scripts).

Casting can also play a significant role in the shaping of a film's storyline and sexual action. Thus, every adult film's script draws on the socially available sexual scripts that Gagnon and Simon have delineated—the specific roles, norms, and symbols embodied in the cultural scenarios; the interpersonal scripts that include the social cues, norms, and interpersonal strategies that guide everyday patterns of interaction and that draw on the screenwriter's and/or director's intrapsychic fantasies, desires, and sexual preferences.

The market for which a porn film is made also affects the film's script and the various behavioral/social scripts used by the director and the performers to produce credible sexual performances. Depending on whether the intended audience includes heterosexual males, heterosexual couples, gay men, gay women, or individuals with more specialized preferences (such as those desiring videos featuring she-males, bondage, or wrestling), the film script, cultural scenarios, and interactional scripts will differ significantly. And, of course, the performers' intrapsychic scripts may also differ depending on the type of movie in which they are performing.

Performers not only draw on their personal sexual scripts in order to provide credible sexual performances, but they also adopt personas (which are also porn-industry career-scripts) that shape both characterization and sexual repertoire—and which affect the performer's realization of the film's script and have an impact on the performances of fellow performers (Escoffier 2003). Very rarely are the sexual activities recorded in a commercial pornographic video ever wholly spontaneous. They are written by scriptwriters or verbally coached by directors, or (in conjunction with the director's choreography) partly improvised by the performers.

When I first began to interview the people who work in the gay porn industry, Michael Lucas, who has worked as a performer and currently directs porn videos for his own company based in New York City, asked if I had ever thought of writing porn scripts. Though I hadn't thought of doing so before, over the next week I wrote four or five with a friend. Though none of them was ever produced, it was a useful lesson about what elements go into developing a porn script. Lucas gave me a very strict formula that has been almost universally acknowledged as the correct one—and an important aspect of the production frame. The script must consist of four or five scenes, eight or nine performers, roughly equal numbers of tops and bottoms, and only two of the performers could appear in more than one scene. Lastly, for Lucas, the video must be set in New York City and reflect the ethnic mix of the city. Such generic formulas are important components of the production frame—in part, they are economic constraints. The scripts that my friend and I wrote told archetypical New York stories (a white-collar crime investigation, a story of tourists and taxicab drivers, and the story of an immigrant's arrival in NYC) and presented characters based on locale (tourism, Wall Street, Washington Heights), occupation (NYPD detectives), and ethnic social types (Dominican baseball players, South Asian taxicab drivers). These scripts were "concepts" more than literal scripts; my co-author and I described the sexual action, but we didn't write any dialogue. In the end, Lucas decided not use any of them because he found it more convenient to develop scripts with particular performers in mind.

This story illustrates that "writing" a script for a porn video is not, in itself, sufficient to generate a credible fantasy world. As Lucas suggested, casting is an important part of developing a porn script, and as I have found in my research, so is direction. But though particular performers lend a script some of the performer's unique individual personality, physical desirability, and sexual energy, the formulaic framework incorporates many fairly abstract elements of local knowledge, social and sexual roles, and cultural beliefs to set the stage for the recreation of a sexual fantasy (the writer's). One young director, Doug Jeffries, discovered this as well:

I'm so overbooked I thought, "Let me get rid of this scriptwriting and let me direct somebody else's script." But I can't do it. First of all, I need to live with my script, and secondly, whoever is writing the script doesn't know the performers. I've always had one or two stars in mind who would be the central characters. As Scott Masters from Studio 2000 said to me, when you write these scripts you're not writing for actors, you're writing for the personality of the person you're casting. There's a performer named Cade Devlin, who's streety and boyish. When he works for Falcon and Studio 2000, they always tell him to tone it down. In the movie I did with him, *Looking for Trouble,* I let him be wild, wear jewelry and be a street boy and that's what he was. He was amazing in that movie. (2005)

Ultimately, the realization of that fantasy will require the director's choreography and the actors' sexual performances and draw on their own intrapsychic scripts in order to produce a credible sexual scene.

This suggests the primacy of *mise-en-scene* as the coordinating "script" of porn production. The explicit porn script and the personal sexual scripts of all the porn production's participants are "keyed" (to use Goffman's term from *Frame Analysis*) by the *mise-en-scene*. Keying takes place when a set of conventions and rules by which a given activity (in this case, sexual activity that is meaningful in terms of everyone's daily framework of sexual conduct) is transformed into a pornographic performance and representation—that is, something patterned on everyday sexual activity but that is seen by both participants (and, in this case, viewers) as something else (Goffman 1974, 40–82).

The textbook definition of *mise-en-scene* is "the contents of the frame and they way they are organized," which includes lighting, costume, décor, props, and the set, as well as the actors and their staging; it is everything that the viewers see and the way they are invited to see it (Hillier 1985, 8–11; Gibbs 2002, 5–26). The importance of *mise-en-scene* implies the overwhelming significance of the director as the "auteur" of the porn movie. It is the director who choreographs the sexual action; who casts the performers who co-star with other; who coaches the performers before and during a sex scene; who selects and then steers the videographer; who approves the wardrobes, hairstyles, and make-up of the performers; who selects the set; and who, by such means, evokes the basic fantasy scenario.

Can sex tell the story? Narrative and sexual action

Narrative has a special place in the thinking about pornographic movies. To the degree that all scripts involve a sequence of related events, they are narratives. Most early pornographic films consisted of short sexual episodes unrelated to one another. They were called "loops" because they were often run as looped shorts in a video player set up in a small booths at adult bookstores. In loops, the sexual action provides the narrative, from the initial oral action through various other forms of sexual play (rimming, cunnilingus, bondage, sex toys, anal play) to the concluding intercourse (vaginal/anal) and the money shots. However, with the emergence of feature-length productions, the short sexual episodes are ever more likely to be organized into an overarching narrative or storyline.

Plot-oriented feature-length porn films first emerged as a significant category of adult films in the 1970s. In *Miller v. California* (1973), the U.S. Supreme Court declared that a work was obscene if it was "utterly" without redeeming social worth *and* if it lacked "serious" literary, artistic, political, or scientific value. In the wake of *Miller v. California,* plot offered the adult industry a basis for legally defending sexually explicit film productions because plot allowed the industry to claim that its films—like *Deep Throat, Behind the Green* and *The Devil in Miss Jones,* all strongly narrative porn movies—had some redeeming social worth and "serious" literary or artistic value (O'Toole 1999, 8). Plot also serves as an alibi for those spectators who felt that plot makes porn more intellectually acceptable (O'Toole 1999, 8, 84–89, 209–10).

Today, the review section of *Adult Video News* (*AVN*), the porn industry's trade journal, explicitly distinguishes in its review section between "plot-oriented features" (based on traditional three-act scripts that rely upon acting and dialog) and "all-sex productions" that have no overarching plot structure. The latter films (successors to the earlier era's loops) are also known as "wall-to-wall" productions and by definition consist of a "series of sex scenes that may or may not include a connecting device" (AVN 2003). There are, of course, many specialty genres, such as those devoted to S/M, girl-girl, and fat or foot fetishes, but the vast majority of porn films produced for the general audience are in these two broad categories.

There is a longstanding debate about the compatibility of narrative and sexual action in film (O'Toole 1999, 209–10). Many viewers of adult videos consider a strong narrative to be a distraction and unnecessary—something to fast-forward through. Others find that a strong narrative enhances and heightens the sexual excitement. Some critics consider narrative and explicit sexual action essentially incompatible. *New York Times* columnist Frank Rich has argued that sex acts bring a narrative to a halt—"like the musical numbers in a 1930s musical" (2000).

Cultural theorist Slavoj Žižek also contends that explicit sexual action interrupts the narrative. For example, during the unfolding of a love story, "instead of the sublime Thing, we are stuck with a vulgar groaning and fornication" (1991, 110–11). Without reference to any pornographic films, he concludes that "congruence between the film narrative (the unfolding of the story) and the immediate display of the sexual act is structurally impossible" (111). Žižek concludes that what he calls "the fantasy ideal of pornographers"—to preserve the "impossible harmony" between narration and explicit sexual action—is unattainable; explicit sexual action, to the degree that it involves erections, penetrations, and orgasms that appear to be "real" sex, throws the spectator off-balance and makes it impossible to believe in the fictional reality of the overarching narrative (Williams 2004, 5–6)

The primary weakness of Rich's and Žižek's arguments are their failure to examine or discuss specific pornographic films. Their arguments rely on arbitrarily and hypothetically inserting an explicit sexual scene in the narrative of a commercial romantic film that is not a sexual story. But pornographic narratives are not "love stories"; they are usually stories about sex, sexual adventure, or, as in much gay porn, stories about sexual identity—in which case, the portrayal of sexually explicit action is not necessarily inappropriate. These narratives often explore interplay between sex and the dynamics of power through social roles and stereotypes (for example, gender, age, body type, or sex role) and cultural mythologies (religion, sports, masculinity/femininity), and are often stories of sexual acceptance, transgression, and a utopian freedom from the encumbrances of everyday life to engage in sexual activity.

In *Hard Core*, Linda Williams, appealing (like Frank Rich) to the example of musicals, came to the opposite conclusion:

> The episodic narratives typical of the genre are not simply frivolous pretexts for the display of song and dance; rather narrative permits the staging of song and dance spectacles as events themselves within the larger structures afforded by the story-line. Narrative informs number, and number, in turn, informs narrative. Part of the pleasure . . . resides in the tension between these different discursive registers, each seeking to establish its own equilibrium. (1989, 130)

In William's view, a narrative porn film's sexual scenes function in several different ways: as regular moments of pleasure (to viewers and/or to the film's characters); as representations of sexual conflicts (among the characters); and as resolutions of those conflicts. She argues that "the episodic structure of the hardcore narrative is . . . more than a flimsy excuse for sexual numbers: it is part and parcel of the way the genre goes about resolving the often contradictory desires of its characters" (120–34).

Director Wash West, discussing the possible function of plot in porn movies, has noted, "Most people think that plot is the story, but it is also what the audience wants to happen." In his movie *Naked Highway*, the central characters (played by Jim Buck and Joey Violence) "don't have sex until you've been with them for an hour or so . . . during which they've been having sex with other people. So it builds up [anticipation] with the audience. So often porn will have no suspense because the people meet and five seconds later they're dropping their pants. There's no anticipation" (2002).

Narrative and sexual action are thus not necessarily contradictory aspects of adult filmmaking. Gay porn filmmaker Jerry Douglas, who had written a musical based on Arthur Schnitzler's play *La Ronde* (a series of sexual vignettes analogous to pornographic "loops") realized that sexual action and narrative could be integrated:

> It came to me in a blinding flash very early on, and I just can't imagine why more people didn't see it. It seems to me absolutely transparently obvious. Just in one example: after Rodgers and Hammerstein's *Oklahoma,* the whole idea was to integrate the musical numbers into the fabric of the story.
>
> And in an adult film, I usually know where my sex scenes are going to fall, and then I have to build the libretto or the webbing or whatever you want to call it, around them. If I do it right, the sex scenes will do what a good number in a musical comedy does: it will reveal character, it will push the plot forward, and it will enrich the theme.
>
> How does one go about achieving this, aside from the number of people in any given scene or the location? The answer to me was always, that we fuck for different reasons. We fuck to pleasure ourselves, we fuck to pleasure our partners, we fuck to hurt our partners, we fuck to hurt ourselves, we fuck to show off. There are any number of reasons why we have sex.
>
> What has always interested me was that this is one of the most primal impulses of the human animal. Art, in the history of the Judeo-Christian ethic, has always faded to black just at the time it gets interesting. So, I always try to make each sex scene push the story forward and reveal the state of mind of the characters at any given moment. (2001)

Many of Douglas's films exemplify this approach of situating the sexual action in the context of a story. In her 1989 essay on Douglas's *More of a Man*, Mandy Merck also examines this question. The film tells the story of a young man struggling against the Catholic church's prohibitions of his homosexual desires and portrays the furtive and sometimes degrading ways he gives in to them. Eventually with the counsel of a drag queen (played by noted porn director Chi Chi LaRue) who he meets at a local bar, he achieves sexual self-acceptance and has a liberating sexual experience with an activist during the annual gay pride parade. Merck found that Douglas had successfully managed "to reconcile porn with cinematic narrative," and concluded, in sharp contrast to Rich and Žižek, that it was "remarkably easy to fuse sex with story" (1993, 234).

While most writers on porn have commented on the place of narrative in porn movies (and its converse, the place of explicit sex in film narratives), the discussion has largely focused on the compatibility between explicit sexual action and narrative. Does explicit sexual action disrupt a narrative? Can a scene of explicit hardcore action move the story forward? There is, however, another debate that takes place primarily among the viewers of adult movies: it is whether or not a narrative in a hardcore movie enhances or detracts from the fantasy potential of a sexual scene?

What impact does narrative have on the spectator's fantasy scripts? For the most part, viewers watch pornography in order to become aroused and to masturbate. An individual's relation to plot in pornography may differ according to their situation—as performer, spectator, or author. Performer Gus Mattox recently told an interviewer that "personally I like porn with no plot—that's what I like to watch, but because I'm an actor/writer, it's more fun for me to make porn with a plot" (Shamama 2004, 8). Does narrative impinge on the fantasy potential of a sexually explicit scene? While both narrative frameworks and realistic social contexts are potential sources of fantasy material, they strongly frame the fantasy potential of the explicit sexual scene. Many viewers, however, reject the narrative's framing effect on the sexual scene. Narratives foreclose viewers' ability to engage with certain fantasies that might otherwise be suggested by the sexual action—without the narrative context, the same scene would enable different fantasies. Thus, a hardcore film consisting only of sexual scenes, without any narrative, offers a fantasy potential that is different than one with a story (for more discussion of fantasy potential, see Escoffier, forthcoming).

Sex, genre, and cultural scenarios

Narrative porn movies often appeal to preexisting film and cultural genres, like popular movies, TV shows, novels, or sports events. By adapting them for a pornographic movie production, the filmmakers invoke the underlying sexual implications of the genre. Adopting generic conventions also helps to organize an adult film's narrative components such as characters, setting, plot, and even visual techniques, without requiring in-depth character development or a complex storyline. Most importantly, by adapting or parodying conventional genres, porn filmmakers appeal to society's cultural beliefs encoded in typical storylines, popular social types, and cultural mythologies (for a discussion of traditional film genres, see Schatz 1980).

Gagnon and Simon argue that individuals in their everyday sexual conduct draw upon society's cultural scenarios—romantic narratives, the coming-out process, stories of success, tales of emotional development—for practical clues to performing social roles, interpreting cultural stereotypes (of gender, age, or race), and identifying typical patterns of behavior (Simon and Gagnon 1986, 102–5). As they put it:

> The most basic sources of sociogenic influence are the cultural scenarios that deal explicitly with the sexual or those that can implicitly to put to sexual uses. Such cultural scenarios not only specify appropriate objects, aims, and desirable qualities of self-other relations but also instruct in times, places, sequences of gesture and

utterance and, among the most important, what the actor and his or her co-partici-pants (real and imagined) are assumed to be feeling. (105)

By adapting preexisting film genres and narrative styles, adult films can incorporate in-fluential cultural scenarios to frame the fantasies stimulated by the sexual action.

Jerry Douglas is one of the leading proponents of the narrative approach in adult moviemaking. A graduate of the Yale School of Drama and a playwright, he directed a number of Off-Broadway nude productions in the late sixties and early seventies. His first film, *The Back Row* (1973), was one of the first porn movies that aspired to and in fact achieved professional quality. It offers a vivid portrait of the gay sexual culture in New York City in the early 1970s that emerged and flourished in the wake of the Stone-wall riots and gay liberation. It had a loose, picaresque story of a young visitor from out west (something of a takeoff on the popular John Schlesinger film *Midnight Cowboy*) accidentally encountering and then exploring the somewhat raunchy gay sexual scene in a porn movie theater. Douglas made only two more movies, however, before quitting in frustration over the control of film rights, money, and bookings with unscrupulous theater owners and distributors.

After 1989, when Douglas returned to making porn movies, he brought a new per-spective from his work in musical theater—in particular, one influenced by Rogers and Hammerstein, who revolutionized the American musical by using the musical number to move the plot along: the libretto weaves the songs into the narrative. In Douglas's view of porn narratives, *sex* tells the story. The sex as performed is an aspect of a character's development: it reveals the film's underlying themes and it moves the plot along. Nearly all of Douglas's later movies involve a thoroughly worked-out script, often as long as 60 pages—even the sex is scripted and it is integral to the plot and character development. Thus, the porn movies of Douglas's later career are feature-length productions in which the sex is embedded within a larger story. Douglas frequently quotes his good friend Stan Ward, a fellow porn scriptwriter and former AVN editor: "Sex always takes place in context."

Flesh and Blood (1996), considered by many to be Douglas's best movie, is a porn film noir and is more specifically a tribute to Alfred Hitchcock; it operates fully within the generic conventions of film noir. While film noir, as a genre of film production, flourished in the 1940s and 50s, it became a particularly influential cultural category in the last quarter of the twentieth century, eventually serving as a kind of popular mythol-ogy. In film noir, sexual desire, paranoia, and murder are central elements of film nar-ratives. As film scholar Foster Hirsch noted, "Noir posits an unstable world, in which terror lurks in wait just beneath a deceptively placid reality. . . . In noir no one is safe from himself or from others—and those others include spouses, siblings, neighbors, best friends" (182). In particular, sex is rarely represented in a romantic context, but one in which sexual desire is driven by obsession and provokes criminal acts. "The noir psychopath," writes Hirsch, "is bedeviled, pursued by ghosts from the past, and is often fatally self-divided. Sometimes the . . . motif is presented in a literal way. . . . as stories about good and bad twins" (190).

In *Flesh and Blood,* Douglas exploits many of these motifs and conventions. The film tells the story of Derrick, played by Kurt Young, investigating the murder of his identical twin brother, Erik (also played by Young). Derrick, who mentions that he is engaged to be married soon after his arrival, discovers that his brother left behind a series of betrayed sexual partners, both male and female. His brother's cruel treatment of his partners is revealed through a series of sexually-explicit flashbacks. Initially each character is a suspect. Each declares their love of Eric and each tells Derrick the story of their sexual relationship with Eric in a self-serving way. But the flashbacks reveal the false notes, delusions, and lies in their stories as well as Eric's unscrupulous manipulation of his partners through seduction, misrepresentation, and lies.

Thus, the sexual action of each scene reveals the psychological character of the person who relates the scene and shows us how in each case the narrator's own delusions about Eric's sexuality or about themselves allowed Eric to manipulate them sexually. His sex with Kenny, the young man who claims to be Eric's boyfriend, is not reciprocal—Kenny bottomed for Eric, Eric did not bottom for Kenny—which suggests that Kenny's love was not reciprocated by Eric. The flashback demonstrates that Kenny's vulnerability lies in his romantic naiveté. The bisexual three-way that Marilyn, who claims to be Eric's fiancé, gives as proof of her and Eric's sexual openness and of their trust to one another, instead reveals her self-delusion: Eric only has sex with the man. Eric's sexual manipulation of a young man who insists that he is straight shows that the young man is also self-deluded, about his sexual desires. Each of Eric's suitors fantasize about Derrick as a possible replacement for the murdered brother—another degree of their self-delusion. When the supposedly murdered Erik suddenly comes out of hiding, Derrick must engage in sex with his brother in order to solve the mystery. But like the others, Derrick succumbs to Eric's ruthless domination because he too is self-deluded, about his own sexual desires and about his brother's thirst to destroy. Derrick has risked everything, but he fails.

Few porn films are predicated on the relentless exploration of the characters' delusions about sexual relationships, their sexual desires or identities, or on a narrative that begins with and ends in murder. The title, *Flesh and Blood,* alludes both to family ties and to the mythology of film noir, invoking the claustrophobia of forbidden sexualities, incest, and secrecy. Through the positioning of the camera as a spectator within the internal space of the scene, the dark angular lighting, and the claustrophobic set, Douglas' *mise-en-scène* replicates the visual style and mood of the traditional noir film. Within the film's narrative, the explicit sexual action contributes to the development of each the film's characters, revealing their illusions and in some sense, illustrating the danger of deluding oneself about sexuality—so commonly the topic of traditional film noir.

One extremely common device among porn scriptwriters and directors is to adapt or to parody a mainstream movie, television show, or even book—e.g., *The Rear Factor, Drill Bill,* or *The Bachelor.* Sometimes this goes no further than the title, in which the porn title makes a sexually explicit joke on the original title (All World Studio's *Dawson's Crack* after the WB series *Dawson's Creek*), but in most cases it can involve a full-fledged erotic adaptation of the original.

Among gay porn videos, a recent example is Wash West's *The Hole* (2002), a parody of *The Ring. The Ring* was a 2002 horror movie featuring a nightmarish videotape; its viewers receive phone calls predicting their deaths in exactly seven days. The title of *The Hole,* of course, plays on the significance of anal eroticism among gay men. West's movie follows a group of jocks who see a videotape of obscure images while staying at a rundown motor lodge. In this case, the follow-up phone call warns that the viewers will turn gay in exactly seven days. Thus, the overall concept of the movie plays on the masculinity of athletes and ambivalent erotic appeal of straight jocks to many gay men. There is an added irony on a meta-cinematic level as well: all but two of the main sexual performers in this very popular gay porn film identify themselves as heterosexual (this fact having been discussed in reviews in local gay newspapers and on the many discussion boards and forums devoted to gay porn). There is no doubt that many viewers of *The Hole* will assume that merely performing in this video "predicts" that some the film's heterosexual performers may eventually become gay. On some level, *The Hole* remains a horror movie for those "straight" homophobic viewers who believe that merely seeing a gay porn movie will help make them gay.

Within this comic framework, there is a coming-out story in which the ultimate outcome, though a surprise to the characters, is in every case a positive one. A local reporter (played by Tag Eriksson) investigates reports of these sexual transformations by interviewing the jocks affected and going so far as to view the tape himself. Does he view the tape to investigate the story or to initiate his own transition to a gay identity? It's not clear—nor is his ambivalence completely resolved by the fantasy he has based on a still photograph/video scene of noted straight porn actress, T. J. Hart in a scene with man; the images of both Hart and the man flash before him as he has an orgasm.

This account of *The Hole* gives a sense of the overall concept of the movie and the cultural scenarios invoked in the movie: the coming-out narrative, the supposedly counterintuitive idea of gay athletes and masculine homosexuals, the nonsensical nature of urban legends and their superstitious appeal. But while these cultural notions influence our ideas of sexual identity and affect our fantasies, they are not by themselves erotic or pornographic. It is the sexual performances within the film's *mise-en-scene* that stimulate erotic arousal, abetted to some degree by the extra-filmic awareness of spectators that most of the leading performers in the film are straight. Thus the film provides the fantasy (outside either the story or the film's scenic presentation) of "actually" straight athletes performing homosexual acts—and, within the film's story, turning gay. The sexual scenes implicitly allude to these outside conditions—all the straight actors but one perform as tops (as penetrators in anal intercourse). The one "straight" actor who performs as a bottom is widely rumored to be "really" gay.

What is the "script" in these two porn movies? Certainly, the literal script of each movie probably will not strictly coincide with the fantasy script of every spectator. Yet the director certainly envisions a fantasy script of some sort—presumably his own. The *mise-en-scene* of each film invokes the laws of desire—those fantasies elaborated willy-nilly from our wishes, denials, delights, clashes, daydreams, and memories, both erotic and non-erotic, in order to establish a scene that will arouse the viewer. It is in some ways a hit-or-miss operation—explaining, in part, the routine complaints from viewers of the tedium and repetition of pornographic movies. And, of course, it is not possible to say what role, if any, the literal script or the fantasy script played in the performer's ability to produce a credible sexual performance.

Coaching the libido

Directing a porn film requires a sophisticated sexual imagination and strong sense of the *mise-en-scene* of sexual encounters. Despite the centrality of "porn stars"—as the performers are often referred to—and the significance of casting both for the film's *mise-en-scene* and the marketing, the director plays the most important role in the production of pornographic movies. *Mise-en-scene* involves coordinating all the elements of a film in order to create a credible fantasy world—coordinating the sexual scripts, both literal and figurative, of performers and other members of the production team; the positioning and movements of the camera; and the framing of the sexual action, as well as the editing and sound-mixing in post-production. For the most part, these elements are coordinated by the film's director. These elements provide the raw material for the "fantasy scripts" that the spectator fashions from his viewing of the movie—via scene selection, fast-forwarding, slow motion, and replaying.

One of the contemporary masters of gay porn is Chi Chi LaRue. Far and away the most prolific director in the history of gay porn, since the late 1980s he has also become one of the leading directors of straight porn, being the preferred directors of such leading female performers such as Jenna James and Tara Patrick. He is widely considered the best and most original director of sex scenes in gay porn today.

LaRue is the preeminent director of all-sex porn videos, and he is especially well-known for his orgy scenes. Group sex, particularly if it is a large group, is very difficult to choreograph. All-sex movies and orgies often have no discernable narrative structure, other than that they will start with oral sex and kissing, move on to rimming and fucking, and culminate in the money shots. However, the sexual activities are usually cumulative—the sucking, kissing, and rimming are added step-by-step. Only orgasms bring the sexual narrative to a conclusion.

Everyday sexual scripts, erotic fantasy fragments, and implied narratives of setups are the raw materials of LaRue's *mise-en-scene*. "I don't write stage directions on my scripts," LaRue told me, "only the dialogue. All the sex, all the movement comes out of my head. Sitting right there. . . . I'm a sex director" (2004). The performers' responses to LaRue's improvisatory style are also important:

> I have to give some credit to the performers . . . I was doing an oral scene and the [performers] came up to me and said, "[W]e want to fuck, we don't want this [scene] to be just oral." It was going to be this little, tiny oral movie, and it blew up into this big, giant movie that turned out not just to be oral.

LaRue's improvisational style extends even to the preparation for future movies—visits to the hardware store can yield material for his next film: "I love water sports, so I do as much dirty water sports as I can get away with. . . . I'll go to a hardware store and look at anything weird that's used for gardening or hosing off the driveway and I'll think, "Oh that'll look great up a butt!" and I'll buy and use it in a movie." (Lawrence 1999, 46).

Another aspect notable about LaRue is his directing style. He shouts out instructions ("Go down on him!"), encouragement ("Yeah, that's fucking hot! . . . Harder, harder . . .") and exclamations ("That's hot!") as he coaches the performers step by step through the sexual scene. He literally supplies the "sexual script" to the performers, the videographer, and the film crew, at the same establishing his own sexual script as a framework. While some performers are uncomfortable with his approach, most find LaRue's method valuable. Usually the biggest problems created by this approach occur in post-production, when the sound editor must go through and meticulously strip LaRue's voice from the recorded soundtrack. The immense irony here is, of course, that LaRue's voice will be erased from the audio recording, but the film is nonetheless an expression of his "voice" as a director and as a coach—of sex.

Directing an all-sex movie requires a different approach than the narrative porn feature. It is much more like filming a sports event, as Jerry Douglas points out:

> You can never storyboard a fuck film. The best metaphor I've ever heard is that it's like photographing a football game. You try to cover it from as many angles as you can and don't have the slightest idea of how it's going to turn out. But your eye had damned well better be on the ball, or in this case, the balls. (2001)

Nevertheless, the wall-to-wall sex movies require considerable planning and advanced preparation. These preparations are utilized through the *mise-en-scene* in order to achieve the spectator's potential fantasy script that will arouse him and encourage his orgasm.

All the elements of the all-sex video must be coordinated. One of LaRue's biggest commercial successes was the *Link* series of movies (1997–1999) made for All Worlds Studios. They were shot in a San Francisco leather bar and the performers were dressed in leather, harnesses, chaps, and black denim. The sexual action took place in dark, dimly-lit rooms; in slings; through glory holes; and in an enclosed area of chain-link fencing. There was fisting, a beer enema, and mild water sports. Many of the group sex scenes were performed by muscular, hairy men. The set, the costumes, the casting, and the lighting created an atmosphere of rough sex, of underground and hidden places, and of uninhibited sex. Despite their darkness and sexual intensity, La Rue himself characterized the *Link* movies as "leatherette movies because they're not heavy leather, even though they are total sex pig movies." (Lawrence 1999, 46).

One of LaRue's recent movies, *Bolt* (2004), was initially thought of as another *Link* movie, but which he took in a completely different direction by making it bright and "clean" ("not the sex, the sex is dirty") rather than dark and dingy by using silvers, chromes, and Lucite (LaRue, 2004). In conjunction with *Bolt*, LaRue's company introduced a large industrial-style metallic bolt as a dildo, which is used throughout the movie. Like the *Link* films, *Bolt* is also a "total sex pig movie," though with a different sort of casting—younger men, more men with blonde hair, and men wearing torn white jockey shorts and tank tops rather than leather. Consequently, it conveys a very different erotic atmosphere and mood than the *Link* movies.

While narrative hardcore movies invoke cultural scenarios and symbols by developing the context within which the sexual action places, the set-up and the implied narrative suggested by the set-up is central to the all-sex video. Many all-sex videos are essentially four or five loops with a theme. The set-up scene is always set in some highly charged symbolic and erotic milieu such as the gym, the barracks, the dungeon, the alleyway, or the warehouse, and it suggests an implied narrative that the spectator's fantasy will elaborate on. The director's *mise-en-scene* exploits the erotic and symbolic significance of the set-up. Thus, for example, the widely held belief that sports world is a rampant arena of homoeroticism "implies" a (fantasy) sexual encounter in the locker room or the gym (Miller 2001, 13, 51–52; Pronger 1990, 177–214). The erotic charge of such implied narratives is enhanced by the uniforms, the typical physiques, and the props of various sports. The military environment exercises a similar erotic fascination for the gay male spectator: sometimes it is established by the mere presence of someone who is a marine or a sailor (thus the appeal of Dirk Yates's *Private Amateur Collection*); other times, an implied narrative is created by set design to look like a barracks or a scene of military-like discipline. (Zeeland 1999, 175–86)

Post scripts: A gathering of thoughts

The sexual scripts of everyday life and those that operate within the context of pornographic production are closely related. Everyday sexual scripts are elaborated by the person engaging in sex through an interplay of his or her interactive and intrapsychic scripts and the society's cultural scenarios. In the pornographic film, like everyday sexual encounters, a dialectic of scripts is operating, but in this case, they resemble palimpsests—layers of fantasies, interactive cues, and cultural narratives overlying the deeper layers of the participant's personal fantasies, scripts, and beliefs about social roles. The porn production dynamic starts out from the director's personal sexual scripts and imagination (often embodied by the director/scriptwriter's script) and is enunciated by the *mise-en-scene* (Silverman 1983, 46–53).

The male performers' "sexual scripts" enable them to achieve the erections and orgasms that are central to the genre's expectations—the visible, physiological effects that authenticate the sexual performances that take place within the director's overarching script and direction. Ultimately, the director's *mise-en-scene* integrates the film's visual vocabulary, the implicit or explicit narrative, and the film's sexual action. Veteran performer Rod Barry, discussing the role of the director from the performer's perspective, proposed this formulation:

> Having an eye for the B-roll [i.e., the set-up, dialogue, etc] and sex. How to tie it all together and make people believe that what happened should have happened, based upon the characters built-up from the B-roll—that's my hypothesis. (2005)

The utopian aspect of pornography has to do realizing fantasies without the usual social and physical limitations that commonly inhibit sexual activity. Nevertheless, Barry's perspective reflects the genre's underlying sexual-psychological realism.

The porn production frame transforms (or "keys," as Goffman terms the process) those daily sexual fantasies into material that enables performers and the production crew to record credible sexual performances. The participants in the production of porn movies all, to some degree, organize their behavior on the set—whether they are performers engaging in sex or part of the production crew lighting, filming, or directing the sex—on the basis of their own sexual scripts, but in the production of a pornographic movie, the imagined fantasy script (of the spectator) that is the desired end result of the production process is framed by the director's *mise-en-scene*.

Porn movies attempt to create fantasies that will arouse the spectator and encourage him to engage in masturbation and to produce an orgasm. The director provides, through the *mise-en-scene,* materials for the spectator's fantasy script, which the spectator himself creates via the remote control device: fast-forwarding, slow motion, pause, replay and so on are basically the viewer's techniques of editing via juxtaposition and montage. Pornography is a form of discourse in which sexual acts and fantasies are explicitly examined, tested, and represented in order to be watched, thought about, and engaged.

Acknowledgments

I am indebted to John Gagnon, Matthew Lore, Lesley Fine, Andrew Spieldenner, and Wash West for their comments on earlier drafts. I especially want to thank the many people in the gay porn industry who have talked with me over the years. Above all, I owe an enormous debt to Jerry Douglas, director of many fine porn films and from whose many interviews of directors and performers I learned so much. He has been my teacher and mentor on the subject of making pornography. I would like to thank also Doug Jeffries, Chi Chi LaRue, Michael Lucas, and Wash West, each of them successful and talented directors of porn movies, for talking candidly and in depth about the business of making pornographic movies; to Andrew Rosen, who has illuminated the process of editing porn films; and to my friends Jim Green and Moshe Sluhovsky for giving me a place to stay in Los Angeles, encouraging me, and talking with me about it all. Last but not least, I want to thank John Gagnon for the many thoughtful and enjoyable conversations over the years about sex, pornography, scripts, and my experiences doing research and writing about the gay porn industry.

References

Astruc, A. 1985. What is *mise-en-scene?* In Hillier 1985, 266–68.

AVN 2003. *Adult Video News.* Introduction to reviews: Category explanation. October: 135.

Barry, R. 2005. Interview by J. Escoffier. March 12. Los Angeles.

Barthes, R. 1986. The reality effect. In *The rustle of language,* 141–48. New York: Hill and Wang.

Bazin, A. On the *politique des auteurs.* In Hillier 1985, 248–59.

Braudy, L. 1977. *The world in the frame: What we see in films.* Garden City: Anchor Books.

Cowie, E. 1990. *Sexual difference and representation in the cinema.* London: Macmillan.

———. 1993. Pornography and fantasy: Psychoanalytic perspectives. In *Sex exposed: Sexuality and the pornography debate,* ed. L. Segal and M. McIntosh, 132–52. New Brunswick: Rutgers University Press.

Douglas, J. 2001. Interview by J. Escoffier. October 1. New York.

Escoffier, J. 2003. Gay-for-pay: Straight men and the making of gay pornography. *Qualitative Sociology* 26 (Winter), no. 4. 531–55.

———, ed. 2003a. *Sexual revolution.* New York: Thunder's Mouth.

———. Forthcoming. Porn star/stripper/escort: Economic and sexual dynamics in a sex work career. *Journal of Homosexuality._

Gagnon, J. H. 2004. *An interpretation of desire: Essays in the study of sexuality.* Chicago: University of Chicago Press.

Gagnon, J. H., and W. Simon. 1973. *Sexual conduct: The social sources of human sexuality.* Chicago: Aldine.

Gibbs, J. 2002. *Mise-en-scene: Film style and interpretation.* London: Wallflower Press.

Goffman, E. 1974. *Frame analysis: An essay on the organization of experience.* New York: Harper and Row.

Gordon, G. N. 1980. *Erotic communications: Studies in sex, sin, and censorship.* New York: Hastings House.

Hillier, J. 1985. *Cahiers du cinema, the 1950s: Neo-realism, Hollywood, New Wave.* Cambridge: Harvard University Press.

Hirsch, F. 1983. *Film noir: The dark side of the screen.* New York: Da Capo Press.

Jameson, F. 1981. *The political unconscious: Narrative as a socially symbolic act.* Ithaca: Cornell University Press.

Jeffries, D. 2005. Interview by J. Escoffier. March 15. Los Angeles.

LaRue, C. 2004. Interview by J. Escoffier. October 7. Los Angeles.

Lawrence, D. 1999. *The top 40 films of Chi Chi LaRue.* Los Angeles: Knight Publishing Corp.

Loftus, D. 2002. *Watching sex: How men really respond to pornography.* New York: Thunder's Mouth Press.

Marcus, S. 2003. Pornotopia. In Escoffier 2003a, 380–99.

McNair, B. 2002. *Striptease culture: Sex, media and the democratization of desire.* London: Routledge.

Merck, M. 1993. More of a man: Gay porn cruises gay politics. In *Perversions.* New York: Routledge. 217-235

Miller, T. 2001. *Sportsex.* Philadelphia: Temple University Press.

O'Toole, L. 1999. *Pornocopia: Porn, sex, technology and desire.* New, updated ed. London: Serpent's Tail.

Patton, C. 1988. The cum shot: Three takes on lesbian and gay sexuality. *OUT/LOOK* 1, no. 4.

Pronger, B. 1990. *The arena of masculinity: Sports, homosexuality, and the meaning of sports.* New York: St. Martin's Press.

Rich, F. 2001. Naked capitalists. *The New York Times Magazine,* May 20.

Ross, A. 1989. The popularity of pornography. In *No respect: Intellectuals and popular Culture,* 171–208. New York: Routledge.

Schatz, T. 1981. *Hollywood genres: Formulas, filmmaking, and the studio system.* New York: Random House.

Shamama, J. 2004. Gus Mattox: An interview. *Adam Gay Video XXX Showcase* 12, no. 10: 6–9.

Simon, W., and J. H. Gagnon. 1986. Sexual scripts: Permanence and change. *Archives of Sexual Behavior* 15, no. 2.

Stoller, R. J. 1985. *Observing the erotic imagination.* New Haven: Yale University Press.

———. 1991. *Porn: Myth for the twentieth century.* New Haven: Yale University Press.

West, W. 2002. Interview with B. Scuglia. www.Nightcharm.com/habituals/video/wash/index.html.

Williams, L. 1989. *Hard core: Power, pleasure, and the "frenzy of the visible."* Berkeley: University of California Press.

———. 2004. Porn studies: Proliferating pornographies on/scene: An introduction. In *Porn Studies,* 1–23. Durham: Duke University Press.

Zeeland, S. 1999. *Military trade.* New York: Harrington Park Press.

Žižek, S. 1991. *Looking awry: An introduction to Jacques Lacan through popular culture.* Cambridge: MIT Press.

———. 1997. *The plague of fantasies.* London: Verso.

Pepper Schwartz

6

The Social Construction of Heterosexuality

Much of modern sex research has grown from the social constructionist viewpoint articulated by Simon and Gagnon in *Sexual Conduct*, the pathbreaking book that encouraged a generation of young scholars to look beyond the collection of data points and into the cultural construction of sexual norms, values, perceptions, and behaviors. Way ahead of their time, Simon and Gagnon made all things problematic and asked us to at least understand the cultural lens we used to interpret behavior and gender.

John Gagnon's later work continued to teach us not to take the ordinary for granted. Since this volume is in his honor, it seems appropriate to write on the most ordinarily taken for granted aspect of sexuality that there is: heterosexuality. Not its facts, figures, behaviors, and other statistics, but rather the very fact that it exists as a location on this planet.

I would not be surprised to get a ho-hum reaction to this enterprise. We tend to explain the exotic and problematize the exception. If most people are five foot ten, we try to explain under five feet or over seven. If something is common and normative, we think we understand it, and we certainly feel no need to explain it. But, in fact, that tendency merely constructs a black box, a familiar shape that fools us into thinking we can explain something merely because we come in contact with it every day. This acceptance of the common obfuscates in two ways: we create post hoc justifications about why what exists is supposed to exist (and mistake that for wisdom), and by accepting a "natural order of things" we hide all the nuances of "fact" by inhibiting further investigation or critique. As a result, we have neglected the social construction of heterosexuality as if it was unproblematic—as if we are born, and poof! we are totally and adequately heterosexual, a mere outcome of some natural selection with an invariant program that creates heterosexuality as a uniform product, with no other markers or interesting differences within until other shades of sexual orientation are introduced.

In fact, "doing heterosexuality" is no less problematic than homosexuality—though its punishments are more for failure than for accomplishment—and the norm is enforced and sanctioned differently from exceptional behavior. Reactions to failures of heterosexual enactment are less violently corrected than portrayals of homosexual identity—except, of course, when a failure of adequate enactment causes an attribution of homosexuality, and psychic or physical violence follows in order to preserve normative heterosexual roleplaying along narrowly constructed and strongly idealized stereotypes.

Just what are those stereotypes and idealistic portrayals of heterosexuality? They vary by region of the world, country, and subculture, but they share a common body of work, and those normative expectations are fed to us at the same time we are being breast-fed. Countless research papers have shown that even infants are programmed into adult sexual niches: we are socially constructed as heterosexual as soon as we are propelled out into the world. Hospitals still paste blue or pink bows on babies' heads, and oohs and ahs about the "little man" and baby girl usually quickly include comments on chests, legs, and genitals, creating expectations for the man or woman to be. Baby boys are held less and cooed at less, says the research, not because they are loved less (there is certainly some evidence that they may be loved more in some families) but because they are being handled in a way that preserves their manliness—their heterosexuality—right from the start. Little girls are dressed in brighter colors and frillier outfits because they are supposed to be supremely adorable as part of their core equipment right from the beginning.

Heterosexuality has its grave expectations. They are not articulated all at once—some are never openly articulated—but we all know that a lack of articulation of norms doesn't mean they don't exist. Briefly, I would like to mention some of the presumptions and social scripts that guide our management of heterosexuality, and comment on some of the consequences of our peculiar rules and regulations.

There are several overarching requirements of heterosexuality that I believe organize the major script of being heterosexual in American society. First of all, heterosexuality is confabulated with gender performance. Whatever the culture, its norms about masculinity and femininity are supposed to co-vary with heterosexual enactment, and gender itself is expected to be unambiguous and performed according to the cultural outlines of the moment. Even today, after the sexual and gender revolutions of the late 1960s and 70s, heterosexual dress codes, mannerisms, and body language are still strictly mandated. Although our culture has antiheros who disdain these conventions (most notably located in the worlds of rock and roll, grunge, heavy metal and other communities of art and counterculture), the majority culture creates cultural icons in its magazines, TV shows, movies, featuring models that tell us what exact gender displays portray heterosexual correctness.

Fashion designers and media stars are quite important. They become the cultural trend setters for the young. No one who has observed the fashion impact of Britney Spears, Lindsay Lohan, and other teen idols can deny with a straight face (as it were) that popular culture creates gender norms. And, I should add, it is not just children or

[81]

The Social Construction of Heterosexuality

teens who use movie stars and band members as guides to sexual correctness: the Academy Awards telecast is watched by millions of avid viewers with one of the central agendas of the entire evening being the observation of who wears what, who appears with whom, and how all of this translates into sexiness. Just about every sitcom and drama is a commentary on who is a man's man, who is a man's woman, and how do characters carry off their evocation of male and female sexual power. Even as we note characters as caricatures, they serve as sexual ideals. The fan magazines exist and prosper because millions of Americans want to follow the stars' lives, copy their wedding dress, gossip about their love affairs, and resemble them as much as possible. This goes way beyond casual ogling; stars are the new royals and their lifestyle choices—such as turning to plastic surgery—begin national trends, in this case creating a new acceptance of plastic surgery so that standards of attractiveness in middle-aged women are changing (helped, of course, by television shows making the process as well as the product fascinating. *The Swan* and several other programs actually show operations or stages of recovery, touting the self-determination of the patient while minimizing the pain and possibility of complications. Of course, in the very act of setting standards based on stars, gender roles become more problematic, since it is hard to measure up against the fantasy embodiment of masculinity and femininity.) It is fair to assume that for many who mimic the style and look of a sex god or goddess, the gap between their idol and themselves serves to erode the individual's confidence in competent heterosexual performance. Who can ever be as "male" and macho as Bruce Willis, wisecracking as he incinerates a building full of bad guys, saves his buddy, and beds the astoundingly beautiful women who populate action films? Who can be as charming as Cameron Diaz—perfectly proportioned and the object of everyone's desire? Who can be as winsome and pure of heart as Julia Roberts, a woman leggier than most runway models, in the storybook romances in which she stars? In drama after drama, she offers the eternal portrayal of female heterosexuality: seeking Prince Charming, losing Prince Charming, regaining Prince Charming. The themes of romantic acquisition and loss may be recast within the frame of a professional woman's life, but this reframing pales next to the strong outline of normative female heterosexuality: that is, for a woman, the central and most important theme in her life will be love. Love is the question, love is the answer, and whatever it takes to get it, keep it, maintain it, and cherish it is what the movie is really about.

We venerate and create fantasy masculinity and femininity—often, ironically enough, portrayed through the exquisite acting of gay or lesbian actors—but the truth really doesn't matter. The James Bonds, the lone wolves, and the cynical detectives and cops tell us what male sexuality in America is supposed to look like. The young lovelies and studmuffins of the movies and TV sitcoms tell us what adequate heterosexuality is supposed to look like. The unspoken sub-clause is that the rest of us who could not fit well in the ensemble casts of *Friends*, *CSI*, or *Grey's Anatomy* have a sexuality that is unfinished, inadequate, and somehow unworthy. This is a disastrous recognition for those who have already experienced self-doubt about their masculinity or femininity within their peer group. Most young girls and women are insecure about whether they are attractive, articulate or desirable. Even without comparison to mythic media icons, they struggle mightily to feel sexually worthy. Women turn themselves into wraiths trying to be thin enough, and put themselves in physical jeopardy by paying surgeons to sculpt their bodies so that they can have thighs, abdomens, and breasts that fit the sexual profile of what they believe men want. Women, and increasingly men, spend thousands of scarce discretionary dollars to change their faces and physiques to fit prevailing standards of beauty so that they will be able to compete in the heterosexual mating market or retain spouses who might otherwise stray to better models of masculinity and femininity.

One can't help but reflect on this: while noblemen of the eighteenth century might have had to work at being dandies, twenty-first-century men are spared these indignities. Just being male used to be enough to be granted provisional heterosexual status. However, increasingly, in some sort of cosmic justice, men seem to be following suit: commercial interests have finally realized that having both sexes terminally insecure is better for business than just having one sex feel inadequate, so now men are in the mix of creating better bodies, more hair (on their head; now many men feel required to get electrolysis for the stuff on their back!), and stiffer erections to make sure that they look and act like the cultural cut-outs they believe will ensure their sexual selection by women. The medical establishment is only too happy to oblige these neuroses.

The past decade has seen the collusion of pharmaceutical research with the medical establishment to create a cultural crisis about potency. The new standard of genital adequacy is to have penises that could compete with the fantasy penises in purple passages in X-rated books and movies. Now "rock hard penises" and "hot throbbing members" will actually exist in life as they do on porn stars. The vision of what a penis ought to look and act like can come true by using Viagra, Levitra, or Cialis, even if few men naturally match the size or performance of these porno-penises unaided by a drug. Viagra, so the media and doctors on lease from Pfizer have said, can give you the erection you've always dreamed of, and as a result, a new baseline standard of erections and performance gets created. Penis performance, always a potential problem for men, now invokes new fears: readiness throughout the lifestyle becomes standard. The natural aging of the organ becomes deviant as we try and create genitals that conform to standards created by chemists rather than nature. Male heterosexuality requires a stiff erection unto death. In order to make male heterosexuality unambiguous, we create a new version of what constitutes achievement of competent sexuality.

There is, of course, a female equivalent. Far before Viagra became a global brand, women's and fashion magazines created yearly standards for the year's "look," which often meant a new kind of body. The mass media would launch cover stories announcing "breasts are back" (I'm not kidding—this was a real cover in 2005) or "the six secrets to making him go crazy all night." Women's magazines, and increasingly men's magazines, do not have stories on sex—the magazines are almost *entirely* about mating and dating—and even the products are advertised to help live the good life of a popular sexual being. If we stand back for a moment, it becomes clear that the entire message of advertising is that heterosexuality is *not* natural: it is not easy—and, indeed, it will take everything they can sell you for you to even hope to sustain a decent sexual presentation and the possibility of creating a successful seduction, engagement, and marriage. Being successful—as a body—as an actor—as a heterosexual—is certainly not seen as a fact of nature. No—*it is seen as an act of will.*

Which leads us to the obvious conclusion that, far from being normal, heterosexual identity is fragile. Very fragile. Easily polluted. Given all the possible paths leading to failure of sexual competence, we are warned that we must be very careful in our construction of it.

This ability to fail publicly brings us to our second proposition: that our performance of heterosexuality is supposed to be accepted and applauded by others. All of this dressing up and strutting out is not just to attract the opposite sex—it is supposed to fend off criticism and attribution as a homosexual. Homosexuality and heterosexuality are like twins: no matter how different they become, they are part of the same piece, the same drama. Homosexuality exists in its own right—but if it did not, it would be invented to enforce compliance to proper gender enactment.

Straight men dress in ways to announce their sexuality, much the way the homosexual men often mimic it to announce their own: exaggerating the costumes of masculinity into mating signals for men with men. The two sexualities, considered so polar, actually butt up next to each other, trying to accomplish different things with the same cultural and physical equipment.

But that is the point, is it not? Heterosexual men and homosexual men, have the same socialization, as do heterosexual women and homosexual women, so it takes some work to distinguish our sexual presentation from one another. No wonder then that we have "fey" gay men and "butch" lesbians. Gay men and women need to work hard to create territory that is unambiguously in revolt against heterosexuality because heterosexuality itself is much more subtle and problematic than we pretend it to be. Hence, exaggerated performances exist among both heterosexuals and homosexuals as each group tries to demonstrate who they are to like others and elicit appropriate reactions. Still, no matter how broad a sexual display is, the audience may not react to even the most counternormative gender role if sexuality is not seen as problematic in that area. For example, there are some locales where people seem almost naïvely unconscious. One sees, for example, environments where women present themselves as "butch" and may even have the build and demeanor of a man, and men who are as fey as anyone who ever crossdressed in a San Francisco gay rights parade are benignly unconscious of the thin line they walk in the gender role enactment wars. Part of this is innocence is one of place: residents of small towns that cannot imagine that anyone in their town could be gay and so integrate their friend's and neighbor's generally non-normative gender display into some other social construct ("weird," "eccentric," "not vain," etc.) rather than gayness. Even though the butch farmer's wife may be secretly hankering after the farmer's wife next door, "audiences" may attribute the non-normative gender or sexual display to asexuality rather than homosexuality. As long as the person in question does not claim an alternate sexuality, they may be spared approbation. On the other hand, this is not always the case. The young who resemble disapproved-of, nonheterosexual attributes can justly quake in school halls, worrying that they will be attacked emotionally or physically—or just disdained.

This brings up a third specification: we are supposed to have certain kinds of bodies that reveal our heterosexuality. For all the jokes about "Pat" on *Saturday Night Live* (the person we could not figure out as male or female, who would confuse us by tempting us with a clue as to her "real" gender and then add another clue that would cancel out the first lead), the truth is that the real joke on us was how much anxiety it caused the viewer to watch a character without a gender and/or sexual identity we could identify.

In general, we *hate* the idea that someone is not firmly assigned to a body type and look that telegraphs both gender and sexuality. In fact, it occurs to me that this intolerance of gender ambiguity may be one of the reasons our society hates fat people. Fat pads out physical differences between the sexes; the roundness we associate with women covers both men and women who are fat: breasts and chests look alike, genitals shrink in reference to the greater bulk of the body, and facial contours become more similar. It is another kind of androgyny, and most people are extremely uncomfortable with it when it is so extreme that they cannot distinguish biological sex. Extreme androgyny like Pat is seen as sexual failure—and therefore sexual identity may be imputed as homosexual even though homosexuality really has nothing to do with body type. Still, all kinds of gender ambiguity or cross-referencing the other gender (especially using the other gender's costumes or customs) has been historically grounds for severe punishment (including death, in some countries and during certain periods of history) or humiliation (open season as a target for humor or bullying). Interestingly, temporary trespass of gender/sexual confabulation is allowable for certain kinds of ritual celebrations such as fraternity costume parties, English music hall performances or Halloween. Anyone who wants to continue the joke too long, however, is quickly labeled deviant, and—to show how strong our feelings are—subjected to violence or contempt. Our culture does not want to lose the hard edges of gender, precisely because people depend on the standards of gender enactment to help them delineate heterosexuality from homosexuality. Imprecise as that may be, it is the tool most people use for a quick assessment of sexual identity.

This brings me to a fourth point about heterosexuality, which has to do not with the body, but the psyche: In order to be considered heterosexual, individuals are presumed to be singularly and unproblematically aroused to the opposite sex and the opposite sex only.

Within sexual identity, the heterosexual package includes the idea that heterosexuality is unitary—all or nothing. We are not supposed to have to learn heterosexuality: it is supposed to come with our genitals and gender behavior. Any indication of flexibility (a continuum of arousal and attraction that may be greatest towards people of the opposite sex but has some arousal to same-sex persons) is, even among the most sophisticated of people, seen as discrediting heterosexuality. In some American Indian cultures, bisexuality is acknowledged as having a place in the sexual pantheon and can be seen as a gift; heterosexuality can co-exist with homosexuality in the same person without putting either into question. In most Western societies, however, and in many non-Western societies, same-sex arousal immediately incurs identity reassignment; we do not want to think of our sexuality as polymorphous. Indeed, the Freudian phrase would be "polymorphous perverse": a disordered drive rather than merely a lusty or extensive one. In our society, sexual identity as a heterosexual allows for no trespass of this central vision of unadulterated heterosexuality.

Interestingly, though, we have developed a pragmatic out for some people who can satisfy the gender norms of heterosexuality so satisfactorily that if they choose the right explanation for same-sex behavior we will not discredit them. While, in most cases, we disallow any behavior but heterosexual conduct, we do have a vision of male and female sexuality that allows a "loophole"—if you will, an apt phrase for the conundrum. Indeed, there are men who so satisfy the norms of masculinity that they can get away with non-heterosexual behavior, at least for a time, and not be reassigned a gay identity. These are the men who are so hypermasculine we believe their accounts of a sexuality so brutish that, when they say any hole will do, we believe them! Rock stars who are outrageous in every other respect are often allowed to have both male and female partners and continue to maintain their dominant sexual status as heterosexual. Another common example are men in prisons, men who have a scarcity of females, or men from cultures where maleness is considered so sexually powerful that they can just enforce their definition of the situation on anything as long as they take in certain cultural scripts that protect heterosexual identity. As an example, I once interviewed a Greek man named Spiro who was sexually adept with both men and women. He seemed to have no trouble having both male and female partners without having either leave him because of his bisexual activity. When I asked him how he could have sex with both men and women without being labeled as gay, he replied, "It is no problem. You see we have four types of men in Greece: men who fuck men, men who fuck men and women, men who fuck women, and queers." I was somewhat flummoxed since I knew he had sex with both men and women and would not consider himself "queer." So I asked him, "Who are the people you consider 'queer'?" "Oh," he said. "The queers are the ones who *get* fucked." Or, put another way, Spiro had a culture that created a vision of men as voracious sexual creatures who naturally will have what they can—as long as they are not degraded by taking the female role, a humiliation from which, apparently, one is denied reentry into the club of heterosexual men. If you are a man who wants to have sex with men in Greece, yet do not want to be thought of as homosexual, you can accomplish this goal, as long as you do not blunder into the "female" sexual role. How this translates intrapsychically may be more difficult, except if you are, like Spiro, from a culture where sexually available women are scarce and sex, any way you can get it, is approved of by your friends.

The allowances for women are different, though not entirely. There are some women whose heterosexual credentials are so impeccable that they evoke increased erotic interest in men rather than relabeling when they take on a same-sex lover. Madonna, for example, gave a well-publicized passionate kiss on the lips to Britney Spears which, while it got headlines, did not hurt Madonna's draw as a performer or her perception by fans as an outrageous heterosexual woman. In some parts of the United States there are those who would give erotic points to women who have sex with women even if they are not superstars . . . as long as the sexual encounter is done for the pleasure of men. Women can have sex with women as performers—or as the hors d'oeuvre in a meal that will be consummated in heterosexual intercourse. Simply put, in our contemporary urban culture, situational bisexuality is sexy, but real lesbianism is an affront.

One exemption from that reaction is lesbianism as a heterosexual porno fantasy. Women who look like *Playboy* bunnies, who are voracious sexual creatures—wild enough to do anything—are asked to do the inevitable porno three-way, and doing so does not endanger their heterosexual status. As long as female performers in porno eventually show that they are sexually available to men, their homosexual sex is seen as kinky rather than as deviant. These women never take on a lesbian identity; their job is to be warm-up artists, create sexual titillation, and make sure that the male viewer simply sees them as an erotic surrogate until he "finishes" the "job." The women in porno movies who make love to one another create a drama of female ecstasy that excites the male viewer rather than threatens him. These actresses do not leave the folds of heterosexuality even in fantasy (although, in reality, many of them are stalwartly lesbian). For our purposes, however, what is interesting is that there are these temporary havens for homosexuality—but sexual identity is preserved because of the belief that beautiful, sexy women will be steadfastly immune to female charms when men are available. Furthermore, if the women who have had sex with each other follow convention and don't try to also take on male prerogatives (such as male dress or demeanor), same-sex appetite is seen as an erotic augmentation rather than a substitution. It is an odd erotic peccadillo of male sexuality that almost all female sexual behavior is catalogued as a dress rehearsal for male sexual enjoyment. Only when the male is truly convinced that the woman has absolutely no desire for the male voyeur, does the wrath of homophobia come to rest at lesbian destinations. Lesbians to most men are bisexuals, and bisexuals are heterosexuals-in-waiting; however, this fluid assignment is often not so gently experienced by the women who must decide if there is a sexual central self that is not really performing for men, but instead seeks a way to justify erotic and/or emotional desire for other women.

This relates to the fifth point: that heterosexual arousal is supposed to be strong and unambiguous. This is a very interesting requirement, and it flies in the face of almost every fact we know about sexual performance. More correctly, sexual arousal is always problematic some of the time: there when you don't want it, absent when you are hoping it will overwhelm you. Arousal is highly sensitive to other emotions—fear of rejection, tension, performance anxieties, distraction, and fatigue; in other words, numerous states of mind and body. Additionally, we are affected by subtle cues in the environment or in the other person's behavior that may consciously or unconsciously affect our behavior: the wrong words, the wrong look and suddenly we are deflated; a serious performance problem for men, especially it if happens often and becomes habitual. Many men, reflecting back on their boyhood, have talked about how disorienting it was not to have an erection under conditions one was supposed to (or to have it when one was not supposed to) and the doubts and fears and dysfunction that followed. Because an erection is supposed to be "natural"—both a perk and prerequisite of heterosexuality—its absence, or the presence of ambivalence, is supposed to be instructive of malfunction, or, in the eyes of society, potential deviance. In other words, your status as a heterosexual goes up or down with your penis.

Women have a variation of this theme, albeit not such a publicly noticeable one. For example, in a sexual interaction, women may be quite worried about the presence or absence of lubrication. Some women's vaginas lubricate quite copiously when aroused; other women remain quite dry no matter how aroused they are, or become less lubricated as they age and approach perimenopause or menopause.. Women, like men, vary in the way their body reacts to stimulation. However, in the Book of Heterosexuality, aroused women are supposed to lubricate, and the lack thereof has been known to cause women—and their partners—some worry that the body is the truer source of information than the mind, and that not lubricating indicates lesser sexual interest or excitement. Lubrication, while easily fixable by modern water-based or silicone products, is perceived to be telling the woman (and her partner) something elemental. A standard of competent heterosexuality is unmet. Women have been let off this hook somewhat by being defined as having a mostly reactive sexuality (i.e., "you do not have to be the first to be sexually aroused," "as a woman you are entitled to be only mildly interested until you are aggressively aroused by a man"). In this scenario, if you are *not* aroused, it is not that you are not heterosexual, it is just that this is the wrong person, you are not in love enough, or that your lover is not man enough to arouse you. In general, however, women's heterosexuality is perceived to be awakened by love. Love is supposed to be the motor of women's sexual emotions. In fact, female sexuality is supposed to be so relational that even inappropriate (i.e., homosexual) arousal can sometimes happen without necessarily impacting heterosexual identity. In this perspective, women are turned on because they are in love, and love is the motivating sexual force. Same-sex behavior, rather than exhibiting an essential part of a woman's true nature, is merely another act of true womanhood—female sexuality created by the power of love. Many women who have had extended lesbian relationships in their biography but do not wish to identify as a lesbian may, post hoc, define their same-sex love affair as primarily a love relationship with a sexual component that could only last for the length of that relationship. This vision of self-limiting sexuality (over when the love relationship is over) is not sustained by our culture when it concerns men. One moment of adult non-heterosexual arousal—no matter how passing the moment—is likely to be seen as definitive evidence of a core homosexual set of desires.

Sixth: the appropriate—that is to say, the opposite sex—is supposed to be attracted to us. Sexual identity can be so shaky that it can also be changed by other people's attention to us rather than our own feelings about ourselves. In the movie *In and Out*, actor Kevin Kline is woefully out of touch with his sexual psyche. He is in his early forties and has gone with his girlfriend for years and years without any genital contact. When one of his famous students assumes he is gay—because of inappropriate gender behavior (including, if you will, that he is neat!) and "outs" him, it is the first time he is forced to confront himself. The gay news reporter who is sent to cover the story immediately sees the Kline character as a "closet case." Not one really sexual moment happens that shows Kline demonstrating sexual desire for another man, but the beginning of his uncloseting is not proved by who he is attracted to (or not attracted to, as the case may be) but also by how others see him and by *who* wants him.

Thus, every heterosexual who is not claimed by the opposite sex as a heartthrob in their youth has doubts—and not only because of being ignored or feeling invisible, but also because of sexual aspirations lofted his or her way by other people with insecure sexual identities. Teenagers, young men and women, and women and men with sexually mixed biographies are all unsure of who they are and who they want, and so they all are more likely to project their own lack of ease onto another person.

Straw Dogs, a subtly homophobic film released several decades ago, insinuates that the central figure Dustin Hoffman is emasculated because he cannot control his flirtatious, wayward wife. This does not mean an immediate homosexual label, but it does mean that his character is not adequately heterosexual because he isn't macho enough to make the men fear him when they ogle and sexually harass her. Written to be a "ball buster" by nature, she is humiliated when the men verbally insult her and he does nothing. In turn, the "virile" workmen have nothing but contempt for a man who will not get physically aggressive when other men decline to respect his woman and ogle her without retribution.. The local men hate him for his effeteness and his social class (he has been pilloried by the working-class men fixing his house as being a "poof") and it becomes a war to the death when the working men get more and more contemptuous of him and turn into sexually salivating males who plan to lay claim to the wife. They study

Hoffman and decide that he is a putz because they can see his wife is running around on him, and they are pretty sure he knows that she is. Whether or not he knows or does not know, in their minds he *should* know, and do something about it. They decide to do with her as they will since he is obviously not a manly man who deserves to have his female property respected. In the end, however, in order to protect his home, woman, and life, Hoffman "gets it" and resorts to primordial battle to retrieve his wife and his self-respect. They attack him and he triumphs over them, but in order to do so, it is necessary for him to kill every one of these men. At the end of the film, in the eyes of his wife, himself and the director, the Hoffman character becomes a true man in the deepest sense of heterosexual glory.

For women, the archetypal story is the transformation story—that of a woman not sufficiently self-discovered enough to take on the accoutrements of femininity and win her man. Pure evocations of this theme can be found in the musical *Annie Get Your Gun* when the Annie Oakley character cleans up to try and get her man, or when the Rancher's Daughter in *Rodeo* puts on a dress to go to the dance. The high point of claiming heterosexuality is claiming one's birthright of loveliness and recognizing one's longing for a man. Women do not necessarily get assigned a lesbian identity if they do not put men in as the obvious center of their life, but they may be seen as desexed if they are not adequately heterosexually active.

Being desexed is not an easy place to be sent to, however. Let a woman tell you what it feels like to be invisible—that is, not sexually attractive enough to be noticed as they walk by, enter a room, or try to engage in interactions with men. Women see other women drawing male attention but feel too old, too heavy, too short, too tall, too awkward, too bright—too *something* to get some of that attention themselves. When a woman feels this way, her sexuality is irrelevant and therefore denied her. If she is not desired, she does not exist. Many teenage as well as older women feel consigned to this purgatory where nature or nurture has somehow failed to give them the talents they need to feel fully sexual.

Given how hard all of this is to accomplish, my seventh point is both ironic and laughable: once our sexuality is enacted, it is supposed to be stable and unconflicted. Heterosexuality is supposed to be a rock. Once established, it is not supposed to turn into anything else, which is a comfort to young men and women who may feel that once heterosexuality is initially established, they can relax *if* they become satisfied with the way they look, turn on to people, get turned on to, match the norms of the present gender culture, and so on.

My own research tells me that that reassessment of one's sexual self can occur, and when it does, it is most likely to come through relationships—that indeed our sexuality *is* relational, especially (but not only) for women. The annals of research on sexual identity are full of stories of women who had never had even a same-sex fantasy who unexpectedly became besotted with a specific person and found their sexuality bending towards the bright light of that love. For example, I have interviewed a woman who was having an affair with another woman while her husband, dreadfully ill, was incapacitated for half a year. They met at work and it was love at first sight. They stayed together for years without the husband finding out and the revelation to one of the partners of the extent of her sexual interest was deeply unsettling to her. She could not deny the fact of her love and attraction—and she was 60 years old when she received this new information about herself! Whether the revision of self-identity occurs because of a special partnership or because one is just totally furious with men because of a series of bad intentions or behaviors, it is shocking to most people to realize they have a flexible sexual self. I have interviewed many women who became homosexual not through lust, but through disgust with the men who had disappointed and abused them. Heterosexual identity may not always unravel when a person shuts down because of a disastrous relationship of a love affair that seems to transcend gender, but most people would not be surprised that it had to change.

The fact is that change is shocking to participants. Heterosexual identity—all sexual identity—is considered immutable by most lay people, except insofar as someone's "true" sexuality may be repressed, suppressed, or denied. The cultural prejudice and presumption is that the presence of any homosexual feeling is a dead giveaway of one's sexual essence because homosexual behavior is somehow more a truth of the body than heterosexuality. (The reasoning seems to be that any homosexual behavior demonstrates a true core sexual predilection, since no person would take on the stigma of homosexuality if it were not compulsively necessary.) Both homosexuals and heterosexual have displayed incredulity and downright rejection of an applicant for a new sexual identity or claim when the claim is from a heretofore homosexual male who is now in love with a woman and believes that his sexuality is oriented in a new way. Our culture doesn't even want to believe such a male really feels what he says he feels. Heterosexuality, in this instance, is so weak that it is easily eclipsed and overpowered by homosexuality. In cases of homosexual exploration, even minimal acts are coded maximally, but in cases of heterosexual exploration by gay men, new sexual experience with women is considered trivial and even psychologically distressed. Despite this reaction, from the lay and scientific community alike, there is still some scientific evidence and certainly adequate anecdotal evidence that both men and women can regroup sexual identity in adulthood when a single important emotional relationship refocuses their sexual energy.

Finally, my eighth and last point about heterosexuality is that intercourse is the heterosexual lingua franca and all else is tangential embroidery. Men and women are not just catalogued because of the gender eroticized but how we eroticize our partner of any gender. Our acts define us, not just our psychology. Key among these acts is the central act of heterosexuality, intercourse. Competent and complete heterosexuals are supposed to prefer intercourse to all other acts. Heterosexuals should have intercourse more frequently than other acts; it should be the main location for our ejaculations and orgasms; and, in general, it should be played as the main event in lovemaking, even if there is a very full program of other kinds of sexual behaviors. Indeed, we seem to need to check in with various kinds of studies, to be checked against the facts and figures of normalcy. While the famous Kinsey studies tried to make it clear that, in their opinion, one pattern of "outlets" was as good as another, those famous studies showed means and medians for sexual acts that made the mean not only average but prescriptive.

This presumption continues in modern texts on human sexuality. Questionnaires, which get at only a rough estimate of sexual habits, are given credence way beyond what their crafters ever believed in, and these ballpark figures now not only define heterosexuality, they define "healthy" or "inhibited" heterosexuality, thereby giving heterosexuals new ways to feel insufficient or suspect. A gigantic field of sexual therapy has arisen since the late 1960s (when Masters and Johnson first published their books on actual sexual behavior), and the public has become quite aware of all the ways there are to fail sexual "competency."

In sum, while heterosexuality is seen as natural, naturally organized around intercourse, strongly held, invariant once achieved, and wholly captivating by those who own it, we know, inside our hearts, and in the light of evidence, that none of these suppositions are entirely true. The question I would pose now is, does this obvious social construction of heterosexuality really matter? Does it matter if heterosexuality is much less unitary, stable or scripted than we thought it was?

That's not clear...

We are far more a work in progress—a tender rather than solid template—than most of us are comfortable with. However, our intolerance of ambiguity makes it likely that we wish to overdefine our sexual identity, to not code our homosexual attractions or fantasies if at all possible, and to try like hell to accomplish heterosexuality as best we can. Except for the bravest and culturally independent among us, we want sexual categories, not open-ended choices or a continuum of desire and identity. Because heterosexuality is so hard to achieve and so fragile to sustain, we seem to need to continue to ignore the gradations of sexual reality and construct a sexual persona that gives us peace of mind in the present, if not necessarily for the future.

As for we social scientists, we continue to ignore such discordant data about sexual identification, desire, or fantasy, or believe it only defines a small number of heterosexually functioning men and women. We know that many heterosexuals have occasional same-sex fantasies or dreams of same-sex behavior, but we do not include it to reshape our definition of heterosexuality and its potential plasticity.

This is why the Kinsey scale has remained an academic rather than a popular concept. The scale which goes from 0 to 6, with 0 being totally heterosexual, 6 being totally homosexual, and 3 being you don't care what comes through the door, was revolutionary in the late 1940s and early 50s, when the study was initially done, but arguably could be just as revolutionary today. If we believe, as we might, that heterosexuality is a continuum of sexual desire rather than a bipolar construction, heterosexuality would be more truly described as often co-existing with homosexual desire, fantasy, love, or attraction. But we have intense resistance to trying to know how heterosexuality is actually practiced rather than socially constructed, and this has rather grave costs for everyone:

First, the stereotypes of invariant heterosexuality help us all fail being heterosexual enough, and this causes among many people low self-esteem, miscategorization of their sexuality. and fear of being "deviant." If our sexuality were less prescribed as a central identity and more as a behavior—one open to a multitude of expressions—we would be less immobilized by fear if we thought or did something less common. Indeed, in today's society, there is movement towards a less static vision of heterosexuality. The young, perhaps more with bravado than anything else, are more comfortable with various combinations of ambisexuality and more often than not, unapologetic for their choices.

Second, this same fear encourages some people in our society to discourage extending civil liberties to gays because we are fearful of compromising our heterosexuality. This school wants all the rewards in society to bolster heterosexuality, thereby keeping us more protected from, I guess, ourselves. There are movements to keep gay people from having legal marriage. Could it be that restrictions of same-sex couples originate because we are so unsure about the steadiness of our heterosexuality that we feel extending heterosexual institutions to same-sex couples will endanger heterosexuality itself? This casts heterosexuality as a strangely unpowerful identity, one so weak that if its institutions are shared that marriage will unravel—but there is really no evidence at all that this will happen.

The third and maybe most important response to the perspective I have offered about our present vision of heterosexuality is that of the intrapsychic costs—of the present exaggerated naturalness of heterosexuality. The unannounced and unspoken contradictions of a pure heterosexuality cause great emotional difficulty to many people—especially at tender ages when self-confidence is low. With little reality to lean on, men and women experience extreme discomfort as they must face their fantasies or discordant early behavior. Surely much of our sexual dysfunction, insecurity, and panic comes from these early years of contradictions and high expectations.

My fourth and final point: even if many individuals concretize their heterosexual identity without much suffering or feelings of insufficiency, do we not incur sexual or psychic costs because we see heterosexuality as incongruent with certain kinds of acts or fantasies? For example, can a heterosexual man enjoy (without guilt or fears of sexual deviance) the experience of anal sex or have sex, happily, without intromission? Can a heterosexual woman enjoy a man who is less than traditionally masculine or prefer sexuality without intercourse as the centerpiece of her heterosexual life without feeling that she has betrayed "normal" heterosexuality? Intercourse itself is so central to the proof of heterosexuality that men and women who might enjoy oral sex more might never feel free to downgrade intercourse as the way they generally have the most pleasure. Why shouldn't sexuality be more varied if it is about pleasure and not demonstration of heterosexual membership?

In conclusion, I think it is clear that if heterosexuality were indelible, easy to achieve, and easy to keep, we wouldn't make all this fuss over it. The liberation of all sexualities is the liberation of each one. While political activism may be organized around the integration of homosexuality and homosexuals into the mainstream, it is not clear that there is a mainstream to be integrated into. Rather, there are many people trying to find a sexual identity that integrates their desires, experiences, and fantasies, however diverse they may be. Opening up the definition of heterosexuality will not endanger our welfare. We need to be able to do life as it evolves, creating sexualities that are unique rather than scripted from the one-size-fits-no-one-very-well tradition.

7

Arlene Stein

Shapes of Desire

Are lesbians united by a shared sexual orientation—by their same-sex desires? Do they hold in common the experience of having engaged in sexual activity or having had close, passionate relationships with members of the same sex? Or are they bound together simply by their sense of themselves as outcasts or as rebels against heterosexual society?

The boundaries separating the group called "lesbians" from the rest of women are not at all clearly or immutably marked. Historically, lesbians constitute a group whose central characteristic is debatable and changing—a group about which there is little consensus. For example, there have always been women who have had sexual/romantic relationships with other women who have not labeled themselves on that basis. There have also been women whose actual sexual fantasies or practices don't fit the common social definition of lesbianism—bisexuals, transsexuals, and others—but who nonetheless identify as lesbians. There are many possible configurations of the relationship among desire, behavior, and identity—the possibilities far exceed the capacity of social categories to describe them.

Like ethnic communities, lesbian/gay boundaries, identities, and cultures are negotiated, defined, and produced. The history of lesbian social worlds is in part the story of this production of boundaries, identities, and cultures. These symbolic struggles construct female homosexuality as a social reality; they create images, myths, and fantasies of lesbian love, desire, and fulfillment; and they shape the composition of the group of women called lesbians.

For most of this century, medical experts have been the primary definers of lesbian

An earlier version of this chapter appeared in *Women Creating Lives: Identities, Resilience, and Resistance* edited by Carol E. Franz and Abigail J. Stewart, 1994. Reprinted by permission of Westview Press, a member of the Perseus Books Group.

[93]

existence. Medical discourses labeled homosexuality as a "condition," associated it with gender nonconformity, and constructed lesbians and heterosexual women as two distinct groups. Lesbianism, in the medical conception, is concrete and objective, a condition of being that has clear boundaries. It is something to be "discovered"—something that always exists in the individual. Subjected to the power of such definitions, individuals defined themselves according to these understandings and organized subcultures to support homosexual desire.

In the 1970s, lesbians and gay men introduced a new vocabulary and set of concepts for understanding homosexuality, suggesting that the boundaries separating heterosexuality and homosexuality were in fact permeable. Lesbianism was a matter of identification, not simply desire. One could be a lesbian by becoming "woman-identified," developing "lesbian consciousness," making women central to one's life, and not giving oneself over to men. Lesbians were not "failed women": they were rebels against an oppressive sex/gender system, the vanguard of women's liberation. One could be a lesbian and a woman too. Indeed, rather than posing a threat to one's womanhood, lesbianism strengthened and enhanced it.

The movement from "old gay" to "new gay" signifies the transition from a world in which medicalized conceptions of homosexuality were virtually undisputed to one in which they were roundly challenged, and from a time when lesbians occupied a particular deviant social role, focused upon homosexual desires, to a time when lesbianism became an identity—a conscious basis for self-construction. It marks a movement toward greater consciousness with regard to lesbianism in particular, and to sexualities in general.

From old gay to new

Women of the baby boom, who reached adolescence and young adulthood during the 1960s and 1970s, found themselves poised between two different accounts of lesbianism. The dominant definition of "the lesbian" was a woman with a medical condition or psychological aberration—an isolated individual divorced from the rest of the world. An emergent account considered her to be a woman who made "a lifestyle choice linked with a sense of personal identity, a product of multiple influences rather than traceable to a single cause" (Krieger 1982).[1]

Curious about variations in identities among those women who actually came out as lesbians during this period—a time when American society was in a period of great social ferment, and gender and sexual norms were being publicly contested—I collected the life stories of 25 women in their thirties and forties who came out as lesbians between the late 1960s and the mid-1970s.[2] I wanted to gain a sense of the relationship between the social category "lesbian" and the variations among women who identified with that category at a particular historical moment when the meaning of lesbianism was highly contested. I also wanted to consider how their sense of self may have changed over time.

What I found was that lesbian-identified women of the baby boom shared a strong belief in the value of claiming a lesbian identity. But while "coming out" provided individuals with a "progress narrative" that legitimated and ordered the lesbian experience, the process of identification was a heterogeneous one. So pervasive among women of this age group was this narrative structure that when I asked them how they would describe their sexual identity, most responded by launching into their "coming out" story, which typically began with early childhood, and moved chronologically through time to the present.[3]

Yet they held a variety of understandings of what coming out actually meant. To some women, becoming a lesbian meant "coming home," reengaging with what they believed to be their authentic self, and acknowledging the desires they had long embraced in secret. It permitted them to adopt a surface identity as a lesbian to match the deep sense of difference they already possessed.[4] To others, coming out meant "discovering" their lesbianism. For these women, desire was often not the primary determinant of a lesbian identification; their deep identification as lesbian was preceded by an identification with lesbianism as a sociosexual category. For still others, women whose sexuality was relatively fluid and inchoate, becoming a lesbian meant solidifying both personal and social identities simultaneously. Illustrating these different meanings, here are the stories of three lesbian-identified women of the baby boom generation.

Barb Yerba: "Just the way I am"

Forty-two-year-old Barb Yerba was born in 1949 to a lower middle-class Italian family in New York. She thinks of herself as straddling the "old gay" and "new gay" worlds because she had same-sex experiences before the late 1960s when the lesbian/gay movements expanded the social space open to lesbians and gay men: "I was sort of an old lesbian. To be an old lesbian meant you were out before feminism. I wasn't out to anyone but myself. But I knew when I was eight years old. I probably knew much earlier." Barb experienced desires for other girls early in life, acting upon these desires in isolation and often thinking that she was "the only one." She thinks of herself as having been a tomboy. "I never played with dolls and hardly ever played with girls. I wore boys' clothes at age eight or nine." At fifteen, Barb had a first sexual experience with another girl. It was 1962. At the time, she had no words to describe her feelings.

As an adolescent, she was vaguely aware of the existence of other lesbians, though unaware of the existence of an organized subculture. In recent years, she has made a hobby of collecting lesbian pulp novels, the dime-store fiction sold during the 1950s and 1960s, featuring lurid covers and such titles as *Odd Girl Out* and *Strange Sisters*. These tales of lust, intrigue, and secrecy; of being young and confused and a social misfit remind her of her own adolescence—of "being young and out of control, having all these feelings, and having no place to go to talk about them." Being a lesbian, she says, was a "long stream of unfinished business." Like the characters in her pulp novels, she says, she felt a mixture of fear and exhilaration: "I felt the very same kind of dichotomy. On the one hand, I felt at peace with myself emotionally. This is home. There's this quote from *The Price of Salt*. 'Nobody had to tell her that this was the way it was supposed to be.' This is home after all these years. I knew that this was what I wanted, but I knew that it was a really bad thing." She feels that she has always been a lesbian—that it was not at all a matter of choice. To become a lesbian, she simply "discovered" what was already there.

Barb's first girlfriend "turned straight" after a few years. "She repressed all that stuff." But Barb couldn't. "I never had any doubts." In high school, Barb befriended Lore, the first "flesh-and-blood" lesbian she had ever met. One day, Lore looked Barb in the eye and said, "You are a lesbian." At the time, Barb says, she scoffed at the allegation, "but it planted some sort of seed." Yet claiming a lesbian identity in a social sense—beginning to self-identify as a member of a stigmatized group—was not an easy task. She was sent to a psychiatrist, who told her that she had "trouble relating to people" and prescribed tranquilizers for her to take. Through her teens and early twenties, Barb had a series of relationships with women, but never claimed a lesbian identity in a public sense until a particular incident provided the catalyst for her coming out.

In 1970, while in college, she was living with a girlfriend and several other people in a communal house in upstate New York. One morning, she awoke to hear her roommates discussing whether the presence of Barb and her girlfriend were "warping the household." That was, she said, "the straw that broke the camel's back." Soon after, Barb became involved with a radical lesbian political group. Her first meeting, in 1971, was "like the messiah had come. [. . .] There were all these people who were like me. They were all my age. They were lesbians. I quickly realized I was a feminist as well as a lesbian." Becoming a feminist meant that she could begin to think of her lesbianism in positive terms. It also meant that she could think of her femaleness and her lesbianism as compatible, rather than conflicting. It gave her a sense that she could have a social as well as a personal identity as a lesbian. Barb says that she would be a lesbian regardless of these historical changes, but she imagines that she would have been forced to lead a far more secretive, far more unhappy life.

Barb's narrative exhibits many elements of the "dominant" account; she sees her lesbianism as an orientation that was fixed at birth or in early childhood. Adolescent girls vary in the extent to which they know their desires. Some are not at all aware of sexual feelings, heterosexual or homosexual, whereas others, like Barb, are deeply conscious of them.[5] Girls who are aware of their sexual feelings early on often experience their adolescence as a period in which their embodied sexual desire is simultaneously elicited and denigrated by the dominant culture. One can imagine that lesbian desires typically find no reflection in either the dominant culture or within adolescent peer groups. Indeed, as we have seen, Barb experienced herself as virtually alone in her desires, having no one to discuss them with. She talked about "knowing" she was a lesbian very early on, by age eight, even before she had words to describe her feelings (Tolman 1991).

Barb identified her desires for girls and women at a relatively early age and felt these desires to be powerful and unwavering. When I asked Barb why she is a lesbian, she replied, "It's just the way I am." Indeed, she found the question itself rather curious. Barb sees her adolescent experiences of difference and her eventual homosexuality on a continuum. Her personal identity as a lesbian, she says, was never really in question. As she grew older and began to affiliate with the lesbian community, these connections gave her a social identity as well, a sense of direction and purpose that went beyond the self and a way to counter some of the stigma in the dominant culture. She spoke of the important role that the lesbian community played in allowing her to normalize her sexuality.

But the fact that she experienced her lesbian desires early in life has played a formative role in shaping her sense of self and the meaning her lesbianism holds for her. Indeed, Barb's identity account resembles the "old gay" account, insofar as the experience of secrecy and stigma looms large for those who spent their formative years "managing" their stigma, carefully determining which parts of the self they would reveal to others.

(Recall Barb's comments that she felt like an "old gay" woman because she had lived much of her adult life in the closet.) Because of these experiences, like women of an earlier generation, Barb tended to accentuate the differences between herself and heterosexual women, viewing lesbians and heterosexuals as two distinct categories. She thinks of lesbianism in essentialist terms, as something that is innate, unchangeable, and believes that the only "real" lesbians are "born" lesbians—women like her who have little choice in the matter of their sexuality.

Margaret Berg: "Coming out through feminism"

Margaret Berg had always thought of lesbianism as something that was involuntary; it was an orientation that one either did or did not "have." But when she was in her early twenties, she became aware of the possibility of constructing her own sexuality and choosing lesbianism. As Margaret describes her history, she was one of those women who "came out through feminism."

She grew up in Brooklyn, New York, a red diaper baby, the daughter of Jewish leftist activists. To be a woman in the 1950s and 1960s—even a middle-class white woman, she said—was to grow up with the profound sense of oneself as a second-class citizen. Margaret spoke of the fact that she'd had to feign underachievement in school in order to catch a husband. She said that she'd experienced her heterosexual relationships as largely unsatisfying. "I had all the feelings about men that we all had—we thought they were like zombies. I felt that I took care of all the men I was involved with. I felt like I was much stronger than they were. I felt like I gave much more than I got." She recalls, "We were growing up in a world that was so invalidating of women. I straightened my hair, I was ambivalent about being smart, my physics teacher told my parents: 'She's doing fine for a girl.'"[6]

The women's movement emerged in the late 1960s and gave voice to this alienation, situating these feelings in the context of women's oppression. Margaret compares her exposure to feminism in 1969 to coming out of a cave. "Feminism," she said, was "the most exciting and validating thing that had happened in our lives." It allowed her and others to resolve the dissonance they felt between cultural codes and subjective experience (Ginsburg 1989). Within the context of the movement, Margaret developed an analysis and vocabulary for these feelings and began to see her problems in gendered terms for the first time. She began to believe that she had devalued herself as a woman and underestimated the importance of her female relationships.

Because of their growing idealization of other women, made possible by feminism, women like Margaret withdrew from primary relationships with men. This was less a conscious decision than the product of the growing separation between men's and women's social and political worlds, at least among the young, predominantly middle-class members of what was loosely called the "movement." At the time, she was romantically involved with a man, but as her women friends became more and more central, he became more peripheral. With time, she recalled, "most of my friends were women, all of my friends were feminists, men were not part of my life. It was all very seamless."

When Margaret became involved in her first lesbian relationship, she said, "The only gay women I knew (and we wouldn't call ourselves gay) were my friends and myself." Margaret met a woman, Jennifer, who eventually moved into her apartment. The world they traveled in was that of liberated sexuality and free use of drugs. There was, she says, "a real sense of barriers breaking." She was drawn to Jennifer as a kindred spirit, an equal. "There was a certain reflection of myself I found in her." Margaret recalls that Jennifer had "much more self-consciously identified homoerotic feelings," whereas hers were more about sexual experimentation and rebellion.

In an effort to try to make sense of her feelings and to find support for them, Margaret began to attend a women's consciousness-raising group devoted to discussing questions of sexuality. Practically overnight, through the influence of gay liberation and lesbian feminism, Margaret's feminist consciousness-raising group transformed itself into a coming-out group. In that group, Margaret was socialized into the lesbian world. She began to think of herself as a lesbian and call herself one. "There was a normative sense about discovering women and male domination and how disgusting men could be. Not to be a lesbian was stupid, masochistic."

She goes on:

> Something called "lesbian consciousness" developed in our heads. It's to reconstruct just how the process occurred. We talked about "coming out" every four or five weeks. That term started having more and more ramifications as our lives changed. Not just making love with a woman for the first time—but every new situation where you experienced and/or revealed yourself as gay .

Within the context of a coming-out group, Margaret carved out a place for herself within the lesbian subculture. Earlier, coming out had referred almost exclusively to the process of disclosure. But now women who had never experienced themselves as deeply and irrevocably different, but who shared a sense of alienation from gender and sexual norms, could also claim lesbian identities by developing "gay consciousness." In the discourse of lesbian feminism, feminism and lesbianism were conflated. Lesbianism was revisioned to signify not simply a sexual preference, but a way for women to gain strength and confidence, to bond with other women.

But the political strategy of coming out to others as a means of establishing unity often had the contradictory effect of making differences among women more apparent, and the tension between identity and difference within the coming-out group soon became apparent. Margaret describes the "experiential gap" separating women who were "entering a first gay relationship" and those who were "coming out of the closet" in her coming-out group.

> One woman was quite involved with a man and left almost immediately—it was never clear exactly why she had joined the group, except that she felt good about women. Another woman pulled out because she felt there was a "bisexual" orientation to the group. . . . Her "coming out" was very different from the rest of ours. She wasn't entering a first gay relationship; rather, she was coming out of "the closet;" entering a gay community and acquiring pride in an analysis of who she is. . . . There was a real experiential gap between her and the rest of the group. We had no understanding of the bar scene, of role-playing, of the whole range of experience of an "old gay." I'm sure a lot of this inexperience translated into moralistic arro-

gance—we were a good deal less than understanding when she called her lovers "girls."

Here we see a clash of cultures and two different visions of lesbianism: the old dyke world, which valorized gender roles, and the emergent lesbian feminist culture, which rejected gendered coupledom in favor of the communalized sensuality of the group circle dance.

> We all went to our first gay women's dance together. I was very scared by a number of older women dressed sort of mannishly. Not scared that they'd do anything to me, but wary of being identified with them. I was very relieved when a group of women . . . showed up and we all danced together in a big friendly circle. That was my first exposure to a kind of joyful sensuality that I've come to associate with women's dances. Looking around and seeing a lot of gay women enjoying themselves and each other helped me let go of a lot of my fears and validated the possibilities for growth and pleasure in the relationship with J.

The old gay world conceptualized lesbianism as desire; the new gay world reconceptualized it as "woman identification." Margaret sees the differences primarily in generational terms, evidencing the extent to which other distinctions may have been less salient at the time. For younger women, becoming a lesbian was a matter of developing "lesbian consciousness," developing a personal sense of self as lesbian. For these women, becoming a lesbian and developing a personal identity as a lesbian was not really in question, but living as one and developing a social identity was. But these differences were not solely intergenerational; they also divided women of the baby boom cohort.

Margaret grappled with figuring out her place in the lesbian world. Coming out, she acknowledges, is "an incredibly hard process." She alludes to the conflict between "old gay" and "new gay" conceptions of lesbianism.

> Coming out is an incredibly hard process; many women think there's some magic leap into gayness—that you suddenly lose all fears, doubts, heterosexual feelings. Others are afraid that they weren't "born gay." Come-out groups help women deal with all of those feelings. The existence of the Lesbian Mothers' Group brought home to us that women are not born lesbians; that women who were both wives and mothers could decide to live with and love other women.

After experiencing some doubts about whether or not she herself was "really" a lesbian, Margaret concluded that even seemingly gender-normative women—-wives and mothers—can be lesbians.

Her story suggests that some women used the rhetoric of coming out to claim authenticity and gain membership in the lesbian world. Clearly, this was a very different path to lesbianism from that taken by women whose personal sense of self as lesbian was not really in question—for whom coming out meant coming out of the "closet." If women such as Barb thought of their lesbianism primarily as internally driven, for Margaret and other "elective" lesbians, the adoption of lesbianism as a social identity often preceded the consolidation of lesbianism as personal identity. Unlike Barb, Margaret did not trace her lesbianism to early childhood experiences or have the experience of being "not heterosexual" early on, even if she expressed alienation from heterosexual gender stereotypes. She reported that her sexual interest in men was often conflicted, motivated more by accommodation to male needs and social expectations than by her own desires.

Margaret also differs from Barb in her high degree of self-reflexivity. In general, she framed her lesbianism as the development of "lesbian consciousness"—a political rather than a sexual choice to be involved with women rather than men. Because of her history, Margaret believes that any woman can choose to be a lesbian. However, she recognizes there are different "types" of lesbians, women who exercise greater and lesser degrees of choice.

Joan Salton: "It's an emotional thing"

Forty-six-year-old Joan Salton grew up in the Midwest, the daughter of school teachers. She describes herself as a tomboy as a child. "I was always interested in the things that boys did, not really interested in playing with dolls, the whole works." She remembers herself as a "horny kid" who was interested in sexual experimentation and had sexual experiences with boys at an early age. She became sexually active with boys at age sixteen and with girls at eighteen.

Like many girls her age, she gained her early knowledge of lesbianism from pulp novels and from the literature of psychopathology, and recalls the images she found in books in the library.

> I suppose the people they talked about in those books were much less weird than the descriptions made them out to be. They were really distorted, looking at things under the microscope without any perception of what the person under the lenses was feeling. I didn't relate to that stuff, but I knew all of the words—dyke, lesbian—and I knew it meant me.

Early on, Joan had what she describes as "better" sex with men than with women. But with women, she says, she felt a "depth of emotion" that she "couldn't feel with men." When she reached her early twenties, she began to call herself a lesbian, even as she continued to have affairs with men, though she did not consider them to be "serious." Becoming involved with men, she said, was "sexually possible but emotionally not": "There are some people for whom being a lesbian means something real different. For me it is a passionate lust for women, emotional intensity I feel only with women." Still, along those lines, Joan acknowledges, she made certain choices. "I dumped a guy who really loved me and who I had great sex with, and . . . for a long time afterwards, I sort of regretted it, because after that I had a really hard time finding a woman with whom I had such good sex. But I knew that I couldn't love him. I didn't feel anything for him emotionally." With time, her fragile sense of lesbianism became more solidified, and she came to have little interest in heterosexuality. This coincided, not coincidentally, with the rise of the gay liberation movement, in which she became public as a lesbian, first as an early gay liberation activist, then as a lesbian feminist.

"It was a time of great social ferment," she recalls. "There was a tremendous amount of feeling behind it. It was a time of connecting a lot of ideas with a lot of feelings." It was about affirming identities that were despised by members of the dominant culture and throwing them back in their faces. For Joan, lesbianism was always at least in part about the rejection of social norms—both inside and outside of the lesbian subculture. "There's a part of me that always wants to throw things in for shock value and stir them up a bit." She was a renegade of sorts, even within the movement; once she had an affair with a gay man, another gay liberation activist. Her rejection of the norms of the movement was motivated at least in part by a recognition of the partiality of sexual identifications. Joan was always very conscious of the fact that her own desires do not conform neatly with the binary sexual categories of homosexual and heterosexual.

When asked whether her lesbianism is a choice, Joan replied, "Yes," adding, "but I'm not straight." Joan feels that her lesbianism is a choice insofar as she could choose to deny what she "really" felt. She could choose to be with men if she wished to fit in, but she has made a choice that fitting in is less important than being "who she is."

> What's choice? Is choice what makes you happy? No, I am not a born lesbian. I know I was able to have okay relationships with men, and good sex with men. I also know that nothing compares to being with a woman, emotionally or sexually. So is it a choice? I don't know. . . . Maybe for me [lesbianism] was eighty percent internal compulsion in a certain direction, and twenty percent choice, and maybe for other people it is half and half or something.

Although Joan was not "born" a lesbian, she sees herself as more sexually driven to women than many women who call themselves lesbians, particularly many who came out in the context of feminism. Indeed, she was involved with "one of those women" through the 1970s and was sexually dissatisfied for a long time. Whereas lesbianism was for Joan about passionate sexuality, for her girlfriend, she said, it was about bonding with other women. "It was about making a domestic relationship, making a life together where neither person dominated the other. It was about having a more equal relationship at home where one could be comfortable and not feel squashed by the other person."

As we saw earlier, Barb described her personal identity as a lesbian as preceding her affiliation with lesbianism as a social category, whereas Margaret said the opposite: her affiliation with the lesbian category preceded her consolidation of a sense of "deep" identity. For Joan, separating out the personal and social aspects of lesbian identification and isolating which "came first" is impossible. She talked about her lesbianism in terms of elements that were chosen and elements that were not, and she remained conscious of a disjunction between "doing" and "being"—between engaging in homosexual acts and claiming a homosexual identity.

Joan's lesbianism is a choice insofar as acting upon her desires and claiming a lesbian identity are chosen, since originally she experienced her desires as being at least partly fluid and changing. But at the same time, she is cognizant of the fact that her adoption of a social identity as a lesbian "organized" these desires, diminishing her earlier bisexual inclinations. She began the process of identity formation with a sense of sexual difference that was relatively inchoate, embracing a lesbian identity with some uncertainty and seeing it as a strategic act rather than as a firm expression of who she "is."

Making sense of the accounts

Barb, Margaret, and Joan each represent an alternative account of lesbian identity. Although certainly not an exhaustive sample of different ways of "being" lesbian, their stories illustrate how lesbian identification presented a symbolic resolution of a problem each woman faced at a particular historical moment.

For Barb, becoming a lesbian meant that she could affiliate with the social category "lesbian," disclose that affiliation to others, and build a social world around the desires she had for so long kept private. For Margaret, becoming a lesbian was largely a matter of developing a personal sense of self as a lesbian to match her affiliation with lesbianism as a social category. She did not have a closet—a subjective sense of herself as highly deviant—to overcome; she was not highly driven toward women in a sexual sense. Finally, Joan's experience combined elements of both Barb's and Margaret's stories. Like Barb, she began the process of identity formation with a sense of sexual difference, but she differed from Barb in that her sense of difference was initially relatively inchoate and unformed. She recognized homosexual desires relatively early, but these coexisted with heterosexual desires. Joan saw her embrace of the social category "lesbian" as a strategic act, motivated at least in part by her deeply felt desires for other women, rather than as a firm expression of who she "is."

Through interacting with other self-identified lesbians and by gaining access to different accounts, these women formed a sense of personal and social identity. These accounts were derived from the dominant culture and from lesbian/gay subcultures. A woman coming of age in the late 1960s and early 1970s had access to a wider array of accounts and ways of being a lesbian than women from earlier generations, when sexual knowledge came almost exclusively from medical discourse. However, this does not imply that all individuals had an open-ended ability to reconstruct themselves as they pleased.[7] Indeed, each woman brought to the coming out process a sense of self that was already partially formed.

Individuals' early experiences of difference or similarity in relation to the dominant heterosexual culture figured prominently in their narratives. Their feelings of difference were often related to the age at which they became conscious of their desires for other girls and women. The early-developing lesbian, such as Barb, seemed to incorporate a greater sense of "differentness" within her sense of self. Margaret and other later-developing lesbians were often very conscious of this, whether or not they named it as such. They were also conscious of how they differed from women who had come out before feminism and gay liberation. "Old dykes," particularly those who were very visibly butch, symbolized for them what they might become if they shunned heterosexuality, but they also embodied a kind of protofeminism—a willingness to go against the social grain.

Coming out can be seen, then, as two distinct but overlapping processes: the development of a personal identity as lesbian, or individuation, and the development of a social identity as lesbian, or disclosure. Most analyses of "coming out" focus on the process of disclosure, assuming that the person is fully individuated before disclosure occurs. But for many women, as I have shown, the process of individuation follows disclosure. For others, individuation and disclosure occur simultaneously, each influencing the other.

What these life stories reveal, to quote Karla Jay and Joanne Glasgow, is that "the word lesbian is not an identity with predictable content . . . it is a position from which to speak" (1990, 6). Individuals bring to the process of sexual identity formation a sense of self that is at least partly formed, and they use the available accounts, or repertoires of meaning, to make sense of this self. These images, or accounts, are themselves historical constructions. As women construct their identities, they are acutely aware of those around them, and they select images to emulate or reject, fitting themselves into different lesbian worlds.

Notes

1. Ken Plummer (1981) called the first account the "orientation" model and the second the "identity construct" model; they are also referred to, respectively, as essentialist and constructionist conceptions of homosexuality. Lillian Faderman (1991) wrote that lesbians of this generation were divided between the "essential" and "existential" varieties, glossing over the complex ways in which individuals utilize elements of both accounts that I hope to show.

2. In 1991, when most of the interviews were conducted, the women ranged in age from 33 to 47. Two-thirds of them were white.

3. On the confessional mode of sexual narratives, see Plummer 1995 and Zimmerman 1990.

4. I have adapted the concepts of "surface" and "deep" identities from Arlie Hochschild's 1983 work on emotional labor, *The Managed Heart*.

5. Beth Zemsky (1991) cited studies that indicate that the mean age for women to recognize and pronounce (at least to themselves) that this sense of difference and disquiet has something to do with lesbianism is approximately fourteen. There may be some correlation between lesbian identity and gender identity insofar as "butch" or more masculine-identified lesbians were less likely to see their sexual identities as being elective than feminine-identified women. But the reasons for this are unclear. Is it because "mannish" lesbians were more "essentially" lesbian in orientation? Or is it because butches were the most identifiable lesbian figures since they stood out, often from an early age, and were more apt to be labeled lesbian by family members and other authority figures? For whichever reason, or combination of reasons, gender inversion is a symbolic marker of lesbianism and a warning to women who step out of their prescribed roles that the taint of lesbianism will follow them (see Newton 1984).

6. For a sense of how dominant cultural norms shaped the lives of teenage girls in the 1950s and how girls resisted these norms, see Breines 1992.

7. See also Burch 1993. This would seem to imply the necessity of "bringing the body back in," acknowledging that bodily sensation and function play a role, albeit one that is always mediated by culture and subjectivity. Also see Vance 1992. In this sense, I depart from the tradition of interactionist studies exemplified in which the importance of physical experience is downplayed, such as Barbara Ponse's *Identities in the Lesbian World* (1978). On the history of sexual theorizing in relation to this question, see Stein 1989.

References

Breines, W. 1992. *Young, white and miserable: Growing up female in the 1950s*. Boston: Beacon Press.

Burch, B. 1993. *On intimate terms: The psychology of difference in lesbian relationships*. Urbana: University of Illinois Press.

Davies, P. 1992. The rule of disclosure in coming out among gay men. In *Modern homosexualities: Fragments of lesbian and gay experience*, ed. K. Plummer, 75–83. London: Routledge.

Faderman, L. 1991. *Odd girls and twilight lovers: A history of lesbian life in twentieth century America*. New York: Columbia University Press.

Ginsburg, F. 1989. Dissonance and harmony: The symbolic function of abortion in activists' life stories. In *Interpreting Women's Lives: Feminist theory and personal narratives*, ed. The Personal Narratives Group, 59–84. Bloomington: Indiana University Press.

Hochschild, A. 1983. *The managed heart: Commercialization of human feeling*. Berkeley: University of California Press.

Jay, K., and J. Glasgow. 1990. *Lesbian texts and contexts: Radical revisions*. New York: New York University Press.

Krieger, S. 1982. Lesbian identity and community: Recent social science literature. *Signs* 8, no. 1: 91–108.

Newton, E. 1984. The mythic mannish lesbian: Radclyffe Hall and the New Woman, *Signs* 9:557–75.

Plummer, K. 1981. Homosexual categories. In *The making of the modern homosexual*. Totowa, NJ: Barnes and Noble.

———. 1995. *Telling sexual stories: Power, change and social worlds*. London: Routledge.

Ponse, B. 1978. *Identities in the lesbian world: The social construction of self*. Westport, CT: Greenwood.

Stein, A. 1989. Three models of sexuality: Drives, identities, and practices. *Sociological Theory* 7 (Spring):1–13.

Tolman, D. L. 1991. Adolescent girls, women and sexuality: Discerning dilemmas of desire. *Women and Therapy* 11, Nos. 3/4: 55–70.

Vance, C. 1992. Social construction theory: Problems in the history of sexuality. In *Sexualities: Critical assessments*, ed. K. Plummer, 356–71. London: Routledge.

Zemsky, B. 1991. Coming out against all odds: Resistance of a young lesbian. *Women and Therapy* 11, Nos. 3/4: 185–200.

Zimmerman, B. 1990. *The safe sea of women*. Boston: Beacon Press.

Shari L. Dworkin and Lucia F. O'Sullivan

8

"It's Less Work for Us and It Shows Us She Has Good Taste"

Masculinity, Sexual Initiation, and Contemporary Sexual Scripts

Why is it that kissing is seen as sexualized, "natural" foreplay to Americans and Europeans while it is virtually unknown among the Balinese, the Siriono of South America, the Thonga of Africa, and the Lepcha of Eurasia (Tiefer 1990)? Why is it that the deep kiss is central to romance in many Western cultures, while the Tinguians place their lips near the other's face and inhale vigorously, and the Lapps kiss the mouth and nose at the same time? Why is it that young men in Papua New Guinea believe that young boys need to be inseminated with the semen of older men in order to grow into manhood while same-sex sexual experiences are not part of normative adolescent male scripts in the United States (Williams et al. 1996)? While members of Western societies tend to embrace the popular belief that biology explains one's sexual object choice ("it's just natural") or what individuals do in sexual encounters ("the parts just fit"), the above examples underscore how sex—and the ways it becomes scripted—is also immanently cultural.

Script theory is one useful window into the cultural construction of sexual life. It posits that sexual scenarios are guided by mutually shared conventions that help actors to enact a sexual situation interdependently. One of the benefits of using such a theory is that it moves away from the common biologism that can all too easily overlook the cultural complexities of sexual practices, fantasies, identities, and desire. Simon and Gagnon (1984, 1987) and Gagnon (1990) argue that there are three interrelated levels of sexual scripts that simultaneously operate in sexual interactions and can account for the production of sexuality as a social activity. The first level of the sexual script comprises the social norms or standards that dictate appropriate sexual behavior in sexual interactions (cultural scenarios) acquired through collective life, from such diverse sources as schools, peers, media, religion, family, sport, and cultural discourse. At the second level, individuals translate or improvise on these more general cultural scenarios within specific social contexts (interpersonal scripts). It is here where individuals take into account one another's needs, wants, and desires as they negotiate their own. Finally, motivational elements produce commitment to a particular sequence of sexual actions and mediate multiple goals, fantasies, and desires (intrapsychic scripts). Core to this view is the contention that human sexual behavior cannot be understood independently from the sociocultural factors that shape individuals.

Many argue that scripts are gendered in heterosexual sex and relationships. According to proscriptions contained in "traditional" gender scripts, men are socialized to initiate and orchestrate sexual interactions, whereas women are socialized to be restrictors or responders, simultaneously concerned about harming their sexual reputations and fulfilling men's sexual needs (Gagnon 1990; O'Sullivan and Byers 1992; Schwartz and Rutter 1998). Research has also demonstrated the existence of a widespread sexual double standard that offers men greater sexual freedom and rights of sexual determination than women (Blanc 2001; Gupta 2001; Gupta and Weiss 1993; Seal and Ehrhardt 2003). Even though men tend to enjoy greater privileges in sex, such as an emphasis on their pleasure and an allowance for multiple partners, there are costs to masculinity too. Researchers have found that restrictive constructs of masculinity lead to men's own self-objectification during sex, which can lead to performance anxiety and a feeling of pressure to be "ready" for sex much of the time with any available partner, pursuing opportunities to the end (Brod 1995; Fracher and Kimmel 1995; Seal et al. 2000). At the same time, women are often castigated within a madonna/whore dichotomy—spurned both for being too receptive ("she's too easy" or "she's a slut") and for being frigid if they "don't give it up" easily enough (Schwartz and Rutter 1998; Staiger 1995). In short, research clearly underscores how "strait-jacketed" definitions of heterosexual masculinity and femininity translate into sexual scripts and can constrain both women's and men's interactions in heterosexual interactions.

In order to see the persistence of a dominant cultural script, one only has to imagine departing from it. How would men really feel if women wanted to initiate sex every single night? How would women react if men felt less compelled to push through to penile-vaginal penetration and instead enjoyed mutual oral sex for most of their sexual repertoire? At what point would a man be viewed as "abnormal" if he wanted his female partner to initiate sex *much more* than he does? How would these desires be perceived and received? Why?

The above scenarios are not meant to suggest that sexual scripts do not vary across individuals, over time within the same culture, or across cultures (Schneider and Gould 1987; Whittier and Melendez 2004). Indeed, there is some suggestion that sexual scripts may be shifting for both heterosexual women and men (Ortiz-Torres, Williams, and Ehrhardt 2003; Segal 1995). Researchers argue that contemporary femininity has outgrown anachronistic notions of sexual passivity and responsiveness to men's advances to include assertiveness in sexual initiation, pleasure-seeking, influencing or coercing reluctant male partners, and negotiating safer sex (Anderson and Aymami 1993; Anderson and Sorensen 1996; Exner et al. 2003; Kamen 2003; O'Sullivan and Byers 1992, 1993, 1996). Researchers have also documented how men have internalized shifts in contemporary masculinity in a manner that pushes male sexual scripts beyond sex as a conquest or instrumental outcome to include emotionality, commitment, and love (Seal and Ehrhardt 2003; Seal, Wagner-Raphael, and Ehrhardt 2000).

However, despite some documentation of flux in gender scripts in recent years, tra-

ditional scripts are in fact said to continue to characterize many heterosexual relationships in Western countries (Hynie et al. 1998; Ortiz-Torres et al. 2003; Seal and Ehrhardt
2003). While numerous studies have documented some changes concerning femininity
and sexual initiation, (Kamen 2003; Ortiz-Torres et al. 2003; O'Sullivan and Byers 1992;
Segal 1995), it is less frequent that researchers focus their attention on parallel shifts in
contemporary masculine norms in heterosexual sexual scripts. This absence in the literature is somewhat surprising, as numerous contemporary scholars have made note
of how heterosexual men are changing in analyses of "involved" fathers, the expressive
"New Man," the "metrosexual" (who identifies as heterosexual yet looks sexually more
fluid), and the commodified "boy toy" (Coltrane 1996, Connell 1995; Dowsett 2004;
Heywood and Dworkin 2003; Messner 1997; Miller 2001), yet few have considered
how such broader cultural shifts may be having an impact on heterosexual men's sexual
scripts.

The data presented here are part of a larger study developing methods to assess
power and gender roles in heterosexual relationships. To more closely examine contemporary heterosexual men's sexual scripts, we employ the concept of disjuncture to describe how there can be a difference between what men currently do and what men want
to do in terms of sexual initiation with their female partners. In the first phase of this
larger study, we conducted in-depth interviews with men and women in heterosexual
relationships after they had completed three weeks' of diary data cataloguing their sexual experiences with their primary partner. These results explore the themes that arose
in the in-depth interviews with the men in our sample. The analysis centers on the ways
that men characterize patterns of sexual initiation in their primary relationships; the
meaning that men give to their currently practiced patterns of sexual initiation; the
range of sexual initiation patterns that men desire; and the rationales men offer for desired initiation patterns when these differ from what is currently practiced. These questions underscore how disjunctures between current and desired practices challenge us
to consider the simultaneity of the cultural, interpersonal, and intrapsychic realms in
sexual scripts. Such an analysis also sheds light on the shifting nature of contemporary
gender relations.

Participants and interviews

Thirty-two men ranging between the ages of 18 and 24 were recruited from a college
in New York City. All were involved in an ongoing sexually active heterosexual relationship. The men reported having been in their current relationships an average of 30
months (range: 5–48 months). Corresponding to the demographics of residents in the
neighborhood, almost one-third of the sample described their race as African Ameri-
can/black, half were white, and twenty percent identified as other. In terms of ethnicity,
less than one-quarter of the men reported that they were Hispanic or Latino. Less than
half of the sample were born in the United States, one-quarter were from a Spanish-
speaking country, one-fifth were from Europe, and the remaining men reported other
origins. The majority of the sample grew up in what could be considered working-class
and lower middle-class families.

Most participants had never been married, were not currently living with their partners, and approximately half of the sample reported that their current relationship was

their first serious relationship. The men reported engaging in vaginal intercourse an average of 17.5 times in the preceding two months (range: 2–60). Only three men reported other sexual partners during the preceding two months. Across their lifetimes, the men reported an average of 6.6 sexual partners (range: 1–20). There were no differences across racial/ethnic groups in terms of the number of lifetime sexual partners or condom use.

Interviews were conducted by a male project staff member with training and experience in conducting sexuality-related interviews, and each interview took approximately forty-five minutes to complete. To begin the coding process, excerpts of transcribed interviews corresponding to men's actual and desired patterns of sexual initiation and perceived reasons for such patterns were extracted. The men's reported patterns of initiation were coded as "male-dominated," "egalitarian," and "female-dominated" according to whether participants described sexual initiation as mostly or solely self-initiated, shared (50/50), or mostly or solely initiated by their female partner.

Current and desired practices: Disjunctures between what men do and what they want?

Three main patterns characterizing men's current and desired sexual initiation emerged. The most common pattern of men's current sexual initiation was male-dominated whereby men reported that they were more likely to initiate sex (N=18, 56.3%). However, 13 of the 18 men (72.2%) reporting this pattern also reported desiring a more "egalitarian" pattern, whereas only 5 (27.7%) of those who practiced a traditional pattern desired to sustain male-dominated initiation. A second common pattern of sexual initiation was female-dominated (N=8, 25%). One-half of the men who currently reported female-dominated initiation desired to sustain female-dominated initiation patterns, while the other half sought to move to a more shared pattern with female partners. A third pattern of initiation was egalitarian (50/50 initiation) with a desire to sustain the same. A very small number of subjects fit into other configurations. For example, one interviewee who currently practiced an egalitarian initiation pattern desired female-dominated initiation.

Current male-dominated/desired egalitarian

Contrary to depictions of men seeking to control sexual encounters with women, among the 18 (of 32) men who stated that they initiated sex all or most of the time, only five wished to maintain this arrangement (see Table 1). When asked to provide rationales for current practices, these were generally explained in terms of "natural" gender differences or individual psychologies and personality differences. For instance, men stated that current patterns took their current form because "I'm the man," "She's a girl," "It's not in her nature," "She's kind of shy," "We have stylistic differences" or "I'm more aggressive." While five of these men expressed wishes to maintain these patterns since they viewed themselves as "more dominant" or "more of a top," most men who practiced traditional initiation patterns desired more equal initiation with their female partners. Here, three main themes characterized men's desire for shared initiation, including preferring to be more of an object of desire to female partners, wanting to "share the work" of initiation, and desiring sexual egalitarianism in the relationship.

Table 1. Current vs. desired sexual initiation practices

| | Desired Practices | | | |
Current Practices	Male-Dominated	Egalitarian	Female-Dominated	Totals
Male-Dominated	5	13	0	18
Egalitarian	0	4	4	8
Female-Dominated	0	2	4	6
Totals	5	19	8	N=32

Preference for men to be an object of desire

Nearly all of the men who currently practiced traditional sexual initiation patterns stated that they sought more egalitarian initiation so as to perceive themselves as an object of desire to their female partner. Men expressed feeling more wanted when women initiated sex. Although perceiving oneself to be an object of desire has frequently been associated with the cultural constitution of femininity and vulnerability, and has not previously been a central part of constructs of heterosexual masculinity (Connell 1987, 1995), it appears that this is not the case in this contemporary sample of college-aged men from a community college campus. Men openly described a preference to be more of an object of desire specifically through female sexual initiation. They confessed that they were not certain of their desirability if their female partner merely "accepted" advances in a traditional script:

> When she initiates, I feel like she actually wants me. And she actually, like, wants to do things with me, as in like . . . as when I initiate things. I . . . I . . . think she wants me? But I'm not completely sure, because . . . she doesn't like . . . start. Like, she tells me she does want to, but . . . I feel more confident that she does when she initiates.

Another man stated that

> I've felt lonely—I know she's not gonna start it. I would like for her to come to me. It's hard to um, just always initiate it myself. There were a couple of times when she came to me and it was a rush, exciting.

Other men agreed, linking this to the eroticism of having a woman in control of initiation and sex in general:

> I would like her to be in control more. More dominant I guess. I think it's attractive. I remember one time . . . she actually grabbed my butt and threw me on the bed. It was a rush. It felt like . . . I guess the word is "erotic" or something.

At the same time that men enjoy the benefits of knowing that they are objects of desire to their female partners, gendered sexual scripts do seem to limit the extent to which some men will accept female initiation. It seems that women may have to negotiate carefully the boundaries of what constitutes initiating "too much." For example, one man explains that

> as I told you, in a lot of cases I initiate and when she does it, it's like something different—so it's more interesting to me. It's exciting . . . so I like it. But I think if my wife initiates it all the time that wouldn't be so exciting or interesting, because . . . I don't know. This is my personal opinion, but I think that the man should be the initiator. I don't know why. Perhaps that's sounds prejudiced, I don't know.

Thus, at the same time that popular discourse is rife with the ways in which men fantasize about being sexually devoured by women, it is not uncommon for men to report that repeated female initiation would be quite uncomfortable. In this way, cultural scenarios structure the possibilities and limits of interpersonal scripts. Here, definitions of manhood may be challenged when women take on "too much" of a continued active role in the initiation process. Another example reveals how initiation is not simply a gendered expression of desire but a form of control. For example, one man explained that he desires for his female partner to initiate sex more, but he realized that he controls the initiation through having her over at his place more.

> I think . . . when I came over her house once before, she initiated too. Because it's different. Like, when she comes over my house . . . I'm in control. But when I come over her house—but I don't come over her house as often as she comes to my house—she's mostly at my house. So . . . maybe this is a factor that could be causing the difference in . . . who's initiating—whose house it is. Because she would initiate it at her house, and then it would be more often than if she was in my house.

Such control might not be easily relinquished by men despite an overtly stated desire for more equal initiation. In this example, this woman is "mostly at my house" where the male partner then enjoys control over the initiation.

Several men also noted the intersubjective nature of scripts by underscoring that men did not facilitate women's initiation more given that men were responding to the perception that female partners wanted male initiation. For example, when asked why this couple currently practiced male-dominated initiation, he replied, "Well, I think she . . . I think she thinks that, the man . . . the man has to do it." Another man replied that when his girlfriend initiated once, it wasn't that he disliked it, but rather, that she disliked it. He explained that she stated to him, "I don't like it that way. And what's wrong with you?"

Thus, both women and men may be commonly responding to cultural expectations that masculinity is—and should be—synonymous with sexual initiation. At the same time that some women may not desire to give up the perceived benefits of traditional scripts, some men may be challenging traditional scripts in a number of ways.

Sharing the "work" or labor of initiation

Within some couples who practiced male-dominated sexual initiation patterns, men described current practices through a discourse of a division of labor that needed to be shared more equitably. These men stated that sexual initiation was work, and they seemed either resentful or tired of its demands. For example, one man stated that he preferred "a mix of initiation. I dislike doing all the work . . . it *feels* like work." Other men agree: "Initiating every day becomes a little tiresome. I don't have a problem if she initiates it."

Previous research lends insight into the above narratives. First, there can be a sharp difference between the sea of cultural images that depict sex as lively, fun, delicious, and free-spirited, and the reality that many women and men engage in sex that they find tiresome, laborious, and/or do not want to have. That is, researchers have described how women and men commonly feign interest in sex, do not feel desire when their partners do, or give in to sex given perceived obligations to fulfill the other person (O'Sullivan and Allgeier 1998). Second, it is intriguing to take note that sex is being narrated by men above through a discourse of a division of labor given that feminists have long argued for more equitable divisions of labor (household chores, emotion work) between women and men in heterosexual relationships (Coltrane 1996; Hochschild 1989; Kroska 1997). It difficult to ascertain if these narratives are part of men's sincere frustrations with their partner's lack of initiation, a commitment to gender equality across different realms of the relationship, or if such complaints are occurring in an inequitable division of labor that already tends to favor men overall (Coltrane 1996).

Desiring more egalitarian sexual gender politics

A minority of men explicitly linked their desire for an egalitarian initiation pattern to a rejection of traditional scripts and to a rejection of inequitable power arrangements between women and men. For example, one man disagreed with narrow definitions of femininity or masculinity, particularly given his social class and upbringing:

> I think initiation was up to, um, both partners. It's not the male's or the female's initiation. And, and it's up to both partners. There's . . . no particular gender as pertaining to the role as initiator, I think I don't believe in the . . . the man as the sole provider. I don't believe that the woman has to . . . you know, stay home and not work. I don't believe in, uh, the man make all the decisions. I don't believe in the wife bein' submissive. I believe in a kinda . . . give and take there . . . And I just grew up believin' that it's a . . . 50–50 type of thing.

Current Female-Dominated/Desired Female-Dominated

Another common pattern of initiation in the sample was female-dominated initiation with a desire to maintain female-dominated initiation. Unlike rationales for traditional patterns of initiation where men indicated that these practices were related to "nature" or personality differences with one's partner, rationales for female-dominated initiation included: offering women the opportunity to express desire and meet women's need to satisfy men, men's fatigue at having their common sexual advances rejected, or men's medical problems. For example, when asked why the current pattern of initiation was female-dominated, men mentioned themes such as "she likes to satisfy me as well," or "I am the second person she's had sex with so she's like into it . . ."

Another man reported that

> Uh . . . I think one reason . . . like I take . . . I take anti-depressants, which like . . . kind of like, makes your sex drive go down? And I think it's somewhat that . . . and she generally always wants to.

Finally, men described female-dominated patterns as a way to solve the problem of being rejected by female partners when they initiated sex: "Because when I tried to initiate, I got shot down, so you just give up. And that's why she initiates most of the time."

At the same time, two-thirds of the men who experienced female-dominated initiation wanted to sustain the current pattern. When asked why, some men explained that they were tired of feeling rejected when they initiate sex, even though they want to continue female-dominated patterns:

> I would want it to be . . . that way, you know—her initiating—but in a more equal sense, where . . . I don't have to worry about like, you know, um . . . is she gonna shoot me down?

A few men reported that they were tired of "being accused" of wanting sex all the time as men, and that female-dominated initiation helped to ease accusations or assumptions about what men are like: "It's better like that [*her initiating more*], like you know? You initiate it too much, they start thinking that's all he wants, you know? Let them initiate it."

Some men also made note of the importance of the interpersonal realm in initiation decisions. This particular interviewee offered that women and men are cognizant of how they should negotiate their own desire among shifting levels of desire in the couple in order to keep arrangements equitable:

> Um . . . I'm fine with her initiating. [*Laughs.*] I think it's good. I think sometimes she feels like she initiates it . . . too much of the time. That I should initiate it more often. Um . . . I guess ideally, it would be better if I wanted to do it more often—or if she wanted to do it less often—and then the balance would be closer to not her wanting to do it as much.

In this case, the male partner's comments reveal assumptions about the gendered nature of desire. If the female partner is initiating sex more, she is read by the male partner as having more desire, and he argues that it would be "better" if he wanted to do it more—or if she wanted to do it less. This quote may replicate the finding that both women and men may still feel that men are (or should be) more responsible for sexual initiation. Alternatively, it may indicate that egalitarianism is the more desirable state of sexual equilibrium for some.

Current egalitarian/desired egalitarian

The third most frequently occurring pattern of initiation was egalitarian with a desire for the same. Similar to participants in other sexual scripts research (Seal and Ehrhardt 2003), men regarded a pattern of more egalitarian initiation as being a function of time in the relationship. Here, it was perceived that men initiated more sexual activities in the beginning of the relationship, but that their female partners initiated more once they felt safe or more comfortable with male partners. For instance, one man reported that his partner "became more comfy with time. She was too shy—at the beginning. But . . . after we broke the ice, then it's the same . . . for the both of us."

When asked about desired configurations of initiation, this group of men reported the same pattern of responses as men who practiced male-dominated initiation, but desired egalitarian initiation: they enjoyed being the object of desire, and preferred to experience mutual desire. For instance, one man explained:

> I think it's perfect the way it is, 'cause if I always . . . like if I was always the initiator, I would feel as though she doesn't find me attractive and she doesn't . . . she doesn't like want me. Like, I . . . I'm glad that she wants me as much as I want her, 'cause any other way it would be too much of either side, you know? Because if I . . . if I didn't initiate as much as she did, she would feel bad. She wouldn't think I find her attractive, you know? So . . . it's good this way.

Sexual initiation appears to be a signifier of one's interest to or attraction towards one's partner, perhaps just as much as it is an expression of sexual release or intimacy. At the same time, limits were again placed on men's acceptance of female initiation. For example, some men who desired female initiation also clearly described an ambivalence about this due to the performance anxieties it elicits. For example, when asked how he would want sex to begin, one man stated that

> Yeah, I wouldn't like any other way. Some of . . . the times when I feel like she's the initiator, like I don't expect her to. Like one time she was in a room and I went to the bathroom. No one was in the room, but she was doin' her paper. And when I came back to the dorm, she was naked and she said, "I'm ready." And . . . I felt . . . I felt kind of . . . uncomfortable. Usually when . . . when she initiates, I have this thing I guess is in my unconscious—that I have to be like . . . I have to perform . . . like now. And right now! Like . . . all kissing and hugging aside. Like, I have to be erect—we have to have sex—so . . . I guess there's a certain amount of pressure to that.

In addition to viewing the above narrative as a potential precursor to performance anxiety, it is also possible to interpret this occasion as one where an individual might consent to unwanted sexual activity given "pressure." That is, researchers have uncovered how both women and men agree or appear willing to have sex when in fact they experience little interest or desire to engage in an initiated sexual activity. O'Sullivan and Allgeier (1998) found that 26% of men and 50% of women reported consenting to unwanted sexual activity over a two-week period of diary collection. For the most part, women and men justified this on the basis of wanting to satisfy a partner's needs, promoting intimacy, or avoiding relationship tensions. It is intriguing to note that at the same time men are handed the pressures to be "ready for sex" at all times, they also narrate such tasks through a discourse of labor that is tiring and/or perhaps not wholly desired.

Other men expressed concerns that they could not keep up with the desire of their female partners and pushed to normalize desire towards egalitarianism if the women initiated "too much." For example, one man described that

> Well . . . I don't have a problem if she initiates it. I don't have a problem. It's just that . . . every day . . . becomes a little . . . kinda tiresome. I was like, "You know what? Let's slow it down just a tiny little bit, you know? I'm not goin' anywhere, you know? As long as you're not going, I'm not goin' anywhere. So . . . let's just slow it down a little bit."

Current egalitarian/ desired female-dominated

A final pattern was egalitarian initiation with a desire for female-dominated initiation. Here, men stated that current patterns were shared, but that they were afraid that their sexual advances would be rejected and would therefore rather have their female partners come to them. For example, one man explained:

> She's not afraid to initialize [sic] it, you know? I can get shy, and I'm . . . I'm afraid of rejection, you know? I don't wanna initialize and she's not in the mood. So sometime I tend to wait to see how she's feeling or I'll wait to see what kind of vibe, you know, is in the room. That's . . . that's when she and I were living together . . . she used to do most of the initializing. But now it's a mutual thing. I would rather her, because like I said, just because of the fact that I'm afraid a rejection . . . I would rather she initializes it, because I see that she doesn't have a problem with it either so. . . .

Such narratives may be consistent with research findings that examine performance anxieties as part of a fear of rejection during sex (Bordo 1999; Brod 1995; Fracher and Kimmel 1995). Here, an egalitarian pattern of initiation is not preferred over a female-dominated pattern because female-dominated initiation may be perceived as wholly eliminating the risk of rejection. Alternatively, as has been noted, perhaps both men's and women's desires are oriented around constituting the self as a successful object of desire through an initiating partner.

Discussion

A popular website for dating, match.com, recently featured an article titled "10 myths women have about men." Myth number eight was listed as "men don't like women who make the first move." The site reported a young man responding to the myth with the retort, "Sure we do . . . It's less work for us and shows us you have good taste." While this comment is not dissimilar to the narratives of sexual initiation as labor that were examined here, it is vital to engage with the additional questions that arise as a result of such statements. For example, even though the comment seems to imply that it is very acceptable for women to initiate sex, and it is clear that this might make men feel more desirable, there is the commonly posed question of how comfortable men actually are with female sexual initiation. Our results indicate that men in relationships feel comfortable if women initiate "once in awhile" or "more" than currently, but "not too much." An interesting question remains: why does a certain amount of female initiation begin to challenge the boundaries of definitions of manhood in the same way that "too much" female intelligence or too much musculature does (Dworkin 2001)? More importantly, why might such responses about what is "enough" or "too much" for women be common within sexual scripts at this particular historical moment? What do such statements signify about the state of gender relations more generally?

Our study set out to extend sexual scripts work from the past by simultaneously examining the cultural, interpersonal, and intrapsychic realms that shape men's sexual initiation patterns. To do so, we asked men to discuss not only their current initiation patterns but also the meanings they attributed to these arrangements and their satisfaction with current arrangements. We also asked men to explain their desires to depart from current practices. Such an emphasis allowed us to uncover disjunctures between current (actual) and preferred (ideal) practices in sexual scripts, demonstrating some of the numerous ways in which men wrestle with, critique, adhere to, and remake "traditional" gender norms.

The results revealed several main patterns of actual and ideal initiation. Most of the men currently practiced male-dominated patterns of initiation, but sought more egalitarian sexual initiation that included preferences to be an object of desire to female partners or to share the labor of sexual initiation. One-quarter of the sample currently experienced female-dominated patterns. Most of these men desired to sustain these patterns, although rationales for current practices seemed to emerge from having previous sexual advances rebuffed, or concerns that women would perceive men as wanting sex too much of the time. Some men also currently practiced egalitarian patterns of initiation with a desire to sustain the same, given an enjoyment of being a desired object in the partnership, wanting to share sexual labor, or wishing to produce more egalitarian arrangements in other facets of the relationship. Such narratives underscore the interrelationship between the intrapsychic realm (preferring to "know" one is an object of desire), cultural scenarios (drawing on what women and men are supposed to do, and shifting such definitions to draw new sexual divisions of labor in the relationship) and the interpersonal realm (facilitating desirable identities through sexual initiations).

The finding that so many men made mention of a preference to be an object of desire to female partners deserves further attention. Historically, heterosexual femininity has largely been constituted as becoming a successful object of desire (Bordo 1995; Connell 1987; Lorber 1995; Tolman, Striepe, and Harmon 2003), with being desired being equated with success as a woman. Being an object of desire for heterosexual men is much more contentious in the private realm, as it has traditionally indicated vulnerability, has been a signifier of male homosexuality, and can be linked to other forms of gender subordination (Bordo 1999; Connell 1987; Eck 2003). Objects of desire have generally been historically defined by a (simplistic) dichotomy of feminine and masculine opposites that form the basis for (some) heterosexual sexual practices (Connell 1987, 1995; Pringle 1990; Weeks 1985). Such categories are now contested and "at play" in a field of shifting power relations that commonly include heterosexual men as sexualized in media imagery, as bodily commodities, and as objects of desire in post-industrial consumer culture (Heywood and Dworkin 2003, Dworkin and Wachs forthcoming; Bordo 1999; Dowsett 2004; Messner 1992; Miller 2001).

Broader social trends shed light on the common contemporary expression of men seeking to be an object of desire. Here, mass media exposure to an array of proliferating images assists in the constitution of both women and men as bodily objects. Researchers argue that as a result of a continual supply of sexy signifiers, it is now

> publically permissible for men to be passively gazed upon and desired. Consequently, this can apply to all men, and that historical achievement is a dangerous and destabilizing shift in Western sexual formations, for it blurs the generally accepted gender distinctions between men and women, and generates uncertainty as to what appropriately constitutes the masculine and the feminine. In this way, sexual desirability is revealed as a product of active processes of social change, rather than the "laws of nature." (Dowsett 2004, 73)

Sexual scripts offer us one window into these "active social processes" given that scripts allow insight into how individuals negotiate the cultural, interpersonal, and intrapsychic realms simultaneously. A fertile area for future sexual scripts research is the role that media plays in constituting (or challenging) beliefs in the above realms. At the same time, researchers can and should use scripts work to intervene on the sometimes problematic consequences that result from increasing pressures to successfully make oneself into a sexualized bodily object. For example, researchers have already noted how men are increasingly suffering from body image issues and body dysphorias that result from objectification—such findings are both distinct from and similar to women given larger cultural trends concerning "body panic" (Dworkin and Wachs forthcoming; Klein 1993; Pope et al. 2000)

Although many men in this sample expressed a desire to shift from male-dominated to more egalitarian or female-dominated patterns of initiation, there are numerous ways to interpret these desires. Many of the men came from working-class and lower working-class families and as such, may have experiences growing up in households where both women and men had to work, extending their understanding of shared labor into the sexual realm (Collins 1990). Despite the common belief that working-class and lower working-class men hold traditional gender ideologies, much sociological work has underscored how working-class men and men of color are more prone to sharing power in certain realms. For example, men of color have been found to do more household labor and child care than do white men (John and Shelton 1997; Stohs 2000). Future researchers might therefore also further explore how flexible heterosexual men's sexual scripts are concerning masculinity in sexual initiation across socioeconomic status, as some researchers find more traditional attitudes about gender roles in lower socioeconomic couples (Seal et al. 2000) while the above research points to the reverse.

Results examined here may also mean broader shifts in gender relations towards more companionate norms, a stretching of traditional scripts for both women and men, a desire for egalitarian relationships (with or without the influence of the feminist movement), or social structural shifts in women's or men's power that may make sexual scripts more flexible. Such possibilities may also mean a reinforcement of old rules: a discourse of women pleasing men (no matter who initiates) and questions as to whether sexual egalitarianism can or will translate into egalitarianism in other realms (e.g., household labor and child care).

At the same time, there are more critical interpretations. As sociological researchers have noted, "How do we explain the gap between what many men say" (that they are in favor of egalitarian arrangements) "and what they do"? Indeed, "it may be in men's interests to change their words, but not to change their behaviors in any substantial manner" given the possible "reality" of men's "privileges" (Messner 1993, 726). Even in the event that men view their sexual (or other) choices as constraining for themselves or others, it may be the case that "these problems are more accurately viewed as the costs of being on top," and this "does not necessarily signal a desire to cease being on top" in broader social or institutional terms (Messner 1993, 730). It may be the case that men strategically deploy gender egalitarian discourse in the sexual realm while also enjoying the various benefits of women's changing status over time. That is, women's increased immersion in the occupational structure, increased contributions to household income, and little change in their already disproportionate levels of household labor may now be coupled with increased pressure to or willingness to initiate sex. This may mean that images of superwomen (juggling multiple realms) might now also extend to expectations for women in the bedroom. Simultaneously, future research need not simply focus on initiation but should also flesh out the degree of egalitarianism in all sexual activities—for example, whether increased pleasure for women is an emphasis within these potentially more egalitarian scripts. Nonetheless, our results indicate that some men do not simply reproduce initiation patterns consistent with reductive cultural notions of hegemonic masculinity and emphasized femininity (Connell 1987, 1995).

There are several limitations to the current study. The analysis is based on self-reports of one member of the couple, without corresponding reports from the other member. Researchers have found that men and women offer different reports concerning household labor, child care, and sexual practices (Coley and Morris 2002; Coltrane 1996; Liu and Detels 1999; Ochs and Binik 1999; Seal 1997), and it is therefore preferable to interview both members of the couple. However, our confidence in the validity of the findings is bolstered by the fact that interviews were preceded by three weeks of detailed diary data collection, allowing for the opportunity for interviewers to discuss men's sexual behavior with diaries in-hand, offering less risk of recall bias (Graham et al. 2003). It may also be the case that men tend to over-report female initiation given interactionist pressures to "do gender" (e.g., enact masculinity) and constitute their own desirability during interviews (Anderson and Sorenson 1996; West and Fenstermaker 1995; West and Zimmerman 1987). Finally, social desirability biases may lead men to over-narrate discourses of egalitarianism. However, we designed the current study to push past reifications of gender norms by asking men not simply about present arrangements, but also about departures from traditional scripts and discrepancies between current and desired practices. By probing men about what is currently practiced and what they desire, and why, we find that new opportunities for analysis among all three levels of sexual scripts emerge.

Although this was a small, exploratory analysis, our findings suggest the need to consider that traditional norms of masculinity and femininity may not deterministically lead to desires for traditional scripts. Our results are consistent with gender studies scholars who seek to conceptualize gendered power not as cohering in a unified and singular gender role with static power relations within a sexual script, but rather to see gender relations as more fluid, dynamic, negotiated, and contested (Heywood and Dworkin 2003; Connell 2002; Messner 1997, 2002; E. Morrell 1998; R. Morrell 2001). In this study, men negotiated internally and with their partner among traditional, egalitarian, and female-dominated strategies—both current and desired forms. This analysis indicates how women's and men's everyday interactions might not simply derive from larger cultural scenarios but might actively reproduce, contest, or shift the gender order (Messner 1992). Scripts work that includes the complexity of men's and women's actual and desired gendered lives across multiple levels of the sexual script may prove more effective than past attempts that privilege any single realm at the expense of the remaining two.

Acknowledgments

This research was supported by NICHD Grant R01 HD41721 (Principal Investigator: Lucia F. O'Sullivan) and by a training grant from the National Institute of Mental Health (T32 MH19139 Behavioral Sciences Research in HIV Infection; Principal Investigator, Anke A. Ehrhardt, PhD). The authors are grateful to Michael A. Messner, Susie Hoffman, Theresa Exner, Michael Kimmel, Anke A. Ehrhardt, and Isabel Howe for their careful reads and suggestions.

References

Amaro, H. 1995. Love, sex, and power: Considering women's realities in HIV prevention. *American Psychologist* 50:437–47.

Amaro, H., and A. Raj. 2000. On the margin: Power and women's HIV risk reduction strategies. *Sex Roles* 42:723–49.

Anderson, P. B., and W. Sorensen. 1996. Male and female differences in reports of women's heterosexual initiation and aggression. *Archives of Sexual Behavior* 28, no. 3: 243–53.

Anderson, P. B., and R. Aymami. 1993. Reports of female initiation of sexual contact: Male and female differences. *Archives of Sexual Behavior* 22, no. 4: 335–43.

Blanc, A. 2001. The effect of power in sexual relationships on reproductive and sexual health: An examination of the evidence. In *Power in sexual relationships: An opening dialogue among reproductive health professionals*, 1–13. New York: Population Council.

Bordo, S. 1995. *Unbearable weight: Feminism, Western culture, and the body.* Berkeley: University of California Press.

———. 1999. *The male body: A new look at men in public and private.* New York: Farrar, Straus, and Giroux.

Brod, H. 1995. Pornography and the alienation of male sexuality. In *Men's lives,* ed. M. S. Kimmel and M. A. Messner, 393–404. Boston: Allyn and Bacon.

Byers, E. S. 1996. How well does the traditional sexual script explain sexual coercion: Review of a program of research. In *Sexual coercion in dating relationships,* ed. E. S. Byers and L. F. O'Sullivan, 7–26. New York: Haworth Press.

Campbell, C. A. 1995. Male gender roles and sexuality: Implications for women's AIDS risk and prevention. *Social Science and Medicine* 41:197–210.

———. 1999. *Women, families, and HIV/AIDS.* Cambridge: Cambridge University Press.

Coley, R. L., and J. E. Morris. 2002. Comparing father and mother reports of father involvement among low-income minority families. *Journal of Marriage and Family* 64, no. 4: 982–97.

Colllins, P. H. 1990. *Black feminist thought: Knowledge, consciousness, and the politics of empowerment.* New York: Routledge.

Coltrane, S. 1996. *Family man: Fatherhood, housework, and gender equity.* New York: Oxford University Press.

Connell, R. W. 1987. *Gender and power.* Stanford: Stanford University Press.

———. 1995. *Masculinities.* Berkeley: University of California Press.

———. 2002. *Gender: Short introductions.* New York: Polity Press.

Dowsett, G. W. 1994. Baring essentials: Science as desire. *Sexuality Research and Social Policy: Journal of NSRC* 1, no. 1: 69-82.

Dworkin, S. L. and F. L. Wachs. Forthcoming. *Size matters: Body panic, health, and consumer culture.* New York: NYU Press.

Dworkin, S. 2001. "Holding back": Negotiating a glass ceiling on women's strength. *Sociological Perspectives* 44, no. 3: 333-50.

Eck, B. 2003. Men are much harder: Gendered viewing of nude images. *Gender and Society* 17, no. 15: 691–710.

Exner, T. M., S. L. Dworkin, S. Hoffman, and A. A. Ehrhardt. 2003. Beyond the male condom: The evolution of gender-specific HIV interventions for women. *Annual Review of Sex Research*14:114–36.

Exner, T. M., P. S. Gardos, D. W. Seal, and A. A. Ehrhardt. 1997. Heterosexual men in the AIDS epidemic: The forgotten group. *AIDS and Behavior* 3:347–58.

Fracher, J., and M. S. Kimmel. 1995. Hard issues and soft spots: Counseling men about sexuality. In *Men's Lives*, ed. M. S. Kimmel and M. A. Messner, 365–74. Boston: Allyn and Bacon.

Fullilove, M. T., R. E. Fullilove, K. Haynes, and S. Gross. 1990. Black women and AIDS prevention: A view towards understanding the gender rules. *Journal of Sex Research* 27, no. 1: 47–64.

Gagnon, J. H. 1990. The explicit and implicit use of the scripting perspective in sex research. *Annual Review of Sex Research* 1:1–43.

Gómez, C. A., and B. V. Marín. 1996. Gender, culture and power: Barrier to HIV-prevention strategies for women. *Journal of Sex Research* 33, no.4:355–62.

Graham, C. A., J. A. Catania, R. Brand, T. Duong, and J. A. Canchola. 2003. Recalling sexual behavior: A methodological analysis of memory recall bias via interview using the diary as the gold standard. *Journal of Sex Research* 40, no. 4: 325–32.

Gupta, G. R. 2001. Gender, sexuality and HIV/AIDS: The what, the why and the how. *SIECUS Report* 29:6–12.

Gupta, G. R., and E. Weiss. 1993. Women's lives and sex: Implications for HIV prevention. *Culture and Medical Psychiatry* 17:399–412.

Hayden, S. 2004. 10 myths women have about men. msn.match.com/msn/article. aspx?articleid=1186.

Heywood, L., and S. L. Dworkin. 2003. *Built to win: The female athlete as cultural icon.* Minneapolis: University of Minnesota Press.

Hochschild, A. 1989. *The second shift.* New York: Avon Books.

Hynie, M., J. E. Lydon, and S. Wiener. 1998. Relational sexual scripts and women's condom use: The importance of internalized norms. *Journal of Sex Research* 35, no. 4: 370–80.

John, D., and B. Shelton. 1997. The production of gender among black and white women and men: The case of household labor. *Sex Roles* 36:171–93.

Kamen, P. 2003. *Her way: Young women remake the sexual revolution.* New York: Random House.

Klein, A. 1993. *Little big men: Bodybuilding subculture and gender construction.* New York: SUNY Press.

Kroska, A. 1997. The division of labor in the home: A review and reconceptualization. *Social Psychology Quarterly* 60:304–22.

Laumann, E. O., and J. H. Gagnon. 1995. A sociological perspective on sexual action. In *Conceiving sexuality: Approaches to sex research in a postmodern world,* ed. R. Parker and J. H. Gagnon, 183–214. New York: Routledge.

Laumann, E. O., J. H. Gagnon, R. T. Michael, and S. Michaels. 1994. *Social organization of sexuality: Sexual practices in the United States.* Chicago: University of Chicago Press.

Liu, H., and R. Detels. 1999. An approach to improve validity of responses in a sexual behavior study in a rural area of China. *AIDS and Behavior* 3, no. 3: 243–49.

Logan, T. K., J. Cole, and C. Leukefeld. 2002. Women, sex, and HIV: Social and contextual factors, meta-analysis of published interventions, and implications for practice and research. *Psychological Bulletin* 128:851–85.

Lorber, J. 1995. *Paradoxes of gender.* New Haven: Yale University Press.

Messner, M. A. 1992. *Power at play: Sports and the problem of masculinity.* Los Angeles: Houghton Mifflin Press.

———. 1993. "Changing men" and feminist politics in the United States. *Theory and Society* 22:723–37.

———. 1997. *The politics of masculinity: Men in movements.* Thousand Oaks, CA: Sage.

———. 2002. *Taking the field: Women, men, and sports.* Minneapolis: University of Minnesota Press.

Miller, T. 2001. *SportSex.* Philadelphia: Temple University Press.

Morrell, R., ed. 2001. *Changing men in Southern Africa.* Pietermaritzburg, South Africa: University of Natal Press.

Morrell, E. 1998. Of boys and men: Masculinity and gender in Southern Africa studies. *Journal of Southern African Studies* 24, no. 4: 605–30.

Ochs, E. P., and Y. M. Binik. 1999. The use of couple data to determine the reliability of self-reported sexual behavior. *Journal of Sex Research* 36, no. 4: 374–84.

Ortiz-Torres, B., S. P. Williams, and A. A. Ehrhardt. 2003. Urban women's gender scripts: Implications for HIV. *Culture, Health, and Sexuality* 5:1–17.

O'Sullivan L. F., and E. R. Allgeier. 1998. Feigning sexual desire: Consenting to unwanted sexual activity in heterosexual dating relationships. *Journal of Sex Research* 35, no. 3:234–43.

O'Sullivan, L. F., and E. S. Byers. 1992. College students' incorporation of initiator and restrictor roles in sexual dating interactions. *Journal of Sex Research* 29, no. 4: 435–46.

———. 1993. Eroding stereotypes: College women's attempts to influence reluctant male sexual partners. *Journal of Sex Research* 30, no. 3: 270–82.

———. 1996. Gender differences in responses to discrepancies in desired level of sexual intimacy. *Journal of Psychology and Human Sexuality* 8, no. 1/2: 49–67.

Plummer, K. 1982. Symbolic interactionism and sexual conduct: an emergent perspective. In *human sexual relations: Towards a redefinition of sexual politics,* ed. M. Brake, 223–44. New York: Pantheon.

Pope, H., K. Phillips, and R. Olivardia. 2000. *The Adonis complex: The secret crisis of male body obsession.* New York: Free Press.

Pringle, R. 1990. Absolute sex? Unpacking the sexuality/gender relationship. In *Rethinking sex: Social theory and sexuality research,* ed. R. W. Connell and G. W. Dowsett, 76–101. Philadelphia: Temple University Press.

Pulerwitz, J., S. L. Gortmaker, and W. DeJong. 2000. Measuring sexual relationship power in HIV/STD research. *Sex Roles* 42, no. 7/8: 637–60.

Schneider, B. E., and M. Gould. 1987. Female sexuality: Looking back into the future. In *Analyz-*

ing gender: A handbook of social science research, ed. B. B. Hess and M. M. Ferre, 120–53. Newbury Park, CA: Sage Publications.

Schwartz, P., and V. Rutter. 1998. *The gender of sexuality.* Thousand Oaks, CA : Pine Forge Press.

Seal, D. W., and A. A. Ehrhardt. 2003. Masculinity and urban men: Perceived scripts for courtship, romantic, and sexual interactions with women. *Culture Health and Sexuality* 5: 295–319.

Seal, D., L. I. Wagner-Raphael, and A. A. Ehrhardt. 2000. Sex, intimacy, and HIV: An ethnographic study of a Puerto Rican social group in New York City. *Journal of Psychology and Human Sexuality* 11, no. 4: 51–92.

Seal, D. W. 1997. Interpartner concordance of self-reported sexual behavior among college dating couples. *Journal of Sex Research* 34, no. 1:39–55.

Segal, L. 1995. *Straight sex: Rethinking the politics of pleasure.* Berkeley: University of California Press.

———. 1997. *Slow motion: Changing masculinities, changing men.* New Brunswick: Rutgers University Press.

Simon, W., and Gagnon, J. H. 1984. Sexual scripts. *Society* 22:53–60.

———. 1987. A sexual scripts approach. In *Theories of Human Sexuality*, ed. J. H. Geer and W. T. Donohue, 363–83. New York: Plenum.

Sobo, E. 1993. Inner-city women and AIDS: The psychosocial benefits of unsafe sex. In *Sexuality across the lifecourse*, ed. A. Rossi, 63–97. Chicago: University of Chicago Press.

Staiger, J. 1995. *Bad women: Regulating sexuality in early American cinema.* Minneapolis: University of Minnesota Press.

Stohs, J. H. 2000. Multicultural women's experience of household labor, conflicts, and equity. *Sex Roles* 42:339–55.

Tiefer, L. 1990. *Sex is not a natural act and other essays.* Boulder: Westview Press.

Tolman, D. L., M. I. Striepe, and T. Harmon. 2003. Gender matters: Constructing a model of adolescent sexual health. *Journal of Sex Research* 40, no. 1: 4–12.

Wagner, L. I., D. W. Seal, and A. A. Ehrhardt. 2001. Close emotional relationships with women versus men: A qualitative study of 56 heterosexual men living in an inner-city neighborhood. *Journal of Men's Studies* 9, no. 2: 243–56.

Weeks, J. 1985. *Sexuality.* New York: Routledge.

West, C., and S. Fenstermaker. 1995. Doing difference. *Gender and Society* 9, no. 1: 8–37.

West, C., and D. H. Zimmerman. 1987. Doing gender. *Gender and Society* 1, no. 2: 125–51.

Whittier, D., and D. K. Melendez. 2004. Intersubjectivity in the intrapsychic sexual scripting of gay men. *Culture, Health, and Sexuality* 6, no. 2: 131–43.

Williams, S. P., P. S. Gardos, S. Ortiz-Torres, S. Tross, and A. A. Ehrhardt. 2001. Urban women's negotiation strategies for safer sex with their male partners. *Women and Health* 33:133–48.

Wingood, G. M., and R. J. DiClemente. 2000. Application of the theory of gender and power to examine HIV-related exposures, risk factors, and effective interventions for women. *Health Education and Behavior* 27, no. 5: 539–65.

Barry D. Adam

9

Relationship Innovation in Male Couples

Sexual Conduct in many ways marked out new territory, taking the study of sexuality away from the biomedical individualism that still passes as "science" especially in HIV risk studies (Adam 1996), turning the psychoanalytic view of sexuality as primal cause on its head, and conceptualizing it as an underdetermined unfolding interaction, rather than an acting out of childhood predestination (Gagnon 1999). John Gagnon and William Simon drew our attention to sexuality as an interplay of cultural scenarios with interpersonal and intrapsychic scripts. The ways in which gay men develop enduring connections with each other happens in the social space delineated by Simon and Gagnon, as they draw on often fragmentary and conflicting social scripts, cope with sometimes hostile environments, and explore new alternatives in rapidly changing sociohistorical contexts.

 Several theorists have been struck by the new freedoms available for same-sex relationships in the late twentieth and early twenty-first centuries, and how lesbians and gay men are perhaps "condemned to freedom" in the sense of innovating relationships without many of the signposts familiar to heterosexual kinship, but are at the same time now able to avail themselves of new opportunities for constructing relationships without much of the "baggage" of patriarchy and traditional gender expectations. As Henning Bech (1997, 142) remarks:

> no societal norms stipulate that two men must live in a one-to-one relationship, nor is it dictated by financial necessity or demands to safeguard succession and continue the lineage. The partners are also from the outset equal in a specific sense, i.e., in terms of gender. No financial disparity has been brought into the relation-

Reproduced with permission from Barry Adam, "Relationship innovation in male couples," *Sexualities* 9, no. 1 (2006): 5–26. © Sage Publications, 2006, by permission of Sage Publications Ltd.

ship on the grounds of gender difference, nor any socially prescribed role alloca-tion regarding the scope or nature of work in or outside the home, or concerning emotional and sexual give-and-take. Finally the partners are not merely of the same sex and gender but are of the male one.

As a result, Bech contends, male couples construct their relationships without many of the guidelines or regulations, like monogamy, that impose upon heterosexual rela-tionships. Michel Foucault (1994, 159–60) was among the first to raise "the question of gay culture . . . a culture that invents ways of relating, types of existence, types of val-ues, types of exchanges between individuals which are really new and are neither the same as, nor superimposed on, existing cultural forms." At a time when gay and lesbian movements were still struggling to claim social space for themselves, Foucault was turn-ing his attention from the problem of sexual repression to the question of what kinds of cultural forms could emerge on these new sites. Jeffrey Weeks, Brian Heathy, and Catherine Donovan (2001, 5) typify contemporary lesbian, gay, bisexual, and transgen-dered (LGBT) relationships as sites of "positive and creative responses to social and cul-tural change, which are genuine 'experiments in living.'"

At the same time, these new freedoms and opportunities scarcely exist in a free field, but rather have come about in a particular historical context (Adam 2004). While LGBT communities have opened space for dyadic development and experimentation, many men do not find the contemporary gay scene conducive to, or supportive of, such relationships. This paper reports on a set of men who have entered into relationships of a year or more, but in a companion study of single men, many expressed a view that the commercial scene encouraged superficial sexual contact and had difficulty find-ing a more enduring partnership. In addition, at the time of the interviews reported here, same-sex relationships had become part of a public debate around legal recogni-tion, with governments and courts moving actively to include them in legal regulations. In Ontario, same-sex relationships had recently acquired legal "common-law" status, thereby conferring most of the rights and responsibilities of marriage on gay and les-bian couples. Soon afterward, an Ontario court directed municipalities to issue mar-riage licenses to same-sex couples who so choose, and the Supreme Court of Canada subsequently affirmed lower court decisions, directing the national parliament to open marriage to same-sex couples, which it did in 2005. Indeed, the marriage debate has oc-cupied so much of the public sphere that it has overshadowed recognition of the diverse forms of relationship innovation evident in these interviews.

The question of monogamy

Among the options that male couples may adopt is sexual exclusivity, but it is by no means a "given." The research literature reports divergent findings regarding rates of sex-ual non-exclusivity, no doubt related to the virtual impossibility of obtaining genuinely random samples of the gay population, varying definitions of relationship, differences in location and in the age profile of respondents, and sampling during different time periods. Though there has been a good deal of speculation on the effect of the AIDS epi-demic on the rate of sexual exclusivity among gay men, there is very little firm evidence in the area. Philip Blumstein and Pepper Schwartz's (1983, 288) largely pre-AIDS study of male couples found that 82% had been nonmonogamous sometime during their relationships. For many, this occurred in a context of "open relationships" characterized by mutually agreed nonmonogamy. They also found, however, that behavior often varied considerably from overt policy: many of the men in open relationships, in fact, acted on their agreement infrequently, while a significant number (43%) of men in relationships with no mutual understanding on non-monogamy, had additional sexual partners beyond their primary partner (see also Kurdek 1988). David Blasband and Letitia Peplau (1985, 407) also found that many men in "open" relationships did not act on this option, while as many as 74 percent of men in "closed" relationships "had nevertheless had sex with at least one other person." Joseph Harry's (1984, 116) study found that "approximately 90 percent of the respondents in relationships of greater than five years' duration reveal some non-exclusiveness compared to about 66 percent of relationships of less than a year's duration." Letitia Peplau and Susan Cochran (1988) report, from their study of 128 university-based men in southern California, that 41% were currently in an "ongoing 'romantic/sexual relationship.'" Of these men, 54% said they had had sex with someone other than their primary partner during the past two months (212). Peplau, Cochran, and Mays's (1997) study of African American gay couples (N=325 individuals) reported a comparable rate of nonmonogamy with slightly more than half indicating an open relationship, but 65% indicating that they had, in fact, had nonmonogamous sex since their primary relationships began. In a study of British gay men (Hickson et al 1994:198), 43.7% of relationships (N=110) were reported to be "closed"; 56.3% "open." They found that "at least one regular sexual partner plus other partners is the most common sexual relationships configuration." Danielle Julien, Élise Chartrand and Jean Bégin (1996) report that 62% of the 41 Québécois couples that they interviewed reported having had sex with outsiders. And Paul Appleby, Lynn Miller, and Sadina Rothspan (1999, 87) found among the couples they interviewed that, in 35 percent, one partner reported sex outside the relationship and in 43 percent, both partners did.

Nonmonogamy is not an indicator of relationship failure among gay men. Indeed, Lawrence Kurdek and J. Patrick Schmitt (1988, 230) found that "partners in open and closed gay relationships were equivalent in intimacy, security, satisfaction, and commitment," a finding confirmed by Blasband and Peplau (1985), Myers et al. (1999), and Yip (1997). Blumstein and Schwartz (1983, 274), as well as Kurdek (1991) and Harry (1984), even found an association between sexual openness and longevity among gay men's relationship. As well, Hickson et al. (1994:200) found that among closed relationships, monogamy is "not a restrictive rule but an active choice" and that "men view their sexual exclusivity as contingent, not necessary." There are indirect indications that consistency of mutual understanding rather than openness or closedness per se are related to relationship satisfaction and perhaps to safer sex practice as well (Julien, Chartrand, and Bégin 1996; Wagner, Remien and Carballo-Diéguez 2000).

The vast research literature emerging from HIV studies confirms a diverse range of "regular" and "casual" partners typical of gay men, but presents them almost exclusively in terms of descriptive statistics, allowing little insight into how these relationships work. Just how gay men manage sexual pluralism and negotiate safety is largely an unresearched area. Blasband and Peplau (1985, 407) recommend in their conclusion that "future research might profitably investigate the processes by which couples negotiate agreements in their relationships." My experience in teaching a course in gay and lesbian studies to undergraduates is that young gay men are themselves very often puzzled about how relationships might happen, vacillating among different models that they try to apply to their lives by piecing together various discourses about relationship and marriage found in the larger culture. Matt Mutchler's (2000) study of gay and bisexual youth in Los Angeles revealed their personal struggles around often contradictory sexual and relationship discourses. Romance scripts that prescribe a relationship trajectory of dating, falling in love, sexual exclusivity, and lifelong commitment often run up against male-gendered scripts of sex as adventure, pleasure, and exploration without commitment. Both of these scripts need to be sorted through in everyday life in relation to safe-sex prescriptions. In addition, the structure of the contemporary gay world often means that young gay men have little direct contact with older men in couples and so have little insight into how their relationships work. As Terry Trussler, Paul Perchal, and Andrew Barker (2000, 300) found in interviewing young men in Vancouver, "the men in our study talk about desire for both monogamous relationships and casual sex at the same time as if it is the central problem of their lives."

Research design

This paper is part of a larger project on the implications of different sexual and relationship modes for vulnerability to HIV transmission (Adam et al. 2003), and draws its evidence particularly from responses to the question, "Do you have a mutual understanding regarding sex outside your relationship?" The study reported here relies on interviews with 70 men in same-sex relationships of a year or more who were selected to represent a wide diversity in relationship length, HIV status, ethnocultural background, age, social class, and educational level. They were recruited by advertising in the gay press, making appeals at meetings of gay organizations, and through the distribution of recruitment leaflets at gay bars and special events in the Ontario cities of Toronto and Windsor. This paper focuses on the formation of sexual relationships with primary and secondary partners.

Genuinely random samples of gay and bisexual men are virtually unachievable; the numbers reported here refer to the participants in this study and cannot be generalized to gay men as a whole. The duration of their relationships ranged from one year (the minimum required for participation in the study) to 23 years (median = 3). For 50 of the 70 study participants, we interviewed one member of a couple; for the other 20, both partners are included in the sample. Since processes of coming to agreement were themselves at issue in this research, we did not want to limit our sample only to couples characterized by high levels of mutual agreement, a possible characteristic of partners in which both members were willing to agree to participate in research. Forty-six were currently living together; the remainder (22) lived apart due to the demands of work or schooling, or by mutual agreement. (Two gave no response.) All of those living apart, however, considered themselves to be in a couple relationship. The participants ranged in age from 20 to 60 years old (mean = 34 years old). The sample was relatively well-educated: 12 had a graduate degree and 33 had completed university. Of the remaining men, 3 had not finished high school, 8 had finished high school, and 14 had some university or college education. Although 16 earned more than $60,000 (Canadian dollars) per year, 13 earned less than $10,000. Another 12 earned between $10,000–19,999;

15 earned between $20,000–39,999; and 14 earned between $40,000–59,999. Most of the participants (42) had tested negative for HIV; of these, 5 had a partner who was HIV-positive. The remaining men were HIV-positive (26), 15 of whom had HIV-negative partners. One did not report his sero-status and one had not been tested. The first-named ethnicities given by study respondents were British (20), French (3), other European (13), Asian (16), Latin American (7), African or Afro-Caribbean (5), Canadian or American (3), Jewish (2), and aboriginal (1). The men were recruited from Toronto (65) as well as Windsor (5) areas.

After being briefed on the overall objectives of the study and signing a consent form, study participants were then interviewed, typically for an hour and a half. Interviews were transcribed and organized using QSR N6 qualitative research software. In the interview quotations below, the tag line identifies the respondent's occupation, age, ethnicity, and relationship length. For men with more than one ethnic identity, the first-mentioned ethnocultural identification is listed.

Building trust in new relationships

Eighteen (26%) of the men who participated in this study reported a commitment to sexually exclusive monogamy as an organizing principle of their relationship, a proportion comparable to previous studies reported in the research literature. What is most striking about this set of men is the relative newness of their relationships. While some men report monogamy in relationships of five, seven, and even seventeen years in duration, most of the monogamous relationships have not yet reached the three-year mark. Several expressed adherence to a clear and simple principle:

> We don't have sex outside the relationship. We both sort of share the same value system. [social worker, 28, Irish, 1 yr]

> We don't have it [sex outside of the relationship]. That's our understanding. If there was any cheating, it's over. [accountant, 33, German, 3 yr]

Monogamy, however, was rarely simply a taken-for-granted presumption. Gay men often enter relationships with a sense of exploring uncharted territory, assessing options, and determining whether monogamy is the preferable course of action. Without clear social norms governing the way that relationships are "supposed" to unfold, men in couples often feel their way toward an arrangement, sometimes by weighing a series of considerations and negotiating a mutual understanding, but just as often through uncovering or running up against conflicting assumptions that have to be sorted through or ironed out.

Monogamy, of course, ties into romantic discourses prevalent in the environing heterosexual culture that provide widely esteemed models about how relationships are "supposed" to happen. As this man remarks:

> He said that if we were going to have a relationship, it's only based on the both of us, and just the both of us. . . . [and] I realized that this was somebody that I would like to spend the rest of my life with. [unemployed, 27, South Asian, 7 yr]

Another makes explicit reference to his parents as a model for conducting his own relationship with a male partner:

> It's monogamous and it's a trust thing and it's off limits. You know my parents are married for 35, I don't know, 40 years or whatever and my mom still looks at guys and my dad still looks at women and it just, it's off limits [banker, 40, English, 2.5 yr]

A few search out monogamy particularly in reaction to what is perceived to be the ephemerality of sexual relationships prevalent in the gay world, and think of monogamy as a refuge in which to protect a valuable, but potentially fragile, relationship with another man:

> I've seen a lot of the gay life and same sex relationships and for the most part I was always dissatisfied with ever wanting to have a relationship and I never did for years because I thought men are promiscuous; they want to have fun. [professional, 33, British, 2 yr]

Others point to the example of friends whose relationships dissolved, ostensibly because of their sexual connections outside of the relationship, as a reason for practicing monogamy themselves. These men, then, seek a durable monogamy, referring at times to models prevalent in the wider (heterosexual) culture or to a desire for protection from temptation offered by the gay scene.

Monogamy often shows itself in the speech of study participants as an accomplishment, rather than a presumption, and as a provisional rule-of-thumb subject to revisiting. Monogamy is often counterposed to an active consideration of alternatives in the narratives of men in relationships:

> I'm more wary of someone who says "I want monogamy" on day one, because well . . . How can you know that? and we've just met. And I've found through experience that there are people who talk a lot about monogamy and they are the very ones that fool around. Even in our relationship we joke a lot about you know, "Oh, he's cute, let's take him home." Now whether or not any of us would even do that . . . [unemployed, 32, French Canadian, 1.5 yr]

Understandings about monogamy appear to come, at times, with "back-up" qualifiers ready to deal with the occasion when practice may violate principle—that is, "If anything did happen . . .":

> We had established that we were in a monogamous relationship. . . . If anything did happen, that we would talk about it. We discussed what we both were looking for in a relationship and we did want to continue a long term relationship that was monogamous, just the two of us. [student, 21, Latin American, 1.5 yr]

Sexual exclusivity carries with it implications for vulnerability to HIV transmission. It impacts deciding whether condoms remain necessary inside the relationship, or conversely, whether lack of condom use is to be read as a sign of monogamy, of "negotiated safety," or of irresponsibility. (The implications for HIV risk-taking are discussed in greater depth elsewhere (Adam et al. 2003).)

For men in same-sex relationships, monogamy appears to be a question that is not often resolved with any finality. Several couples reported extensive and ongoing discussions about it. In some, it is a source of tension:

> We have both agreed that we want monogamy, it's a monogamous one [relationship] and that's the way it is. . . . I made the mistake of mentioning a fantasy of a third person and we had a fight and he left. [disability pensioner, 44, British, 1.5 yr]

> Monogamy is a difficult thing especially in the gay community so I was kind of pushing towards having an open relationship but he said . . . that wasn't what he was into, and he's very much the person that I want to spend the rest of my life with, so we agreed to be monogamous. I think I'm comfortable with monogamy now. . . . My partner's pretty insistent about monogamy so it was a challenge at the beginning, but it's fine now. [nurse, 32, German, 6 yr]

A partner in the longest-term monogamous relationship in this study says:

> [There] really shouldn't be any sex outside the relationship. A couple of times we had some arguments and I'd say, "You know, I don't . . . want this. Maybe we should just be friends and we'll go out and do our own thing," but it's never gone beyond that. [teacher, 49, European, 17 yr]

Monogamy, as a firmly held principle for organizing relationships, appears to be more common among men in early stages of relationship development, younger men who refer to heterosexual models, and men whose formative years were passed in cultures with no, or limited, autonomous gay worlds. These latter men, like younger men, tend to draw their blueprints for successful relationships from heterosexual models they grew up with, and from the social prescriptions promoted in the larger culture. Alternatively, some men experience the sexual consumerism evident in the commercial bar-and-bath scene as antithetic to relationships of any duration, and opt for monogamy as a means of providing secure space for developing a sense of couplehood. Still, the narratives of the participants in this study frequently communicate a sense of monogamy as something provisional, tentative, and subject to change, even among those who nevertheless seek to construct a firm and enduring monogamous relationship for themselves. The voices documented in this study point toward monogamy as a ground for building trust in a relationship, while nonmonogamy appears to arise more in couples in relationships of greater duration, who feel confident of their relationship, and are thus ready to deal with "risks" posed by sexual interaction with other men.

Monogamy discourses and practices

Another sector of the men in this study express a view of monogamy in contention: as an ideal to which practice should aspire, as a uncomfortable pretence, or an unnecessary constraint. Some men acknowledge a gap between practice and the monogamy regime, either in themselves, in their partners, or in both. It is a gap that might be managed through silence. Putting words to deeds requires reassessments: is the relationship about to give way, or is monogamy itself the problem? Some understand sex with others in terms of "slips," "cheating," or exceptions, thereby honoring monogamy in the breach; others reach toward an understanding (made explicit in couples dealt with in the next section of this paper) where recreational sex is separated from emotional commitment to their partner.

In some instances, the gap between presumption and practice is managed with a "don't ask, don't tell" policy where a sexual contact outside the relationship may be thought of as exceptional or experimental. Some settle into a longer term pattern of "open secrets," tacit acknowledgments, or implicit silences where an arrangement may be intuited or perceived-to-be without having been spoken:

> I'm actually trying to work out staying monogamous with him as much as I can. . . . I would like to be monogamous. I have sex outside of the relationship even though I haven't told him. . . . I sort of understood that he doesn't want to know anything about . . . any details. [white-collar, 37, Eastern European, 7 yr]

> Some of my encounters I feel funny about because I do have a partner and my partner doesn't know about them. I mean, he suspects but he doesn't know about them. . . . but I also believe that gay men living together 18 years—and there's lots of them in this city—they're all out playing. I could take you to a bathhouse in Toronto and half the bathhouse, half the people in the bathhouse have partners and we all chuckle. We all know. [retired, 40s, British, 18 yr]

Nonmonogamous practices may be grounded on a distinction between recreational sex and love, an opposition that often later becomes explicit in male couples:

> I told you I have been in the sauna twice. I have had a lot of fun, but it's just only something occasional. I mean I don't have to tell my boyfriend, "Well, I had occasional sex today," so I don't mention it. . . . I don't feel guilty. I feel great with myself because I still love him. Yeah with my partner it's involved with feelings, feelings, but in the sauna it is just sex. [unemployed, 32, Latin American, 3 yr]

For couples working with implicit or explicit monogamy rules, recognition of divergent practices may occasion conflict:

> Yes, if I don't shove it in his face, I can get away with blue murder. If any of his friends see me and report back to him then I'm a dead man. . . . He leaves a couple days here and there on business or whatever and he is so paranoid that I'm going to bring home a thousand men and have a group orgy that he refuses and/or lies when he's coming back so it minimizes the amount of time I would have to arrange such a perverted onslaught of hedonism. [artist, 34, African American, 3 yr]

Many men in couple relationships, however, soon question the "rules" that designate "wronged" or "betrayed" parties. Aware of alternative arrangements widespread in gay communities, the monogamy question may be reopened, though not without some trepidation:

> I caught him cheating on me, so like a child I went and cheated on him, and after that's said and done as far as I know, we haven't done anything more. . . . It's in the process where he's been trying to talk me into having an open relationship. I don't want to smother him and make it so that we have to break up in order that he can explore, you know, that side . . . but again, I'm concerned, you know that . . . he'll bump into someone, that they'll have a great time, and suddenly I'll be on the back burner. [disability pensioner, 32, Canadian, n.d.]

Agreeing about disclosure may be one method to manage the potential risk posed by sexual connection outside the relationship:

> What happened was early in the relationship, when I was slipping, I would wait two or three, four weeks and say, "You know where I was that night? You know a couple weeks ago? Well I kind of slipped that night," and I tried to slough it off because it had time behind it, and I'm out of the shame now and . . . so we got clear that we needed to . . . make it clear [i.e. disclose] within 24 hours. [blue-collar, 36, Canadian, 8 yr]

In the following instance, monogamy is redefined. Partner A remarked simply:

> We trust each other and, you know, we decided we're not going to go out with anybody else.[technician, 37, South Asian, 1 yr]

Partner B revealed, however, that he was already married. From his viewpoint:

> She [wife] knows him [partner A] and she loves him, so basically, I would say that I'm a lucky person because I've got two people. If you're going to get into this relationship, it's going to be just both of us and I explained this to him, what my life is all about and he told me about his, and he said, "Okay, if this is going to be a long term relationship it has to follow these kind of things. It's just going to be like that." We accepted each other's rules and regulations and that's fine. [manager, 30s, Southern European, 1 yr]

The potential gap between monogamy ideals and practices sets up a semiotic snare (Adam et al. 2000; Sobo 1995) that may leave a partner vulnerable to HIV transmission:

> I think my partner assumes like, monogamy, which I also do. I know that the reason why, say, we're having unprotected sex is because he guarantees to me that . . . we're in a monogamous relationship. . . . I hate to see all that trust that he put on me. It's like, but if I fool around with someone else, you know, I'm obviously not going to say anything. [student, 25, Southeast Asian, 2 yr]

The following participant described a lengthy odyssey of relationship renegotiation that explicitly recognized the risk posed by the monogamy semiotic snare:

> I read a really good article in the *Village Voice* that talked about two couples. Both started HIV-negative and one couple ended up HIV-positive over time. . . . So one couple's relationship was, if you fool around outside the relationship, the relationship's over, and the other couple's attitude was if you fool around outside the relationship, we'll talk about it and deal with it. So it was the couple that said if you fool around the relationship it's over, they're the ones that became HIV-positive. Because I think the best condoms like the best relationships occasionally leak. And I think that if you have an agreement at home that you don't want to know if the relationship has leaked, the only thing that happens is you don't get told. [designer, 49, Jewish, 20 yr]

Monogamy then has simplicity on its side and it purports to defend the couple from outside threats, but at the same time, many men chafe at its limitations, and the potential gap between words and deeds poses other dangers in the form of HIV transmission.

Adventure and experimentation

The solution to the "monogamy problem" for many couples is to have sex together with a third man. In this study, in fact, more couples had experience with three-way relationships than with sexual exclusivity. Several men in monogamous relationships remarked that the three-way was under active consideration but had not yet been tried:

> What I want to do is I want this relationship to grow using monogamy, and then perhaps branching out and experimenting. A year from now, I might be [ready], six months from now, I might be. But right now, I think the relationship is too, too young, to negotiate on it. [manager, 41, South Asian, 1 yr]

This respondent describes monogamy as a habit that he and his partner fell into, but at the same time they find the possibility of a three-way intriguing:

> It's sort of been an ongoing dialogue, that's just increased over time, that if we were to have sex outside the relationship that it would be the both of us with a third. [white-collar, 30s, southeast Asian, 21/2 yr]

Three-ways are premised on agreement in the couple concerning whom to introduce into the relationship. One man expressed regret that the three-way route was, therefore, not open to him and his partner:

> I know that he has seen other people. He knows that I see other people. And like I said, there's no discussion about it. . . . We don't share the same taste for people. People that he likes, I don't like. People that I like, he doesn't like. So finding a third person will be extremely difficult. Ideally I would love to have a monogamous relationship and [be] totally exclusive. [banker, 36, Latin American, 5 yr]

Many more have taken the next step. This is the experience of a couple who had tried it once:

> We had the one experience and we thought about maybe trying it again some-time in the future, when we're both ready and for something different, you know, because it could be interesting. It could be quite erotic bringing a third person. . . . When I met him, it was like, "You better be good with me. You better not cheat," and this kind of thing and "It's just a monogamous relationship" and "I think that open relationships are disgusting." Now that we've known each other long enough . . . we wanted to experiment . . . because I think he's less scared than he used to be. [student, 20s, German, 2 yr]

Another describes a special occasion when the first step toward a third was taken:

> We were monogamous just with each other, probably 6 or 7 years, something like that. . . . He was a friend of ours and it was . . . [partner's] birthday and we went out for dinner and he must have asked [partner] what he wants for his birthday and he sort of said, "You." So we ended up having sex with him. We had sort of walked around it, we tiptoed around it, without really discussing it. I was attracted to this person as well so it wasn't really an issue for me. [designer, 49, Jewish, 20 yr]

Not every couple finds three-way experiments to be satisfactory. More than one decided to discontinue after one or several tries with a third man:

> We're both monogamous. It's since we started out. We just really don't want to be with other people and it's just a question of trust. . . . We've tried, we've experimented with other people but we can't just, we can't bear the thought of the other person being with another person. [teacher, 30, Southeast Asian, 4 yr]

> We just really didn't like having people in our bed. So we ended up . . . trying the bathhouse scene and didn't really work for us. . . . Not saying that it will never happen again but until the relationship is where we want it to be with each other, having sex with other people is not going to happen. [unemployed, 39, English, 3 yr]

This couple chose to experiment while on vacation. Being in another country provided a safe space in which to try out openness. Afterwards, they decided the emotional toll was too great:

> We just thought we'll call it a kind of vacation. . . . We'll come back and we'll talk about being monogamous again and maybe we'll just use the sleeping-with-the-other-guy-thing—do that while we're on vacation. The repercussions . . . it didn't work out; it took us quite a while to become committed to each other because of the excitement and the mood of sex with strangers. [blue-collar, 36, Canadian, 8 yr]

And another couple simply lost interest:

When we were doing the threesome . . . that's when I said, "Look, let's just have an open relationship and if you want to have sex with other people that's fine, cause I'm not enjoying this any more." He said, "Okay," and never did. We never had another threesome. [small business owner, 32, Scottish, 9 yr]

Some couples arrive at a satisfactory accommodation of additional partners into the relationship, usually by developing a set of (sometimes tacit) understandings that curb the destabilizing potential of a third man. Others find the wiser course of action to be withdrawal from triple relationships because relationship with a third man proves to be competitive with the sexual and emotional focus of the primary couple.

Two plus one

Couples in this study who found three-way relationships satisfying typically did not form triads of three equal members. Third parties are usually temporary, secondary relationships, and rely (as do the "open" relationships described in the next section) on managing a distinction between recreational sex and sex with love. Three-ways provide for additional sexual opportunities in a manner that can be read as open and "above board" by both partners; only secret, individual sex is defined as threatening to the relationship:

Yes, the only rule we have it that you're not allowed to bring anybody home unless if I'm going to have a threesome. . . . We make clear that this person can become a sexual partner or even a friend, we make it clear that what we want to have is just to have fun but we are not looking for a boyfriend. [white-collar, 36, Spanish, 4 yr]

We have one rule: three way or no way. That way you're not cheating on me—I'm not cheating on you—if we're doing anything, we're doing it together. It's something we both agree on that—because [partner] is 29, young and cute, and I'm 49 and find people who like the old one and not the young one, or somebody who likes the young one and not the old one, and so we talk and if it's not a mutual attraction all the way around then forget it. [retired, 49, French, 2.5 yr] [confirmed by partner, unemployed, 29, American, 2.5 yr]

We can't have sexual partners without the other being part of it. We draw a clear distinction between something that's just sex, and fun, versus what we have in the rest of our relationship, which is pretty emotionally involved. [professional, 28, Southern European, 3 yr]

Thus, making a three-way work out successfully may require careful communication:

If we mutually agree that we like them, fine, then we take them home. We always communicate how we're doing and how we're feeling. Even during the act. . . . We will never have sex with them again even if we really had a good time because . . . We know that that can cause problems because we've seen it with other couples. [professional, 31, Eastern European, 3 yr]

Distinguishing primary
from secondary relationships

Without ready-made rules or models with which to construct relationships outside of the monogamy regime, gay men in this section have nevertheless arrived at workable arrangements that include ongoing, emotionally committed relationships and short-term sexual adventures. While these relationships might be termed "open," none are anarchic free-for-alls. All have a set of tacit and/or explicit understandings that differentiate the primary partner from others and typically communicate priority for the partner in house. At the same time, these are not relationships put together in a way that mirrors heterosexual marriage or depend on the entire discursive complex that defines the monogamy regime. Rather, they are premised on the uniquely gay social institutions developed in gay and lesbian communities most common in urban environments of advanced, industrial nations. They partake of the quick-sex opportunities available in these environments without compromising romantic commitment. Whether sex outside the couple happens together or individually, open arrangements found themselves on particularly male discourses distinguishing sex-as-play from sex-as-love:

> Emotionally monogamous, absolutely. The fact that I have sex outside the relationship and he may or may not have sex outside the relationship in absolutely no way takes away from that fact that we are completely and totally committed to each other and totally in love and we will spend the rest of our lives together and we both know it. . . . I consider sex outside the relationship to be completely, 100% recreational. I know for a fact that he has had a few experiences outside . . . the relationship. . . . I would always either go to the other person's place or to a public place like a bathhouse or something like that. In the two threesomes, they were both mutual friends. [lawyer, 41, Irish, 3 yr]

The bifurcation between love and play, however, is not automatic, guaranteed, or always easy in practice. Each of the men in this study discussed "rules," whether tacit or overt, that helped realize the distinction in everyday life and communicate priority to the primary partner. What arises from these narratives is a remarkable lack of commonality concerning what those rules are to be. It appears that having a game plan is what counts, more than which game plan it is. Disclosure, for example, may be a ground rule for one relationship:

> If the other person does know that I'm going to have sex with someone else and he's not involved, as long as he knows about it, then those are kind of our ground rules. But I have to say 90% of the time we have sex with others together. When we have encounters with people it's just for the sex. . . . We both know that it's not going to lead to anything else. [professional, 38, Southern European, 22 yr]

As R Jeffrey Ringer (2001, 147) remarks, disclosure "prevents the announcement of an outside-sexual episode from being perceived as a threat to the relationship":

Well, if we go and sleep with somebody else, it's our motto that we have to tell each other. We just have one rule. [manager, 28, British, 2 yr]

On the other hand, not saying much at all works for other couples (examples above). Many couples observe rules to assure that the introduction of a guest into the home does not displace the other partner in his own space, by keeping the third man out of the couple's bed or out of the home altogether:

I have no problem with my partner . . . going to the tubs; [he] goes about once a month, and I have no problem with that. We have a deal though that we do not have sexual experiences with other people at our home. . . . The answer is NO to someone coming over here and no to having an affair with someone. . . . I don't want to start seeing in the mailbox, like, love letters from . . . someone because that's going to create problems. [disability pensioner, 43, Irish, 22 yr]

Alternatively, each partner is expected to sleep at home, and not at the home of another man:

We just have to come home at the end of the evening; we don't stay overnight. I'm not a jealous type, nor is my partner and I'm really not afraid that he's going to run off with somebody so he can go out and have sex. In fact recently, since I've been immobile here, he's been very good at taking care of me, but I've encouraged him to go out and seek sex, and go to the baths. . . . This fellow that comes over for a three-way now comes over for a two-way because I don't participate so I mean I still encourage him to come over and have sex with my partner, I mean that's not an issue. We trust one another. [manager, 48, British, 13 yr]

These respondents succinctly articulate two other common principles: no second dates; sex out of town is okay. No sleepovers either at our house or his house:

No second dates. (Interviewer: And how did you come to that policy?) *Queer As Folk*[1]. . . . I go on tournaments and what not. You're supposed to be promiscuous out of town aren't you? [disability pensioner, 42, Canadian, 2 yr]

You can't take anyone home, that's an explicit rule. Some of the implicit rules are . . . if one person is unhappy with who the other person is seeing, then pretty much they shouldn't see him. I think we try, although I think I'm better at this than he is, try not to schedule visits with other people when both of us are free. [lawyer, 37, Northern European, 5 yr]

When I was away . . . he went to the bathhouse and he had sex with three guys. If I'm away for a couple weeks then it's understandable. [accountant, 35, East Asian, 5 yr]

One couple had arrived at a point that carries the bifurcation to its extreme:

We never bring anybody home. We always come home. We never stay over any-where. When we've had threesomes it often ended up that one of us would leave because we were unhappy. And the other two would continue and that would cause problems so we just decided not to do it. I mean, we're very, we're very committed to each other. We just don't have sex together. So um, we understand that we're not looking to replace each other. If I find that I start feeling too affectionate to them I'll stop having sex with them. [instructor, 46, Jewish, 10 yr]

Consistent with the existing research literature on gay couples, it is noteworthy as well that arrangements that grant explicit permission to partners for sex outside the pri-mary relationships may not necessarily be acted on. Perhaps more important than what these arrangements say about sex or monogamy is how they communicate respect for, and affirm, the masculine autonomy of each partner to *choose* his own course of action, and to *choose* to prioritize his primary partner even in the context of a wealth of other options:

We try not to set limits on each other. We told each other the times we have [had outside sex], yeah. Well, we've talked jokingly about having a three-way. We have specified that it would be okay to go to a bathhouse in town. Now, would I person-ally feel comfortable going to a bathhouse? The answer is no. I don't like bath-houses. [economist, 30, African American, 1 yr]

If we would like to have sex with somebody else you can, but the fact that we have permission makes it no fun anyway, so [*laughs*]. . . . If I don't care that he's doing it then it's not fun for him. [small business owner, 32, Scottish, 9 yr]

[Partner is] the type of person that when we first got together, I knew very well that if I told him not to have sex with other people, that would be the first thing he would do, because he's the type of person, you just can't tell him what to do. [designer, 49, Jewish, 20 yr]

Generally, such arrangements appear to work well over the long term, and perhaps help explain the correlation between longevity and openness in male couples:

It's very open. I mean we've had sex singularly, we've had sex together, and again, I go back to what I said earlier, sex is sex, it has nothing to do with the relationship. And basically that's how my whole relationship is built. If he goes out and has sex with a guy, and they're getting their rocks off, he's not going to go home with him and they're not going to start up a relationship. [professional, 60, British, 13 yr]

Of course the open relationship is not risk-free. The distinction between primary and secondary partner can implode, and when it does, a sense of anguish and betrayal can come back:

We were seeing one fellow over an extended period of time, who became a friend of ours and . . . I guess it was like I was out on the beach collecting shells and I didn't notice the tide was coming in. It was up around my knees before I noticed that [partner] and [third man] had fallen in love. I wasn't quite prepared for that, because it wasn't supposed to work that way. . . . I didn't mind him having sex with others. I wasn't thrilled with him having love relationships with other people. I felt very threatened. [designer, 49, Jewish, 20 yr]

Finally, study participants were asked, as part of the interview process, about sex with women. The vast majority responded that women were not part of their sex lives, or had not been for a long time. One man was married at the same time as he had a male partner, and another had had a lengthy episodic relationship with a woman at the same time as he was having a relationship with a male partner (neither of whom he lived with). Two others considered sex with women a possibility contained within a general agreement sanctioning sex outside the couple relationship, but did not report having acted on it. Finally two other men remarked that they avoided sex with women because women do not observe the opposition between sex-as-play and sex-as-love and would therefore pose a risk to their current relationship.

Living apart together

A few of the couples in this study did not live together. For those who had never lived together, most of the issues raised by the monogamy question had not come up. Their approach was essentially indistinguishable from single men:

I guess we just leave it up to your own discretion. [unemployed, 45, British, 1 yr]

We don't live together. . . . We can go our separate ways and meet somebody. [waiter, 42, Afro-Caribbean, 1 yr]

Others experienced separation due to work or schooling. In these instances, "out of town" rules typically came into play:

My lover's 2000 miles away. We had this understanding that we're separated for more than a month, and so he has needs, I have needs. As long as we keep it safe, you know we're allowed to do it . . . At first we weren't sure, you know, how that would work for us, but then after we got into it, we realized, we didn't feel jealousy, we were fine with it, we were both participating. It was fine, actually it was exciting. We enjoyed it. . . . [Partner] and I have gotten to a point in our relationship where we're so committed and we've been through so much together that our relationship has gone beyond the jealousy and the sexual, it's very deep you know so, we honestly do not feel threatened by anyone. He's my soul mate, he's my best friend and that's why those things don't bother me [professional, 42, Latin American, 4 yr]

Discourses of romance, autonomy, and adventure

Among the men in this study, monogamy scripts appeared most commonly among younger men and/or men new to gay relationships, and among men whose formative years have been in cultures with limited or absent autonomous gay worlds. A policy of sexual exclusivity prevailed especially among men in the "honeymoon" phase of their relationship—that is, in the first two years. Sexual exclusivity provided a context for foundation-building in relationships, and time for the development of mutual trust. Some couples found monogamy worked for them over the long term, but was often contested in many others that treated it as a passing phase, developed "exemptions," or struggled to arrive at new accommodations.

What is not easy to discern from these interviews is the degree to which these tendencies are shaped by age or generation. Older men and men in longer relationships are more likely to have been part of the Stonewall generation influenced by gay liberation and by public debates questioning monogamy, while younger men have been more exposed to the struggle for marital rights. Whether this means that today's younger men will adhere more strongly to monogamous ideals as they age, than have today's older generation, remains to be seen. What is perhaps noteworthy from these interviews is how little the couples in this study referred explicitly to public debates around gay marriage as relevant or influential in the ways in which they conduct their own relationships.

The social space provided by gay worlds in advanced, industrial nations such as Canada has allowed for the creation of indigenous sexual cultures among lesbians and gay men that have taken their own autonomous path of development apart from (if still a part of) the courtship and family practices of the heterosexual hegemony. Gay sexual cultures, especially in major cities, provide opportunities for sexual self-expression and for communication networks among homosexually-interested men, permitting the emergence of innovative arrangements in sexual and emotional connections among men. It must be noted, all the same, that this study reports on men who have successfully formed a couple relationship; many men experience gay sexual culture as an efficient delivery system for "fast food" sex but express varying degrees of distress or loneliness at not being able to find a deeper emotional connection with another man.

Relationship innovation occurs at the nexus of several different discursive strands. The men in this study do not want to give up the promise of romantic love, and many expressed impassioned commitments to the other men in their lives. But in an all-male environment, they also show allegiance to particularly masculine discourses of autonomy and adventurism, insisting on a right to sexual self-determination and attraction to the sense of affirmation and pleasure experienced with other men.

The men in this study identified one other as their partner, a man with whom most (but not all) lived and who provided emotional security and a home base. From this center, many ventured out together or separately to include other men, but often with safeguards in place to ensure the primacy of partner and household. Secondary sexual relationships often matured into extended friendship networks. Says this respondent:

> In terms of the overall picture, it's been quite positive in that we've met some great people all over the place through sex and in many cases those relationships are no longer sexual relationships and they just developed into really good friendships. [lawyer, 37, Northern European, 5 yr]

It is noteworthy that while a discussion around "polyamory" continues in the lesbian press, the only male study participant to raise this idea in interview did so a result of having had a lesbian therapist. It may be that men conducting simultaneous relationships of similar emotional and sexual quality have not adopted polyamory as a concept, or may not present themselves for a study of this type because they do not think of themselves as having a "couple" relationship. In terms of this study, the two-plus-one model of relationship was widespread, while polyamory among men appeared to be fleeting. Clearly there is still research to be done that focuses specifically on triple (as opposed to couple) relationships.

The vitality of relationship innovation among gay men is such that the wave of relationship recognition in advanced, industrial nations such as Canada is likely to be just a beginning, not an end, in taking account of the diversity of relationships entered into by gay men. While legal recognition is an indispensable step in providing the tools necessary for the well-being of male and female couples, its extension out of heterosexual models will not include the wealth of relationship innovation already under way.

Acknowledgments

This paper results from a larger study on HIV risk-management funded by Health Canada. Co-investigators: Winston Husbands, James Murray, and John Maxwell, with the assistance of Elmer Bagares and Danielle Layman-Pleet. I would like to thank Adam Green, Mary Bernstein, and VoonChin Phua for their comments. The views expressed here are solely those of the author and do not represent the views or policy of Health Canada.

Note

1. *Queer as Folk* (U.S. version) has an episode where two lead characters determine the ground rules of sex outside their relationships.

References

Adam, B. D. 2000. Age preferences among gay and bisexual men. *GLQ* 6, no. 3: 413–34.
———. 2004. Care, intimacy, and same-sex partnership in the 21st century. *Current Sociology* 52, no. 2: 265–79.
———. 2006. Infectious behaviour: Imputing subjectivity to HIV transmission. *Social Theory and Health* 4:168–79.
Adam, B. D., and A. Sears.1996. *Experiencing HIV.* New York: Columbia University Press.
Adam, B. D., A. Sears, and E. Glenn Schellenberg. 2000. Accounting for unsafe sex. *Journal of Sex Research* 37, no. 1: 259–71.
Adam, B. D., W. Husbands, J. Murray, and J. Maxwell. 2003. *Renewing HIV prevention for gay and bisexual Men.* Toronto: AIDS Committee of Toronto.
Appleby, P., L. Miller, and S. Rothspan. 1999. The paradox of trust for male couples. *Personal Relationships* 6:81–93.
Bartos, M., J. McLeod, and P. Nott. 1993. *Meanings of sex between men.* Canberra: Australian Government Press.
Bech, H. 1997. *When men meet.* Chicago: University of Chicago Press.

Blasband, D. and Peplau, L. 1985. Sexual exclusivity versus openness in gay couples. *Archives of Sexual Behavior* 14, no. 5: 395–412.

Blumstein, P., and P. Schwartz. 1983. *American couples*. New York: Morrow.

Connell, R. W., M. D. Davis, and G. W. Dowsett. 1993. A bastard of a life. *Australian and New Zealand Journal of Sociology* 29, no. 1: 112–35.

De Cecco, J. P., ed. 1988. Gay relationships. New York: Haworth.

Foucault, M. 1994. *Ethics: Subjectivity and truth.* Vol. 1 of *The essential works of Michel Foucault, 1954–1984.* Ed. P. Rabinow. London: Allen Lane.

Gagnon, J. H. 1999. Sexual conduct. *Sexualities* 2, no. 1: 115–26.

Harry, J. 1984. *Gay couples.* New York: Praeger.

Hickson, F., P. Davies, A. Hunt, P. Weatherburn, T. McManus, and A. Coxon. 1994. Maintenance of open gay relationships. In *The family and HIV*, ed. R. Bor and J. Elford. London: Cassell.

Julien, D., É. Chartrand, and J. Bégin. 1996. Male couples' dyadic adjustment and the use of safer sex within and outside of primary relationships. *Journal of Family Psychology* 10, no. 1:89–96.

Kurdek, L. 1988. Relationship quality of gay and lesbian cohabiting couples. *Journal of Homosexuality* 15:93–118.

———. 1991a. Correlates of relationship satisfaction in cohabiting gay and lesbian couples. *Journal of Personality and Social Psychology* 61, no. 6: 910–22.

———. 1991b. Sexuality in homosexual and heterosexual couples. In *Sexuality in close relationships*, ed. K. McKinney and S. Sprecher. Hillsdale, NJ: Lawrence Erlbaum.

Kurdek, L., and J. P. Schmitt. 1988. Relationship quality of gay men in closed or open relationships. In De Cecco 1988.

LaSala, M. 2000. Gay male couples. *Journal of Homosexuality* 39, no. 2: 47–71.

Mutchler, M. 2000. Sexual scripts, masculinity tensions, and HIV among gay youth. In *Gay masculinities*, ed. P. M. Nardi. London: Sage.

Myers, T., D. Allman, L. Calzavara, K. Morrison, R. Marchand, and C. Major. 1999. Gay and bisexual men's sexual partnerships and variations in risk behaviour. *Canadian Journal of Human Sexuality* 8, no. 2: 115–26.

Peplau, L. and S. Cochran. 1988. Value orientations in the intimate relationships of gay men. In De Cecco 1988.

Peplau, L., S. Cochran, and V. Mays. 1997. A national survey of the intimate relationships of African American lesbians and gay men. In *Ethnic and cultural diversity among lesbians and gay men*, ed. B. Greene. Thousand Oaks, CA: Sage.

Plummer, K. 1982. *Documents of Life.* London: Allen and Unwin.

Plummer, K. 1995. *Telling sexual stories.* London: Routledge.

Ringer, R. J. 2001. Constituting nonmonogamies. In *Queer families, queer politics.* New York: Columbia University Press.

Smith, R. and R. Brown. 1997. The impact of social support on gay male couples. *Journal of Homosexuality* 33, no. 2: 39–61.

Sobo, E. 1995. *Choosing unsafe sex.* Philadelphia: University of Pennsylvania Press.

Trussler, T., P. Perchal, and A. Barker. 2000. Between what is said and what is done. *Psychology, Health and Medicine* 5, no. 3: 295–306.

Wagner, G., R. Remien, and A. Carballo-Diéguez. 2000. Prevalence of extradyadic sex in male couples of mixed HIV status and its relationship to psychological distress and relationship quality. *Journal of Homosexuality* 39, no. 2: 31–46.

Weeks, J., B. Heathy, and C. Donovan. 2001. *Same sex intimacies.* London: Routledge.

Yip, A. K. T. 1997. Gay male Christian couples and sexual exclusivity. *Sociology* 31, no. 2: 289–306.

David Wyatt Seal, Lucia F. O'Sullivan,
and Anke A. Ehrhardt

10

Miscommunications and Misinterpretations

Men's Scripts about Sexual Communication and Unwanted Sex in Interactions with Women

Introduction

The wealth of research addressing men's sexual coercion of women has been generated almost entirely within the last two decades. In one of the earliest and most influential studies, Koss and colleagues (1987) found that 15% of the women in a national sample of U.S. college students reported an experience that constituted rape and 4% of the college men surveyed indicated that they had perpetrated rape. Studies examining sexual coercion more broadly (i.e., use of verbal or physical means to obtain sexual activity without consent) find much higher rates among women. For example, in the landmark 1997 National Institute of Justice study, 56.5% of a national sample of college women reported having experienced some form of sexual coercion (Fisher et al. 2000). Rates are even higher in community samples, especially among poor or immigrant populations (Frye et al. 2001).

Sexual scripts and coercion of women by men

Scripts are cognitive schema characterizing a particular sequence of events, such as going out on a first date or going to a movie. They refer to the organization of mutually shared conventions that allow two or more actors to participate in a complete act involving mutual dependence (Gagnon and Simon 1973; Simon and Gagnon 1986). Sexual scripts are theorized to play a key role in how we understand and enact sexual behavior (Littleton and Axsom 2003). The literature on scripts has focused on a normative or "traditional" sexual script for heterosexual interactions that positions men as initiators of sexual activity and women as the reactors or "gatekeepers," the latter responsible for controlling the pace of sexual intimacy between a couple (Brooks 1995; Byers 1996; Simon and Gagnon 1986; Tiefer 1995). Men are expected to pursue ever-higher levels of sexual intimacy, even to the point of using pressure or coercion to counter a partner's resistance (Littleton and Axsom 2003).

Although clearly limited in the extent to which these stereotyped roles characterize many heterosexual interactions, the traditional sexual script has provided a conceptual framework for much of the research in the field. Despite a wide range of operational definitions, such as "sexual aggression," "rape," "coercion," and "unwanted sex," researchers have established that a relatively high proportion of women across samples have had at least one lifetime experience of sexual coercion by men (see Spitzberg 1999 for a review). Studies investigating men's experiences of sexual coercion by women generally indicate that such experiences are far less prevalent than women's experiences of coercion by men, and unlikely to result in some of the more severe emotional and psychological consequences that women often experience (O'Sullivan, Byers, and Finkelman 1988). Thus, in this respect, the body of literature on sexual coercion appears to support this aspect of the traditional script for heterosexual relationships.

Yet evidence suggests that men do not regularly pressure women into sex despite typically higher levels of sexual interest and initiation compared to women (Byers and Lewis 1988). That is, most men stop their sexual advances when requested to do so by a woman (Byers and Lewis 1988; Byers 1988; Byers and Wilson 1985). The majority of men and women reported that most of the sexual behavior they were involved in (both on recent dates and during their lifetimes) was wanted, not coerced (Hannon et al. 1995), calling for a closer scrutiny of the ways in which scripts incorporate sexual coercion.

Studies of miscommunication about sexual interest and consent

There has been a recent growth of research focused on the components of sexual coercion, as well as on the interactions that conform in some but not all respects to sexual coercion. Researchers have documented that some people at times do engage in unwanted sexual activity without their partners knowing that the activity was unwanted, complicating the issue of sexual consent. This is especially likely in relationships where sexual "precedence" has been established. Having a shared sexual history is often viewed as preempting one's rights to validly resist or refuse future sexual access (Monson, Langhinrichsen-Rohling, and Binderup 2000; Shotland and Goodstein 1992). Women report acquiescing to male partners' demands to avoid negative consequences, such as rejection or fights, or to maintain the relationship (Basile 1999; Livingston et al. 2004). Moreover, research indicates that most unwanted sexual behavior is preceded by some type of *wanted* sex behavior (Hannon et al. 1985; Wade and Critelli 1998), further complicating the demarcations between coercive and noncoercive elements in the traditional sexual script. Sawyer and colleagues (1993) found that the majority of men and nearly 40% of women agreed that willing participation in lower levels of intimacy (e.g., oral sex, mutual masturbation) comprised consent for higher levels (e.g., vaginal intercourse). Delineating wanted from unwanted sex in a given interaction becomes difficult if individuals do not communicate clearly or attend carefully to their partners' communication.

Other studies have shown that both women and men sometimes freely consent to, and feign interest in, unwanted sex. Such behavior is not in response to partner demands, but attributed to other reasons, such as wanting to promote intimacy or reduce relationship tension (O'Sullivan and Allgeier 1998). "Token resistance" is another form of sexual miscommunication that involves refusing a sexual advance despite interest and intention to engage in the activity (Muehlenhard and Rodgers 1998; Osman 2003; Walker 1997). Although the use of token resistance is generally rated positively in established relationships (O'Sullivan and Allgeier 1994), its use can potentially lead to conflictual sexual situations, especially when mediated by rigid cultural norms (Hall et al. 2000). Men who think that women fake disinterest may come to believe that women prefer men who are dominant and can turn a "no" into a "yes" (Berger et al. 1986). Krahé and colleagues (2000) found a strong link between men's beliefs that women engage in token resistance and reported aggression against female partners. In contrast, "sexual teasing" is a form of miscommunication that involves expressing interest in engaging in sex with a potential partner when the communicator has no real intention of having sex (Meston and O'Sullivan 2005). This form of provocation is intended to frustrate or cause tension in the target. Although both women and men report engaging in sexual teasing (Meston and O'Sullivan 2005), women are far more likely to report this behavior than are men. Sexual teasing also may be linked to coercion. College women who more strongly endorsed a belief that it is improper for women to "lead men on" were more likely to indicate that date rape in some scenarios was justified (Muehlenhard and MacNaughton 1988).

Misinterpreting a partner's sexual cues

Misinterpreting a partner's sexual cues can have a range of consequences—some of them dire. Many men report receiving mixed messages and being confused about their partners' desires (Wade and Critelli 1998), a situation that can lead to unwanted and possibly nonconsensual sexual activity. Abbey (1982) hypothesized that males' traditional responsibility for initiating sexual activities may cause them to optimistically interpret ambiguous information as evidence of sexual attraction and responsivity. Men's readiness to interpret ambiguous cues as indicative of a woman's sexual interest is well-documented (Abbey 1987; Abbey and Harnish 1995; Harnish, Abbey, and DeBono 1990; Willan and Pollard 2003).

Being the recipient of unwanted or coercive sexual advances is not limited to women. Men also report being pressured into sexual relations by women, and often acquiesce to the pressure to demonstrate or preserve their masculinity (Krahé, Scheinberger-Olwig, and Bieneck 2003a; Muehlenhard and Cook 1988; Struckman-Johnson 1988). Further, evidence suggests that both women and men initiate and refuse sex and may behave coercively when refusal occurs (Krahé, Waizenhofer, and Moller 2003b; O'Sullivan and Byers 1993; Struckman-Johnson, Struckman-Johnson, and Anderson 2003).

Conceptual framework for understanding sexual communication

Collectively, these studies suggest that many conflictual sexual interactions between men and women may result from miscommunication and misinterpretation of receptivity cues rather than outright sexual coercion. Although the traditional sexual script positions men as the initiators and aggressors in heterosexual interactions, more recent studies suggest that egalitarian scripts are becoming normative, with greater convergence in men's and women's roles in Western societies (Alexis 1999; Schwartz and Rutter 1998; Seal and Ehrhardt 2003; Seal, Wagner, and Ehrhardt 2000). Although researchers have noted the importance of developmental (Laumann et al. 1994; Simon, Eder, and Evans 1992) and cultural (Ortiz-Torres, Serrano-Garcia, and Torres-Burgos 2000; Seal and Ehrhardt 2003; Seal et al. 2000; Wyatt 1994) influences on the individual expression of scripts, most research has involved predominantly white, middle-class, college-educated, or young married samples (Metts and Spitzberg 1996; Ortiz-Torres et al. 2000).

The societal transition in normative scripts creates the potential for conflict. Traditional heterosexual scripts clearly delineated shared expectations about men's and women's roles in sexual interactions (Gagnon and Simon 1973; Simon and Gagnon 1986). As nontraditional scripts become more normative, men and women have to create new, less familiar, and untested scripts. The creation of new scripts increases the likelihood that partners will not share common expectations about their shared sexual experiences. The possibility of deliberate miscommunication of one's intentions and willingness creates further confusion about the expected or "scripted" course of events.

The current study

Data reported in this article were collected as part of a larger study that explored heterosexual scripts among an ethnically diverse sample of urban men (Seal and Ehrhardt 2003). Specifically, we report on men's narratives about (1) their experiences with situations in which they thought that their partner was sexually interested, only to realize that they had misperceived their partner's availability cues; (2) their unwanted sexual experiences with women; and (3) their experiences within a steady relationship when one partner wanted to have sex but the other did not. A narrative approach posits that humans are natural storytellers and that their stories integrate people's construction of events occurring over time. A primary aim of the narrative approach is to explore people's stories for the insights they provide into the identity of the storyteller and the culture in which the storyteller lives (Murray 1997).

Method

Participants

One hundred heterosexually active men were recruited men from STD/health clinics and from social networks in inner-city neighborhoods in New York City to participate in a semi-structured qualitative individual elicitation interview that explored the men's perceptions of the scripts guiding courtship, romantic, and sexual interactions with women. Study participants were recruited from geographic areas of the city characterized by an elevated number of AIDS cases, increased rates of drug use and poverty, and decreased social and health services.

We recruited a sample that was heterogeneous with respect to age, race/ethnicity, education, and income (see Table 1). Over three-fourths of the men self-identified as African American/Black or Latino. The median education was some post-high school

Table 1. Sample characteristics (N=100)

Recruitment Sites:
    STD or health clinic   48%
    Community group   52%
Age:
    18–23   37%
    24–28   34%
    29+   29%
Race/Ethnicity:
    Black/African American   58%
    Latino   21%
    White   13%
    Other   8%
Country of Origin:
    United States   63%
    Trinidad/Jamaica   30%
    Other   7%
Income:
    Zero   26%
    1–10,000   15%
    10,001–20,000   31%
    20,001–30,000   16%
    30,000+   12%
Occupation:
    Unemployed   33%
    Full-time student   10%
    Lower socioeconomic status   29%
    Higher socioeconomic status   28%
Education:
    Less than high school diploma   15%
    High school diploma   23%
    Vocational or technical degree   12%
    Some college   30%
    BA/BS   13%
    Post BA/BS   7%
Relationship Status:
    Not currently involved in a steady relationship   32%
    Unmarried, involved in a steady relationship   46%
    Engaged   5%
    Legal or common-law marriage   17%
Number of Children:
    Zero   63%
    One   19%
    Two   10%
    Three or more   8%

vocational training or college. The majority of the sample (72%) had an annual income of $20,000 or less, and a third reported current unemployment. Most of the men were born in the United States, Trinidad, or Jamaica. About two-thirds of the men were involved in some type of steady relationship. Slightly over a third of the men reported having children.

Recruitment and interview procedures

In the STD/health clinic setting, men were individually approached in the waiting room and told about the study. Interested participants were immediately enrolled and interviewed in a private clinic room. Non-clinic participants were recruited through various key contacts who introduced the researchers to their personal social network (e.g., a soccer team). An overview of the study was presented to the members of each social network as a group, and individual participation was solicited. Interested participants were scheduled for interviews at private locations chosen by the participants. In both settings, most individuals approached were willing to participate. Each participant received $10 for the interview. No individual identifiers were collected to ensure participant anonymity.

Interviews were conducted by an ethnically diverse (Puerto Rican, Trinidadian, and Caucasian) research team experienced in the administration of qualitative interviews related to sexual behavior and HIV. All interviewers received extensive training in the interview protocol prior to conducting the fieldwork. Interviews were monitored by a senior researcher experienced with qualitative methodology to ensure protocol adherence. The interview team met regularly to discuss field issues and problems with protocol fidelity.

In this article, we report on three topics of interest:

Misperceived sex. Tell me about situations in which you thought a woman wanted to have sex, but you realized at some point that you had misread her desire for sex.

Unwanted sex. Tell me about situations in which you had sex with a woman, but really didn't want to.

Non-mutual sex. Within your current (last) steady relationship, tell me about times when one partner wanted to have sex but the other didn't.

For each topic, follow-up probes were used to elicit additional details about men's experiences, including the interpersonal scripts guiding the interaction, the nature of the man's relationship to his female partner, and his affective and behavioral responses to the situation.

Data analysis procedures

Interviews were audiotaped and transcribed. We analyzed men's narratives for themes pertinent to these *a priori* questions, as well as other themes that emerged in the data:

1. What were the situational and relational contexts in which these three different types of conflictual sexual interactions with women occurred?
2. What were men's perceptions of the interpersonal scripts guiding these interactions in terms of who initiated them, controlled the pace, and set the limits?
3. What were men's affective and behavioral reactions to these experiences?

Principles of Grounded Theory Analysis (Corbin and Strauss 1990; Strauss and Corbin 1994) guided our analyses. We initially examined the transcripts to identify primary coding categories as well as a range of themes present within each category. Identified coding categories and themes were organized into a formal codebook, and illustrative quotes relevant to these themes were extracted. Next, transcripts were content-coded. New themes that did not appear to fit into the original codebook were discussed by the coding team and modifications were made when deemed appropriate. When suggested by associations, overlap, or diversions in the data, thematic categories were refined, merged, or subdivided.

Summaries were initially rated by two members of the data analysis team. Interrater discrepancies were discussed until consensus about the appropriate code was obtained. Decision trails were noted and documented to assure that interpretations were supported by the data (Hall and Stevens 1991; Sandelowski 1986). This process was repeated until the study raters consistently achieved 80% or greater concordance, after which the summaries were rated by a single evaluator. Ten percent of the remaining summaries were randomly selected for independent evaluation by the two raters. The overall concordance rate was .84 across the interviews that were evaluated by both raters. Most of the discrepancies involved the omission of a minor theme by one of the coders rather than disagreement about a major theme.

Results

Below, we present key themes that were identified in the men's narratives about the three types of conflictual sexual interactions with women.

Misperceived cues: I thought she wanted to have sex with me

Separate from experiences with non-mutual sexual desire within ongoing sexual relationships, most of the men reported situations in which they believed that their partner wanted to have sex, only to realize later in the sexual sequence that they had misinterpreted their partner's availability cues. These situations typically occurred with casual or newer sexual partners.

Women are very complicated when it comes to sex. Many men indicated that women's sexual availability cues could be difficult to interpret: "Women are very complicated when it comes to sex. Sometimes they are just being friendly. That doesn't mean they want to go to bed with you." Another man said that sometimes he will want to have sex with a woman, but her desires are "hard to figure out," which makes "me shy and makes me pull back" as he does not "know what to do."

Was she just being friendly? Men recognized that a woman's friendliness did not necessarily mean that she wanted to have sex with him. However, they expressed difficulty distinguishing between friendliness and sexual availability cues. One man commented about a woman at his work who he described as "flirtatious": "Some people are just that way . . . A lot of people are very flirtatious and sometimes you misread a flirtatious gesture as a very sexually directed thing, even though it usually isn't sexual." Another man asserted that he could tell when a woman was sexually available: "I can just see right in their eyes, and by the way they keep coming closer and closer to you and they start giggling." However, he then added, "It seems very simple, but sometimes I am wrong. She could just want to be your friend."

Some men reported that they have never misinterpreted a woman's sexual availability cues as "I never initiate unless I'm 100% sure it's okay, and then sometimes I still don't initiate." Another man said, "I don't push nobody into nothing. I wait until they tell me they want to do it. I never really kissed nobody first; they always kiss me first."

Letting me know she is not interested. Men indicated that women used a range of strategies to express sexual disinterest. Common rejection strategies included saying "no," physically pushing men away, and "giving you stories that doesn't [sic] add up to the situation, giving you excuses." Most men reported acceptance of their partner's rejection. One individual related, "One night the opportunity presented itself and I made a move . . . just kinda very gently and very nicely, and was rebuffed. I kind of put my tail between my legs and walked away—I felt like an idiot." Another man commented that "it's no big deal" if a woman doesn't want to have sex: "There's supposedly seven women to one man in this world so I'm looking for those seven women and for those (men) who aren't using their seven, I'm after them for leftovers."

A woman's "no" should be respected, but does her "no" mean "yes"? Most men believed that a woman's "no" should be respected: "(You can) either get blown away by it or you can take it in stride." Another man observed that most women do not play "hard-to-get"; rather they are just not sure if they want to have sex. Thus, he said that when a woman once changed her mind about having sex with him, "I stopped myself. I calmed myself down. She said she didn't want it to lead to sex, you know, she's not that type of person. I just stopped and we continued on from there." However, men also believed that "women [could be] kinda funny. They'll tell you 'yes' and they mean 'no.' Or, they will tell you 'no' and they mean 'yes.'" Another man said, "That's a tricky question 'cause sometimes a woman keeps saying 'no' and she means 'yes' . . . If they say 'no' while they are moving closer to you, they really want you to continue. Body language tells you what they really mean."

In these situations, some men "just ask. Because I don't want nobody say I forced myself on them, and they come out and say sex harassment or rape. So I just ask you. If you tell me no, well, I leave you there." Other men reported physical persistence:

This is what I'd do if a girl says "no." I'll be like alright. I might chill for a few seconds, and then I'll start kissing on her neck. You do what you got to do to get in her pants or whatever. And then if she says "no" again, I'll keep trying. I won't like jump over them. I just keep trying, then she just be with it [in the mood]. Some girls will be like "no." They be like, "I said no." So you just be like "alright"... You win some and you lose some.

Men also reported situations in which they believed that their partner "was just playing games with me . . . She's telling me she would like to sleep with me and she only waiting for me to make that move and stuff like that. And when I do make that move, she reject me." Another man related a specific situation involving a "cute, hot" partner: "She was totally aggressive, totally going nuts on me, everything but penetrating her vagina . . . all of a sudden, she was like, no, no, no, what do you think is going on here?" About the incident, he added: "Golly, we're running around like a bunch of horses, buck naked in my apartment. I just kinda figured."

Although some men took rejection passively, other men expressed frustration and anger with women who they believed had deliberately led them on. One man related an experience he had with a female friend with whom he was watching an x-rated video. She "acted like she wanted to have sex . . . and was giving me signals all along." Then, he stated, "When we there, she suddenly said 'I didn't come here for this.' . . . The whole thing almost turned ugly." He said he accused the woman of being "frigid," "made of rock," and a "teaser." Another man indicated that when a woman is "leading you to believe that she want it and you reach that point, boom, 'no,' it's a difficult feeling . . . you do get blue balls, a painful thing."

But what if I have already penetrated her? Men were divided about whether a woman's "no" was still valid if he and his partner were naked, had engaged in oral sex, or had initiated penetrative vaginal sex. Some men believed that "the point of no return is for kids. If you're an adult, you have to have some kind of control." Another man indicated that "I've actually gotten all naked and they tell me no and I act like OK, you know. I don't have to force her, you know, to give me some. However, other men felt differently. Some men felt that being naked is "the point of no return." Another man felt that the point where a woman should not refuse to have sex is "when she sees the man has an erection." Another man said:

It was awkward. I just felt like she was playing me, like she was leading me on, and then when I wanted to have sex, she was like, no, so I was thrown off. She undid my pants, and she was doing things down there [performing oral sex], and she was undoing her clothes, and I was like alright, and then when it came time to do things, she was like, no, and then she got mad and jumped up and put her stuff on. I was like, what did I do? She just said she didn't want to have sex at that time.

A few men expressed confusion as to whether it is rape if a man has his penis inside of a woman's vagina and she tells him to stop, but he thrusts his penis once or twice more before withdrawing. Or, the woman tells him to stop when he is ready to ejaculate and it is too late to stop the ejaculation. One man wondered whether he had committed rape by today's definitions:

I learned after a while. But you know a lot of times I probably did rape if you follow what they're calling it [rape] now. I don't know why they say it was rape. They never used to call it rape. Back then everybody used to keep it quiet. But now I just think different today. You figure the signals she giving you [means] go ahead and then things happen and then she come and say she ain't [wanting sex]. It's very embarrassing. It's degrading.

Other men's comments were suggestive of coercion as well, although they did not perceive their actions to be coercive. One man said that there were times when he was "really kind of persistent and into pressure" even though it "wasn't exactly her preference." However, he spontaneously added that he never felt like "I raped her." Another man asserted that "I haven't misread a woman yet. I guess I've been lucky." However, he went on to say, "I have done it sometimes when the female didn't really want to do it. She just laid there."

Men's unwanted sexual situations

Forty of the one hundred men reported unwanted sexual experiences with women. In general, these interactions occurred with casual partners and could be characterized as female-initiated and controlled. Typically, the men had not anticipated that sex would occur in the specific situation, nor did they expect to develop close emotional relationships with the women. The men's reasons for labeling these sexual interactions as unwanted could be grouped into two basic categories: partner characteristic concerns and relationship concerns.

Partner characteristic concerns. The most frequently cited reasons for the men's experiences of unwanted sex focused on negative partner characteristics. Many men reported discomfort with sexually aggressive women. One man said, "I have had a woman who was absolutely ridiculous. She would invite you over and you come over and she would start taking your clothes off." He said he would resist, but she would tell him "you're going to have to fuck me right now . . . You're going to have to do it now. You're either going to do that or you're gonna fight." Similarly, some men reported discomfort with women who were very assertive when initiating condom use. One man related a story about a woman who he knew casually. He said that she drove him to a highway and parked. Then, she pulled a condom out of her bag. Although the respondent said that he knew what she wanted, he asked "What is that for?" She said, "I want you to put this on." The man replied "No, I don't want to," to which his partner said, "Why not?" The respondent then told her, "Because I don't like the way you just turned yourself out, pulling out a condom. You a ho? Are you a prostitute? What the hell is wrong with you?" The man then said that his partner's action of pulling out a condom indicated that she had obviously thought ahead about having sex, which showed that she was "dirty."

A few men reported unwanted sexual experiences with older women, some of whom were mothers of friends. One participant said when he was 16 and "having sex a lot," he'd had sex with a friend's mother: "I felt, damn, I hang out with this guy and I had sex with his mother . . . I felt bad that I had sex with one of my friend's mothers and that fucked me up." Other men reported discomfort with women who could not be sexually satisfied: "I felt like I was tiny in her because she was very open. Making love to her was like making love to the air. So it was like, damn she was a real slut. That's about the only one . . . I couldn't satisfy her." Another man related an incident with a woman he met in a club one night, later going to her house. He said that "she was making the scene like I was really gonna enjoy the sex." However, he added that when "I finally put my penis in her vagina, her vagina was so big, and so I had to like fight with it. That kinda turned me off."

Other undesirable partner characteristics that made sexual interactions unwanted included lack of physical attraction ("it looks good on the outside, but when they take off the clothes it's like a different thing"), concern about contracting a sexually transmitted infection from a partner who they did not know well or who was deemed "easy" or "promiscuous," and who had poor hygiene:

> We was getting physical. I wanted it at that point, but after we got naked, the stench gave me a turn off. At that point, I realized I don't want it. I guess she still believe that I wanted it, but at that point no is no. I didn't want to have anything to do with it.

Relationship concerns. Unwanted sex narratives related to relationship concerns typically occurred with women toward whom the men held positive feelings, but with whom they did not want steady relationships. Sex in these contexts represented relational commitment and was not wanted as a result. Some men feared that having sex in these situations would ruin their friendships with these women. A man who'd had sex with a friend said:

> It was an uncomfortable circumstance because after you have to face yourself. It was like a guilty feeling because it was like I forced myself to do it and then I had to turn around and try to explain to that person that it was just a little need, but it wasn't that great of a need. She wanted it more. I just did it with her to satisfy her. It wasn't nothing. It was her. It was a strange feeling. It was hard to explain it to her because you know you're messing with that other person's feelings and you really don't know the kind of feeling that they have for you at that time and then you have to go and try and change that.

A few unwanted sexual interactions involved primary female partners, and focused on a female partner's desire to use a condom against the male partner's preference ("We hadn't used a condom in awhile and all of the sudden she want me to use a condom. So I just said 'forget it,' and rolled over and went to sleep") and the male partner's lack of sexual desire due to fatigue or general lack of interest ("There have been times when I said I'm sorry I'm not in the mood 'cause I don't feel like doing nothing. I just want to get some sleep").

Men's reactions to unwanted sexual interactions with women. In about a third of men's unwanted sexual narratives, the men reported that sex did not occur, whereas in the remaining narratives, men reported that sex occurred. Most frequently men reported that they were unable to resist their partner's aggressive sexual advances. One man related a sexual encounter with a woman that he described as "intimidating" and "uncomfortable." The participant said that, at age 18, a supervisor of his at work began staring at him and making direct sexual comments toward him. He said she intimidated him and he tried to avoid her. However, he stated that one day, when he went to pick up his paycheck from her, she locked the door behind him and began fondling him. Eventually, they had sex. The participant indicated that he continued to have sex with this woman in order to get her to stop pressuring him.

A few men said they continued with unwanted sexual relations when breaking up with a sexual partner presented a possibility of danger: "I had some women threaten me. I had some women put guns in my face talking about I ain't gonna be with no other women if I ain't gonna be with them."

In other cases, men reported that they were either too drunk or too high to resist their partner's advances: "If I really didn't want to, I wouldn't do it . . . [However, when] you're in that state [drunk or high], sometimes you don't think when you're high, you just do it [have sex]." Physical arousal was another reason men said they could not resist unwanted sexual opportunities: "I was weak. I didn't really mean 'yeah.' I really meant 'no.' My heart says 'no,' but other parts of my body were saying 'yes.' Just weak. I'd call that a weakness."

Men also reported having unwanted sexual relations in order to avoid rejecting a woman's sexual interest and possibly hurting her feelings. One man described situations where he was at home with a woman, feeling comfortable, watching a video, and the woman gave him signals of her sexual interest (e.g., "Asking me to turn out the lights so she can see the video better; touching me"). He described these signals as "very obvious where she's letting me know that she's making herself available and then I could move with her or at least try to initiate sex with her." The participant said that sometimes these relationships could be "uncomfortable," especially if he did not desire a relationship with the woman. He admitted that sometimes he would have sex with the woman "simply because the opportunity is there." At other times, this participant said he has sex because "if they (women) have gone that far and really do want sex, then maybe you should just go ahead and do it with them . . . Unlike men who are used to being rejected, I think women take rejection much harder than men." He later added that he does not like to reject women and "if I do, I try to do it in a way that's very gentle. I don't just say I'm not interested in you. I'll just say 'Oh, I'm really tired tonight' . . . I'll make up an excuse."

A few men reported having sex in response to gender norms that dictate that men should pursue all sexual opportunities: "I didn't really want to fuck her, but sometimes a man's got to do what a man's got to do." Other men indicated an obligation to have sex due to the receipt of gifts or money:

> A lot of older females figure if they buy you this and that, it's like you on call at any time. "I [the woman] call when I want it. I want you [the man] to be there, right then." . . . The gifts they was giving me, my mother couldn't afford to give me. It was legal. You're not going to refuse it if somebody give you a million dollars. If somebody buys you a nice shirt, you're not going to refuse it. You're crazy if you do, especially if you are poor. So you go and have sex with her even if you don't really feel like it.

Some men reported having sex due to peer pressure. One man related an interaction that he had with an older woman he knew casually from the neighborhood who asked him to buy her a beer. "She was giving me a signal and I obviously was trying to ignore her because I wasn't interested." However, he said his friends at the bar chided him for being "cheap" and urged him to buy her a beer. So, he bought her a beer, and then she asked him to take her home as she was drunk. At her apartment, the woman begged him to stay, so he "just had to get on top of her and do it, but I didn't really want to do it" as "I wasn't comfortable with her." He later commented, "I won't say that she's a whore or that she does it for money, prostitution or anything, but she slept with a couple of guys already I know." In retrospect, he thinks the woman and his friends had the whole episode planned: "It's like they knew what was happening and I was the only dumbass that didn't know what was going on."

When unwanted sex is post-sex regret. In a few cases, men's narratives about their unwanted sexual experiences reflected post-sex regret about the encounter. One man described a casual encounter that he had experienced as follows:

> I regret that. I wish I hadn't done it. . . It was kinda a waste. I just think I just was kinda bowled over because she was really attractive. But I didn't really like the person . . . Even when I see her [now], I don't want to talk to her. It's just, "Oh, Jesus Fuckin' Christ, here she comes."

Another man expressed post-sex concern about being exposed to a sexually transmitted infection. He said that when he was having sex with his partner, she was screaming and talking dirty, which both excited and scared him. However, he soon discovered that she was a very "loose, easy, rough, and promiscuous girl," and he regretted not using a condom for fear of getting a disease: "I began to think, God knows who the fuck has been in this thing [her vagina], and I haven't used a condom."

Men explain never having experienced unwanted sexual interactions with women. Among men who reported that they have never experienced unwanted sex, some reported that "it just had never happened." Other men reported that sex is never unwanted because they "always want sex." Another man reflected:

> I'll never say I've slept with a woman and I didn't wanna do it because I did it. I knew I wanted to do it, but probably when after thinking . . . Most guys have sex with a woman, you wanted to have sex with her. Nobody forced you into that situation. You went ahead and did what you had to do so I think that kinda remorse—to think that "oh man, I shouldn't have done that," that's bullshit. Don't do something and then think about the consequences after you commit the crime.

Non-mutual sexual desire

In the area of steady sexual relationships, most of the men shared experiences when they had been aroused but their partner did not desire sex. One man explained:

My girlfriend complains that every time I come over here we have to have sex. The relationship is young. We now started to discover each other. Of course I want sex every time. Sometimes she wants to dance or cuddle, but I'd rather have sex. We're young now. We can have sex. Let's have sex. When I'm old, we can sit and talk.

Many men also reported that their partner sometimes desired sex when they did not: "I don't consider myself a very sexual person or wanting sex all the time 'cause I usually don't. She wants to have sex all the time and she loves it. She just couldn't get enough." Few men reported that sexual desire was always mutual: "It's a normal thing. When it's time to go to bed, before we go to sleep, it's time to have sex. That's already understood by both of us. She's always in the mood and so am I." Frequently cited reasons for a lack of mutual sexual desire included "not being in the mood" or being "too tired." Other reasons included a general lack of sexual interest, a preference for cuddling, or being too busy or preoccupied.

I'll get you in the mood anyway. In most narratives, men said the partner desiring sex would try to stimulate his/her partner subtly through physical contact (e.g., massage or kisses) designed to get the disinterested partner in the mood:

I will just initiate. I will just start touching her, holding her. I start kissing her neck or going down to the spots I know is gonna get her aroused. I just get her hot. I will take off her panties and her shirt. She gets in the mood and doesn't seem to mind. After that, we just have sex . . . Other times, she is hungry and sometimes she will get on top of me kind of thing and sort of initiate. Just kinda bumping and grinding kind of thing. Really kissing me very deeply. Just really progressing, touching all over the body, not just erogenous zones. Slowly, but surely, I might as well be having sex.

In many cases, men indicated that people feel "obligated to have sex because you're in a relationship . . . If you really have love for a person and want that person to be happy, you try to fulfill all the needs of that person."

In situations in which a person's attempt to get his/her partner in the mood was unsuccessful, men said the most common response from the aroused partner was to give up:

If you want it [sex] so bad, you'll try to do some things like kissing and fondling to coax this person into giving it up. But if they don't want to do it, they don't want to do it, and there's not much you can do. You'll have to wait to the next time or when they're ready.

A partner's failure to become sexually aroused usually was not associated with negative feelings: "Sometimes I won't be feeling good and she'll want it, and since I'm not feeling good, I won't. And sometimes she's tired, so she won't. It doesn't create any problems."

I won't take "no" for an answer. In about a third of the narratives, more conflictual strategies were reported, including the use of pressure and persistence. Typically, these narratives involved male sexual desire accompanied by female resistance:

> After I watch one or two pornos, I'm a little bit horny. I tell her get over here. I want you right now . . . I might let her slide during her period, but if she has a headache, here's two aspirin, god damn it, let's go!

In many cases, men reported that their partner would acquiesce to their sexual demands:

> There's not supposed to be negotiations for sex. If I have to negotiate for sex, I don't want it. If I want my sex and my girl is there, then I go get some. If she's asleep and I wake her up in a nice way, then we get into it. She turn over and we get tight. She comes and she proceeds to make me aroused and then we have sex. It's just like that.

Men reporting more coercive responses often indicated that if a partner did not acquiesce to their sexual demands, then they would threaten to have sex with a different partner: "She don't have a choice because all I care about is me. If she won't have sex with me when I want, I will call my other girl who will satisfy my desires." On a related note, women often were overtly blamed for their male partner's infidelity: "Her lack of desire makes me go out there and do things I don't want to do [cheat]." Alternatively, some men would demand that their partner perform other sexual activities: "If she's not interested in [vaginal] sex, I'll settle for oral sex . . . Got to compromise. You know, I'd be like, 'Come on baby, you do this for me, oral sex, and I'll leave you alone.'"

Frustration, rejection, anger, and disappointment. Conflictual resolutions were likely to be accompanied by feelings of frustration, rejection, anger, and disappointment:

> It pisses me off when she doesn't get aroused. I can't make love to her when she's not in the mood. I don't want her to be a dead fuck. I don't want to just be fucking a log, you know, dead. I want her to participate, hug, you know, feel aroused, moan, groan. Her on top of me. Me on top of her. I like her to express her sexual desires as well as I'm expressing my sexual desire toward her. So I just get mad and leave if she doesn't want to have sex.

Other men said failure to respond to a partner's sexual overtures suggested infidelity: "There may have been times when I was physically tired. The last thing I wanted to do was have sex, but women just don't want to hear that shit. She thinks you been messing with someone."

Discussion

We investigated men's narratives about occasions in which they had miscommunicated or misinterpreted sexual interest in interactions with women. An urban sample of ethnically diverse men provided a set of rich insights into their intentions and motivations guiding their participation in conflictual sexual interactions, as well as their reactions, reasoning, and interpretations of these situations. Their narratives help clarify the extent to which the traditional sexual script characterizes the sexual lives of this group of men, and possibly other groups of men like them, although the study itself was not designed to generalize beyond our participants.

The men's narratives revealed their considerable uncertainty about the appropriate sexual scripts and gender roles to which they should adhere. The men were aware that the traditional heterosexual script depicting men as the sexual aggressors and women as the sexual gatekeepers was changing and may no longer be the dominant norm. However, the deterioration of the traditional gender script as the dominant norm for heterosexual interactions made the men less certain of how they should act in these situations. For example, the men exhibited a growing awareness of a more current sexual norm which posits that a woman's "no" is to be respected and that continued male sexual advances could be construed as sexual coercion. Yet, the men also expressed uncertainty about whether a woman's "no" was still valid if partners were naked, had engaged in oral sex, or had initiated penetrative vaginal intercourse.

The rape attribution literature indicates that many instances of unwanted and forced sex are not defined as sexual coercion if depicted as fitting the traditional sexual script (Littleton and Axsom 2003). Similarly, some have argued that sexual coercion operates through mechanisms of "normal" heterosexuality, despite employing discursive or adversarial dichotomies of male and female roles (Gavey 2003; Hird and Jackson 2001). Many of the narratives in our study suggested that many men clearly had lost their metric for judging normal or expected scenarios, leaving them uncertain about expected gender roles and behavior.

The men also were asked to describe experiences in which they had engaged in sexual activity with a woman when they did not really desire sex at that time or with that partner. In these scenarios, men might be expected to indicate that they were never in such situations because they always wanted to engage in sex, or to report feeling pressure to engage in unwanted sexual activity in order to preserve or enhance their masculinity, in line with the traditional sexual script. We found that somewhat less than half of the men (40%) reported engaging in unwanted sexual activity; the majority indicated they always wanted to have sex or that this experience had just never occurred. Our findings are consistent with previous research in which 25–30% of heterosexual men reported nonconsensual sexual interactions (Krahé et al. 2003a). Among the men who reported experiences of unwanted sex, the typical interaction took place with new or unfamiliar female partners. Interestingly, the men described their lack of desire as centering around concerns about partner characteristics and being uninterested in establishing a relationship, rather than physical or circumstantial reasons, indicating that these men did not feel compelled to pursue all sexual opportunities that arose. Further, the men's reasons for having unwanted sex were similar to the ways that women report coercing men into having sex (Krahé et al. 2003b).

Clear links to sexual coercion arose in the men's narratives about situations involving discrepancies in sexual desire between partners in a steady relationship. When faced with a reluctant partner, some men insisted that their female partners acquiesce to their demands for sex, and saw such compliance as the man's right in the relationship. This "right" appeared more explicitly connected to rules regarding regular access to one's sexual partner rather than the prerogatives granted men in relation to women generally. In situations in which a man misinterpreted a casual partner's desire for sex, the men were typically far more accepting of these partners' refusals. Collectively, these findings correspond to our understanding of "implicit contracts" (O'Sullivan and Allgeier 1998) that appear to develop in relationships, delineating rules about responding positively and consistently to a partner's sexual advances even when one is not immediately interested in sex.

Although our findings offer insight into men's perceptions of misperceived and misinterpreted interactions with women, it remains difficult to disentangle conceptual issues associated with desire, acquiescence, consent, compliance, and coercion. Recall may be hampered by the consolidation of memory in line with the outcomes of a given interaction (Shotland and Hunter 1995), as well as biases in recall of negative information about oneself or one's partner. At the core, we need to know more about how people communicate and negotiate in sexual encounters. Part of the difficulty in delving into these issues is the heightened emotional valence associated with deconstructing the components of disagreements around sex, lack of desire, feelings of rejection, or loss of face. Although a narrative approach can be a powerful tool for eliciting information about the personal and cultural meanings of behavior, a limitation of this method may be the extent to which the men's stories were influenced by social desirability or self-presentation biases. These biases were evident in our data, but we also note that the men disclosed potentially embarrassing or negative personal experiences, suggesting that these biases were not always present. Further, we posit that men would be most likely to self-monitor around these aspects of scripts that they perceived to be governed by strong social norms—the identification of which was a key goal of our study. Thus, even exaggerated stories would offer insight into our questions of interest.

Another limitation of the current study is our recruitment of a convenience sample, although we note that our participants were diverse with respect to a range of demographic characteristics and were recruited from an urban, community setting. The study is also limited by its focus on men only. Future research could extend this effort by comparing the perspectives of both members of a couple. We need to better understand similarities and differences in the way that men and women perceive their heterosexual interactions, and the ways that these perceptions interact to influence dyadic sexual communication, decision-making, and behavior. Research has suggested that women and men who privately endorse more egalitarian roles and scripts will still behave in accordance with more traditional roles in order to conform to their perceptions of their partner's script preferences (Ortiz-Torres, Williams, and Ehrhardt 2003; Seal and Ehrhardt 2003). This may be particularly true for interactions with newer or casual partners with whom idiosyncratic interpersonal scripts have not yet become habitual, or interactions with established partners that involve transitional or novel experiences (Metts and Cupach 1989; Metts and Spitzberg 1996).

Examining misinterpretation and miscommunication of sexual interest and desire expands our understanding of experiences of unwanted sexual activity and sexual coercion. Most research addressing links to sexual coercion has focused on individual characteristics, including attitudes and beliefs (Burt 1980; Malamuth, Heavey, and Linz 1993), behavioral factors (Abbey et al. 2001; Hersh and Gray-Little 1998; Malamuth

1996), personality traits (Fernandez and Marshall 2003; Senn et al. 2000; Lindsey, Carlozzi, and Eells 2001), and childhood abuse experiences (Simons, Wurtele, and Heil 2002; Widom 2000). Although these factors have important explanatory power, they characterize precipitating factors at the individual level rather than at the dyadic level of a couple's interaction. Understanding the dyadic influences on heterosexual interactions may ultimately help identify points of intervention and enable both men and women to better communicate their respective emotional and sexual needs and fulfill those of their partners (Alexis 1999; Campbell, 1995; Metts and Cupach 1989; Seal and Ehrhardt 2003; Seal et al. 2000). Changes in harmful sexual scripts that engender or support the use of sexual coercion require broad and sustained public health efforts. Such research will support efforts to ensure healthier outcomes in couple interactions.

Acknowledgments

Data collection and coding were supported by National Institute of Mental Health center grant P50-MH43520 to the HIV Center for Clinical and Behavioral Studies (Anke Ehrhardt, PhD, Principal Investigator) and by NRSA training grant 5T32-MH19139 to Behavioral Sciences Research Training in HIV Infection (Zena Stein, MD, Program Director). Data analysis and manuscript preparation were supported by National Institute of Mental Health center grant P30-MH52776 to the Center for AIDS Intervention Research (Jeff Kelly, PhD, Principal Investigator).

The authors thank the HIV Center's Psychosocial/Qualitative Core, Ed Dunne, Lydia Leon, Deborah Palmer-Seal, Verron Skinner, Samantha Williams, and all the other team members for their invaluable contributions to the success of this project. Gratitude also goes to Chelsea STD Clinic/New York City Department of Health, and the Young Men's Health Clinic/Columbia-Presbyterian Medical Center for their assistance.

References

Abbey, A. 1982. Sex differences in attributions for friendly behavior: Do males misperceive females' friendliness? *Journal of Personality and Social Psychology* 41:830–38.

———. 1987. Misperceptions of friendly behavior as sexual interest: A survey of naturally occurring incidents. *Psychology of Women Quarterly* 11:173–94.

Abbey, A., and Harnish, J. 1995. Perception of sexual intent: The role of gender, alcohol consumption, and rape supportive attitudes. *Sex Roles* 32:297–313.

Abbey, A., P. McAuslan, T. Zawacki, A. M. Clinton, and P. O. Buck. 2001. Attitudinal, experiential, and situational predictors of sexual assault perpetration. *Journal of Interpersonal Violence* 16:784–807.

Alexis, E. 1999. Exploring a new paradigm in gender communication. *Toward a New Partnership* 5:1–4.

Basile, K. 1999. Rape by acquiescence: The ways in which women "give in" to unwanted sex with their husbands. *Violence Against Women* 5:1036–58.

Berger, R., P. Searles, R. Salem, and B. Pierce. 1986. Sexual assault in a college community. *Sociological Focus* 19:1–26.

Brooks, G. R. 1995. *The centerfold syndrome: How men can overcome objectification and achieve intimacy with women.* San Francisco: Jossey-Bass Publishers.

Burt, M. R. 1980. Cultural myths and supports for rape. *Journal of Personality and Social Psychology* 38:217–30.

Byers, E. S. 1988. Effects of sexual arousal on men's and women's behavior in sexual disagreement situations. *Journal of Sex Research* 25:235–54.

———. 1996. How well does the traditional sexual script explain sexual coercion? Review of a program of research. *Journal of Psychology and Human Sexuality* 8:7–25.

Byers, E. S., and K. Lewis. 1988. Dating couples' disagreements over the desired level of sexual intimacy. *Journal of Sex Research* 24:15–29.

Byers, E. S., and P. Wilson. 1985. Accuracy of women's expectations regarding men's responses to refusals of sexual advances in dating situations. *International Journal of Women's Studies* 8:376–87.

Campbell, C. A. 1995. Male gender roles and sexuality: Implications for women's AIDS risk and prevention. *Social Science and Medicine* 41:197–210.

Corbin, J., and A. Strauss. 1990. Grounded theory method: Procedures, canons, and evaluative criteria. *Qualitative Sociology* 13:3–21.

Fernandez, Y. M., and W. L. Marshall. 2003. Victim empathy, social self-esteem, and psychopathy in rapists. *Sexual Abuse: Journal of Research and Treatment* 15:11–26.

Fisher, B. A., L. E. Daigle, F. T. Cullen, and M. G. Turner. 2003. Reporting sexual victimization to the police and others: Results from a national-level study of college women. *Criminal Justice and Behavior* 30:6–38.

Frye, V., N. El-Bassel, L. Gilbert, V. Rajah, and N. Christie. 2001. Intimate partner sexual abuse among women on methadone. *Violence and Victims* 16:553–64.

Gagnon, J. H., and W. Simon. 1973. *Sexual conduct: The social origins of human sexuality.* Chicago: Aldine.

Gavey, N. 1993. Technologies and effects of heterosexual coercion. In *Heterosexuality: A feminism and psychology reader*, ed. S. Wilkinson and C. Kitzinger, 93–119. London: Sage.

Hall, J., and P. Stevens. 1991. Rigor in feminist research. *Advances in Nursing Science* 13:16–29.

Hall, G. C. N., S. Sue, D. S. Narang, and R. A. Lilly. 2000. Culture-specific models of men's sexual aggression: Intra- and interpersonal determinants. *Cultural Diversity and Ethnic Minority Psychology* 6:252–68.

Hannon, R., D. S. Hall, .T. Kuntz, S. Van Laar, and S. Williams. 1995. Dating characteristics leading to unwanted versus wanted sexual behavior. *Sex Roles* 33:767–83.

Harnish, R. J., A. Abbey, and D. K. DeBono. 1990. Toward an understanding of the "sex game": The effects of gender and self-monitoring on perceptions of sexuality and likeability in initial interactions. *Journal of Applied Social Psychology,* 20:1333–44.

Hersh, K., and B. Gray-Little. 1998. Psychopathic traits and attitudes associated with self-reported aggression in college men. *Journal of Interpersonal Violence* 13:456–71.

Hird, M. J., and S. Jackson. 2001. Where "angels" and "wusses" fear to tread: Sexual coercion in adolescent dating relationships. *Journal of Sociology* 37:27–43.

Koss, M. P., A. A. Gidycz, and N. Wisniewski. 1987. The scope of rape: Incidence and prevalence of sexual aggression and victimization in a national sample of higher education students. *Journal of Consulting and Clinical Psychology* 55:162–70.

Krahé, B., R. Scheinberger-Olwig, and S. Bieneck. 2003. Men's reports of nonconsensual sexual interactions with women: Prevalence and impact. *Archives of Sexual Behavior* 32:165–75.

Krahé, B., R. Scheinberger-Olwig, and S. Kolpin. 2000. Ambiguous communication of sexual intentions as a risk marker of sexual aggression. *Sex Roles* 42:313–37.

Krahé, B., E. Waizenhofer, and I. Moller. 2003b. Women's sexual aggression against men: Prevlance and predictors. *Sex Roles* 49:219–32.

Laumann, E. O., J. H. Gagnon, R. T. Michael, and S. Michaels. 1994. *The social organization of sexuality: Sexual practices in the United States.* Chicago: University of Chicago Press.

Lindsey, R. E., A. F. Carlozzi, and G. T. Eells. 2001. Differences in the dispositional empathy of juvenile sex offenders, non-sex-offending delinquent juveniles, and nondelinquent juveniles. *Journal of Interpersonal Violence* 16:510–22.

Littleton, H. L., and D. Axsom. 2003. Rape and seduction scripts of university students: Implications for rape attributions and unacknowledged rape. *Sex Roles* 49:465–75.

Livingston, J. A., A. M. Buddie, M. Testa, and C. VanZile-Tamsen. 2004. The role of sexual precedence in verbal sexual coercion. *Psychology of Women Quarterly* 28:287–97.

Malamuth, N. M. 1996. The confluence model of sexual aggression: Feminist and evolutionary perspectives. In *Sex, power, conflict: Evolutionary and feminist perspectives*, ed. D. M. Buss, and N. M. Malamuth, 269–95. New York: Oxford University Press.

Malamuth, N. M., C. Heavey, and D. Linz. 1993. Predicting men's antisocial behavior against women: The "interaction model" of sexual aggression. In *Sexual aggression: Issues in etiology and assessment, treatment, and policy,* ed. N. G. Hall and R. Hirschman, 63–97. New York: Hemisphere.

Metts, S., and W. R. Cupach. 1989. The role of communication in human sexuality. In *Human sexuality: The societal and interpersonal context*, ed. K. McKinney and S. Sprecher, 139–61. Norwood, NJ: Ablex Publishing Corporation.

Metts, S., and B. H. Spitzberg. 1996. Sexual communication in interpersonal contexts: A script-based approach. In *Communication yearbook* 19, ed. B. R. Burlson, 49–61. Thousand Oaks, CA: Sage Publications.

Monson, C. M., J. Langhinrichsen-Rohling, and T. Binderup. 2000. Does "no" really mean "no" after you say "yes"? Attributions about date and marital rape. *Journal of Interpersonal Violence* 15:1156–74.

Muehlenhard, C. L., and S. W. Cook. 1988. Men's self reports of unwanted sexual activity. *Journal of Sex Research* 24:58–72.

Muehlenhard, C. L., and J. S. MacNaughton. 1988. Women's beliefs about women who "lead men on." *Journal of Social and Clinical Psychology* 7:65–79.

Muehlenhard, C. L., and C. S. Rodgers. 1998. Token resistance to sex: New perspectives on an old stereotype. *Psychology of Women Quarterly* 22:443–63.

Murray, M. 1997. A narrative approach to health psychology: Background and potential. *Journal of Health Psychology* 2:9–20.

Ortiz-Torres, B., I. Serrano-Garcia, and N. Torres-Burgos. 2000. Subverting culture: Promoting HIV/AIDS prevention among Puerto Rican and Dominican women. *American Journal of Community Psychology* 28:859–81.

Ortiz-Torres, B., S. P. Williams, and A. A. Ehrhardt. 2003. Urban women's gender scripts: Implications for HIV. *Culture, Health, and Sexuality* 5:1–17.

Osman, S. L. 2003. Predicting men's rape perceptions based on the belief that "No" really means "Yes." *Journal of Applied Social Psychology* 33:683–92.

O'Sullivan, L. F., and E. R. Allgeier. 1998. Feigning sexual desire: Consenting to unwanted sexual activity in heterosexual dating relationships. *Journal of Sex Research* 35:234–43.

———. 1994. Dissembling a stereotype: Gender differences in the use of token resistance. *Journal of Applied Social Psychology* 24:1035–55.

O'Sullivan, L. F., and E. S. Byers. 1993. Eroding stereotypes: College women's attempts to influence reluctant male partners. *Journal of Sex Research* 30:270–82.

O'Sullivan, L. F., E. S. Byers, and L. Finkelman. 1998. A comparison of male and female college students' experiences of sexual coercion. *Psychology of Women Quarterly* 22:177–95.

Meston, C. M., and L. F. O'Sullivan. 2005. Such a tease: Intentional sexual provocation within heterosexual interactions. Manuscript submitted for review.

Sandelowski, M. 1986. The problem of rigor in qualitative research. *Advances in Nursing Science* 8:27–37.

Sawyer, R. G., S. M. Desmond, and G. M. Lucke. 1993. Sexual communication and the college student: Implications for date rape. *Health Values* 17:11–20.

Schwartz, P., and V. Rutter. 1998. *The gender of sexuality.* Thousand Oaks, CA: Sage Publications.

Seal, D. W., and A. A. Ehrhardt. 2003. Masculinity and urban men: Perceived scripts for courtship, romantic, and sexual interactions with women. *Culture, Health, and Sexuality,* 5:295–319.

Seal, D. W., L. I. Wagner, and A. A. Ehrhardt. 2000. Sex, intimacy, and HIV: An ethnographic study of a Puerto Rican social group in New York City. *Journal of Psychology and Human Sexuality* 11:51–92.

Senn, C. Y., N. Verberg, S. Desmarais, and E. Wood. 2000. Sampling the reluctant participant: A random-sample response-rate study of men and sexual coercion. *Journal of Applied Social Psychology* 30:96–105.

Shotland, R. L., and B. A. Hunter. 1995. Women's "token resistant" and compliant sexual behaviors are related to uncertain sexual intentions and rape. *Personality and Social Psychology Bulletin* 21:226–36.

Shotland, R. L., and L. Goodstein. 1992. Sexual precedence reduces the perceived legitimacy of sexual refusal: An examination of attributions concerning date rape and consensual sex. *Personality and Social Psychology Bulletin* 18:756–64.

Simon, W., and J. H. Gagnon. 1986. Sexual scripts: Permanence and change. *Archives of Sexual Behavior* 15:97–120.

Simon, R. W., D. Eder, and C. Evans. 1992. The development of feeling norms underlying romantic love among adolescent females. *Social Psychology Quarterly* 55:29–46.

Simons, D., S. K. Wurtele, and P. Heil. 2002. Childhood victimization and lack of empathy as predictors of sexual offending against women and children. *Journal of Interpersonal Violence* 17:1291–1307.

Spitzberg, B. H. 1999. An analysis of empirical estimates of sexual aggression victimization and perpetration. *Violence and Victims* 14:241–60.

Strauss, A., and J. Corbin. 1994. Grounded theory methodology. In *Handbook of qualitative research,* ed. N. K. Denzin and Y. S. Lincoln, 273–85. Thousand Oaks, CA: Sage Publications.

Struckman-Johnson, C. J. 1988. Forced sex on dates: It happens to men too. *Journal of Sex Research* 24:234–40.

Struckman-Johnson, C. J., D. Struckman-Johnson, and P. B. Anderson. 2003. Tactics of sexual coercion: When men and women won't take no for an answer. *Journal of Sex Research* 40:76–86.

Tiefer, L. 1995. *Sex is not a natural act and other essays.* Boulder: Westview Press.

Wade, J. C., and J. W. Critelli. 1998. Narrative descriptions of sexual aggression: The gender gap. *Journal of Social and Clinical Psychology* 17:363–78.

Walker, S. J. 1997. When "no" becomes "yes": Why girls and women consent to unwanted sex. *Applied and Preventive Psychology* 6:157–66.

Widom, C. S. 2000. Understanding the consequences of childhood victimization. In *Treatment of child abuse: Common ground for mental health, medical, and legal practitioners,* ed. R. M. Reece, 339–61. Baltimore: Johns Hopkins University Press.

Willan, V. J., and P. Pollard. 2003. Likelihood of acquantaince rape as a function of males' sexual expectations, disappointment, and adherence to rape-conducive attitudes. *Journal of Social and Personal Relationships* 20:637–61.

Wyatt, G. 1994. The sociocultural relevance of sex research. *American Psychologist* 49:748–54.

PART III

SEXUAL BEHAVIOR

Edward O. Laumann, Jenna Mahay, and Yoosik Youm

11

Sex, Intimacy, and Family Life in the United States

Redefining union formation

Family demographers have traditionally defined "union formation" as simply the point at which a person was married. More recently, they have added cohabitation to their analyses. But, as several scholars have pointed out, even this expanded definition of union formation is no longer adequate given the dramatic transformation of intimate ties over the last several decades in the United States, particularly the decoupling of marriage and sex (Raley 2000; Mahay and Laumann 2001).[1] Americans now spend a larger proportion of their lives outside of marriage, but they are certainly not abstaining from sex or committed intimate relationships in these intervals. In fact, while age at first marriage is increasing, age at first intercourse is decreasing; and Americans, as a result, spend more of their lives in non-coresidential sexual relationships.

As sexual ties have become increasingly organized outside of marriage, the meaning of marriage itself has changed. The expectation that sex, cohabitation, and childbearing are the defining elements of marriage has changed, with marriage no longer being seen as the only socially acceptable relationship for these activities. Goldscheider and Waite (1991) also emphasize the fact that independence from one's parental family no longer requires marriage. In our view, the family demographers' conception of intimate union formation must accommodate this changing reality to include non-coresidential sexual relationships (cf. Mahay and Laumann 2001; Raley 2000).

The formation of romantic and sexual partnerships is a critical issue because the ways in which these relationships are formed and maintained have consequences for whether or not they lead to cohabitation, marriage, or singlehood, and, in turn, their duration. They also have consequences for the quality of life associated with cohabitation, marriages, or singlehood. For example, a couple's mutual friends and kin may help keep their relationship afloat by helping to sustain mutual trust and emotional support, resolve conflicts, and provide pertinent information about the partners' personal histories, including the risk of transmitting disease (cf. Youm and Laumann 2002). Conversely, their disapproval of the relationship may effectively challenge its continued existence. The environing social network around an intimate couple may even exert influence on the couple's negotiation of the division of household labor (cf. Youm and Laumann 2003).

Thus, a better understanding of sex, intimacy, and the family requires us to include the unions that people form prior to cohabitation and marriage in our definition and study of union formation (Mahay and Laumann 2001; Laumann et al. 1994, 225–68). While not all romantic relationships lead to marriage, almost all marriages in the United States today begin with a romantic relationship. An individual must first find and choose a potential partner, develop a romantic relationship, and from there decide whether to continue dating, to move in together, to get married, or to simply end the relationship and look for someone else. Thus, marriage and cohabitation depend on many things, including individual attitudes, the ability to find a partner, the involvement of social networks, the ways of meeting one's partner and developing the relationship, and the subsequent internal dynamics of the relationship that determine whether or not it leads to marriage. Since most demographers study only marital and cohabitation unions, they are in a sense selecting the dependent variable. We know relatively little about the formation of sexual relationships and the dynamics that make up sexual marketplaces, which are only loosely coupled with the cohabitation or marriage markets (cf. Laumann et al. 2004).

We propose to address three interrelated themes in the following discussion, by (1) reviewing the emerging perspective on sexual exchange in sexual partnerships that incorporates biological, psychological, social, and cultural considerations in shaping sexual conduct over the life course; (2) noting the growing importance of intimate union formation more broadly conceived to include dating and singlehood in accounting for the changing structure of long-term unions among U.S. adults; and (3) showing how the growing diversity in patterns of union formation across the major race and ethnic groups in the United States can be understood as emerging from the dynamics of sexual partnership formation operating under different social and cultural constraints.

Understanding sex and intimate unions

Figure 1 displays schematically our perspective on the social organization of sexuality that has animated a series of studies that we have conducted over the past fifteen years, based on population-based surveys of the United States, China, and the Chicago metropolitan area (cf. Laumann et al. 1994; Laumann and Michael 2001; Laumann et al. 2004; Parish and Laumann n.d.). Each individual—the respondent or focal person (ego) and the partner (alter)—is embedded in a network of family and friends who become stakeholders in the social and sexual behavior of that person and have influence on choices about the sex partner and sexual practices. Each individual brings his or her own personal characteristics and perspectives on sex and its practice and meaning, and each individual has a history of experience (or inexperience) that influences those preferences and judgments. Potential sex partners meet, interact, negotiate, form expectations, and

Figure 1. A schematic outline of the model of sexual exchange

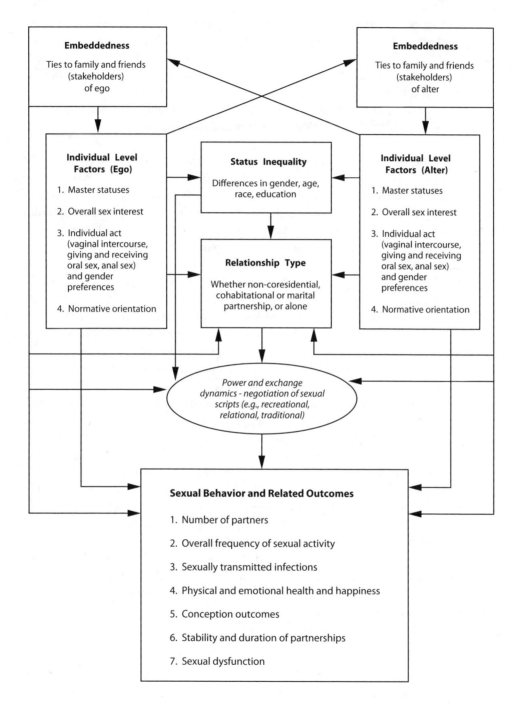

Source: Laumann et al. 1994, 545.

make decisions about their sexual behavior in the context of other decisions about their partnerships and their nonsexual behavior. The partnerships themselves have attributes that affect sexual behavior, as is evident when one compares the dramatically different patterns of sexual behavior among married and cohabiting couples vs. dating and un-partnered (i.e., single) individuals. The reported sexual behavior, in short, is specific to the sexual partnership and affected by it. The partners and their social network interpret that behavior. It also has consequences: some anticipated, others not so; some desired, others not so; some quite private, others quite public. The figure is not a full-fledged model because we have not yet melded the many important factors adequately to specify a formal model.

In a further specification of the model, we decompose "relationship type," a focal point in figure 1, into a multistate representation of the four possible relationship types and the 12 transitions that are possible to make from one relationship type to another: single, dating, cohabiting, and married, as depicted in figure 2 (Mahay 2002). This is our expansion of the conception of union formation into an exhaustive and comprehensive delineation of the alternative relationship statuses that can be occupied by an adult for varying periods of time over the life course.[2] The demographers' traditional focus only on transitions between single and marriage and cohabitation do not allow us to examine the intimate union formation processes that lead to these outcomes. By including dating in our analysis of union formation, we can specify the probabilities of transitioning between the four statuses over a given period of time (in our case, within the next three years) and determine how these probabilities change over the life course. For example, including "dating" as a state in the multistate analysis of union formation will reveal whether older women's lower rate of marriage is because older women are less likely to date than younger women, or whether it is just less likely for their dating relationships to turn into marriages. Moreover, we can determine the total expected amount of time spent in each of these four states over the life course and whether the expected amount of time in each state differs according to the state in which one starts. Since figure 1 hypothesizes that relationship type is associated with a variety of outcome variables, especially those related to quality of life and health risks, we believe that we expand greatly the reach of the model in explaining important features of social behavior and its consequences over those that restrict attention exclusively to cohabitation and marriage. Unfortunately, however, large-scale data sets needed for an accurate multistate analysis, such as the U. S. census, have not collected the requisite data on sexual relationships outside of marriage or cohabitation. This has led to a privileging of these more "legitimized" types of relationships at the expense of a better understanding of the intimate union formation processes that lead to marriage and cohabitation.

Data sources

We will be drawing from two principal data sources for the empirical analysis below. First, the National Health and Social Life Survey (NHSLS), conducted in 1992, is a national probability sample of 1,410 men and 1,749 women between the ages of 18 and 59 years living in households throughout the continental United States. It accounts for about 97 % of the population in this age range—roughly 150 million Americans. It excluded people living in group quarters, such as barracks, college dormitories, and pris-

Figure 2. Multistate representation of singlehood, dating, cohabitation, and marriage

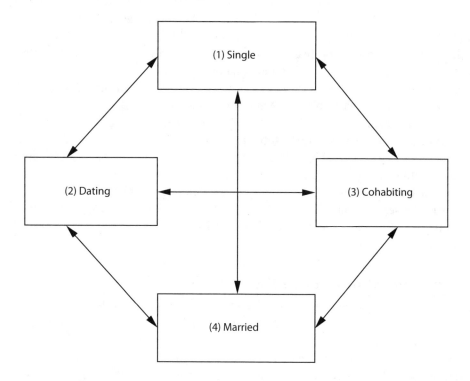

ons, as well as those who did not know English well enough to be interviewed. The sample completion rate was greater than 79 %. Checks with other high-quality samples (e.g., the U.S. Census Bureau's Current Population Survey) indicated that the NHSLS succeeded in producing a truly representative sample of the population. Each respondent was surveyed in person by experienced interviewers from NORC (National Opinion Research Center), who matched respondents on various social attributes such as race and ethnicity, for an interview averaging 90 minutes. Extensive discussion of the sampling design and evaluations of sample and data quality are found in Laumann et al. 1994.

Second, the Chicago Health and Social Life Survey (CHSLS), conducted principally in 1995 with a small supplementary sample in 1997, has a multi-level sampling design. It consists of a total sample of 2,114 in Chicago and its environs, including a representative sample of Cook County (which includes the city of Chicago and its inner suburban ring) with a probability sample of 377 men and 513 women between the ages of 18 and 59 years. In addition, cross-section samples of four selected neighborhoods with about 325 respondents apiece were conducted to facilitate the exploration of locally organized sexual markets. We use only the data from the Chicago/Cook County sample in this paper. NORC followed in nearly all details the procedures employed in the national sample, achieving a completion rate of 71 %. The interview schedule replicated most of the questions from the NHSLS, but included additional questions that let us explore in much greater detail the sexual partnering process over time. Two important departures from the NHSLS design were (1) the use of Spanish-speaking interviewers so that we could include recent immigrants who lacked facility in English, and (2) the use of computer-assisted program interviewing (CAPI) that permitted the respondent to enter his or her own answers to the more sensitive items in the protocol. Research by Turner et al. (1998) have demonstrated that CAPI procedures are likely to enhance the disclosure of socially sensitive information (e.g., disclosure of same-gender behavior or interests) because of the enhanced privacy and confidentiality of the interview.

What distinguishes these surveys from other surveys of sexual behavior is their unremitting, extensive focus on the specific sexual partnerships in which particular sexual activities are conducted and their timing. Every feature of the sexual partnership is explored, from the ways in which the partners became acquainted (e.g., by self-introduction or through mutual friends and acquaintances), the physical and social venues of the meeting places, the social characteristics of the partners and the members of their respective social (non-sex-based) networks, the timing of different developmental events in the sexual relationship, including initiation and termination, bargaining and negotiating over sexual events, and the subjective evaluation of the quality of the partnership.

Some pertinent empirical findings

Looking at relationship type from a more longitudinal perspective, table 1 reveals that the categories typically used by family demographers do not reflect the underlying dynamic aspects of sexual partnering that result in different relationship histories and experiences of people in these categories. For example, almost half of those in the "Never Married, Single" category are currently in an ongoing sexual relationship (i.e., rows 2 + 5 + 7 = 47.1), while the other half are not. This is not a distinction that is typically made, but it makes an important difference in one's mental and physical health, and also for one's future chances of cohabiting or marrying, since one typically must develop a romantic relationship before cohabiting with or marrying a partner. Further differences in the experiences of those in the "Never Married, Single" category are revealed by the fact that about one-fourth of both men and women in this category have cohabited at least once, and about one-third of those who have cohabited have done so more than once. Thus, those in the "Never Married, Single" category actually reflect a wide range of experiences. Similarly, of people who are currently "Cohabiting," 30% have been previously married and 20% have not been previously married but have previously cohabited with someone else. Thus, these seemingly straightforward, taken-for-granted categories belie the variation in the relational history of people in these categories that are likely to influence future relationships.

As suggested by figure 1 and shown in table 1, the relational histories by which individuals end up in these categories vary systematically by individual master status categories, such as race/ethnicity and age.[3] For example, 30% of those who are "Never Married, Single" between 45 and 59 years of age have never had a sexual partner, compared to only about 10% of those who are younger. And, the proportion of those who are "Never Married, Single" who are currently dating steadily decreases from 54% for those 18–24 to only 19% for those aged 45–49. Of those who are currently married, only half of those 18–24 did not cohabit before marriage, compared to almost 90% of those who are 45–59 years old. Among those who are 18–24 and are married, about 46% lived with their spouse before marriage, and 10% lived with another partner before they married their spouse. Among those who are 45–49 years old and currently married, only 10% lived with their spouse before marriage, and 2% lived with another partner before marriage. Among those who are currently divorced and single (not cohabiting or remarried), 57% of people 35–44 are currently dating, while only 32% of people 45–59 are currently dating.

In terms of race and ethnicity, while about one-third of African Americans and Hispanics who are "Never Married, Single" have cohabited in the past, less than one-quarter of whites in this category have ever cohabited. Thus, this category reflects a different set of experiences for African Americans and Hispanics than it does for whites. In addition, among those who are currently married, 16% of African Americans cohabited with someone other than their spouse before they were married, compared to only 7% of whites and 1% of Hispanics.

Table 2 reports the data in table 1 as percentages of the total population marginals so that the reader can more readily determine the relative proportions of the population at large with particular master status attributes like gender, age, and race that fall into particular relationship status combinations. Thus, we can learn that 27% of the men are "Never Married, Single"'s while nearly 19% of the women in the United States fall into this category. Only 3.2% of the men and 2.3% are single with no sex partners ever. Even some of these can be expected to shift from the status of a virgin given time (look at the declining percentages across age for row 1 under "Never Married, Single").

Approaching the matter of relationship volatility from another vantage point, Mahay (2002) estimated the transition probabilities of moving from one relationship status to another (as depicted in figure 2) by three-year age intervals for a representative sample of residents of Chicago, aged 18 to 59, in 1995, using multistate analysis (Preston, Heuveline, and Guillot. 2000). She had to use this database as it is the only one with the necessary detail about relationship statuses and their duration; unfortunately, it is a relatively small sample and, as a result, subject to large sampling errors. This means that detailed breakdowns of the estimates would be misleading, but several aggregate results are, in fact, very robust and reliable. The result of this exercise is to estimate that approximately one half of an urban adult's lifetime between 18 and 59 in the United States is spent in single or dating relationships, and the remainder is spent in cohabitation (about 9% of the total age interval in question) or in marriage (about 43% of the age interval). Such a finding—suggesting that half of American adult lifetimes are spent in relationship statuses almost wholly ignored by official government statistics— provides further warrant for reconsideration of these efforts. Below, we will demonstrate that many facets of people's quality of life and health status are differentially associated with these relationship statuses.

Table 3 can only be regarded as suggestive because it is based on the same modest sample drawn from only one metropolitan area, Chicago in 1995.[4] Unfortunately, there are no other empirical studies of which we are aware that provide the necessary information to draw the distinctions we believe are important in studying intimate union formation. The table further focuses attention on the complexity of the partnering patterns among the several relationship status categories by gender and race, suggesting that even the addition of the dating status does not fully capture the manifold character of inti-

Table 1. Life course patterns of singlehood, dating, cohabitation, and marriage by selected variables

Subcategory Percent Distributions for Adults 18-59, NHSLS

	Total	Gender		Age			
		Men	Women	18-24	25-34	35-44	45-49
Never Married, Single							
(1) Single (no sexual partners ever)	12.0	11.7	12.4	10.7	10.7	11.7	30.2
(2) Single-Currently Dating	34.1	35.5	32.5	46.1	28.7	18.1	11.6
(3) Single-Dating-Currently Single	27.9	28.9	26.6	27.9	24.2	31.9	39.5
(4) Single-Dating-Cohabiting-Currently Single	9.1	8.0	10.5	6.3	11.9	11.7	9.3
(5) Single-Dating-Cohabiting-Currently Dating	8.7	8.0	9.6	6.0	11.9	12.8	2.3
(6) Single-Dating-Cohabiting-Dating-Cohabiting-Currently Single	3.9	3.5	4.3	1.9	5.7	6.4	2.3
(7) Single-Dating-Cohabiting-Dating-Cohabiting-Currently Dating	4.3	4.5	4.0	1.3	7.0	7.5	4.7
Total %	*100*	*100*	*100*	*100*	*100*	*100*	*100*
N	*700*	*377*	*323*	*319*	*244*	*94*	*43*
Never Married, Cohabiting							
(8) Single-Dating-Cohabiting	69.3	63.3	73.9	75.0	64.2	50.0	100.0
(9) Single-Dating-Cohabiting-Dating-Cohabiting	30.7	36.7	26.2	25.0	35.9	50.0	0.0
Total %	*100*	*100*	*100*	*100*	*100*	*100*	*100*
N	*114*	*49*	*65*	*52*	*53*	*6*	*3*
Married							
(10) Single-Dating-Married	71.8	72.6	71.3	50.0	61.5	72.3	89.2
(11) Single-Dating-Cohabiting-Married	20.9	18.9	22.4	39.8	28.4	19.2	8.8
(12) Single-Dating-Cohabiting-Dating-Cohabiting-Married	4.9	5.8	4.3	6.1	6.9	6.0	1.1
(13) Single-Dating-Cohabiting-Dating-Married	2.4	2.7	2.1	4.1	3.2	2.5	0.9
Total %	*100*	*100*	*100*	*100*	*100*	*100*	*100*
N	*1220*	*514*	*706*	*98*	*405*	*364*	*353*

Divorced, Single

(14) Single-Dating-Married-Currently Single	42.5	34.1	46.9	0.0	21.2	32.9	62.3
(15) Single-Dating-Married-Currently Dating	31.8	35.3	30.0	40.0	28.9	39.0	27.4
(16) Single-Dating-Cohabiting-Married-Currently Single	11.0	11.8	10.6	40.0	21.2	9.8	5.7
(17) Single-Dating-Cohabiting-Married-Currently Dating	14.7	18.8	12.5	20.0	28.9	18.3	4.7
Total %	100	100	100	100	100	100	100
N	245	85	160	5	52	82	106
Divorced, Cohabiting							
(18) Single-Dating-Married-Dating-Cohabiting	66.7	65.0	67.9	100.0	52.4	68.8	90.0
(19) Single-Dating-Cohabiting-Married-Dating-Cohabiting	33.3	35.0	32.1	0.0	47.6	31.3	10.0
Total %	100	100	100	100	100	100	100
N	48	20	28	1	21	16	10
Remarried							
(20) Single-Dating-Married-Dating-Remarried	43.9	43.6	44.2	33.3	26.8	36.1	60.8
(21) Single-Dating-Married-Dating-Cohabiting-Remarried	36.0	32.7	38.4	66.7	39.3	42.2	27.8
(22) Single-Dating-Cohabiting-Married-Dating-Remarried	4.2	5.9	2.9	0.0	3.6	3.6	5.2
(23) Single-Dating-Cohabiting-Married-Dating-Cohabiting-Remarried	15.9	17.8	14.5	0.0	30.4	18.1	6.2
Total %	100	100	100	100	100	100	100
N	239	101	138	3	56	83	97
Other							
(24) 3 or more Cohabiting partners or spouses	73.6	83.4	65.7	73.9	78.1	71.9	72.4
(25) Other	26.4	16.6	34.3	26.1	21.9	28.1	27.6
Total %	100	100	100	100	100	100	100
N	565	253	312	23	137	231	174
Total N	3131	1399	1732	501	968	876	786

Note: The data used in this table are from the NHSLS cross-section sample only (not the oversample). Percent distributions are unweighted.

Table 1. (cont.) Life course patterns of singlehood, dating, cohabitation, and marriage by selected variables

Subcategory Percent Distributions for Adults 18-59, NHSLS

	Race/Ethnicity			Degree		
	White	African American	Hispanic	<HS	HS Degree	Some College
Never Married, Single						
(1) Single (no sexual partners ever)	13.6	6.3	7.1	16.7	15.8	9.6
(2) Single-Currently Dating	35.1	39.8	21.4	31.3	26.3	37.7
(3) Single-Dating-Currently Single	28.2	21.1	37.5	27.1	28.1	27.6
(4) Single-Dating-Cohabiting-Currently Single	8.9	10.9	10.7	9.4	10.5	8.7
(5) Single-Dating-Cohabiting-Currently Dating	6.9	14.1	12.5	10.4	8.8	8.4
(6) Single-Dating-Cohabiting-Dating-Cohabiting-Currently Single	3.5	3.1	8.9	5.2	4.7	3.3
(7) Single-Dating-Cohabiting-Dating-Cohabiting-Currently Dating	3.9	4.7	1.8	0.0	5.9	4.7
Total %	*100*	*100*	*100*	*100*	*100*	*100*
N	*493*	*128*	*56*	*96*	*171*	*427*
Never Married, Cohabiting						
(8) Single-Dating-Cohabiting	73.6	63.2	66.7	54.6	70.0	75.4
(9) Single-Dating-Cohabiting-Dating-Cohabiting	26.4	36.8	33.3	45.5	30.0	24.6
Total %	*100*	*100*	*100*	*100*	*100*	*100*
N	*72*	*19*	*12*	*22*	*30*	*61*
Married						
(10) Single-Dating-Married	72.5	54.6	78.4	77.0	72.7	70.4
(11) Single-Dating-Cohabiting-Married	20.2	29.3	20.5	18.5	21.3	21.3
(12) Single-Dating-Cohabiting-Dating-Cohabiting-Married	4.9	12.1	0.0	3.0	4.4	5.4
(13) Single-Dating-Cohabiting-Dating-Cohabiting-Dating-Married	2.4	4.0	1.1	1.5	1.7	2.9
Total %	*100*	*100*	*100*	*100*	*100*	*100*
N	*984*	*99*	*88*	*135*	*362*	*720*

Divorced, Single						
(14) Single-Dating-Married-Currently Single	44.3	45.0	12.5	48.0	49.4	37.3
(15) Single-Dating-Married-Currently Dating	31.7	27.5	43.8	16.0	27.7	37.3
(16) Single-Dating-Cohabiting-Married-Currently Single	10.9	10.0	18.8	16.0	12.1	9.7
(17) Single-Dating-Cohabiting-Married-Currently Dating	13.1	17.5	25.0	20.0	10.8	15.7
Total %	100	100	100	100	100	100
N	183	40	16	25	83	134
Divorced, Cohabiting						
(18) Single-Dating-Married-Dating-Cohabiting	67.6	50.0	66.7	77.8	61.1	66.7
(19) Single-Dating-Cohabiting-Married-Dating-Cohabiting	32.4	50.0	33.3	22.2	38.9	33.3
Total %	100	100	100	100	100	100
N	37	4	6	9	18	21
Remarried						
(20) Single-Dating-Married-Dating-Remarried	45.4	37.5	37.5	36.4	50.6	40.4
(21) Single-Dating-Married-Dating-Cohabiting-Remarried	34.7	37.5	50.0	48.5	34.8	33.3
(22) Single-Dating-Cohabiting-Married-Dating-Remarried	4.1	8.3	0.0	3.0	2.3	6.1
(23) Single-Dating-Cohabiting-Married-Dating-Cohabiting-Remarried	15.8	16.7	12.5	4.0	11.0	23.0
Total %	100	100	100	92	99	103
N	196	24	16	33	89	114
Other						
(24) 3 or more Cohabiting partners or spouses	74.1	69.5	69.2	74.1	78.7	70.6
(25) Other	25.9	30.5	30.8	25.9	21.3	29.4
Total %	100	100	100	100	100	100
N	433	82	39	112	150	299
Total N	2398	396	233	432	903	1776

Note: The data used in this table are from the NHSLS cross-section sample only (not the oversample). Percent distributions are unweighted.

Table 2. Life course patterns of singlehood, dating, cohabitation, and marriage by selected variables
Total Column Percent Distributions for Adults 18-59, NHSLS

		Gender		Age			
	Total	Men	Women	18-24	25-34	35-44	45-49
Never Married, Single							
(1) Single (no sexual partners ever)	2.7	3.2	2.3	6.8	2.7	1.3	1.7
(2) Single-Currently Dating	7.6	9.6	6.1	29.3	7.2	1.9	0.6
(3) Single-Dating-Currently Single	6.2	7.8	5.0	17.8	6.1	3.4	2.2
(4) Single-Dating-Cohabiting-Currently Single	2.0	2.1	2.0	4.0	3.0	1.3	0.5
(5) Single-Dating-Cohabiting-Currently Dating	2.0	2.1	1.8	3.8	3.0	1.4	0.1
(6) Single-Dating-Cohabiting-Dating-Cohabiting-Currently Single	0.9	0.9	0.8	1.2	1.5	0.7	0.1
(7) Single-Dating-Cohabiting-Dating-Cohabiting-Currently Dating	1.0	1.2	0.8	0.8	1.8	0.8	0.3
Subtotal %	*22.4*	*27.0*	*18.7*	*63.7*	*25.2*	*10.7*	*5.5*
Never Married, Cohabiting							
(8) Single-Dating-Cohabiting	2.5	2.2	2.8	7.8	3.5	0.3	0.4
(9) Single-Dating-Cohabiting-Dating-Cohabiting	1.1	1.3	1.0	2.6	2.0	0.3	0.0
Subtotal %	*3.6*	*3.5*	*3.8*	*10.4*	*5.5*	*0.7*	*0.4*
Married							
(10) Single-Dating-Married	28.0	26.7	29.0	9.8	25.7	30.0	40.1
(11) Single-Dating-Cohabiting-Married	8.1	6.9	9.1	7.8	11.9	8.0	3.9
(12) Single-Dating-Cohabiting-Dating-Cohabiting-Married	1.9	2.1	1.7	1.2	2.9	2.5	0.5
(13) Single-Dating-Cohabiting-Dating-Married	0.9	1.0	0.9	0.8	1.3	1.0	0.4
Subtotal %	*39.0*	*36.7*	*40.8*	*19.6*	*41.8*	*41.6*	*44.9*

Divorced, Single							
(14) Single-Dating-Married-Currently Single	3.3	2.1	4.3	0.0	1.1	3.1	8.4
(15) Single-Dating-Married-Currently Dating	2.5	2.1	2.8	0.4	1.6	3.7	3.7
(16) Single-Dating-Cohabiting-Married-Currently Single	0.9	0.7	1.0	0.4	1.1	0.9	0.8
(17) Single-Dating-Cohabiting-Married-Currently Dating	1.2	1.1	1.2	0.2	1.6	1.7	0.6
Subtotal %	*7.8*	*6.1*	*9.2*	*1.0*	*5.4*	*9.4*	*13.5*
Divorced, Cohabiting							
(18) Single-Dating-Married-Dating-Cohabiting	1.0	0.9	1.1	0.2	1.1	1.3	1.2
(19) Single-Dating-Cohabiting-Married-Dating-Cohabiting	0.5	0.5	0.5	0.0	1.0	0.6	0.1
Subtotal %	*1.5*	*1.4*	*1.6*	*0.2*	*2.2*	*1.8*	*1.3*
Remarried							
(20) Single-Dating-Married-Dating-Remarried	3.4	3.2	3.5	0.2	1.6	3.4	7.5
(21) Single-Dating-Married-Dating-Cohabiting-Remarried	2.8	2.4	3.1	0.4	2.3	4.0	3.4
(22) Single-Dating-Cohabiting-Married-Dating-Remarried	0.3	0.4	0.2	0.0	0.2	0.3	0.6
(23) Single-Dating-Cohabiting-Married-Dating-Cohabiting-Remarried	1.2	1.3	1.2	0.0	1.8	1.7	0.8
Subtotal %	*7.6*	*7.2*	*8.0*	*0.6*	*5.8*	*9.5*	*12.4*
Other							
(24) 3 or more Cohabiting partners or spouses	13.3	15.1	11.8	3.4	11.1	19.0	16.0
(25) Other	4.8	3.0	6.2	1.2	3.1	7.4	6.1
Subtotal %	*18.1*	*18.1*	*18.0*	*4.6*	*14.2*	*26.4*	*22.1*
Total N	*3131*	*1399*	*1732*	*501*	*968*	*876*	*786*

Note: The data used in this table are from the NHSLS cross-section sample only (not the oversample). Percent distributions are unweighted.

Table 2. (cont.) Life course patterns of singlehood, dating, cohabitation, and marriage by selected variables
Total Population Percent Distribution for Adults 18-59, NHSLS

	Race/Ethnicity			Degree		
	White	African American	Hispanic	< HS	HS Degree	Some College
Never Married, Single						
(1) Single (no sexual partners ever)	2.8	2.0	1.7	3.7	3.0	2.3
(2) Single-Currently Dating	7.2	12.9	5.2	6.9	5.0	9.1
(3) Single-Dating-Currently Single	5.8	6.8	9.0	6.0	5.3	6.6
(4) Single-Dating-Cohabiting-Currently Single	1.8	3.5	2.6	2.1	2.0	2.1
(5) Single-Dating-Cohabiting-Currently Dating	1.4	4.6	3.0	2.3	1.7	2.0
(6) Single-Dating-Cohabiting-Cohabiting-Currently Single	0.7	1.0	2.2	1.2	0.9	0.8
(7) Single-Dating-Cohabiting-Cohabiting-Currently Dating	0.8	1.5	0.4	0.0	1.1	1.1
Subtotal %	*20.6*	*32.3*	*24.0*	*22.2*	*18.9*	*24.1*
Never Married, Cohabiting						
(8) Single-Dating-Cohabiting	2.2	3.0	3.4	2.8	2.3	2.6
(9) Single-Dating-Cohabiting-Dating-Cohabiting	0.8	1.8	1.7	2.3	1.0	0.8
Subtotal %	*3.0*	*4.8*	*5.2*	*5.1*	*3.3*	*3.4*
Married						
(10) Single-Dating-Married	29.7	13.6	29.6	24.1	29.1	28.6
(11) Single-Dating-Cohabiting-Married	8.3	7.3	7.7	5.8	8.5	8.6
(12) Single-Dating-Cohabiting-Dating-Cohabiting-Married	2.0	3.0	0.0	0.9	1.8	2.2
(13) Single-Dating-Cohabiting-Dating-Married	1.0	1.0	0.4	0.5	0.7	1.2
Subtotal %	*41.0*	*25.0*	*37.8*	*31.3*	*40.1*	*40.5*

Divorced, Single

(14) Single-Dating-Married-Currently Single	3.4	4.6	0.9	2.8	4.5	2.8
(15) Single-Dating-Married-Currently Dating	2.4	2.8	3.0	0.9	2.6	2.8
(16) Single-Dating-Cohabiting-Married-Currently Single	0.8	1.0	1.3	0.9	1.1	0.7
(17) Single-Dating-Cohabiting-Married-Currently Dating	1.0	1.8	1.7	1.2	1.0	1.2
Subtotal %	*7.6*	*10.1*	*6.9*	*5.8*	*9.2*	*7.6*

Divorced, Cohabiting

(18) Single-Dating-Married-Dating-Cohabiting	1.0	0.5	1.7	1.6	1.2	0.8
(19) Single-Dating-Cohabiting-Married-Dating-Cohabiting	0.5	0.5	0.9	0.5	0.8	0.4
Subtotal %	*1.5*	*1.0*	*2.6*	*2.1*	*2.0*	*1.2*

Remarried

(20) Single-Dating-Married-Dating-Remarried	3.7	2.3	2.6	2.8	5.0	2.6
(21) Single-Dating-Married-Dating-Cohabiting-Remarried	2.8	2.3	3.4	3.7	3.4	2.1
(22) Single-Dating-Cohabiting-Married-Dating-Remarried	0.3	0.5	0.0	0.2	0.2	0.4
(23) Single-Dating-Cohabiting-Married-Dating-Cohabiting-Remarried	1.3	1.0	0.9	0.9	1.2	1.3
Subtotal %	*8.2*	*6.1*	*6.9*	*7.6*	*9.9*	*6.4*

Other

(24) 3 or more Cohabiting partners or spouses	13.4	14.4	11.6	19.2	13.1	11.9
(25) Other	4.7	6.3	5.2	6.7	3.5	5.0
Subtotal %	*18.1*	*20.7*	*16.7*	*25.9*	*16.6*	*16.8*
Total N	*2398*	*396*	*233*	*432*	*903*	*1776*

Note: The data used in this table are from the NHSLS cross-section sample only (not the oversample). Percent distributions are unweighted.

Table 3. Patterns of sexual partnering over twelve months by gender, race, and relationship status (excluding single status)

			Just one partnership (STD last year: 1.7%)	Multiple short-term partnerships (STD last year: 8.8%)	Long-term partners with short-term concurrent partnership (STD last year: 0%)	Long-term partners with long-term concurrent partnership (STD last year: 3.8%)	N
Men	White	Dating (37%)	46	21	24	9	70
		Cohabiting (8%)	60	7	27	7	15
		Married (56%)	97	0	1	2	106
	Black	Dating (54%)	21	21	33	24	42
		Cohabiting (14%)	45	9	9	36	11
		Married (32%)	97	0	1	2	25
Women	White	Dating (29%)	65	3	17	16	65
		Cohabiting (7%)	93	0	7	0	15
		Married (64%)	98	1	1	1	143
	Black	Dating (60%)	67	6	6	21	78
		Cohabiting (18%)	96	0	4	0	24
		Married (23%)	93	0	3	3	30
		N	475	34	62	53	624

Source: Chicago Health and Social Life Survey (1995)

mate union formation in the contemporary United States. Here, we take into account partner turnover in the past twelve months, noting that a substantial majority (65%) have had only one sex partner during the year (and 15% have had none) but that 20% have more than one in various permutations, including serial monogamy and short- and long-term concurrent partners. Moreover, these patterns of concurrency are socially organized: African American men are five times more likely to be in long-term concurrent partnerships—a form of polygamy—than white men are. Being married is substantially more likely among white men and women, while dating and cohabiting are substantially more likely among black men and women, reflecting their greater likelihood of being in one of the nonmarried relationship statuses and the resultant greater volatility in the pattern of union formation.

The dating, cohabitation, and marriage markets

Demographic trends

The above patterns, observed in contemporary surveys about sexual partnering, need to be put into historical context. Both men and women in the United States are marrying later than at any other time in this century (Cherlin 1992). While the age at first marriage generally declined in the first half of this century, the rise in the age at first marriage has been dramatic in the last four decades. Female age at first marriage has been rising by about one year per decade for the last four decades (Kiernan 2000, 67). Between 1960 and 1999 the median age of first marriage for white women increased by almost five years, from 19.9 to 24.5, and for white men the median age increased by over four years, from 22.2 to 26.6 (Fitch and Ruggles 2000, 70). And, in 1999, about one-fourth of 29-year-old white women and 31-year-old white men had not yet married. This suggests that an unprecedented proportion of this generation will *never* marry, since the proportion of whites never married follows a pattern similar to the trend in age at first marriage with a twenty to thirty-year lag (Fitch and Ruggles 2000, 70).

For African Americans, the delay in first marriage has been even more striking. The median age at first marriage increased to 28.6 for African American men, and 27.3 for African American women (Fitch and Ruggles 2000, 70). This represents a six-year delay for African American men and a seven-year delay for African American women since the 1960s. And, in 1990, about a quarter of 35-year-old African American women had never married, and a quarter of 35-year-old African American men had not yet married.

The coinciding rise in cohabitation suggests that *union* formation has not been delayed as much as one might infer from the marriage rates. However, while cohabitation does indeed account for a substantial proportion of the decline in marriage among these groups, it does not explain all of it. In addition, because cohabitation is relatively unstable (40% of cohabiting unions break up without the couple getting married), the number of years spent in a union before age 25 has still substantially declined (Bumpass, Sweet, and Martin 1990).

A second trend resulting in higher rates of unmarried men and women is the increasing rate of divorce. The divorce rate has risen slowly but steadily since at least the middle of the nineteenth century through the end of World War II. During the 1950s, the divorce rate fell modestly, but in the 1960s, the annual rates rose sharply. Divorce rates peaked in 1979, and then declined slightly in the 1980s. Although estimations vary somewhat, it is projected that today over half of all marriages will end in divorce. While the annual rate of death for married persons has declined at the same time that the annual rate of divorce has been rising, the rising divorce rate since 1970 has pushed the total dissolution rate well above its historical high (Cherlin 1992).

The third demographic trend resulting in higher rates of unmarried older men and women is the declining rates of remarriage. In the early 1960s, when the divorce rate rose sharply, the remarriage rate for divorced people also rose. But in the 1970s, while the divorce rate still soared, the remarriage rate fell, and it has remained low and relatively stable through the 1980s (Cherlin 1992). The rate of remarriage has declined among divorced women of all ages, although the declines were greatest among women under age 25 at the time of divorce—a 51% drop between 1965 and 1980 (Bumpass, Sweet, and Martin 1990).

Although divorced women are less likely to remarry, they are just as likely to be cohabiting with new partners. But, as mentioned above, cohabitation is less stable than marriage, and even when people do get remarried, the rate of divorce for remarriages is substantially higher than for first marriages (Cherlin 1992). While about 30% of first marriages end in separation or divorce within ten years, 37% of remarriages dissolve within the first ten years. Thus, about 16% of the 1970 birth cohort are projected to experience a second divorce (Cherlin 1992).

Finally, the decoupling of sex and marriage was further facilitated by the contraceptive revolution inaugurated by the introduction of an effective birth control pill in 1960 (Westoff 1977) and the legalization of abortion in 1973,[5] as well as by changing norms about out-of-wedlock childbearing.

Paralleling the preceding discussion of changing trends in marriage, cohabitation, and divorce over the past several decades, we observe dramatic changes in the normative and behavioral climate regarding the initiation of sexual activities across age cohorts over the past forty years (cf. Laumann forthcoming). Figures 3a through 3e tell a consistent story. Average age at first intercourse has dropped 2 years, from 19 to 17 (see figure 3a). While most women wanted to have their first sexual experience when it happened, there was a 38% increase in the percentage of women who went along with their first sexual experience even though they would have preferred not to (figure 3b). More detailed analysis reveals that this increase in disapproval of first sexual experiences can be attributed primarily to the very early teen years in which these events took place and the feeling that strong peer pressure "made them go along with it" (cf. Laumann et al. 1994, 327–33). Figure 3c reveals the transformation of these early sexual events: the first sex partner who was or became the spouse declines from 45% among the 50- to 59-year-olds to only 6% among the 18- to 29-year-olds! The percentage of first sex partners who were not well known to the respondent nearly doubled, from 17% to 36%. Viewing the matter from another vantage point, figure 3d plots the frequency of sex with the first sex partner by age cohort. Here again we observe a steady decline in the percentage of persons who report still having sex with their first sex partner and a sharp increase in the percentage of persons who had sex with their first sex partner less than 10 times, with 56% among the 18 to 29 year olds falling into this category. Finally, figure 3e depicts a steady increase in the percentage across the age cohorts expressing approval of premarital sex, rising from 54% among the 50- to 59-year-olds to over 80% among the 18- to 29-year-olds.

Relationship status and quality of life

Finally, perhaps the most important question for the majority of the population is "how are these relationship statuses related to quality of life?" It must be kept in mind that relationship statuses are associated with a wide range of factors that may also affect quality of life, such as age, socioeconomic status, health, social competence, and substance abuse. There are substantial differences in quality of life experienced by people who have different relationship histories. For example, in most comparisons of single persons with persons occupying a relationship status that involves the presence of a sex partner, the latter report enjoying higher levels of health, happiness, or physical/emotional satisfaction than the single persons (cf. Waite and Joyner 2001). (To be sure, singles are much less likely to report ever having had a sexually transmitted disease than the other relationship configurations.) Such a pattern disfavoring singlehood, with the exception of experiences with STDs, suggests that people experience strong incentives to move out of singlehood into one of the other relationship statuses. While being involved in a sexual relationship may increase levels of happiness, it may also be the case that those who are unhappy or unhealthy may have a more difficult time sustaining a sexual relationship with a partner.

The differentials in quality of life between statuses seem to be quite orderly, and in general, favor the more permanent or stable relationship status—that is, married status

Figure 3a. Age at first intercourse by age cohort

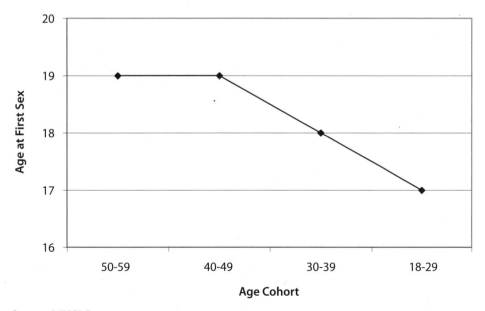

Source: NHSLS

Figure 3b. Percent of women whose first sexual event was not wanted at the time by age cohort

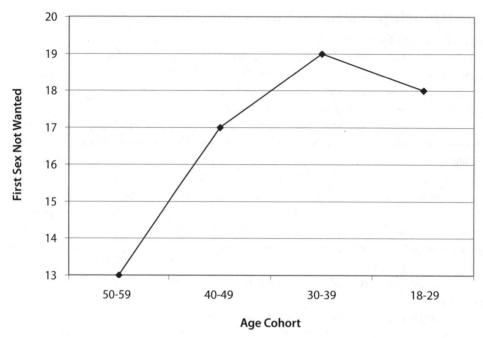

Source: NHSLS

Figure 3c. Status of first sexual partner by age cohort

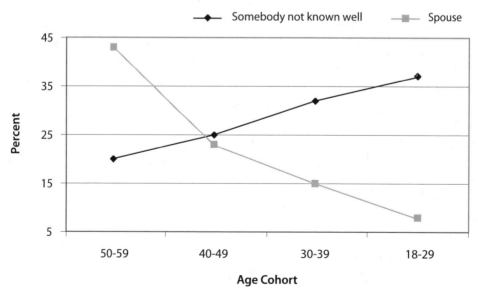

Source: NHSLS

Figure 3d. Frequency of sex with first sex partner by age cohort

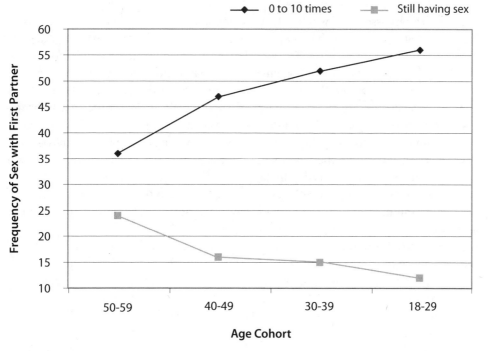

Source: NHSLS

Figure 3e. Approval of premarital sex by age cohort

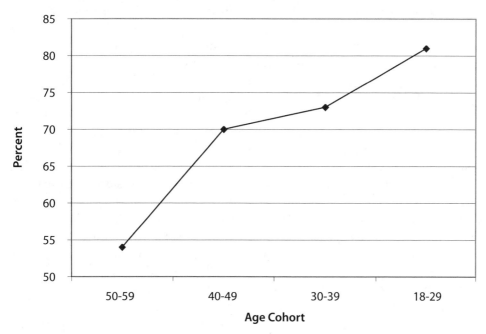

Source: NHSLS

is "better in quality of life" when compared to cohabiting, and cohabiting is "better" when compared to dating (see Waite and Joyner 2001). Part of this ordering can be accounted for as a result of the more limited number of recent and potentially concurrent sex partners associated with the focal respondent in the more enduring relationship statuses—that is, the lower the competition for the focal person's sexual attention, the higher the levels of satisfaction. The most adverse status for quality of life, however, is the absence of a sexual partner altogether (cf. Laumann and Youm 2001).

Interestingly, however, there is a gender difference in the ordering of the level of happiness by relationship type. For never married men, the biggest increase in happiness occurs between the single and dating status, with a slight decline for cohabiting, and then an increase to the highest level of happiness among those who are married. For never married women, on the other hand, there is no increase in happiness from single to dating, and even a slight decline in happiness. The jump in happiness for women occurs between dating and cohabiting, and then from cohabiting to where it reaches its highest level in marriage. Apparently, for never married men, happiness appears to be associated with simply being in a sexual relationship, while for women, level of commitment appears to be more important (see Waite and Joyner 2001 for a detailed analysis of the association of relationship type, commitment, and physical and emotional satisfaction). It is also interesting to note that more single women than single men report being "Very/Extremely Happy," despite the fact that single men are much more likely to have had a sexual partner in the last year. In fact, about one-fourth of single men had two or more partners in the last year, compared to only about 16 % of single women.

Conclusions

The central claim of this paper is that the transformation in the social organization of sexuality in the United States over the past fifty years has had profound implications for the formation of intimate unions. This transformation is rooted in the disembedding of sexual activities from their close association with fertility as the result of the early 1960s contraceptive revolution that conferred unprecedented control over the likelihood of pregnancy on individual decision-makers instead of on biology. Romantic, sexually active relationships no longer have to be conducted under the shadow of unwanted pregnancy and the socially sanctioned imperative of being married in order to have children. With the declining age of sexual maturation from over 16 years of age to nearly 12 over the course of the last century (Frisch 1985), the increasing age at first marriage to 26 for men and 24 for women, the 50/50 likelihood of divorce and the decline in the rates of remarriage, Americans currently face the prospect of spending nearly half of their adult life between 18 and 59 single (with no sex partner) or in non-coresidential dating relationships. While family demographers have recently been paying increasing attention to cohabitation in addition to their focus on marriage, they have failed to take sufficient notice of the growing significance of singlehood and dating relationships in accounting for the dynamics of intimate union formation within various population subgroups. This is an especially serious oversight because of the growing discrepancies in the patterns of union formation among African Americans, Hispanics, and whites.

What is more, this transformation in the social organization of sexuality in the United States has been highly gendered—that is, men and women experience very different trajectories across the various relationship statuses over their life course (Laumann and Mahay 2002). In some sense, men have, for a much longer historical period, been much more likely than women to be sexually active earlier in their adolescence, accumulate more partners over their life time (6 versus 2 for women) (Laumann et al. 1994, 172–224), engage in premarital sex with partners that they have no intention of forming a long-term relationship or marrying, and have overlapping or concurrent partners within committed relationships like cohabitation or marriage. While there is some suggestion that women are "catching up" with men with respect to some of these matters (e.g., becoming sexually active earlier),[6] and engaging in premarital sex with partners they do not intend to marry (although they are still much more likely than men to report that they are in love with them), they are much more likely than men to spend longer periods of time in single status, especially at ages beyond 40. By age 70, 70% of women will neither have a sex partner nor much prospect of finding one, whereas only 35% of men will be without a sex partner (cf. Laumann et al. 1994, 91; Mahay and Laumann 2001). The gender gap with respect to subjective preferences for selected sexual practices (Laumann et al. 1994, 148–71) and normative orientations toward sexuality (Laumann et al. 1994, 509–40) appears to be robust and persistent, despite notable variations across race and ethnic groups. These differentials are important because they set the gendered terms in which negotiating and bargaining are framed (cf. Youm and Laumann 2003) and affect the likelihood of making transitions from one relationship status to another (figure 2).

In comparison to western European, economically developed countries, the population of the United States has an exceptionally high prevalence of sexually transmitted diseases (cf. Michael et al. 1998). This is especially surprising because it is well known that public opinion in the United States about sexual matters is among the most conservative in the world (cf. Widmer, Treas, and Newcomb. 1998; Laumann 2002). How could a sexually conservative population be so prone to the spread of STDs? Here is a case where reasoning from central tendencies or averages can be very misleading. Analysis of the distribution of normative attitudes about sexual matters in the U. S. population suggests that there is, in fact, an extensive polarization of views that set adherents of traditional, religiously inspired notions about sexuality and the need for restraint in sexual expression against adherents of sexually liberal, hedonistic views that celebrate the joys of sex. In the middle can be found the majority of the population who embrace the view of moderation in all things sexual. The strongly held views of the polar extremes are embraced with enthusiasm by distinctive population subgroups (Laumann et al. 1994, 509–40) that are concentrated in different regions of the country, making for brouhahas over public health policies regarding sexuality a regular, recurring feature of the political landscape (cf. Laumann, Gagnon, and Michael 1994; Ericksen 1999). Fights over sex education in the schools, condom advertising in the public media, condom distribution in public places, abortion, and teenage pregnancy are only some of the issues that command public attention in inconclusive debates (cf. Michael 2001).The resulting lack of coherence in public health policy is manifest in the hodgepodge of public-health half measures that vary greatly from locality to locality and the impacted dissemination of STDs in specific race and ethnic groups (cf. Laumann and Youm 1999). How else could one account for the wild variations in the prevalence of specific STDs from subgroup to subgroup in the United States. For instance, rates of gonorrhea among African Americans are twenty to thirty times higher than the white rates, while rates for viral STDs are highest among higher-educated whites.

There are enormous differences in the prevalence of STDs among persons with particular relationship status configurations. We suggest the systematic inclusion of the more comprehensive set of relationship statuses (including dating and single statuses) in population-based data-gathering would greatly enhance our understanding of the dynamics of STD transmission in the population at large and thus contribute to the formulation of more effective intervention strategies.

Finally, we believe there is a pressing need to recognize the fundamental heterogeneity of the dating relationship status. Our data suggest that there are distinctive patterns of dating, ranging from strict serial succession of dating dyads (where one terminates one dating relationship before starting another—a form of serial monogamy), to short-term concurrency in dating relationships (the pattern apparently preferred by whites) to long-term and recurrent concurrency among dating partners (approximating a form of polygamy—a form that is already well established in the African American population in lieu of marriage). There is, of course, also the overlay of concurrency in cohabitation and marriage to be considered. Since as much as a quarter of one's pre-60 adult life is spent in dating relationships, it will behoove us to understand these phenomena more fully, especially as they are so self-evidently related to the dynamics of disease spread and constitute the critical precursors for transitioning to other relationship statuses. Understanding the consequences of concurrency in sexual partnerships for triggering termination and transition to other relationship statuses and for other health and quality of life outcomes is a critical next step in the research enterprise.

Acknowledgments

A version of this paper was presented at the XV International Sociological Association World Congress of Sociology, Brisbane, Australia, July 8–13, 2002. The authors are listed in alphabetical order.

Notes

1. The lack of research on sexual relationships as part of the union formation process is no doubt also in large part due to a lack of reliable, broadly inclusive data on sexual partnerships. Large-scale data sets often used by demographers, such as the U.S. Census and Current Population surveys, have collected data only on cohabitation and marital relationships, rather than sexual relationships. In this way, government definitions of important or legitimate relationship statuses have conventionalized and privileged marriage and (only in the recent past) cohabitation as relationship statuses worthy of study.

2. While this conception is intended to include both opposite-gender and same-gender sexual partnerships, the empirical materials in the paper will refer only to opposite-gender relationship statuses because we lack sufficient numbers of respondents who report same-gender partnerships to sustain a valid and reliable statistical analysis. Less than three percent of the male respondents in the National Health and Social Life Survey (NHSLS, Laumann et al. 1994 (especially chapter 8 on homosexuality)) reported at least one same-gender partnership in the past twelve months. This translates into only 39 men. The number of women with at least one same-gender partnership in the past year is only 24. (See Laumann et al., 1994,

311.) While as many as nine percent of men reported some same-gender experience in their lifetime, over 40% of these men reported such experiences occurring only during their adolescence (before 18).

3. See Laumann et al. 1994, 30–34 for an extended discussion of the concept of master statuses and master relationships.

4. One bias we know these data reflect arises from the fact that the twelve largest central cities in the U.S. are known to have higher concentrations of single persons than elsewhere.

5. This was the occasion of the Supreme Court's controversial decision in Roe v. Wade that asserted that a woman's right to have an abortion was protected by the U.S. Constitution. See Michael 2001 for an extended discussion of the changing prevalence of abortion in the United States in the wake of the Supreme Court decision.

6. There has been about a year decline in the average age of first intercourse over the past 40 years, but there is still roughly a six-month differential between white men and women. The differential for age of first intercourse is larger in the African American population—about a year and half—and more persistent over time. The white differentials by gender seem to be converging more rapidly than in the African American community. See Laumann et al. 1994, 325.

References

Bumpass, L., J. Sweet, and T. C. Martin. 1990. Changing patterns of remarriage. *Journal of Marriage and the Family* 52:747–56.

Cherlin, A. 1992. *Marriage, divorce, and remarriage.* Cambridge: Harvard University Press.

Ericksen, J. A. (with S. A. Steffen). 1999. *Kiss and tell: Surveying sex in the twentieth century.* Cambridge: Harvard University Press.

Fitch, C., and S. Ruggles. 2000. Historical trends in marriage formation. In *Ties that bind: Perspectives on marriage and cohabitation,* ed. L. J. Waite, C. Bachrach, M. Hindin, E. Thomson, and A. Thornton, 59–88. Hawthorne, NY: Aldine de Gruyter.

Frisch, R. E. 1985. Fatness, menarche, and female fertility. *Perspectives in Biology and Medicine* 28, no 4: 611–33.

Goldscheider, F., and L. Waite. 1991. *New families, no families: The transformation of the American home.* Berkeley: University of California.

Laumann, E. O. Forthcoming. Love, sex and public morality in the United States: Moving to the right? In *Morality and public life: Is America in moral decline?* ed. M. R. Zinman. Lawrence: University Press of Kansas.

Laumann, E. O., S. Ellingson, J. Mahay, A. Paik, and Y. Youm, eds. 2004. *The sexual organization of the city.* Chicago: University of Chicago Press.

Laumann, E. O., J. H. Gagnon, and R. T. Michael. 1994. A political history of the National Sex Survey of Adults. *Family Planning Perspectives* 26 (January/February): 34–38.

Laumann, E. O., J. H. Gagnon, R. T. Michael, and S. Michael. 1994. *The social organization of sexuality: Sexual practices in the United States.* Chicago: University of Chicago Press.

Laumann, E. O., and J. Mahay. 2002. The social organization of women's sexuality. In *Handbook of women's sexual and reproductive health,* ed. G. M. Wingood and R. J. DiClemente, 43–70. New York: Kluwer Academic Publishers.

Laumann, E. O., and R. T. Michael. 2001. *Sex, love, and health in America: Private choices and public policies.* Chicago: University of Chicago Press.

Laumann, E. O., A. Paik, and R. C. Rosen. 1999. Sexual dysfunction in the United States: Prevalence, predictors, and outcomes. *Journal of the American Medical Association* 281, No. 6 (February 10): 537–44, 584.

Laumann, E. O., and Y. Youm. 1999. Race/ethnic group differences in the prevalence of sexually transmitted diseases in the United States: A network explanation. *Sexually Transmitted Diseases* 266 (May): 250–61.

———. 2001. Sexual expression in America. In Laumann and Michael 2001, 109–47.

Mahay, J. 2002. Family formation over the life course: Processes of change and strain. PhD diss., University of Chicago.

Mahay, J., and E. O. Laumann. 2001. Meeting and mating over the life course: A new approach to understanding union formation. Paper presented at the annual meeting of the American Sociological Association, Anaheim, CA, August.

Michael, R. T. 2001a. Abortion decisions in the United States. In Laumann and Michael 2001, 377–438.

———. 2001b. Private sex and public policy. In Laumann and Michael 2001, 463–91.

Michael, R. T., J. Wadsworth, J. A. Feinleib, A. M. Johnson, E. O. Laumann, and K. Wellings. 1998. Private sexual behavior, public opinion, and public health policy related to sexually transmitted diseases: A U. S.–British comparison. *American Journal of Public Health* 88, no. 5: 749–54.

Parish, W., and E. O. Laumann. n.d. The patterning of sexuality in China. Manuscript.

Preston, S. H., P. Heuveline, and M. Guillot. 2000. *Demography: Measuring and modeling population processes.* Malden, MA: Blackwell.

Raley, R. K. 2000. Recent trends and differentials in marriage and cohabitation: The United States. In *Ties that bind*, ed. L. Waite, 19–39. New York: Aldine de Gruyter.

Turner, C. F., L. Ku, S. M. Rogers, L. D. Lindberg, J. H. Pleck, and F. L. Sonenstein. 1998. Adolescent sexual behavior, drug use, and violence: Increased reporting with computer survey technology. *Science* 280, no. 5365: 867–73.

Waite, L., and K. Joyner. 2001. Emotional and physical satisfaction with sex in married, cohabiting, and dating sexual unions: Do men and women differ? In Laumann and Michael 2001, 239–69.

Westoff, C. F. 1977. The contraceptive revolution. Princeton: Princeton University Press.

Widmer, D., J. Treas, and R. Newcomb. 1998. Attitudes toward non-marital sex in 24 countries. *Journal of Sex Research* 35:349–58.

Youm, Y. 2000. Trust in U. S. families: Its effects on the formation and dynamics of families. PhD diss., University of Chicago.

Youm, Y., and E. O. Laumann. 2002. Social network effects on the transmission of sexually transmitted diseases. *Sexually Transmitted Diseases* 29, no. 11:689–97.

———. 2003. The effect of structural embeddedness on the division of household labor: A game-theoretic model using a network approach. *Rationality and Society* 15, no. 2: 243–80.

David Knapp Whittier
and Rita M. Melendez

12

Sexual Scripting and Self-Process

Intersubjectivity among Gay Men

Sexual scripting theory is a conceptual framework offered to examine the social construction of sexuality (Simon and Gagnon 1984, 1986, 1987). The theory distinguishes between three interrelated levels of social life involved in the scripting of sexuality—cultural scenarios, interpersonal relations, and the intrapsychic. With this heuristic, sexuality is examined as it occurs at interdependent levels of social life: first, the direction—the who, what, when, where, and how of sexuality—existing at the level of culture and helping to form human activity, such as social norms and definitions provided by social institutions; second, how people orchestrate sexual interactions, as in sexual intercourse; and third, how the individual actor uses and creates cultural expressions of sexuality; for example, their particular sexual fantasies and the role these play in their sexual lives. A way to examine and account for social change is contained in this three-tiered conceptualization (Simon and Gagnon, 2003; Whittier and Simon, 2001).

Following Kenneth Burke (1968), sexual scripting theory uses the metaphor of drama (Gagnon 1973, Simon 1996) to capture the means by which individuals act out and experience their sexuality.[1] With this viewpoint, human sexual activity is motivated by culture and the imagery serves to counter the natural science model and physical characterization of sexuality. Humans are motivated by social and cultural forces more so or as much as they are by physical influences. Elements of the theatre, such as the stage, scene, props, script, audience response, and the actors' performances are important to the vibrant construction of sexual activity. Actors are constantly involved in producing society and sexuality. Even the script is interpreted and enacted differently by actors depending upon their unique life histories, experiences, and backgrounds. Plum-

This chapter is an extension and expansion of the article "Intersubjectivity in the intrapsychic sexual scripting of gay men." *Culture, Health & Sexuality* 6, no. 2 (2004):131–43. *www.tandf.co.uk/journals/titles/13691058.asp*

mer (1982) notes that a common misuse of sexual scripting theory has been the application of cultural stereotypes to individual behavior, ignoring the interaction between culture, interpersonal encounters, and the individual. He states:

> In the hands of some researchers, it has become a wooden mechanical tool for identifying uniformities in sexual conduct—the script determines activity, rather than emerging through activity. What is actually required is to show the nature of sexual scripts as they emerge in encounters (Plummer 1982, 228, emphasis in the original).

In this chapter, we present the reports of the sexual thoughts, fantasies, and activities of some gay-identified men. This chapter demonstrates that, as Simon and Gagnon (1984, 54) argue, the intrapsychic is "the symbolic reorganization of reality in ways to more fully realize the actor's many-layered and sometimes multi-voiced wishes." This article concentrates primarily on intrapsychic scripting as an underdeveloped but necessary part of sexual scripting theory. The intent isn't to dismiss or refute the importance of institutional sources and interpersonal negotiations, but to illustrate intrapsychic sexual scripting more fully.

The self and sexuality in sexual scripting theory

Sexual scripting theory is a framework for thinking about and studying sexuality as well as a conceptualization of the modern self. The interrelationship between the three analytic levels of sexual scripting theory points to both social change and individuation in modern sexuality. "The 'self' that most contemporary individuals experience . . . is in fact the product of the widespread decline in the isomorphism between cultural scenarios, available interpersonal scripts, and assurances of intrapsychic satisfaction" (Simon and Gagnon 1987, 370). The realm of sexuality is one domain in which the "self" takes on special importance within modernity. As definitions for sexuality grow and diversify within culture, the potential relationships between individual motives and cultural scenarios increase in number and complexity. For example, contemporary sexuality does not merely constitute a means to reproduction but serves many other social purposes like intimacy and relationships (D'Emilio and Freedman 1988; Giddens 1992). Emphasis is placed on individual sexuality, for instance, as a legitimate pursuit of personal pleasure (D'Emilio and Freedman 1988; Seidman 1991). Some analysts have noted that sexuality has become a harbinger of "character" and representative of beliefs, values, and morals in social life (Gecas and Libby 1976). Moreover, in modernity, sexuality becomes increasingly regarded as a distinct and highly significant social domain within which individuals may anchor themselves (Giddens 1992; Lichtenstein 1977; Stoller 1979; Person 1987). Consequently, sexuality becomes a social location for the "true self" and individuals become increasingly self-reflexive in the domain of social meanings that is termed "sexual." For Simon and Gagnon (1987), all this significance attributed to sexuality is sociogenic.

Two related processes endemic to modernity, individuation and sexualization, help create intrapsychic sexual scripting—the "realm of self-process" (Simon and Gagnon 1987, 364). In symbolic interactionism, "self-concept" references all thoughts as feelings of oneself as an object—the products or consequences of self-awareness (Gecas and Burke 1995, 42). Sexual interests have previously been examined as "lists" of characteristics or traits that researchers have preordained as representative of the intrapsychic sexual realm (Anderson and Cryanowski 1994; Anderson, Cryanowski and Espindle 1999; Bem 1974; Breakwell and Millward 1997; Garcia 1999; Jemail and Greer 1977). However, these "lists" often reinforce cultural scenarios and stereotypes. Highly structured and predetermined measures ensure that the intrapsychic or the private realm of individuals will be filtered through the cultural or public realm of the researcher. Likewise, a focus on cultural scenarios and how people act them out sexually (e.g., as with sex/gender roles and "scripts") is a simplistic usage of sexual scripting theory. More complex phenomenon are involved in the construction of culture, selves, and sexuality. Although individuals construct intrapsychic scripting from cultural meanings, these meanings are altered, combined, and translated into individual-level meanings—which, as such, are not completely synonymous with cultural scenarios as culture is carried and developed, in part, in the everyday activities and uses of individuals (DiMaggio 1997; Swidler 2001). For this reason, it is important to examine the processes by which individuals manage their sexual lives. What is needed are ways of studying sexual intrapsychics and subjectivities that do not reduce them to preordained categories (di Mauro 1995) and means of analyzing how individuals manage the cultural scenarios surrounding them in their sexual lives, especially those which occur in sexual practice or interpersonal sexual scripting. Attention to individual sexual meanings, desires, and erotic interests may be replacing a reductionistic focus on sexual identities (Garnets and Peplau 2000; Levine 2003; Rust 1993; Whittier and Simon 2001). According to Longmore (1998, 53), "what is missing from the literature are conceptualizations and measures of the sexual-self concept from a symbolic interactionist perspective." Individuals, at the level of the intrapsychic, are also involved in scripting or creating sexuality. As Plummer notes, "we tell stories about ourselves in order to constitute ourselves" (1995, 172).

Sexual scripting theory clarifies the relation between personal and situated (social-contextual) meaning by distinguishing between intrapsychic sexual scripting, interpersonal sexual scripting, and cultural scenarios for sexuality. Therefore the methods employed in this study were chosen to examine meaning, particularly that of the individual, because meaning is central to sexual scripting and symbolic interactionism.

Recruitment

Men were recruited face-to-face in gay-identified locales such as bars and gyms. Interested friends of those interviewed were occasionally recruited via a chain method. The men were told that the interviews would be longitudinal and that they would need to meet with the first author weekly to discuss their thoughts and feelings surrounding (solitary) masturbation and interpersonal sexual encounters. Participants were not recruited so as to "represent" gay men. Rather, they were recruited for their willingness to participate in in-depth discussions of their sexual lives.

Participants

Each of the 23 gay-identified men participated in a longitudinal series of audiotaped interviews. Three were in their 20s, five in their 30s, eleven in their 40s, two in their

50s, and two in their 60s. Two participants identified themselves as Latino and the rest as white. To help keep participants' identities confidential, pseudonyms replace actual names in the excerpts presented below.

Interviews

The first author used unstructured, longitudinal interviews to elicit meanings, attributions, perceptions, fantasies, wishes, and desires. Consistent with the goals of ethnography, a thick record and saturation of personal sexual meanings, thoughts, fantasies, desires, and behaviors were aimed for as the intended outcome of the data collection to aid the analysis.

Following Carspecken's (1996) method for critical ethnography, only a few broad questions were used in the interviews, so as to limit the effects of the researcher's preconceived notions of what might be an important and relevant line of inquiry. In the first session, each man was asked to tell "the story of his life" from his birth to that moment in time, devoting special attention to sexual history. After this initial interview, the men completed an average of 6.5 follow-up interview sessions in which they were asked to recall, in as much detail as possible, any self-defined sexual experience since their last interview, including (solitary) masturbation and sexual encounters with others. As the participant recalled each experience or story, neutral probes were used to extract the participant's perceptions, feelings, attitudes, and desires. An example of a typical probe is, "Can you recall anything else you thought about that?" The first life/sexual history interview lasted approximately two hours, and each subsequent follow-up sexual diary interview lasted approximately half an hour.

Analysis

Interview data were analyzed using a modified grounded theory approach (Strauss and Corbin 1990), making use of aspects of Carspecken's (1996) critical ethnographic method and guided by interpretivist traditions in qualitative research (Lincoln and Guba 1985). Unlike traditional grounded theory, the approach did not assume an inexperienced orientation to the data on the part of the investigator.

Multiple reports were collected over time to encourage participants to articulate their implicit beliefs and theories to the extent that these became apparent to them in their sustained considerations of their sexual thoughts, desires, feelings, and activities. Longitudinal reports were required so that the ethnographer could examine the record for back- and fore-grounding of sexual meanings—a process described as a dialogic reconstruction (Carspecken 1996).

Each of the transcripts and notes were examined for evidence of dialogic reconstructions. Transcripts and notes were further organized into three overarching themes: 1) the importance of intersubjectivity; 2) the burdens intersubjectivity brings to sexual identity; and 3) the methods participants use to alleviate these burdens. Gender, race, class, and age were common themes mentioned by the participants and further identified by the authors as significant social statuses by which participants commonly talked about their sexual experiences. Social categories of gender, race, class, and age are social practices as well as structures, stratifications, and statuses. These are social practices in that people take up and (re)create gendered, raced, classed, and aged meanings for sexuality. People create culture just as they are created by culture (DiMaggio 1997; West and Fenstermaker 1995). Because these social categories were often used by interviewees to describe their experience, they were also used as analytic themes to organize the larger theme of intersubjectivity and to help highlight how individuals use social status categories in a nuanced manner to make sense of their sexual lives.

Results

When talking about their sexual lives, both past and present, all the men spoke about intersubjectivities—what they thought others thought of them. Intersubjectivity functions both as a burden and an avenue to sexual excitement. Findings reported here concentrate on individuals and how they manage intersubjectivity to minimize the fear of rejection, define sexual excitement, and increase personal, sexual pleasure.

Importance of intersubjectivity to desire

Many of these men were concerned with what they think other men think of them. Many participants discussed how their attraction to some other men began only after they perceived an interest from the other. One participant, Ramon (25 years old, Latino), spoke about getting sexually excited after realizing that he was the object of other men's interest. He said, "[they were] just totally turning me on as they were talking to me and making me feel really comfortable like they were really genuinely into me and I was not really having to, you know . . . like to work the scene." Ramon experienced his own sexual excitement through the thought that other men found him sexually exciting. Almost irrespective of the qualities of these men, Ramon founds himself sexually attracted to them because they were attracted to him. Ramon's experience reflects a seemingly common intersubjective occurrence.

The importance of intersubjectivity is also observable when some men talked about the emotional and relational aspects of their sexual partners. In these cases, relationships with other men are a way of affirming positive self-definitions. For example Kevin (46 years old, white) only sleeps with men he loves. He insisted he could not sleep with anyone who does not want a lasting relationship (even if only as a friend); indeed, to do so would not only be a negative characteristic of his potential partner but of himself. Kevin stated he does not want to be regarded as a "blow-up doll," demonstrating his need to be in a relationship that involves more than just sex.

> If I get an indication that this is just going to be a quick blowjob or a fast fuck or something like that, generally I wasn't interested. If it's . . . you want to talk . . . you want to let me find out a little bit about you . . . you want to find out something about me. Is this a strict . . . Is this strictly a physical thing, also . . . and there is some of that not only because the romance but there are some people out there who are extraordinarily beautiful on the outside and hideously ugly as soon as they open their mouths. And I don't particular want to associate with those people.

Kevin essentially affirms his own likeability and sincerity through his partners, as well as his (perceived) ability to know his partners "true" selves. Kevin's moral boundaries are mirrored in how he thinks about his sex partners.

Although Kevin concentrates on achieving a long-lasting relationship with the men he sleeps with, others seek short-term sexual gratification with one-time partners they might never see again. Although these men seem to avoid long-lasting relationships with other men, their short affairs often have a relational aspect to the meanings attributed to these sexual encounters and further exemplify the importance of intersubjectivity. For example, Robin (36 years old, white) said his favorite encounters in bathhouses involve talking with men as an essential element of his attraction as well as a requisite for a sexual encounter with them.

> I loved talking . . . Sometimes I would go to the baths because I could do . . . I could sort of get both of it. If you get the right kind of guy you can talk for a really long time and have sex too. And that was neat too. I mean, I met him at the baths and we talked for a long time while we were having sex and playing around. It was just . . . I mean I remember that experience to this day because that was the first time that I ever just like really, you know, locked into someone and seemed to relate, you know, in that way.

Robin is not interested in a mere sexual organ, but rather in someone who verbally connects with him. Robin's belief that he got something more than just genital contact in the bath house made the sexual encounter the epitome of excitement for him.

Another participant, Corey (37 years old, white) goes to adult bookstores for one-time sexual encounters. He gets a heightened sense of sexual pleasure from the idea that he is pleasing his partner above and beyond that partner's previous experience. Corey went into a bookstore with the decided notion that he would pay attention to what turns him on sexually. He described performing fellatio on men through glory holes and wanting them to make bodily gestures and sounds to show him they are interested and excited. When he feels they are not, he loses interest. He says, "Generally, just with all guys, my major thing that I care about doing is whatever pleases my partner." Performing analingus is another turn on and method Corey uses to reinforce positive feedback from his sexual partners:

> I have this idea that not many people do it [analingus] and so it . . . so it's . . . kind of exciting to be somebody who will do it when not many . . . when not that many people do it. And . . . but I really like it. Because I know that it is such . . . I mean, I can remember the first few times, you know, when I was young and people would do it to me, how really neat it felt. And so . . . for me it's nice to be able to make somebody feel what I have experienced before.

Corey derives sexual excitement when he feels he provides this rare sexual service. He feels that he obligates men to be grateful to him and in so doing creates the impression for himself that he is special and unique to them. He says,

> My real motivation was real selfish because I wanted to have sex. I wanted to feel somebody's body next to mine. And then I'm there and the thought is, "Oh, wow, I am really providing a service here that somebody enjoys."

But at the same time there is also a selfish thing too. I mean with this guy, I knew I was aware of, "Oh, if he picked me . . ." Me . . . suck his cock would be a small boost to [my] self esteem because I perceived him as a this . . . the kind of looking guy that could have nine out of ten guys that wanted him.

Clearly, there is a symbolic, if not "committed," relationship between the subject and object in Corey's sexual exchanges and excitement. Performing fellatio on this man would mean more to Corey than simply a good sexual experience—it would enhance his evaluation of himself. Fellatio on this man is "selfish" because it provides more benefits for Corey (good feelings about himself) than he can return, and it provides for Corey's personal pleasure and excitement.

The burdens of intersubjectivity to desire

Other men avoid relationships or the thought of relationships completely. For some, the problem of intersubjectivity is a major factor in their sexual lives. Many men devise means of dealing with sex that preserves sexual excitement by engaging in processes that sidestep the possibility of intersubjectivity. For example, Thomas (32 years old, white) is concerned with finding an intimate partner, but feels threatened about exposing himself emotionally to someone who might reject and hurt him—what he calls the "rejection factor." Phone sex is "safe sex" because "there's no rejection there": "He is not going to reject me if he sees me and I'm not his type. And I'm not going to reject him because I don't see him." Through commercial phone sex, Thomas maintains human contact on a sexual level without any fear of rejection from the other. To further alleviate his fear of rejection, Thomas often enacts different roles over the phone, highlighting his ability to leave his "true" self behind and engage in a sexual encounter where he does not feel judged.

Other men also cope with intersubjectivity by avoiding ongoing relationships. Erik (44 years old, Latino), for example, is wary of the competition and commitment that cruising in a gay bar represents to him and is consequently more interested in obtaining sex in adult bookstores. The "scene" here helps to set out this meaning. He says,

> I guess I have a pretty strong sex drive. I want to have sex, but I don't want any type of emotion involved right now . . . I like the safety that I feel there. I like whenever I open a booth door and a guy invites me in, I like that feeling of approval that feels good to know that he approves of me. Um, I like that feeling of conquering somebody.

The bookstore represents a place where Erik is "in control"—the "alpha dog." Erik's sense of sexuality is fulfilled and approved in the bookstores without any of the risks of rejection or injured emotions. He feels that the bookstores give him a sense of sexual "approval" without having to invest his own emotions. He is able to continue to have meaningful sexual contact with men that are neither long lasting nor potentially hurtful.

For other men, the burdens of intersubjectivity affect them in their long-lasting relationships. Robin, for example, feels that his boyfriend's under-enthusiasm during sex makes him less attractive.

> And even when we have sex right now, I mean he is just so off-putting about it. He does not really get into it. And that makes me feel less attractive. And that makes the sexual encounter less than ideal to me because I think ideally, you know, have my, you know . . . my penis adored or praised or whatever.

Robin wants his partner to be sexually excited by him. Robin's sense of himself as a sexual being is reflected through his perception of his partner's excitement for Robin during sex. Lacking perception of his partner's excitement for him, and somewhat like Thomas, Robin fantasizes about having sex on stage as a means of relieving himself of some of these burdens of intersubjectivity. In this imagining, sex lacks the connotations of personal motives that would bother Robin, such as cheating on his boyfriend or a possible rejection, while simultaneously enhancing positive thoughts like having sex with good-looking and even famous people.

Bob (42 years old, white) seems to have a way of engaging in sexual interactions that minimizes the role of the other and thoughts about evaluations of Bob as a sexual object. This is a mode that is different from what he experiences with his lover wherein he is very concerned to negotiate emotional supports and verbal approvals. In his "minimization" mode, Bob continually describes his sexual encounters as "playing" (a common term used by some U. S. gay men for recreational sex), and his description of the sexual encounter is reminiscent of playing in the sexual action—a way of being sexual that is fairly unconcerned about the selves involved. It is sex that is romantic and full of affection by virtue of his stance toward and actions he takes in it, not from the stated feelings of one for the other.

> And I was enjoying touching him. And it was just like having the favorite toy that you want to have there, right there to play with. And you can play with it as much as you want.

When asked to talk about who the people in the scene are and what they expect of each other, Bob points out that, to him, sex is "not a narrative, it is an event."

> There's no story. There's nothing going on. And some people sit and watch them for hours. But if it's real life going on in front of me, I can watch it for hours. If I can get in and touch and be a part of it, I love that.

His mode of being sexual is facilitated by a "still shot," as in a photograph, frozen in the eternal—not tied to a series of actions like a video, but focused heavily on a frozen frame in his mind that captures sexuality for him. A baseball pitcher on television turns to pitch a ball, and in the instant that the pitcher turns, Bob snaps a shot of the pitcher's profile and it becomes a spur to masturbation for him:

> And the couple of times that I jacked off this week were both times I was watching TV and it was something visual that triggered me. One time I was watching the World Series and Don had gone upstairs to watch something else because he doesn't like baseball. So I was sitting downstairs . . . just laying on the sofa watching TV and this pitcher was pitching and he's just real studly. He's long and lean and

dark and a great profile. And when . . . when they pitch, they turn a lot . . . And I love . . . I love the profile. And I love the . . . this part of the man's torso, you know the upper body and the face and the neck.

Bob's mind substitutes variations of the still shot to keep himself aroused, side-stepping intersubjectivity by keeping the baseball player's frozen image in his mind. There is no need for the baseball player to approve or disapprove of Bob; the entire process of approval takes place in Bob's mind.

Bob is not concerned with achieving orgasm. He expressed that getting close to others is his goal, not so much obtaining an orgasm. When he does talk about his interest in having an orgasm, it is described as "utilitarian," where he comes when the others do because "I know when men cum the energy goes 'eeii' [down]." Surely the "turn on" of Bob's stillshot is a container of much more complexity than even this rather thick description, full of meaning and emotion.

Cultural meanings and sexual intersubjectivities

Gendered preferences

In Bob's description of the baseball player, his sexual desire is framed by the gender system and surrounded by his understanding of masculinity. He recalls sex partners that have roughly the same "look." The "look" is part of the composition. These are all essentially the same photo: "The Marlboro man, masculine, the Adam's apple, thin, tough, working class, uncomplicated, very nice, not obviously gay, hairy chest, smokes and drinks." Desiring a man who fits his image of masculinity, Bob freezes an image and conjures up thoughts of men and touching them, thereby heightening Bob's experience of masculinity and sexuality.

Other participants also experience gender intersubjectively, and gender was relevant in three ways. First, gender expression was a way some men felt sexual and attractive to other men. By expressing their sense of what it means to be a man, these men felt that other men would find them attractive, thus affirming their own sexual desirability. For example, Robin talked about going out with his boyfriend to a bar. He said, "I dressed like . . . I haven't done it in years but I dressed like cowboy hat, boots and stuff. I think that made me feel really uh . . . really masculine. You know, that really turned me on." Robin thought that this got him more attention than he usually garners. For Robin, dressing up as a cowboy increased his sense of acceptance and desirability because it connoted manliness; it also decreased Robin's sense that others would reject him.

Second, sexual encounters are ways some men affirm their own gender status. By having sex with a particular type of man, they can express masculine and feminine traits. For example, Erik's preference for straight, white businessmen amplifies his masculinity and sexual pleasure. At the adult bookstores Erik frequents, he has anonymous sex with men he perceives as his type. He discusses how he makes these men's faces touch the dirty floor and how he feels he is "breaking their façades." Erik considers these sexual encounters as a form of domination over them; getting sexual pleasure by enacting, in sex, what he perceives to be his masculinity. Erik also enjoys placing what he perceives to be "nelly" (effeminate) men in abject positions. On the other hand, he expresses nurturing emotions and interests towards sex partners he assumes to be kind, masculine, and unassuming. In doing so, Erik breaks with what he sees as status differences and the judgments of his partners. Erik's sense of his sexuality and masculinity is complex, and it varies somewhat in its manifestation with different partners and situations.

While most men deal with intersubjectivity in relation to "masculinity," at least one man, Corey, deals with the problem of intersubjectivity by perceiving and focusing on "femininity."

> My zodiac sign is Virgo, which is the feminine energy and it just all makes sense. I grew up believing that women were passive; they were the ones that gave pleasure, that did things that they didn't necessarily want to do to please their man. And so then I thought because Virgos generally manifest feminine energy, well this all makes sense why I imagine myself in these situations or find myself in them.

As noted previously, many men deal with intersubjectivity by trying to please their partners sexually. Corey understands his desire to please his partner as a feminine characteristic. He views his feminine nature as innate.

Third, their sexual scripting was framed by institutional gender scripts, such as "hegemonic masculinity" (Connell 1987). For example, Ramon affirms his masculinity in his sexual relations with other men. He wants to be in control of the relationship, and for him control means "being the man." It does not denote making his partner do the dishes or clean the house; it does, however, mean being the "top" (or inserter) in anal intercourse. He likes his partners to be bigger than he is and to be able to "throw around," "manhandle," and "tear up" these masculine men. He says, "I carry myself well. And my fantasy is to be with a guy that is equally that way or bigger but that I could have control of." To be in control of a highly masculine man is basic to Ramon's sense of his masculinity. The men Ramon has relationships with reflect his masculinity and are essential to his sexual gratification. Ramon simultaneously experiences being sexual and masculine, as the two reinforce each other.

Race and desire

Race is also a fundamental social structure that helps determine how people experience their sexual desire. Some men had specific preferences for men of a particular race. Most preferred their own race. Kevin said, "I prefer Caucasians . . . I don't find black men attractive." However, exceptions to this pattern probably provide the clearest and most illustrative examples of how racial meanings matter in sexual self-concepts. For example, Corey feels he has a special affinity for men of Middle-Eastern descent, which he associates with masculinity, and Ben (late 50s, white) exclusively prefers young Asian men.

Robin is not concerned about the race of his partners and seems to have an almost moral egalitarian stance toward having sex with men of different races. He is adamant about enjoying diversity. Having partners of different races affirms his view of himself as being open to diversity and not constrained by judgments of appearances. Robin often speaks out against the "looksist" system and views racial diversity as an affirmation of his egalitarian world view. Not only does he not judge others based on their looks, but he also feels that the partners he chooses do not judge him by his looks. Lack of interest in race is one way Robin deflates the importance of appearances. By choosing men with diverse racial backgrounds, Robin affirms a moral code he has acquired or established

in his life, which also serves the additional purpose of reducing possible negative intersubjective experiences. Someone who rejects Robin based on his looks is not worthy of
Robin's attention in the first place.

Race can also serve as a type of "pre-filter" for potential partners. Ramon, who is
Latino, has an almost exclusive interest in white men. When asked what he likes about
white men, he says:

> They're probably open-minded like I am enough to cross race . . . maybe. Because
> they are kind of like me, because I'm a very open-minded, very laid-back, very ma-
> ture, and educated in the sense that I understand that, you know, we are all human
> beings. Every time I met a white guy who liked me, that is exactly the way they are.
> Just like me . . . that to me is very respectful and it turns me on. [Emphasis added.]

Race filters out the men Ramon would not be interested in because they would not have
the traits he finds appealing. Race also serves as a verification of Ramon's own qualities—laid-back, open-minded, and educated. Ramon noted that, while on a trip to Atlanta, white men were hitting on him at a gay bar. "I got a lot of enquiry. I mean a lot
of people like were like coming on to me because they just thought like, 'What are you?
Like are you Mexican or Indian? What are . . . ?' Just, I was kind of exotic to them, I
guess." Because white men were interested in Ramon's race, he felt special and experienced his sexuality through his race and its appeal to white men.

Where Ramon enjoys the experience of having white men seek him out, Whitney
(51 years old), a white participant, only seeks sex with black men. He says:

> I was looking for a black man. That is basically all I am interested in. That is the
> number one qualification. I . . . I sometimes feel like I am not . . . well, I know I am
> not as picky about looks . . . as I would be with white men or with men of other
> races.

When asked to talk about his attraction to black men, Whitney says that there are many
different qualities; he cannot describe the things he finds attractive about black men's
looks. Above all, Whitney appreciates what he perceives as a "lack of guilt" surrounding
sex among black men. He says, "Sex in general, I think it's much more accepted and a
whole lot less guilt, no matter what you are doing." Because he perceives black men as
having fewer judgments about sex in general, he believes that he himself is less likely to
be the object of negative perceptions by black men.

Social class

Social class is also a framework where intersubjectivity is situated and organized and
can be viewed in light of sexual self-concepts. The insinuation of social class into other
statuses is difficult to untangle. For Erik, race and class combined to represent the established white world. Rough sex with white men in adult bookstores is a way Erik makes
the white world sit up and take notice that he is visible and a presence in their lives.
These feelings may stem from early experiences Erik had growing up in a predominantly
white world. Erik explained his attraction:

I was so attracted to men with wedding rings on . . . They were in the established white world, you know. You know, thinking about it, when I was a kid being in that elementary school, and I was the only Latino kid and trying to get into the white world, to blend in. It was sort of like getting revenge, sort of like getting into the white world. I mean, you'd see these guys in their little shirt and ties and their suits, and they'd have this persona of perfection, um, together. They were together guys, you know, they weren't upset. They didn't cry, so together, and to be able to pull down his pants and lift up those starched shirts, and you're in control, you know. Seeing them moan and lose their inhibitions and call out your name begging, you know, to keep doing what you're doing, that was a turn on to me. Usually, those guys would just literally zip up and turn their backs. They didn't say thanks or see you or pat you on the ass, but for that little time to be able to break that façade, to me, that was a hell of an accomplishment. And for them to reciprocate to me, my existence, if they called me up or they acknowledged that I existed, that was an accomplishment, you know. [Emphasis added.]

Erik's attraction to white men interacts with his previous experiences with white men. Because he perceives white men as the establishment that was disempowering (and demasculinating) him, Erik wishes to affirm his power (sexually) with these men.

Ramon also merged issues of race and class in discussing his sexual self, often mentioning his attraction to white men:

I care about him a lot as a person because he's just . . . he's intelligent and he is just, you know. I don't know why . . . I've got this thing. I don't know why this thing . . . I'm always attracted to white boys.

In this quote, Ramon goes from discussing a specific partner to describing his overall taste in men. "Intelligence" seems to operate as a code for Ramon, denoting someone who is educated and carries himself well—social status or class. Perhaps, for Ramon, having sex with white men verifies his class mobility. Ramon has worked hard to be a part of the established world, being the first in his family to go to college and to graduate school—accomplishments that are reflected in Ramon's sexual preferences.

Unlike Erik and Ramon, Bob is attracted to men whom he perceives as "blue-collar" or working-class. Bob relates this attraction to his upbringing: "There's a safety, there's a feeling of comfort, a feeling of belonging, too, because I was raised in that environment. I was raised in a blue-collar environment, and I'm comfortable with that." Class overlaps with gendered perceptions to represent the ideal man Bob would like to have a relationship and feels comfortable with. Class frames individual sexual meaning in that it connotes men Bob finds attractive.

Sexual self-reflections on age

These men also conceive of their sexual selves in relation to the social category of age. Because age is a significant social category and status in society, many of these men could not think of themselves as sexual beings without taking into consideration "age" and what it means to them. Age is a cultural scenario that organizes their sexual selves and desires. Age is a social practice in the domain of sexuality as they experience aged sexual definitions of the situation, self-concepts, desires, and behaviors.

At least two distinct groups of men who participated in this study expressed life-long sexual interests in men who differed from them in terms of their ages. Brent (early 50s), Thomas, Todd (mid-30s), Erik, David (late 40s), and Corey had all been primarily interested in men older than themselves when they were younger, but as they aged, the gap between their own ages and that of their partners closed. Warren (early 50s), Ben, Rick (early 50s), and Kevin have a substantial sexual interest in men who are younger than they are, and the gap between their own age and that of their partners has widened over the course of their lives.

The record of Kevin's thoughts and experiences provide some clues as to the meaning and imbrications of age on his own sexual desires, concepts, and activities. While younger,

> I preferred people my own age and I actually preferred . . . I guess I'm a narcissist at heart. There have been a couple of times when my fantasies have been, say, [to] meet my exact double or have maybe a magic mirror and have my reflection step through and have sex with myself.

This image of himself frozen in a time includes connotations of sex that are also, as discussed above, very much about romance, intimacy, trust, and the nice, friendly attitude and personality of the other (and, in his reflection on those values, of himself).

> He is young, he's a guy, which is a big plus for me. He is a young, good-looking young man, a very good-looking young man. Uh . . . Very, can be very, very sweet. Can be very, very tender and thoughtful.

Thoughts of a particular young man have been a spur to Kevin's masturbation over the last few years, although Kevin has never actually had sex with him. When the young man tells Kevin personal details, Kevin feels the young man trusts him, which gets Kevin sexually excited. Kevin "gets off" on the thought of being trusted and special to this young man.

> It was something he could tell. Something he wanted to share. Especially with me . . . When he is around me he doesn't feel like he needs those defenses. . . I think that is also tied in with making love. When somebody gives themselves to me or I feel like I am going to give myself to them, that like . . . To me that is the strongest show of emotion and trust uh . . . holding onto them uh . . . being tender with them. Knowing that either you or . . . either they are giving me pleasure or um . . . they are getting pleasure from me.

However, although the young man makes Kevin feels special, Kevin realizes his age keeps them apart.

> He and I had talked about it, and I really wasn't his type. I was a little too old for him anyway, which just broke my heart, in more ways than one.

But Kevin is able to manage this discrepancy and the problem it poses for intersubjectivity by living it in the realm of fantasy, in a way that does not implicate himself.

> And of course in my fantasy there is no rejection. That is the nice thing about fantasy. There is no rejection in my fantasies; I can go ahead and do the things that I can't, that I couldn't.

It seems that age brings to Kevin a safe set of boundaries for sex like trust, intimacy, and control.

> He [the younger fantasy lover] wants me to enjoy him just as much as I want him to enjoy me. Because it is me, it is even more special. I am the one in control. A lot of people think that okay this is the dominant person, [but] there have been times when I have felt like, no, I am the one that is controlling what is going on right here. And I am the one that is making sure that uh . . . [Kevin's lover] or whoever enjoys this, or doesn't enjoy it.

Kevin feels that social connotations of relations based on age denotes trust on the part of his younger love interest. This is further reflected in another common masturbatory fantasy related by Kevin—the first-time sexual encounter. Kevin often fantasizes about having sex with someone who has never had either penetrative or receptive sex. This fantasy represents for Kevin the idea that the other trusts him enough to make him his "first" sexual experience.

Discussion

Despite a body of empirical research on desire, "not a great deal is known about the beliefs that guide people's behavior with respect to sexual desire. Some researchers believe that sexual desire may mean different things to different individuals and moreover, that sexual desire is often confused with other needs and desires" (Regan and Berscheid 1999, 73). This paper demonstrates that sexual desire *reflects* rather than is "confused with" other needs and desires. Indeed, this paper argues that sexual desire is expressive of culture and perceptions of interpersonal expectations. It offers a useful reminder that sexual desires are not merely present in people's lives, but *emerge* as part of their lives.

The content of individual sexual fantasies and desires expresses and constitutes (at the level of the individual) the sexual culture and institutionalized arrangements surrounding each individual in the world. For example, imagining the view of the other toward the self (or intersubjectivity)—especially with regard to major social statuses such as gender, race, class, and age—commonly appeared in men's sexual self-conceptions and intrapsychic sexual scripting.

With selves and sexuality implicated, "it is not surprising that the major organizing principle of sexual scripting is the *minimization* of the risk of failure" (Simon and Gagnon 1987, 373, emphasis added). Even in the "disembodied" context of Internet sex chat, Waskul, Douglass, and Edgeley found that people "locate personhood in a safety zone by neutralizing, reducing or containing meaning," a process they refer to as the "enselfment of meaning" (2000, 394). The ambiguity of much sex talk between people may reflect attempts to save face, hedge commitments, and minimize risks (Gecas and Libby 1976; Schwartz 1994; Cavan 1966).

Moreover, sexual desires may be directly expressive of our values and beliefs. Herdt (2000, 527) notes that "conceptions of attraction are closer to what anthropologists have called 'values' —the general disposition to desire and merit an ontological state or a culturally valued social role" and "to participate in a collective system of valued objects that lie halfway between the individual and culture." Similarly:

> Individual erotic preferences are certainly not created solely by the social structural arrangements. But the integration of the preferences into a system of personal values, motives, and self-image very much depends on historical conditions. (Kon 1987, 279–80)

The process through which individual sexual desire emerges is useful to examine because it helps reveal the sociocultural complexity of sexuality and the grammar of sexual practices. Sexuality is framed by social institutions and, as practiced, it helps to create these institutionalizations.

Sexual scripting theory exists as a useful tool for examining sexuality; however, many sex researchers have marred its usefulness through simplification and misunderstanding. A common use of the theory is one in which cultural scenarios are viewed as directly constructing an individual's sexuality in a way that makes sexuality overdetermined by social structure and culture without specifying the processes or mechanisms by which this might occur. Some sexuality researchers concentrate on behaviors and physiologies rather than on the meanings involved in sexual scripting—a focus on behavioral outcomes and teleologies of the sexual which tend to draw attention away from the processes.

Our point about symmetrical sexual scripting is not dissimilar from the debate in symbolic interactionism regarding the importance of social structure versus process (LaRossa and Reitzes 1993; Longmore 1998). As it is appropriately equipped, we strive to emphasize linkages of social structure with identities (Stryker 1980) as well as managed self-meanings or even something like Burke's internal process of self verification (Burke and Reitzes 1981) using sexual scripting theory. We emphasize social process, but we recognize that the split is more synthetic and analytic than a description of "reality." There is no social structure without process and vice versa. Sexual scripting theory and symbolic interactionism are alternative ways of studying sexual intrapsychics and their relation to the interpersonal and cultural realm. At its core, symbolic interaction examines the meanings people create with others rather than the lock-step enactments of scripts or texts handed to them by culture. Similarly, it is doubtful that we will learn much about sexuality from highly structured survey items created with selected meanings for individuals to choose from because these instruments specify the sexual. Like sexual scripting theory, symbolic interactionism places emphasis on self-reflexivity and the ongoing production of sexual and social life.

The interactions between the cultural, interpersonal, and intrapsychic spheres make sexuality a moving and ever-changing target. "Each level of the scripting process influentially contextualizes the other, but rarely with the power to provide a comprehensive understanding of the other (Simon and Gagnon 2003, 493). The urgency of epidemics of sexually transmitted infections, teen pregnancy, and the need to understand sexuality and methods of altering sexual behavior has led not only to an increased awareness of scripting theory but also to cultural determinism. Our intent has been to highlight the interplay between the three spheres of scripting theory (in particular, between the cultural and intrapsychic spheres) and to offer a useful reminder that very individual sexual desires are not merely motives in people's lives, but emerge as part and parcel of the rest of their social interactions. The focus on categories of sexual behaviors and identities draws attention away from the processes and meanings involved in sexual scripting. As Simon and Gagnon (2003, 496, emphasis added) modestly state, "a scripting approach, at best, is not a terminal point but merely *a beginning.*"

This article explored sexual desire by examining the importance of intersubjectivity as a process involved in intrapsychic sexual scripting; however, a complete explanation of intrapsychic sexual scripting is far too complex for any single paper to describe completely. Surely other processes occur and can be identified in individuals' intrapsychic sexual scripting and these can be further understood in relation to interpersonal sexual scripting, and cultural scenarios. The development of sexual scripting theory through thoughtful applications in empirical research is likely to offer a coherent field for judging and testing ideas about sexual desire that take into consideration sociocultural structures and processes that constitute sexuality as much as biologies, physiologies, and epidemiological constructs of sexuality such as "men who have sex with men" and "multiple sex partners." The theory can systematically address Plummer's (1975) concern of examining the sources used to build up sexual meaning. Further development of sexual scripting theory must direct attention to mutually interacting aspects of the sexual, including the individual, interpersonal, and cultural conditions.

Acknowledgments

This research was supported in part by the Sexuality Research Fellowship Program of the Social Science Research Council with funds provided by the Ford Foundation, by an appointment to the Research Participation Program sponsored by the Centers for Disease Control and Prevention (CDC) and administered by the Oak Ridge Institute for Science and Education through an agreement between the Department of Energy and the CDC, and the Program In Human Sexuality Studies at San Francisco State University. We thank the study participants for their involvement and numerous anonymous reviewers for their comments. We also thank Phil Carspecken and the late Bill Simon for analytic advice and direction.

Note

1. There have been other influences as well: Ernest Burgess, Michel Foucault, David Riesman, and Robert Stoller (see Simon and Gagnon 2003) as well as that of symbolic interactionism (see Plummer 2003; Simon and Gagnon 2003).

References

Anderson, B. L., and J. M. Cryanowski. 1994. Women's sexual self-schema. *Journal of Personality and Social Psychology* 67:1079–85.

Anderson, B. L., J. M. Cryanowski, and D. Espindle. 1999. Men's sexual self-schema. *Journal of Personality and Social Psychology* 76:645–61.

Bem, S. L. 1974. The measurement of psychological androgyny. *Journal of Consulting and Clinical Psychology* 42:155–62.

Breakwell, G. M., and L. J. Millward. 1997. Sexual self-concept and sexual risk-taking. *Journal of Adolescence* 20:29–41.

Burke, K. 1968. Dramatism. *International encyclopedia of the social sciences*, VII, ed. D. L. Sills, 445–52. New York: The Free Press.

Burke, P. J., and D. C. Reitzes. 1981. The link between identity and role performance. *Social Psychology Quarterly* 44:83–92.

Carspecken, P. 1996. *Critical ethnography in educational research.* New York: Routledge.

Cavan, S. 1966. *Liquor license: An ethnography of bar behavior.* Chicago: Aldine.

Connell, R. W. 1987. *Gender and power: Society, the person, and sexual politics.* Stanford, California: Stanford University Press.

DiMaggio, P. 1997. Culture and cognition. *Annual Review of Sociology* 23:263–87.

di Mauro, D. 1995. *Sexuality research in the United States: An assessment of the social and behavioral sciences.* New York: Social Science Research Council.

D'Emilio, J., and E. Freedman. 1988. *Intimate matters: A history of sexuality in America.* New York: Harper and Row.

Gagnon, J. 1973. Scripts and the coordination of sexual conduct. *Nebraska Symposium on Motivation* 21:27–59.

Garcia, L. 1999. The certainty of the sexual self-concept. *Canadian Journal of Human Sexuality* 8:263–70.

Garnets, L. and L. Peplau. 2000. Understanding women's sexualities and sexual orientations: An introduction. *Journal of Social Issues* 56:181–92.

Gecas, V., and P. J. Burke. 1995. Self and identity. *Sociological perspectives on social psychology*, ed. K. S. Cook, G. A. Fine, and J. S. House, 41–67. Boston: Allyn and Bacon.

Gecas, V., and R. Libby. 1976. Sexual behavior as symbolic interaction. *Journal of Sex Research* 12:33–49.

Geer, J. H., and W. T. O'Donohue, eds. 1987. Theories of human sexuality. New York: Plenum.

Giddens, A. 1992. The transformation of intimacy: Sexuality, love and eroticism in modern societies. Stanford: Stanford University Press.

Herdt, G. 2000. On the development of sexual attraction. Archives of Sexual Behavior 29:527–29.

Jemail, J., and J. Greer. 1977. Sexual scripts. In *Progress in sexology: selected papers from the proceedings of the 1976 International Congress of Sexology*, ed. R. Gemme and C. C. Wheeler, 513–22. New York: Plenum Press.

Kon, I. 1987. A sociocultural approach. In Geer and O'Donohue 1987, 257–86.

LaRossa, R., and D. Reitzes. 1993. Symbolic interactionism and family studies. In Sourcebook of family theory and methods: A contextual approach, ed. P. G. Boss, W. J. Doherty, R. LaRossa, W. R. Schumm, and S. K. Steinmetz, 13–166. New York: Plenum.

Levine, S. B. 2003. The nature of sexual desire: A clinician's perspective. Archives of Sexual Behavior 32:279–85.

Lichtenstein, H. 1977. The dilemma of human identity. New York: Jason Aronson.

Lincoln, Y., and E. Guba. 1985. Naturalistic inquiry. Beverly Hills, CA: Sage.

Longmore, M. 1998. Symbolic interactionism in the study of sexuality. Journal of Sex Research, 35:44–57.

Person, E. 1987. A psychoanalytic approach. In Geer and O'Donohue 1987, 385–410.

Plummer, K. 1975. Sexual stigma: An interactionist account. London: Routledge.

———. 1982. Symbolic interactionism and sexual conduct: An emergent perspective. In Human sexual relations: Towards a redefinition of sexual politics, ed. M. Brake, 223–44. New York: Pantheon.

———. 1995. Telling sexual stories: Power, change and social worlds. New York: Routledge.

Plummer, K. 2003. Queers, bodies and postmodern sexualities: A note on revisiting the "sexual" in symbolic interactionism. Qualitative Sociology 26:515–30.

Regan, P., and E. Berscheid. 1999. Lust: What we know about human sexual desire. Thousand Oaks, CA: Sage.

Rust, P. 1993. "Coming out" in the age of social constructionism: Sexual identity formation among lesbian and bisexual women. Gender and Society 7:50–77.

Seidman, S. 1991. Romantic longings. New York: Routledge, Chapman and Hall.

Schwartz, P. 1994. Love between equals. New York: Free Press.

Simon, W. 1996. Postmodern sexualities. London: Routledge.

Simon, W., and J. H. Gagnon. 1984. Sexual scripts. Society 22:53–60.

———. 1986. Sexual scripts: Permanence and change. Archives of Sexual Behavior 15:97–120.

———. 1987. A sexual scripts approach. In Geer and O'Donohue 1987, 363–83.

———. 2003. Sexual scripts: Origins, influences and changes. Qualitative Sociology 26: 491–97.

Stoller, R. 1979. Sexual excitement: Dynamics of erotic life. New York: Pantheon.

Strauss, A., and J. Corbin. 1990. Basics of qualitative research: Grounded theory procedures and techniques. Newbury Park, CA: Sage.

Stryker, S. 1980. Symbolic interactionism: A social structural version. Menlo Park, CA: Benjamin Cummings.

Swidler, A. 2001. Talk of love: How culture matters. Chicago: University of Chicago Press.

Waskul, D., M. Douglass, and C. Edgeley. 2000. Cybersex: Outercourse and the enselfment of the body. Symbolic Interaction 23:375–97.

West, C., and S. Fenstermaker. 1995. Doing difference. Gender and Society 9:8–37.

Whittier, D., and W. Simon. 2001. The fuzzy matrix of "my type" in intrapsychic sexual scripting. Sexualities 4:139–65.

PART IV

SEXUAL POLITICS

Gilbert Herdt

13

Sexual Development, Social Oppression, and Local Culture

Introduction

As a result of immense historical and social change in culture and science over the past 20 years, a paradigm shift is rapidly occurring in the social and health sciences: scholars and policy-makers are examining the effects of social oppression and structural violence on the sexual lives of people around the world. The work of John Gagnon, over decades, has made clear the importance of his perspective and its theoretical underpinnings and I wish to dedicate this essay to John—esteemed mentor, friend, and ally in the field of sexuality and social change.

Sexual inequalities—the forms of indignity, social disadvantage, stigma, discrimination, and violence perpetuated or based upon sexual conduct, sexual identity or perceived sexual orientation, or membership in a sexual category or sexual culture—remain common in the United States and other societies. Concomitantly, protection of sexual health and rights remains poorly developed in many countries, including the United States. Increasingly, sexual researchers are examining the sociopolitical conditions that create sexual inequalities, which in turn contribute to disparities in sexual health and services among sexual minorities and people of color (Teunis n.d.). While this new social analysis that has looked deeply at social oppression and sexuality among adults and adolescents is critical to sexuality research in the twenty-first century, thus far children and childhood sexuality have been understudied, due to historical, cultural, and scientific barriers. This paper examines both the historical barriers that impeded this change and the epistemology and shifting paradigms in the social sciences, especially anthropology, that have emerged to support study of the long-neglected effects of social oppression upon young people's sexuality.

Historically, sexuality research as well as policy have consistently emphasized the

An earlier version of this chapter appeared in *Sexuality Research and Social Policy* 1 (2004):1–24. By permission of the National Sexuality Resource Center.

individual, not the culture—sometimes to the extent that it appeared as if people lived outside of time and space, or what I have elsewhere referred to as the "lone child" model of sexual development (Herdt 1990, 1991). Sexual development research has long been burdened by the cultural notion that sexual differences inhere in the individual and are essential (i.e., removed) from social influence, a paradigm with intellectual sources in psychoanalysis, medical sexology, epidemiology, and of late, evolutionary psychology. This paradigm has largely ignored the roles of institutions, custom, beliefs, attitudes, knowledge, sexual decision-making, sexual risk-taking, and sexual behavior—in short, the totality of sexual culture (Herdt 1999) (Gagnon and Simon 1973; Rubin 1984; Vance 1991). Stated differently, there have been few advocates for culture as a decisive factor in sexual health interventions in American society (Parker 2004). Psychology in particular has regarded sexual development and sexual health as outcomes of individuals removed from the social surround; consequently, sexual desire, behavior, infection, and health have been viewed as resulting from internal drives, and variably as signs of personal or moral weakness, biological fitness, or reproductive health or morbidity (Abramson and Pinkerton 1995; Gagnon 1990; Moran 2000). Perhaps this hegemonic trend was itself the product of a historically old tradition of folk psychology and expressive individualism in the United States that promoted individual feelings and associations at the expense of culture and community (Bellah et al.1985).

Of greatest import for the present chapter is the fact that social oppression was completely omitted until recently from accounts of young people's sexuality. Change was seen to be a product of social forces that imposed unique constraints upon the individual, and samples were selected in a manner that precluded cultural diversity by class and race, as explained below. Whether focused upon the individual or society, however, the individual and social difference theories of young people's sexual development typically ignored social oppression and the roots of sexual inequality, both in the United States and globally. Thus, social oppression has been omitted from narratives of gender inequality, sexual coercion, dating patterns, unintended pregnancy, and the double standards facing young women (Tolman 2003). Of late, scholars examining the forces of structural violence in human life have turned to the classic text on social oppression, Paulo Freire's *Pedagogy of the Oppressed* (1970), as a general guide to analyzing the roots of social difference and social oppression in particular. However, it is noteworthy that Freire never discusses sexuality in his work.

Leading scholars such as John Money have long warned of the deplorable hiatus in the study of childhood sexuality, correctly insisting that within the United States childhood sexuality was the last great taboo of research in sexuality (Langfeldt 1981). How little the situation has changed in the twenty-first century, and how much the field continues to suffer as a result. Due to the political and social barriers that thwart past and present studies of sexuality, the United States has lacked the scientific freedom and the necessary data to reconceptualize childhood sexuality. Moreover, the continuing challenges from extremist organizations regarding discussions of childhood sexuality, sexual abuse, and sex education has disrupted efforts at rational scientific discourse (e.g., the attacks on Judith Irvine's 2002 book, *Harmful to Minors*). While colleagues in Europe have been much more able to pursue these investigations, they too have also encountered barriers. Gagnon and Parker (1995) have suggested that the "Americanization" of sexuality study after World War II—a shift in the focus of sexuality research from Europe to the United States—probably further undermined childhood sexuality research. No wonder it has been impossible to rethink childhood sexual theory and method, given the fundamental void of data on children and childhood sexual development.

Nonetheless, in the 1990s the new paradigm of "structural violence" came into focus as a lens through which to understand these issues, most critically in links between HIV infection and poverty. Paul Farmer defines structural violence as "the host of offences against human dignity," including poverty, racism, and inadequate health care (2002, 8). Consideration of sexuality gradually entered into the studies of structural violence, overcoming the silence and stigma of prior generations of mental health professionals, not to mention communities (Bayer 1981). One year later, sexual and social health policy included references to social oppression and long-term structural factors that affect adult sexual health and well being (Díaz 1998; Parker and Aggleton 2003).

So far, however, structural violence has still been neglected as a lens for understanding the social oppression of children and young people, particularly in relation to examining the ways in which forces such as poverty, heterosexism, and homophobia compromise the integrity of sexual development. Some have asked what difference it would make to study social oppression if, as the individual differences/essentialist sexuality model argues, childhood sexual development comes from within the individual (reviewed in Herdt and McClintock 2000). Previously, the answer has been, "Not much."

By the end of the twentieth century, however, a new set of answers to such questions was taking shape in sexuality study. Consider the frequently heard argument today that "abstinence-only" sexuality education is the preferred model for prevention of unintended pregnancy and HIV/STDs in the United States and globally. This model assumes the individual difference perspective and typically ignores the social surround, especially the impact of structural violence. For example, while the official U. S. government policy promotes abstinence-only sexuality education policy (since passage of the Welfare Reform Act of 1996), researchers and sex education experts such as Doug Kirby (2001) have raised serious questions about the effectiveness of this policy and its claims. This policy was implemented largely in the absence of research and empirical evidence. Nevertheless, the U. S. government is today exporting abstinence-only policies to other countries as if the conditions of childhood sexuality were everywhere the same, and as if social oppression did not matter. Uganda, importantly, is being trumpeted as a success story for abstinence-only approaches, while in fact the specific history of the HIV epidemic in that country and a variety of other prevention factors merit study (see Herdt 2004) in explaining changes in that country. Clearly the forces of social suffering are not being considered in such accounts of the responses of people in Uganda. We shall consider this example further below.

It is time to rethink theories of sexuality from the perspective of a social difference paradigm, which would allow consideration of the contributions of culture and society to sexual development and of the expanding role played by social meaning systems and social practices as defining features of sexual cultures (Gagnon 1991; Herdt 1999). Sociocultural theory can help embed the study of young people's sexuality within its real-world contexts, wherein social suffering and even "survival sex" are parts of daily life that constrain the choices and life circumstances widely experienced by young people globally (Preston-Whyte et al. 2000).

Sexual essentialism and individual difference theories

In the first decade of the new century, sexuality in general and childhood sexuality in particular are still represented in popular culture, and all too often in science as well, as a function of individual differences. We can call this the nineteenth-century model of sexual essentialism. It argues that everything sexual is the product of individual development and internal or innate mechanisms, such as sexual drives, cognitive and behavioral predispositions, sexual identity mechanisms (e.g., innate sexual orientation), gender differences, behavioral capacities (e.g., the ability to bond), and personal or eccentric personality traits (such as nurturance or aggressiveness). Typically this mode of sexual essentialism treats gender as internally driven (Tiefer 1995), rather than as mediated by folk theories of development, local moral codes of conduct, sexual subjectivity, and sexual standards as defined by sexual cultures (Herdt 1996), which has resulted in sexual and gender hierarchies that have oppressed women and minorities and impeded human potential and optimal development (B. Miller 1992).

Sexual essentialism historically included the reduction of all aspects of human gender and sexuality to intrinsic and unlearned mechanisms of human evolution and development regardless of culture and context. Some of the most interesting problems in science and society over the past century have been debated within this paradigm (Abramson and Pinkerton 1995). One need only think of the mission of Margaret Mead: at the suggestion of anthropologist Franz Boas, the founder of American anthropology, she was sent to Samoa to question the innate character of adolescent development, emotions, and sexuality. The publication of the resulting case study was pivotal to the formation of cultural relativism and the history of anthropological theory. Freudian developmentalism—or rather the reaction to it—was the background to Mead's project, as she stated in her own letters from her fieldwork sites (Mead 1977). Much of the subtext surrounding anthropologist Derek Freeman's 1999 critique of Mead's Samoan study concerned the biologically essential versus the socially learned attributes of childhood sexuality and adolescent development—rather than just the question of scientific truth, progress, and hoaxing, as Freeman had claimed. At stake was the issue of whether local factors of social oppression in Samoa (such as sexual coercion of girls by boys) resulted in the observed development forms that Margaret Mead reported? We will never know the entire answer to this question, but it is noteworthy that this controversy has not stimulated the field very much. Reductive accounts of sexuality do not reside in any single discipline but rather appeal to a widespread tendency in our society to assume a folk model that childhood and young people's gender and sexuality are "drives" or "hormonally" driven. Much like the Freudian developmental model that once reduced sexuality to infantile conflicts, sexual essentialism lives on and indeed has a special appeal.

The obvious implication is that individual difference theory is too reliant upon the internal mechanism model (Shweder 1989). Hence, while science has intermittently concerned itself with the effects of inequality in such areas as racial discrimination and intelligence testing, this critical factor has typically been left out of sexuality studies. Perhaps this is because psychology was for such a long time hegemonic or at least intellectually ascendant in the science of sexuality (Weeks 1985) and thus needed to justify a paradigm, rather than to question it.

Sexual essentialism over the past century has produced counter-reactions as well, such as the analysis of conservative or traditional sexuality (Janice Irvine 2002; Weeks 1985), and new policies regarding sexuality as a human right (Parker, Barbosa, and Aggleton 2000). Nevertheless, sexuality as an innate force remains surprisingly robust in accounts of human development (and of childhood and adolescent sexuality especially), in spite of decades of criticism throughout the twentieth century (Benedict 1938; Gagnon and Parker 1995; Herdt 1981; Herdt 1990; Kinsey, Pomeroy, and Martin 1948; Mead 1961; Rubin 1984; Tiefer 1995; Vance 1991). Moreover, recent studies have made strides in analyzing these forms of reductionism (see Herdt 1991, 1997a; Lancaster 2003; Parker, Barbosa, and Aggleton 2000; Petchesky 2003) though they have not eliminated them. Indeed, evolutionary psychology and genetic theories of sexuality, which tend to derive from such reductionism, are on the rise (Buss 1992). Debates about eugenics, heterosexism, homosexuality, racial purity, and miscegenation remain intellectually alive and privilege the individual difference model, as do evolutionary psychology's accounts of mating, altruism, and related areas (Lancaster 2003).

An important outcome of Freudian developmentalism is a strong concern—some would say preoccupation (Gagnon 2004)—of individual difference theorists with childhood sexual orientation as an expression of intense, continued sexual essentialism. As social analysts such as Carole Vance have pointed out, there is a tendency in research about sexual orientation to sloppy and scientifically dubious thinking, resulting in a variety of special claims, for example, about the existence of a "gay brain" (see Lancaster 2003, chapter 18). Studies such as that of Simon LeVay (1993) provoked excitement about the potential for locating morphological markers of homosexuality in brain structures, only later to be tarnished by methodological and empirical questions (see Lancaster 2003, 240–42). As Murphy has written in *Gay Science* (1997), most of the large amount of sexual orientation research completed in recent decades is not unreasonable, but the influence of homophobia and heterosexism in much of it "spurs worry about sexual orientation research" (225). The level of genetic sexual determinism in relation to sexual orientation reaches its zenith in the article "Parental selection of children's sexual orientation" by Greenberg and Bailey (2001), which conceptualizes genetic screening for homosexual traits by parents before birth, without any discussion of the meaning of homosexuality in local cultures or of the bioethical issues raised by this possibility. To the social theorist, such a model poses a threat both to the civil rights of gay and lesbian persons and to liberal democracy in general.

The social difference model, by contrast, treats sexuality as a product of social environment, socialization, and enculturation across the course of life, and especially as mediated through parents, family caretakers, peers, communities, and major institutions of society (e.g., businesses, religion, schools) that condition the conduct of sexual relations in adulthood. In support of this model, Tiefer (2000) recently stated, "Science is a fully social process, and theory making is an important intellectual contribution to a political debate" (48), and in some sense, this social foundation is inherent in all of science (Kuhn 1970). Nonetheless, since the time of Freud (1905), Margaret Mead (1927), Alfred Kinsey and colleagues (1948, 1953), and Gagnon and Simon (1973), sexuality studies have tended to produce master narratives about what sexuality is and what it does to society. The outcome has been a tug-of-war between the so-called biological "essentialists," who approach sexuality from the perspective of individual differences, and the social "constructionists" who assume the perspective of social differences. The duality is ironic, for as primatologist Martin Pavelka has said, "Perhaps more than any other area of human behavior, sexuality spans the gap between what is normally perceived as biological and what is regarded as cultural" (1995, 17). The roots of this duality reach back to Freud and his grand narrative about sexuality as an individual entity.

The influence of Freudian developmentalism

Historically, sexual essentialism (as represented in individual difference theories of bio-psychosocial sexual development) was based on assumptions of intrinsic traits that were studied in samples that were neither representative of cultural diversity nor attentive to local culture and moral worlds (Gagnon and Simon 1973; Herdt 1999). Freudian developmentalism was both a landmark theory in this regard (Stoller 1968, 1985) and also the most influential perspective on sexual thinking in popular culture (Robertson 1976), and while it has been reviewed many times, there is value to be gained from another brief examination of the gaps in this model of sexual essentialism as they influenced the social study of sexuality.

In the early modern period, religious forces clearly influenced the primary load of cultural meanings surrounding sexuality and procreation (Foucault 1978). The shift, marked by the emergence of sexuality in medicine and science in the late eighteenth century, arose largely in reaction to these religious forces and served to newly organize the definitional understanding of sexuality as a phenomenon of individual bodies and internal states, which had been often diagnosed as abnormal. Nineteenth-century bio-psychosocial theories of sexual differences were located within medicine and sexology, fields that served as the critical historical sources for prevailing cultural ideas surrounding individual sexual development (Moran 2000). Foucault in particular speculated that this historical development led to the classification of new sexual identities and to a clinical codification of ways of speaking (thinking) about particular desires, especially the so-called "perverse" signs of sexuality such as masturbation. This work took place in doctors' offices, clinics, and hospitals, because its focus was on individual symptoms as expressed through what were labeled as abnormalities of perverse pleasures. This organization of sexuality served as the foundation for Freud's grand narrative about the "repressive hypothesis" (Foucault 1978).

When childhood sexuality first entered the intellectual world as a problem a century ago—and we might use Freud's 1905 work as a convenient marker of this theoretical thinking—it was widely assumed that biopsychosocial development, including the development of sexual temperament and gender traits, was intrinsic, evolutionary, and universal. The biopsychosocial building blocks of "sex" and "temperament" were viewed as identical for all humans in all times and places—what anthropologist Anthony Wallace has called the "replication of uniformity" model of human nature (1969). Its preconception assumed racial and evolutionary differences across groups, in line with the racial and hierarchical thinking of Victorian times (Stocking 1997). In addition, academic psychology focused little attention on childhood or adolescent sexuality outside of the United States (Mead 1949; see also Maccoby 1984). Individual difference theory, as formulated in Freud's clinical studies and theoretical essays (1905), were of course the product of the sexual psychology of late nineteenth-century upper middle-class white Viennese individuals (Gay 1998). Their childhood sexuality was grounded in a particular worldview and distinctive kinds of "sexual lifeways" (Herdt 1997a) that constituted particular beliefs and values of sexuality, and sexual stories and behavioral styles through which sexual socialization was created in childhood and then reinforced in adulthood, though this lens remained uncritically examined even by anthropologists until much later (Herdt and Stoller, 1990).

Freudian developmentalism was based upon assumptions of patriarchy, the inherent inferiority of women, and social class privilege (Chodorow 1978). In current jargon, it was profoundly heteronormal (that is, Freud and his followers assumed heterosexuality to be normal and natural for all humans; see Cohler and Galatzer-Levy, 2000). In addition, decades of discussion in psychoanalysis, anthropology, psychology, and literary studies focused upon whether there was or was not a universal Oedipal complex for all humans, and if there was, whether it was the same or different for males and females (Malinowski 1929; Spiro 1982). Anthropologists such as Devereux, following the lead of Margaret Mead (1935) in particular, attempted to modify and more commonly attack this approach and succeeded in establishing the view that sexual customs differ across cultures and gender, and are variable and subject to politics, economics, and religious forces (Whiting, Kluckhohn, and Anthony 1958; reviewed in Wallace 1969). And while childhood gender (Whiting and Edwards 1988) and sexuality (Spiro 1979) were studied during this era, social oppression and factors such as poverty, colonial domination, racism, and sexism were left out of the grand narrative. However, some postcolonial studies in anthropology have examined colonial domination in understanding Orientalism, the use of politics and religion to undermine colonial authority, racialism and sexual colonialism, and representations of the sexual other more broadly (see Comaroff and Comaroff 1991; Gagnon 1997; Said 1972; Stoller 1995).

Note that the paradigm changes that seeped into anthropology and psychology via sexuality study never took hold in general, but lingered on in the study of sexuality (DiLeonardi 1998; Herdt 1990; Tuzin 1991; Vance 2001). Historically, psychoanalysis claimed the territory of childhood sexuality so early on that the giants of anthropology felt compelled to rebut the "just so story" of human evolution and the partial and incomplete account of culture (Wallace 1969). Eventually social and developmental psychology would largely reject its fundamental preconceptions, such as its treatment of individual gender traits and temperament (Maccoby and Jacklin 1974). Nonetheless, the study of childhood sexuality—to the extent it was studied by anthropologists at all up to the 1980s—was the province of socialization, typically investigated by women scholars such as Margaret Mead or Freudian-oriented male researchers who included Edward Sapir, George Devereux, and psychoanalyst Abram Kardiner, the primary figures in "culture and personality anthropology" (Singer 1961; Wallace 1969).

Several of these anthropologists provided rare ethnographies of sexuality (see Herdt 1991 for a re-analysis of Devereux's 1937 classic ethnography of Mohave Indian sexuality that subsumed the clinical pathologies and diagnostic regimes of Freudian developmentalism). Childhood sexuality as a product of culture and socialization remained critical to this scientific period, as reviewed previously by Mead (1961), but none of the studies involved the examination of structural violence or factors such as poverty, and it would be another four decades before anthropological studies of normative sexuality made their debut (Markowitz and Ashkenazi 1998). Their categories and developmental characteristics continued to rely so heavily upon individual difference theory, especially Freudian developmentalism, as to severely compromise the local culture's own folk theories of sexuality and its meaning systems. By the late 1950s and early 1960s, with the rapid decline of influence of Freudian developmentalism in theory and research, academics were in search of a new paradigm.

While psychoanalysis never succeeded in being fully institutionalized in academic departments within American universities, especially the social sciences, its influence upon psychiatry, psychology, and of course popular culture theories of human nature/ sexual nature remained significant until the 1960s, only to re-emerge in postmodern gender theory a generation later (Butler 1993). Its supreme attention to individual bodies and essential or innate forces in development made the local culture or community irrelevant as just another mind heard from, rather than another region of importance. Moreover, as feminist theory has long complained (Chodorow 1978; Rosaldo and Lamphere 1974), power structure and social oppression are not acknowledged in psychoanalytic treatment of sexuality. To paraphrase Foucault (1978), not only was sexual repression in the sense defined by Freud a universal, supposedly free of historical and cultural influence, but the more individual innate dispositions were studied, the less power and society were even considered as relevant to understanding the nature of sexual repression. The "gaze" of the doctor could diagnose and determine what was wrong with the patient internally, yet all but ignore the social reality of the person's sexual development and social life. No wonder Freud's seduction material took the form of a theory of fantasy, rather than of a theory of the reality of possible sexual abuse and incest within the nuclear family, because such cultural conditions were too terrible to imagine in Freud's time (Gay 1998).

What individual difference theory left out

Advances in understanding the biopsychosocial development of sexuality and sexual functioning over the past three decades have been remarkable. Generally, the more rigorous and empirically oriented authorities in the field presently regard "psychoendocrine theories" as providing the best chance of predicting main effects upon development (Meyer-Bahlberg 2000). Clearly, such a view privileges individual difference theory and enshrines sexuality within individuals, but that view does not reveal the full scope of this powerful paradigm.

Previously, biopsychosocial studies were methodologically conducted as if "all things were equal," the epistemological position of sociobiology that ultimately destroyed it (Gould 1981). That is, if the social environment in all times and places was "equivalent" in evolution, or "neutral" as argued by Freud (1905) in the development of sexual desire, then a single theory, and a single methodology, could encompass the claim to universalism. This scientific positivism reached its zenith in the theory of the "universal" Oedipus complex (Freud 1913), a theory which the sociobiologists, interestingly enough, were to reclaim decades later. The anthropologists of Freud's time, notably Alfred Kroeber (founder of the department of anthropology at the University of California at Berkeley, and first protégé of Franz Boas, founder of American anthropology), could not accept such a universalistic claim, for the simple reason that if the purported sexual difference was universal, how then could Freud explain the huge range of culture and cultural variation around the world (Herdt and Stoller 1990)? The culture and personality theorists and psychoanalyst-anthropologists such as Kardiner (1939) never satisfactorily answered the question. John Whiting and colleagues (1958) at Harvard tried to reconcile the problem through an "ecological" model of adaptation and child-rearing variability, but their methodology was criticized and the database flawed. Anthropology was eclipsed in the renewal of sexuality study following World War II.

During this period the famed Kinsey studies established the most important empirical base for understanding sexual behavior and provided a new survey methodology and approach to answering questions about sexuality in mass societies (Gagnon and Parker 1995). The contribution of the Kinsey studies of sexuality in males (Kinsey et al. 1948) and females (Kinsey et al. 1953) to showing behavioral variation in sexual development was enormous. Take note, however, that these surveys excluded African Americans from their samples, and focused upon a single point in developmental time, thus suggesting a more stable and less dynamic picture of social diversity and individual change than was probably the case (Herdt 1990). Moreover, Kinsey's reliance upon the construct of "sex drives" undercut his effort to reform the popular epistemology. As Gagnon and Parker (1995) have well noted, Kinsey's studies changed the methodology from the individual interview to the survey, which enormously altered the source and meaning of the data of sexuality. But did it actually change the popular understanding of sexuality? The public continued to regard sexuality as guided by sex drives and in some sense rooted in individual differences.

Anthropology did not escape the individual difference paradigm either when it came to sexuality. While cultural relativism in general was privileged, psychologizing was looked down upon, and the epistemology that all things human belong in social and cultural context was favored, anthropologists regarded sexuality differently (Herdt 1997a). Sexuality became a function of reproduction, kinship, and family formation (Vance 1991). Too much emphasis in anthropological theories of sexuality was placed upon sex as an individual biological need or as an imperative to reproduce (Herdt 1996), and heterosexual development was equated to marriage, with extramarital affairs treated as matters of individual sexual drives and "personality adjustments," not unlike the perspective of the psychoanalysts (Gregor 1985). The point is that sexology and psychology were not alone in privileging individual differences as the core of sexuality. By the late 1950s and early 1960s, Freudian developmentalism had been eclipsed and the developmental cognitive psychologists were in ascendancy, including those who would pioneer contemporary studies of early sex differences (Maccoby 1984). These cognitive studies were environmentally influenced and sophisticated, but still leaned heavily upon internal states and traits (i.e., biopsychosocial variables) such as hormone levels in the pregnant mother or aggression in the child (Maccoby and Jacklin 1973).

If we compare John Money and Anke A. Ehrhardt's classic, *Man and Woman, Boy and Girl* (1972), which theorizes about and documents the field and state of knowledge in gender identity and sexual development at the time, with Anke A. Ehrhardt's (2000) recent review, two contrasts emerge. First, what was established as an empirical "universal" has been challenged by later empirical studies and methodological critiques (Gagnon 1990). While Money and Ehrhardt's psychosexual work set the standard for years, their studies on hormonal functioning and sexual identity have been challenged or disproved, and in other cases, transcended (McClintock and Herdt 1996; Meyer-

Bahlberg 2000). In short, what previously stood as an empirical claim of "truth" has in some instances come to be seen as a "partial truth" in relation to cultural context and life course changes (Herdt 1990). Second, Money and Ehrhardt's samples were limited. While their work was more social constructionist than is often allowed by critics (but more so outside of the United States than in American society), their samples were not representative. For example, their discussion of Australian aborigines and Melanesian societies was informative and influential, if not entirely correct (Herdt 1991), but their U.S. clinical samples used for understanding gender identity conflict were not representative of the class, ethnicity, and gender variations in the country at the time.

Again, the intellectual history of these studies reveals how human development theories and biopsychology have privileged individual difference theories of biopsychosocial sexual development, stressing intrinsic traits and states, and sometimes the interaction of both, but with little regard for the social surround and no regard for cultural diversity. A fine body of scholarship has consistently refined the understanding of culture and social change in relation to sexuality (see D'Emilio and Freedman 1988; Herdt 1997a; Weeks 1985; and see Parker 1991, 1999, for a rich account of Brazil for comparison). By contrast, Ehrhardt's recent work questions gender inequality, stereotypes, and the need to understand power differences as basic to interpreting gender (1997, 361). In short, inequality and social oppression have entered into biopsychosocial studies of sex to narrate and interpret the researchers' own society.

By now it will be clear that prior studies within developmental psychology (as well as those within the culture and personality school of anthropology and Kinsey's early survey-studies) all emphasized a lone child model of sexuality in which individual developmental differences are taken as a priori and largely separate from the social world (Shweder 1989). The vulgar version of these studies once promoted by sociobiology (Geertz 1973) and currently advanced by evolutionary psychology (Buss 1992) decontextualized development by removing the formation and behavior of the person from the naturalistic settings of the group to the laboratory or imaginary evolutionary settings of prehistory. A more sophisticated approach regards the biological and psychological dimensions of development as separate from the social or moral world of the child, but tries to study both of them (Stigler, Shweder, and Herdt 1990). This approach dualizes the subjectivity of the person and the social surround (Herdt and Stoller 1990).

The White Middle-Class Norm (WMCN)

Methodologically, the field of biopsychology has historically relied upon selected samples of typically white middle-class people—especially college-aged young adults—for its testing ground. Why this mattered was that such samples skewed and misrepresented the range of sexuality in the United States (Laumann et al. 1994) and generally left social oppression out of the picture.

What has created the social conditions for this change in sexuality study? In a single word, diversity; more specifically, the recognition of race, social class, ethnicity or national origin, religion, gender variation, and sexual minority status as key variables in a complex grid of social sexualities or "master statuses" within the United States. Diversity has obviously penetrated the mirage of an idealized White Middle-Class Norm (WMCN). Biopsychosocial theories of individual differences have depended too heavily upon normative development in European and American populations, including school children and college-aged young adults. Today, the vast majority of all biopsychosocial articles, in leading journals such as the *Archives of Sexual Behavior,* typically report samples of WMCN (not to mention *Psychology, Culture and Evolution,* a journal of evolutionary psychology). Adolescent psychology in general, which has its sources in cross-cultural adolescence studies in the Pacific Islands, has virtually ignored this body of cross-cultural evidence (Herdt and Leavitt 1998). What a pity. The Pacific Islands reveal many cases of early and delayed maturation, and early sexual interest, producing different outcomes from cases studied in the West. This is due in part to the godmother of this field, Margaret Mead, whose study was on the right track but did not cast off the WMCN mantle of heteronormativity in two respects: first, her sampling of Samoans was not representative in any meaningful sense of local variation, and second, her privileging of American problems and narratives of adolescent "turmoil" created a WMCN norm against which all other variations were compared (DiLeonardo 1998).

Historically, Western differences were themselves compared to differences among white middle-class people, going right back to Freud, but also to the more relevant studies of adolescence by psychologist G. Stanley Hall (who had invited Freud to the New World), published in 1904 (Moran 2000). The depiction of difference was located in individual white middle-class bodies, which were theorized to be representative of all individuals, without taking note of their sociocultural differences when compared to the then-current populations of people of color. Moreover, the norm of individual development was socially classed—middle-class or upper-class, in general, as reflected in the college samples historically stressed. They were also gendered—again, as in Freud's work, because the modern period of European and North American imagery stresses masculinity as the norm of human sexual nature. (Freud's theory of sexuality, which saw femininity as failed masculinity, failed itself [Stoller 1975].)

Money and Ehrhardt (1972) advanced what today is called an "interactionist" paradigm, considering both gender and sexuality inputs from intrinsic development and the learning environment. This paradigm argued that sex assignment and subsequently social handling by the caretakers primarily determined gender identity as adult outcomes. Subsequent scholars have split apart the paradigm, so that the more biological theorists, such as Bailey and Oberschneider (1997; reviewed in Bem 2000), have promoted the idea that sexual orientation is genetically driven, while cultural theorists have argued that gender and sexual subjectivity are purely the result of social learning. Such arguments are specious because they depend upon the definition of constructs such as sexual orientation as discrete variables or unified entities, which is doubtful; they also conceptualize gender identity as being defined by conformity to group norms, which ignores personal development and resistance to norms (Cohen 1995; Jacobs, Thomas, and Lang 1997). When it comes to complex human conditions—such as 5-alpha reductase deficiency and the third gender related to it (Herdt 1994)—understanding of human sexuality must deal with both individual and social difference factors, both in childhood and later in adult expressions.

As we have observed, a remarkable paradigm change has occurred in the basic perception of childhood sexuality. A generation ago, the study of biopsychosocial development began with the normative study of white middle-class children growing up in suburbs or small towns in the Western world (Elder 1975). Gender and sexuality were defined as distinct domains, with compartmentalized subjectivities and gender always taking precedence, as in the notable work of Maccoby and Jacklin (1973) and Whiting and Edwards (1988). The point is not that the child developmental psychologists were the only scholars to privilege individual difference theory and methodology; rather, as the institutional disciplines for such studies, developmental psychology and sexology had not been creative in understanding the cultural and historical factors that reproduce gender subjectivities.

Aside from the folk reliance upon individual difference theory, there is another cultural factor, politically motivated, that perpetuates individual difference theory. A hundred years after the publication of Freud's (1905) famous theory that children were not sexually naïve, many in the United States still cling to the notion of children as sexually innocent. Anthropologists would interpret this as a way in which the white middle class has perpetuated one of the last great icons of the culture. Paradoxically, this belief perpetuates the taboo on sexuality in children that results in a lack of comprehensive sexuality education and thus, greater risk for sexual abuse and disease as well (Janice Irvine 2002). Again, this iconic belief is still basic to the worldview fostered by middle-class American popular culture.

Social difference theories of childhood sexuality

American and European studies of childhood sexuality remained captive to individual difference theories because they were typically conducted within experimental and developmental psychology contexts that left out local culture and models of rationality (Shweder 1990). Even the anthropological studies of the day ignored history and social change in local cultures (Mead's 1935 study of sex and temperament in three New Guinea societies provides a pivotal case; see Gewertz 1983). Indeed, studies of the cultural construction of all manner of social phenomena excluded sexuality entirely, whereas kinship and marriage were commonly described, being viewed as the bedrock of reproductive heterosexuality, with the apparent (although not real) conformity of exotic cultures, no less than the mother country, to these norms (Herdt 1997a). In the ensuing years, the field of the developmental psychology of children was dedicated to gender study (e.g., Maccoby 1998), not to sexuality, except in the field of sexology (reviewed in Money and Ehrhardt 1972; see Money 1987).

In retrospect, psychological studies largely neglected childhood sexuality, particularly prior to the onset of gonadal puberty (McClintock and Herdt 1996), as it is situated in its own local moral world. Social oppression as it affected childhood sexual development and its developmental sequelae was especially overlooked. Herdt and McClintock (2000) have suggested, for example, that sexual attraction achieves a stable threshold at around age 10, which may be a universal; however, some local cultures place barriers to the expression of these feelings and socially oppress young people in such ways that the development of their sexuality is secondary to survival itself. Recent sexuality research is thus becoming more sensitive to variations in meanings and narratives between individuals and across cultures, moving research, education, and policy closer to the voices and experiences of local cultures and their moral worlds (for examples, see the research of Díaz (2002) on gay Latino males in the United States; Paiva (2002) on Brazilian adolescents; and Tolman (1994, 1996) on adolescent girls and their sexual desires). Thus, a new trend is emerging to deal with interaction between individual differences and social differences, negotiating forces of social oppression and inequality in vulnerable populations (Krieger 1999; Teunis n.d.).

The creation of the construct "gender" earlier in the twentieth century was associated with "temperamental" patterns of being a man or a woman, but slowly its meanings shifted to include social dimensions as well. The effect of this new set of perspectives, situated in the 1920s and 1930s, was profound, though focused more on the family, intimacy and romance, and the creation of social rights for women rather than upon sexual behavior per se (Moran 2000). Intellectual feminism slowly grew in prominence through the first wave in the 1920s, though the more acute change was probably among the elite, rather than the general populace (Stimpson 1996). New studies in the 1960s on women's roles and meaning systems and their lives and place in society began a paradigm of feminist study in the social sciences (Rosaldo 1974). This shift was invigorated by the (second) sexual revolution in the United States (and Western Europe) and by the birth control pill, and led to the middle-class notion among women of the egalitarian sexual script (Ehrhardt 2000). This trend continues as an important social belief in development today (Tolman 1996). In the subsequent decades, overriding concerns about female fertility, contraceptives, abortion, and control of women's reproduction developed that were formative in shaping state-level health policy and in influencing state-funded studies of sexuality (di Mauro 1997; Ginsburg and Rapp 1995). Historically the field of sexology has continued to be defined by such concerns, based as it is in a paradigm that understands sex to be a set of individual difference traits residing inside the individual or her identity (thoughtfully reviewed in Hrdy 2000). It is notable that feminist theory had so little to say about sexuality during this period up to the 1990s (Parker, Barbosa, and Aggleton 2000).

As Crawford and Popp (2003), Ehrhardt (1996), Krieger (2003), and Tolman, Striepe, and Harmon (2003) have suggested, developmental gender differences also play a large role in the formation of childhood and adolescent sexuality and sexual health. Gender (masculinity and femininity) so frequently shapes the roles and goals of parental caretakers and peers and thus defines childhood sexuality and sexual socialization, stunting or even harming adult sexual functioning and intimate relations. Masculinity in particular has played a largely unknown and unstudied part in the impact of gender upon sexual development through what Connell (1995) has called the "live fast and die young" syndrome: the need to take risks, aggress, and impress, and the need to show off and be proud in front of one's peers, often in imitation of media or comic book heroes. This is the cultural material from which warriors are made (Mead 1935); and even after a warrior culture has long since been pacified, these narratives of masculinity live on to profoundly shape the meanings and practices of how boys and girls are socialized into sexual relationships (Gagnon 1991; Herdt 2003).

But all through the period from the 1960s to the 1980s, the field of sexuality studies remained preoccupied with two major concerns: the regulation of unwanted pregnancy, especially among adolescent unwed females (reviewed in Gagnon and Parker 1995; Moran 2000), and the study of orgasm and its psychophysiological correlates in the laboratory (Masters and Johnson 1966). Prior to the AIDS epidemic, the bulk of research funding and population planning, demography, and public health sexuality intervention money went into programs for teenagers and the control of adolescent sexuality through studies of the impact of contraceptives and individual psychological factors on pregnancy and birth (Moran 2000). A long history of this work reveals the extent to which it was controlled by men, its focus was on unwed underclass or poor women of color, it precluded identification of sexual orientation or assumed heteronormal samples, or it focused upon sexual lifestyles labeled as abnormal (Boxer and Cohler 1989; Herdt and Boxer 1993). And thus it remained until the advent of the AIDS epidemic in the 1980s.

HIV and a paradigm of structural violence

The formation of sexual minority groups and increased social activism were significant forerunners to the American response to the AIDS epidemic in the 1980s (Levine, Nardi, and Gagnon 1997). In brief, social ferment and sexual revolution in the 1960s witnessed the emergence of a new critical mass of social movements, including Black Power, second wave feminism, the student movement, and the gay liberation movement (D'Emilio and Freedman 1988; Epstein 2003; Morgan 1970). The American tradition of individual expressionism was given new meaning in the protests and counterculture movements of students and hippies (Bellah et al. 1985). The interpretations of this change extended the gamut—from that of the psychologist, Eric Erickson (1968), who attributed these changes to "identity confusion" and the lack of adequate internalized role models, to social scientists who believed that American society was profoundly flawed and in need of radical change (DiLeonardo 1998; Hymes 1974).

A quick glance at the institutional changes in anthropology during this time is instructive. Following the collapse of colonialism and the failure of the Vietnam War, anthropology experienced an upheaval that was associated with the disruption of traditional theory that had been ahistorical. The anthropological studies previously reviewed showed a marked resistance to examining sexuality and gender inside the United States or to studying sources of social inequality outside of the United States. Margaret Mead's *Coming of Age in Samoa* (1927) is perhaps foundational in this regard, though critics are divided over its contributions. Mead's work, for example, extols the modernism of the times; change in traditional societies was ignored, whereas change at home was focused upon the middle-class. In the words of DiLeonardo (1998), "Mead's America of 1927, then, has an extremely narrow class and race compass" (177). The reactions to this work in the 1960s led to new vistas of study, including gender, but sexuality was still left out of the picture.

What came to be known as "symbolic anthropology" and gender studies, among other areas, led the way in formulating what would become postmodern theory, and in beginning the gradual withdrawal from working abroad to working in the United States and Europe (DiLeonardo 1998). Generally, this new paradigm—as best instanced by the work of Clifford Geertz (1973) and his followers—had little or nothing to say about sexuality, and was silent on young people's sexuality. Ensuing historical shifts in anthropology and cross-cultural studies exerted relentless pressure to change perspective from the local or regional ethnography to the national and global context of neocolonialism (Appadurai 1996; Knauft 1999; Parker 1999). Structural violence and social suffering also became increasingly important themes within anthropological, demographic, epidemiological, and development work (Farmer 1999; Krieger 1999; Parker, Carballo, and Herdt 1991; Scheper-Hughes 1992; Setel 1999). The fading of the once-dominant view of cultural relativism—that local cultures are islands out of time and space, and the exoticization of Otherness—hastened the postcolonial critique and the advance of social critiques (Gagnon 1997; Said 1978). The concomitant change in cross-cultural methodologies is evident; a new awareness of historical records and of the need for history has ushered in experience-near accounts of the voices of local agents confronted with ideologies, oppression, and the state (Manderson 1996; Manderson and Jolly 1997). Slowly, sexuality has come back into anthropology (Herdt 1981; Stoller 1995; Vance 1984; Weston 1993; reviewed in Herdt 2000).

In one sense the two paradigms, individual and social, came to a head in confronting the AIDS epidemic. As the epidemic expanded, the tendency was to individualize and essentialize the location of the pandemic in homosexuals, Haitians, and other categories of blame (Farmer 1993). This blame and shame or finger-pointing precipitated a new paradigm of sexual essentialism, also known as the "health belief model," in which individuals, not cultures, were studied (Levine 1991). A large and growing body of sexuality research was stimulated as a result of this change, both in the United States and globally (Parker and Aggleton 1999). Take note, however, that the grassroots reaction came first, with little academic response. American academics were very slow to respond to the AIDS crisis in the United States, with psychology responding earlier than anthropology, but only after much death and suffering from the epidemic (reviewed in Herdt and Lindenbaum 1992). In another sense, it is clear that this research was at first disconnected from policy (Herdt and Lindenbaum 1992). Still further, the academy here followed the gay and lesbian social movement in responding to the challenges (Levine et al. 1997), though the role of the government was to become large and intrusive in how Lesbian/Gay/Bisexual/Transgender (LGBT) communities defined sexual health (Epstein 2003).

The epidemic forced a response that focused upon the immediate needs of adults who were sick and dying. Quickly a variety of AIDS campaigns and public health efforts began to focus upon adult gay men and bisexual individuals who engaged in high-risk behavior, though these interventions were largely disconnected from communities and sexual cultures. Young people's sexuality was at first ignored (Herdt and Boxer 1993). The majority of these efforts highlighted an individual difference model, as perhaps most famously demonstrated in the flawed "health belief" model of sexual risk-taking (reviewed in Levine 1991). In this model, the individual's own belief about risk and vulnerability was studied as a means to intervene and promote "rational" sexual behavior. Left out of the equation was social oppression—especially homophobia, discrimination, poverty and racism, among other forces. We now know how vital the factor of homophobia is in understanding the effect of social oppression upon risk for HIV (Herek 1997).

Notably, epidemiological methodology became hegemonic in HIV studies, focusing not upon context or social surround, but upon individual behavioral acts (critiqued in Parker, Carballo, and Herdt 1991). Like the emphasis in Kinsey's work from a generation before upon individual sex acts rather than upon their social context (Herdt 1990), there remained a tendency in this model to reduce the social world into a limited set of variables. Much was ignored in this work. For example, only later was it discovered that a young Hispanic man who comes out of a background of sexual abuse in childhood is more likely to engage in risky sexual behaviors that lead to adult HIV infection (Díaz 1998), or that a young woman of color who is constantly pressured by the males in her community to engage in premarital sex without the benefit of contraceptive use is much more likely to have an unintended pregnancy (Rosenthal et al. 2001), and that a young self-identified gay, lesbian, or transgender adolescent whose local culture forbids the expression of same-gender sexuality experiences intense alienation, isolation, and victimization that may well lead to suicide (Paul et al. 2002).

Nevertheless, sexual identity, identity-based social movements, and gay and lesbian sexuality studies in general made important strides as new funding and impetus for studying the sources of sexual infection and effective interventions (including the role of LGBT community formation) was made available (Epstein 2003; Levine et al. 1997). Social and cultural studies of HIV became one of the new processes of transformation in sexuality study (Herdt and Lindenbaum 1992), via social movement theory, feminist theory, gay and lesbian studies, globalization, the emergence of sexual diversity, the development of diverse sexual cultures, and the growth in human rights after the end of the Cold War (see Herdt 1997b; Levine et al. 1997; Parker and Aggleton 2003; Petchesky 2002). These studies in turn paved the way for a context in which to understand a multitude of new sexualities and social communities, including LGBT youth.

The aftermath of the AIDS epidemic was the formation of new behavioral and psychological studies of sexuality (but typically focused on adults, not young people) due to the unprecedented circumstances of the global epidemic. Research, intervention studies, community development, mobilization and coalition building, and social policy studies took a large leap in the effort to stop the transmission of the HIV virus. Within studies of the LGBT community, homophobia and heterosexism emerged as the new lens for understanding social oppression (Herek 1988). Gay and lesbian youth in general, a previously amorphous category, suffered from heightened suicide risk and low self-esteem, it was believed (reviewed in Herdt 1989). Only later were young people, particularly self-identified gay and lesbian youth, to become the focus of research and intervention efforts (Herdt and Boxer 1993). Gay and lesbian culture was a new context that enabled intergenerational social relations and the transmission of knowledge and culture (Herdt 1997b). Studies of gay bashing and homophobia are now more common and feature prominently in social analysis (Herman 1997), while new forms of prejudice against transgender persons have arisen.

On a global basis, the AIDS epidemic stimulated a new set of cultural studies of sexuality as well, as can be seen from the anthologies published on the topic in the 1990s (Brummelhuis and Herdt 1995; Herdt and Lindenbaum 1992; Levine et al. 1997; Parker and Aggleton 1999). Globalization also provided new empirical examples of how sexuality requires a broader lens than in the past; for example, the incredible reform of South Africa's racial and sexual policies after apartheid created unprecedented conditions for identity, gender, diversity, and development in a multi-ethnic society (Gevisser and Cameron 1995). In the midst of this amazing social change, the AIDS epidemic created terrible suffering for young people involved in survival, including the exchange of sex for money (Preston-Whyte et al. 2000). It was evident that researchers must no longer take the Western middle-class norm as the baseline for all childhood sexual development, especially in situations of radical and swift social change.

Within our expanding and diverse Western liberal democracies, it is obvious that we are dealing not with one but rather with multiple sexual cultures, as typified by mainstream suburban and small town middle-class white families, urban people of color, and gay, lesbian, bisexual, and transgender communities, representing cultures that overlap, compete or sometimes complement each other in their visions of human nature and the moral world of sexuality (Herdt 1997a; Weeks and Holland 1996).

Local sexual culture and social oppression

A sexual culture, through its meaning system and social practices, creates and reproduces a well-developed theory or an implicit folk model of sexuality, which among other things explains why and how children grow up to be the adults whose sexual desires, meanings, and practices conform to local sexual customs (Herdt 1999). Such a teleological worldview of human nature/sexual nature provides a charter for the institutions that control or regulate people's sexual behavior, ultimately to reproduce the group and structure the life course. But such a cultural force may, of course, completely ignore social oppression, or justify it as inevitable, natural, or even innate in human development (Herdt 2001; Parker and Aggleton 2003). This is the challenge faced by those who would study young people's sexuality across the world: to analyze how a sexual culture socializes children as intentional agents who subscribe to its folk theory of sexual nature, accepting its contradictions, double standards, and suffering of social oppression. By enacting sexual conduct, the culture is reproduced, and the boundaries of the group are reinforced. Every culture that practices marriage and has a concept of the family, whether in Chicago, Bombay, Paris, rural France, or New Guinea, effectively implements this group-regulating model of sexuality.

The problem of social oppression and sexuality arises again in the form of social hierarchies and forms of power based upon age, wealth, knowledge, gender, and other characteristics that regulate sexual culture and the form of contradictions within traditional cultures. In this area, we need to know not only how the boundaries of a sexual culture and community are drawn (Parker, Barbosa, and Aggleton 1991), but also how the regulation of traditional punishments and stigma can degrade, disempower, and dislocate people. Narratives and observations are critical, complementary dimensions of such an approach. For example, where sexuality is silenced by shame and secrecy, we need to know who has the power to silence, who feels shame, and what is at stake in adhering to or breaking the rules (Herdt 1981). If premarital intercourse between boys and girls is regarded as part of growing up, of being human, and of participating in social reality, then childhood sexual play will be approved in the sexual culture, as it is among the Trobriand Islanders of New Guinea (Malinowski 1929) and the !Kung people of Southern Africa (Shostack 1980). Conversely, if childhood sexual exploration is disapproved, it may form the basis for restriction, punishment, ostracism, and worse (Carrier 1980). Thus are social differences made real and become reality-defining for a culture in relation to the individual's sexual development. And thus too the local folk theory implicitly creates the conditions for departure from social practice, resistance to custom, and definitions of normal and abnormal, pathology and disease, goodness or stigma, and deviance. A sexual culture that maintains childhood sexual oppression and prohibits sexual play in childhood, such as the Sambia of New Guinea (Herdt 1987), frowns upon deviations and punishes those who fail to conform. Consequently, we ought to be skeptical of a normative developmental model based upon middle-class Western samples. When it comes to sexual subjectivity and identity formation, however, I believe that it is even more crucial to be aware of variations and to avoid the assumption of normalities.

A society disrupted by forces of warfare and conquest, political revolution, or eco-logical disaster contains the seeds for social oppression that may impact upon sexual development, introducing discontinuities in sexual development (Herdt 1990). Less ob-vious are the forces of poverty, racism, or heterosexism that disproportionately impact upon minorities or certain social classes or sexual cultures not in the majority, creat-ing conflict, turmoil, uncertainty, and anxiety that inflect sexual development. Among the outcomes of such conditions in contemporary society are sexual abuse, sexual risk-taking that introduces unintentional pregnancy early in development, and exposure to major STDs. As explained previously, research on the development of sexual attraction suggests that young people form stable representations of attraction by age 10. Even be-fore gonadal puberty, then, awareness and conflict surrounding the normative and ac-tual attractions and sexual subjectivies of young people create significant possibilities for discordances between individuals and society (Herdt and McClintock 2000). Indeed, the basic question of what constitutes normative or aberrant development must be re-thought to include considerations of the expected outcomes of disrupted development when it comes to a highly mediated social behavior such as sexual intimacy (Connell and Dowsett 1992), sexual objectification, and oppression (Tolman 2003).

Sexuality in such a hypothetical local culture is no longer purely an internal state, because social upheaval will refract or distort sexual subjectivity, with sexual develop-ment itself becoming the victim or by-product of oppression. Hence, sex becomes less of a middle-class luxury for romance and pleasure or recreation, and less a means of per-sonal development as mirrored in stories of coming out or personal fulfillment (Plum-mer 1995). In these instances, sexual subjectivity pertains instead to accommodation, hierarchy, power, and survival, as reflected most radically in the notion of "survival sex," which is common in oppressed communities (Díaz 2002). Indeed, the very notion of "survival" as in "survival sex" is a critical register for the voices of sexual trauma and confession, such as those narrating stories of incest survivors and rape victims (Plum-mer 1995). Sexual development, in this perspective, is the product of multiple determi-nants so strongly embedded in cultural reality and the social surround that the meaning between inside and outside is ultimately rendered impossible to tease apart for the per-son, even when the social oppression that forms their lived experience is transparent.

But what happens when survival sex becomes the norm (Preston-Whyte et al. 2000) in a culture? Here, new perspectives and ways of rethinking sexual policy must come to the fore. The burdens of social oppression are now exaggerated by growing disparities in wealth and social health policies around the world (Farmer 2003). In these societ-ies, the disrupted lives of children and young people whose poverty and life circum-stances, including having been orphaned by the HIV epidemic, make them victims of unprecedented sexual marketplaces, at least from the perspective of white middle-class people. Alice M. Miller (2000) comments:

> Survival sex that forces youngsters to trade sex for money is far too common
> in oppressed communities, and among women living in marginal communities
> throughout the world. New policies are being put in place to protect against sexual
> trafficking—women and children being moved for "immoral purposes" to "gratify
> the passions of another." (77)

The 1979 Convention on the Elimination of All Forms of Discrimination against Women calls for protections against sexual violence and exploitation, especially violence against women that causes sexual suffering, and the 1989 Convention on the Rights of the Child (CRC) supports positive approaches to sexual development across childhood and youth, for both girls and boys. The AIDS epidemic in world regions such as Africa has compounded these issues many times over. These critical changes that are necessary to study these issues require a new research and policy framework to understand how severe social oppression is impacting young people's sexuality. For this, I would like to return to the issue of abstinence and abstinence-only policies in both the United States and other countries.

Oppression: What social difference theory left out

In the United States, the Surgeon General's Report on Comprehensive Sexuality Education in the United States—his "Call to Action to Promote Sexual Health and Responsible Sexual Behavior"— was a watershed of change (Satcher 2001). It must be remembered, however, that the Surgeon General's report was necessary because of the U.S. government's official policy on abstinence-only sexuality education, a policy largely bereft of scientific credibility (Kirby 2001). Moreover, the U.S. government opposed publication of the report, and it was bitterly contested by right-wing anti-sexuality education organizations (Irvine 2002).

This report never achieved widespread circulation, and there is little reason to believe that it has influenced the sexual health policies of other countries, especially those in which abstinence-only programs are being promoted by the U.S. government. As we have seen, awareness of diversity and diverse sexualities is an important source for understanding sexual development and optimal adult outcomes. In societies such as Uganda, mentioned above, abstinence has a very different meaning than in white middle-class privileged sexual cultures (e.g., suburban New York City). Abstinence is not going to work well or at all for such people until the forces of social oppression are addressed. Thus, the social oppression produced by sexual coercion and shame, stigma, silence, risk-taking, suicidal tendencies, and danger-filled ways of seeking pleasure are all enormously important in understanding the negative influences upon children's sexual development (Long 1997; Parker and Aggleton 2003; Paul et al. 2002).

In the United States, social oppression is linked to power and social inequalities in institutions such as high schools. Throughout much of the twentieth century, the high school was a constant source of conflict in sexuality education and gender and sexual rights (Moran 2000). Perhaps this was because of the intersections of private and public and of individual and state that are common to the shared purpose of public school pedagogy. Abstinence-only education opens up new vistas for understanding the hidden sociosexual oppression of communities played out in classrooms. Young people are its victims and perpetrators, but they act as proxies for the community and, in a larger sense, for the state. The controversy surrounding the Surgeon General's Call to Action has signified the U.S. government's opposition to empowerment in the arena of sexual rights and the empowerment of young people's sexuality. Abstinence-only policies, officially endorsed by the government and paid for from public funds, continue to regard sexual freedom and agency as threats to citizenship and democracy. Moreover, the imagery surrounding these policies in the Welfare Reform Act of 1996 racializes sexuality and stigmatizes poor women of color (Fields n.d.). Such policies impact sexual equality, including the rights of young people and all cultural minorities to achieve the full potential of their sexual well-being and the ability to protect themselves from harm and disease.

Here then is a clear and transparent issue of social oppression, purveyed by the U. S. government, that may serve as a general proxy for understanding the reproduction of structural sexual violence in the United States. Are Americans callous or indifferent to this social oppression? I think not; however, they remain largely unaware of the influence of their government in shaping young people's sexuality through these policies. Moreover, they are ignorant or turn a blind eye to the role of extremist organizations in the promotion of abstinence-only policies. It has long been known that certain fundamentalist religious and traditional right-wing groups (what Janice Irvine 2002 calls the "New Right") have supported abstinence as a "cultural cause." Public opinion polls conducted by a variety of organizations, including SIECUS, consistently demonstrate that Americans want "comprehensive" sexuality education (a concept typically taken to mean more than abstinence-only education and also including teaching about sexual disease prevention), but they are confused about how to achieve or implement this ideal. The public can be manipulated through misinformation and fear by New Right organizations that exaggerate differences and induce divisive sexual speech (Irvine 2002) in local culture and community meetings, such as those of the PTA.

Nonetheless, there is a hopeful sign of late: the emergence of sex and sexuality as linked to positive sexual health in one form or the other. A 1970s draft defines sexual health as

> a state of physical, emotional, mental and social well being related to sexuality; it is not merely the absence of disease, dysfunction or infirmity. Sexual health requires a positive and respectful approach to sexuality and sexual relations, as well as the possibility of having pleasure and safe sexual experiences, free of coercion, discrimination and violence. For sexual health to be attained and maintained, the sexual rights of all persons must be respected, protected, and fulfilled.[1]

This positive trend, one that includes pleasure and prevention within the same frame, is the new "gold standard" of the Surgeon General's Report on Comprehensive Sexuality Education (Satcher 2001), and increasingly it is invoked to strengthen the relationship between sexual cultures, social policies, and the law. Let us hope that this model of sexuality as a human right spreads to encompass both the North and the South, making the analysis of social oppression the key to understanding sexual development and young people's sexual subjectivities.

Conclusion

In this survey, I have reviewed some of the historical barriers that served to thwart the study of social oppression as a force in the development of young people's sexuality. I have argued for the expansion of childhood sexuality studies through biopsychological approaches that are more inclusive of cross-cultural and intracultural diversity. Individual difference theories from this viewpoint need to incorporate consideration of cultural variation and social change, including social oppression. Social oppression in sexual development is common in many places and times and creates an impact on childhood sexual subjectivities and behaviors that has typically been ignored in research and policy. Viewing optimal sexual development as more dependent upon the environment than in past approaches can lead to a belief that sexual health, like good maternal health care, should be a basic human right for our species as a whole.

An individual difference perspective that grew through Freudian developmentalism and reached into the social and psychological sciences was a critical factor. So too was the disdain of sexuality in anthropology and the absence of significant study of variation within contemporary Western societies, the result in part of modernism. The disruption of the AIDS epidemic in the 1980s introduced the conditions for a new paradigm that would study structural violence in relation to sexuality. This paradigm change in turn has influenced subsequent readings of major research and policy, but it has not eliminated contradictions or discontinuities in postmodern societies.

Discontinuity, as Benedict (1938) long ago reasoned, produces developmental outcomes that cannot be explained without understanding the society, the sexual culture, and the local moral world. Sexual discontinuity, in which the child is forbidden knowledge of sex but the teenager or young adult is expected to be an expert practitioner without ever having had sexuality education, is particularly vexing in the United States, Benedict noted. Particular societies can distort the outcomes of sexual behavior development through such forces as segregation, discrimination, racism, sexual shame and silence, censorship, prohibition on childhood sexual play, and condemnation of homosexuality. For example, poor inner-city African American girls typically cannot locate a safe space in which to define for themselves their desires and thus become the agents of their own desires in adolescent development, due to the coercion and pressure of their families, peers, and boyfriends (Fine 1988). Moreover, recent studies of HIV clearly show that HIV risk-taking among poor men of color, especially Hispanic gay men, is greatest when those men suffer from a history of sexual abuse and exploitation, leading to a kind of victimized sexual subjectivity that may spiral out of control (Díaz and Ayala 2000). These examples suggest that when social oppression influences sexual development early on, the outcomes may stunt development and enhance risk and negative outcomes for health, mental health, and sexual functioning perhaps throughout life.

As an anthropologist, I believe that social oppression, inequality, and disparities between groups pose the greatest challenge to science and society. Racism, poverty, heterosexism and homophobia, xenophobia, stigma and scapegoating of people with AIDS, and other negative factors are laced into the intrinsic development of the child and produce alternative outcomes or deficits and even death when compared with other populations. Globalization is having unintended effects of a far-reaching nature as well, in terms of sexual tourism, STDs, and social and sexual movements (Herdt 1997c; Parker, Barbosa, and Aggleton 2000). One of the critical reasons is the lack of social and legal protections. Social and legal protections against sexual injustices of this kind are minimal in the United States, and not surprisingly, knowledge of sexual health and sexual rights needed to advance sexual health and social policy are rather poorly developed as well. Globally, the human rights abuses and sexual and reproductive rights violations that have followed from studies of these issues since the 1994 International Conference on Population and Development in Cairo are chilling and reveal the profound vulnerability of women and children to sexual exploitation (Petchesky 2003).

Sexual cultures create moral worlds that strongly inflect the meaning of sexual development and place children and adolescents whose sexuality is outside of the norm at risk. Theories of sexual development typically describe "normative" processes that assume an "all things being equal" epistemology of social resources and community development. For children and early adolescents coming into sexual awareness who suffer from structural violence—resulting from poverty, racism, heterosexism, religious persecution and anti-Semitism, homophobia and anti-gay violence, the marginalization of transgender people, xenophobic bias against immigrants, ageism, and discrimination against individuals with disabilities—sexuality is not a matter of being normative or equal. It is a matter of survival. While this process may be common to all human development, we have not studied its role sufficiently in the development of sexuality, and hardly at all in situations of social oppression, to understand the outcomes and to determine the social policies necessary to deal with their effects upon human development.

When a sexual culture directs people to objectify others, as when sexual objectification occurs, the results effectively dehumanize others, and when the culture's theory of human nature naturalizes this as necessary in the cosmos or as a result of biology, then a formula has been created for oppression within the group. The hostility may be directed toward categories of objects, whether based on race, gender, religion, social class, sexual orientation, or any other human characteristic (Teunis n.d.). Such a pattern results from long-term structural violence, the tendency of the psyche to engage in the projection of fears and anxieties, and the displacement of aggression and domination, typically by men.

Finally, optimal sexual development is here viewed as being more dependent upon the environment than previously suggested by theorists, and such a revised view places increased emphasis upon the importance of sexual health research that will better inform and help to shape the best practices and policies related to sexuality. Understanding optimal sexual health is the key to the formation of better policy in communities and populations continually impacted by oppression and adversity. In the end the question of how individual resilience emerges out of such social differences is vital to theories about the interaction between sexual culture and individual sexual development. The resilience of the human spirit amidst adversity of all kinds is a thing to behold in this universe. However, it does not occur in a vacuum; we can enhance resilience by linking our research to policy formation in this arena of human development. For all of us who love the study of sexuality and practice the study of development in cultural context, the survival of sex is ultimately not in question, nor is the survival of domination, for both will find a footing in the future. We cannot turn back social change, for change is in the nature of our species, but we can increase the sense of inclusion and belonging in the future by creating, through the best research and thoughtful social policies, the means for people to achieve a better voice in their own sexual and social development and destinies.

Note

1. World Health Organization. 2002. Gender and reproductive rights, working definitions section, para. 3. www.who.int/reproductive-health/gender/sexual_health.html. The WHO web-

site states that its definitions are "presented . . . as a contribution to on-going discussions about sexual health, but do not represent an official WHO position, and should not be used or quoted as WHO definitions."

References

Abramson, P. R., and S. D. Pinkerton, eds. 1995. *Sexual nature, sexual culture.* Chicago: University of Chicago Press.

Appadurai, A. 1996. *Modernity at large.* Minneapolis: University of Minnesota Press.

Bailey, J. M., and M. Oberschneider. 1997. Sexual orientation: Professional dance. *Archives of Sexual Behavior* 26:433–44.

Bancroft, J., ed. 1997. *Researching sexual behavior: Methodological issues.* Bloomington: Indiana University Press.

Bancroft, J., ed. 2000. *The role of theory in sex research.* Bloomington: Indiana University Press.

Bayer, R. 1981. *Homosexuality and American psychiatry.* New York: Basic Books.

Bellah, R. N., R. Madsen, W. M. Sullivan, A. Swidler, and S. M. Tipton. 1985. *Habits of the heart: Individualism and commitment in American life.* Berkeley: University of California Press.

Bem, D. 2000. The exotic-becomes-erotic theory of sexual orientation. In Bancroft 2000, 67–81.

Benedict, R. 1938. Continuities and discontinuities in cultural conditioning. *Journal of Psychiatry* 1:161–67.

Boxer, A., and B. J. Cohler. 1989. The life course of gay and lesbian youth: An immodest proposal for the study of lives. *Journal of Homosexuality* 17:315–55.

Brummelhuis, H., and G. Herdt, eds. 1995. *Culture and sexual risk: Anthropological perspectives on AIDS.* New York: Gordon and Breach.

Buss, D. M. 1992. Mate preference mechanisms: Consequences for partner choice and intrasexual competition. In *The adapted mind,* ed. J. Barkow, L. Cosmides, and J. Tooby, 249–66. New York: Oxford University Press.

Butler, J. 1993. *Bodies that matter: On the discursive limits of sex.* New York: Routledge.

Carrier, J. 1980. Homosexuality in cross-cultural perspective. In *Homosexual behavior: A modern reappraisal,* ed. J. Marmor, 100–122. New York: Basic Books.

Chodorow, N. J. 1978. *The reproduction of mothering.* Berkeley: University of California Press.

Cohen, L. 1995. The pleasures of castration. In Abramson and Pinkerton 1995, 276–304.

Cohler, B. J., and R. M. Galatzer-Levy. 2000. *The course of gay and lesbian lives: Social and psychoanalytic perspectives.* Chicago: University of Chicago Press.

Comaroff, J., and J. L. Comaroff. 1991. *Of revelation and revolution, vol. 1: Christianity, colonialism, and consciousness in South Africa.* Chicago: University of Chicago Press.

Connell, R. W. 1995. *Masculinities.* Berkeley: University of California Press.

Connell, R. W., and G. W. Dowsett, eds. 1992. *Rethinking sex: Social theory and sexuality research.* Philadelphia: Temple University Press.

Crawford, M., and D. Popp. 2002. Sexual double standards: A review and methodological critique of two decades of research. *Journal of Sex Research* 40:13–26.

D'Emilio, J. D., and E. B. Freedman. 1988. *Intimate matters: A history of sexuality in America.* New York: Harper and Row.

Díaz, R. 1998. *Latino gay men and HIV: Culture, sexuality and risk.* New York: Routledge.

———. 2000. Cultural regulation, self-regulation, and sexuality: A psycho-cultural model of HIV risk in Latino gay men. In Parker, Barbosa, and Aggleton 2000, 191—215.

Díaz, R., and G. Ayala. *The impact of social discrimination on health outcomes: The case of Latino gay men and HIV.* New York: National Gay and Lesbian Task Force.

DiLeonardo, M. 1998. *Exotics at home.* Chicago: University of Chicago Press.

di Mauro, D. 1997. Sexuality research in the United States. In Bancroft 1997, 3–8.

Ehrhardt, A. A. 1996. Our view of adolescent sexuality: Risk behavior without developmental context. *American Journal of Public Health* 86, no. 11: 1523–25.

———. 1997. Gender. In Bancroft 1997, 361–62.

———. 2000. Gender, sexuality, and human development. In Bancroft 2000, 3–16.

Elder, G. 1975. *Adolescence in the life cycle: Psychological change and social context*. New York: Halsted Press.

Epstein, S. 2003. Sexualizing governance and medicalizing identities: The emergence of "state-centered" LGBT health politics in the United States. *Sexualities* 6, no. 2: 131–71.

Fine, M. 1988. The missing discourse of desire. *Harvard Educational Review* 2:29–53.

Farmer, P. 1993. *AIDS and accusation: Haiti and the geography of blame*. Berkeley: University of California Press.

———. 1999. *Infections and inequalities: The modern plagues*. Berkeley: University of California Press.

———. 2002. *Pathologies of power*. Berkeley: University of California Press.

Fields, J. n.d. Children-having-children: Racism, innocence, and sexuality education. In Teunis n.d.

Foucault, M. 1978?. *The history of sexuality*. Trans. R. Hurley. New York: Viking.

Freeman, D. 1999. *The fateful hoaxing of Margaret Mead: A historical analysis of her Samoan research*. Boulder: Westview.

Freire, P. 1970. *Pedagogy of the oppresse*d. New York: Continuum.

Freud, S. 1905. *Three essays on the theory of sexuality*. New York: Basic Books.

———. 1913. *Totem and taboo*. 18th ed. London: Tavistock.

Gagnon, J. H. 1991. The implicit and explicit use of scripts in sex research. *Annual review of sex research* 1:1–43.

———. 1997. Others have sex with others: Captain Cook and the penetration of the Pacific. In *Sexual cultures and migration in the eras of AIDS*, ed. G. Herdt, 23–40. Oxford: Clarendon Press.

Gagnon, J. H., and Parker, R. G. 1995. Conceiving sexuality. Introduction to *Conceiving sexuality: Approaches to sex research in a postmodern world*, 3–18. New York: Routledge.

Gagnon, J. H., and Simon, W. 1973. *Sexual conduct: The social sources of human sexuality*. London: Hutchinson.

Gay, P. 1998. *Freud: A life for our time*. New York: Norton.

Geertz, C. 1973. *The interpretation of cultures: Selected essays*. New York: Basic Books.

Gevisser, L., and M. Cameron, eds. 1995. *Defiant desire: Gay and lesbian lives in South Africa*. New York: Routledge.

Gewertz, D. 1983. *Sepik River societies*. New Haven: Yale University Press.

Ginsburg, F., and R. Rapp. 1995. *Conceiving the new world order*. Berkeley: University of California Press.

Gould, S. J. 1981. *The mismeasure of man*. New York: Norton.

Gregor, T. 1985. *Anxious pleasures: The sexual lives of an Amazonian people*. Chicago: University of Chicago Press.

Greenberg, A., and J. M. Bailey. 2001. Parental selection of children's sexual orientation. *Archives of Sexual Behavior* 30, no. 4: 423–39.

Herdt, G. 1981. *Guardians of the flutes: Idioms of masculinity*. New York: McGraw-Hill.

———. 1987. *The Sambia: Ritual and gender in New Guinea*. New York: Holt, Rinehart and Winston.

———, ed. 1989. *Gay and lesbian youth*. New York: Haworth.

———. 1990. Developmental continuity as a dimension of sexual orientation across cultures. In

Homosexuality and heterosexuality: The Kinsey scale and current research, ed. D. McWhirter, J. Reinisch, and S. Sanders, 208–38. New York: Oxford University Press.

———. 1991. Representations of homosexuality in traditional societies: An essay on cultural ontology and historical comparison. *Journal of the History of Sexuality* 1:481–504.

———. 1994. Mistaken sex: Culture, biology, and the third sex in New Guinea. In *Third sex, third gender: Beyond sexual dimorphism in culture and history*, ed. G. Herdt, 419–46. New York: Zone Books.

———. 1997a. *Same sex, different cultures: Exploring gay and lesbian lives*. Boulder: Westview Press.

———. 1997b. Sexual cultures and population movement: Implications for HIV/STDs. In *Sexual cultures and migration in the era of AIDS: Anthropological and demographic perspectives*, ed. G. Herdt, 3–22. New York: Oxford University Press.

———. 1997c. Inter-generational relations and AIDS in the formation of gay culture in the United States. In Levine, Nardi, and Gagnon 1997, 245–82. Chicago: University of Chicago Press.

———. 1999a. Clinical ethnography and sexual study. *Annual Review of Sex Research* 10:100–119.

———. 1999b. *Sambia sexual culture: Essays from the field*. Chicago: University of Chicago Press.

———. 2000. Why the Sambia initiate boys before age 10. In Bancroft 2000, 82–109. .

———. 2001. Stigma and the ethnographic study of HIV: Problems and prospects. *AIDS and Behavior* 5:141–49.

———. 2003. *Secrecy and cultural reality*. Ann Arbor: University of Michigan Press.

Herdt, G., and Boxer, A. 1993. *Children of horizons: How gay and lesbian youth are forging a new way out of the closet*. Boston: Beacon Press.

Herdt, G., and S. C. Leavitt. 1998. *Adolescence in Pacific island societies*. Pittsburgh: University of Pittsburgh Press.

Herdt, G., and S. Lindenbaum, eds. 1992. *The time of AIDS*. Newbury Park, CA: Sage Publications.

Herdt, G., and M. McClintock. 2000. The magical age of 10. *Archives of Sexual Behavior* 29, no. 6: 587–606.

Herdt, G., and R. J. Stoller. 1990. *Intimate communications: Erotics and the study of culture*. New York: Columbia University Press.

Herek, G. M. 1988. Heterosexuals' attitudes toward lesbians and gay men: Correlates and gender differences. *Journal of Sex Research* 25, no. 4, 451–77.

———. 1997. The HIV epidemic and public attitudes toward lesbians and gay men. In Levine, Nardi, and Gagnon 1997, 191–218.

Herman, D. 1998. *The antigay agenda*. Chicago: University of Chicago Press.

Hrdy, S. B. 2000. Discussion paper. In Bancroft 2000, 33–45.

Hymes, D. 1974. *Reinventing anthropology*. New York: Vintage Books.

Irvine, Janice M. 2002. *Talk about sex: The battles over sex education in the United States*. Berkeley: University of California Press.

Irvine, Judith. 2002. *Harmful to minors: The perils of protecting children from sex*. Minneapolis: University of Minnesota Press.

Jacobs, S., W. Thomas, and S. Lang, eds. 1997. *Two-spirit people: Native American gender identity, sexuality, and spirituality*. Urbana: University of Illinois Press.

Kardiner, A. 1939. *The individual and his society*. New York: Columbia University Press.

Kinsey, A., B. Pomeroy, and C. E. Martin. 1948. *Sexual behavior and the human male*. Philadelphia: W. B. Saunders.

Kinsey, A., B. Pomeroy, B., and C. E. Martin, and P. Gebhard. 1953. *Sexual behavior and the human female*. Philadelphia: W. B. Saunders.

Kirby, D. 2003. Do abstinence-only programs delay the initiation of sex among young people and reduce teen pregnancy? *American Sexuality* 1, no. 6. nsrc.sfsu.edu.

Knauft, B. 1999. *From primitive to postcolonial*. Ann Arbor: Michigan University Press.

Krieger, N. 1999. Embodying inequality: A review of concepts, measures, and methods for studying health consequences of discrimination. *International Journal of Health Services* 29, no. 2: 295–352.

Krieger, N. 2003. Genders, sexes, and health: What are the connections and why does it matter? *International Journal of Epidemiology* 32:652–57.

Kuhn, T. S. 1970. *The structure of scientific revolutions*. 2nd ed. Chicago: University of Chicago Press.

Lancaster, R. 2003. *The trouble with nature*. Berkeley: University of California Press.

Langfeldt, T. 1981. Childhood masturbation: Individual and social organization. In *Children and sex*, ed. L. L. Constantine and F. M. Martinson, 63–74. Boston: Little, Brown and Company.

Laumann, E. O., J. H. Gagnon, R. T. Michael, and S. Michaels. 1994. *The social organization of sexuality: Sexual practices in the United States*. Chicago: University of Chicago Press.

LeVay, S. 1993. *The sexual brain*. Cambridge: MIT Press.

Levine, M., P. M. Nardi, and J. H. Gagnon, eds. 1997. *In changing times: Gay men and lesbians encounter HIV/AIDS*. Chicago: University of Chicago Press.

Long, L. D. 1997. Refugee women, violence, and HIV. In *Sexual cultures and migration in the era of AIDS: Anthropological and demographic perspectives*, ed. G. Herdt, 87–106. New York: Oxford University Press.

Maccoby, E. E. 1984. Gender as a social category. *Developmental Psychology* 24:755–65.

———. 1998. *The two sexes: Growing up apart, coming together*. Cambridge: Harvard University Press.

Maccoby, E. E., and C. Jacklin. 1974. *The psychology of sex differences*. Stanford: Stanford University Press.

Malinowski, B. 1929. *The sexual life of savages in northwestern Melanesia*. New York: Harcourt, Brace and World.

Manderson, L., and M. Jolly, eds. 1997. *Sites of desire, economies of pleasure: Sexualities in Asia and the Pacific*. Chicago: University of Chicago Press.

Markowitz, F., and M. Ashkenazi, eds. 1998. *Sex, sexuality, and the anthropologist*. Urbana: University of Illinois Press.

Masters, W., and V. Johnson. 1966. *Human sexual response*. Boston: Little, Brown and Company.

McClintock, M., and G. Herdt. 1996. Rethinking puberty: The development of sexual attraction. *Current Directions in Psychological Science* 5:178–83.

McClintock, M., G. Herdt, and R. Rosenfield. 1998. Preadolescent determinants of sexuality. *Pediatric Update* 19, no. 9: 1–10.

Mead, M. 1927. *Coming of age in Samoa*. New York: Dutton.

———. 1935. *Sex and temperament in three primitive societies*. New York: Dutton.

———. 1949. *Male and female*. New York: Dutton.

———. 1961. Cultural determinants of sexual behavior. In *Sex and internal secretions*, ed. W. C. Young, 1433–79. Baltimore: Williams and Wilkins.

———. 1977. *Letters from the field, 1925–1975*. New York: Harper Colophon Books.

Meyer-Bahlburg, H. F. L. 2000. Discussion paper: Sexual orientation—discussion of Bem and Herdt from a psychobiological perspective. In Bancroft 2000, 110–24.

Miller, A. M. 2000. Sexual but not reproductive: Exploring the junction and disjunction of sexual and reproductive rights. *Health and Human Rights* 4:68–109.

Miller, B., ed. 1992. *Gender hierarchies*. New York: Cambridge University Press.

Money, J. 1987. Sin, sickness, or society? *American Psychologist* 42:384–99.

Money, J., and Ehrhardt, A. A. 1972. *Man, woman, boy, girl*. Baltimore: Johns Hopkins University Press.

Moran, J. P. 2000. *Teaching sex: The shaping of adolescence in the 20th century*. Cambridge: Harvard University Press.

Morgan, R., ed. 1970. *Sisterhood is powerful*. New York: Vintage.

Murphy, T. F. 1997. *Gay science*. New York: Columbia University Press.

Paiva, V. 2000. Gendered scripts and the sexual science: Promoting sexual subjects among Brazilian teenagers. In Parker, Barbosa, and Aggleton 2000, 216–40.

Parker, R. 1991. *Bodies, pleasures, and passions*. Boston: Beacon Press.

———. 1999. *Beneath the equator: Cultures of desire, male homosexuality, and emerging gay communities in Brazil*. New York: Routledge.

Parker, R., and P. Aggleton, eds. 1999. *Culture, society, and sexuality: A reader*. London: UCL Press.

———. 2003. HIV and AIDS-related stigma and discrimination: A conceptual framework and implications for action. *Social Science and Medicine* 57:13–24.

Parker, R., R. M. Barbosa, and P. Aggleton, eds. 2000. *Framing the sexual subject: The politics of gender, sexuality and power*. Berkeley: University of California Press.

Parker, R., M. Carballo, and G. Herdt. 1991. Sexual culture, HIV transmission, and AIDS research. *Journal of Sex Research* 28:75–96.

Paul, J. P., J. Catania, L. Pollack, J. Moskowitz, J. Canchola, T. Mills, D. Binson, and R. Stall. 2002. Suicide attempts among gay and bisexual men. *American Journal of Public Health* 92:1338–45.

Petchesky, R. P. 2000. Sexual rights: Inventing a concept, mapping an international practice. In Parker, Barbosa, and Aggleton 2000, 81–103.

———. 2003. *Global prescriptions: Gendering health and human rights*. New York: Margrave.

Pavelka, M. S. M. 1995. Sexual nature: what can we learn from a cross-species perspective? In Abramson and Pinkerton 1995, 17–36.

Plummer, K. 1995. *Telling sexual stories*. New York: Routledge.

Preston-Whyte, E., C. Varga, H. Oosthuizen, R. Roberts, and F. Blose. 2000. Survival sex and HIV/AIDS in an African city. In Parker, Barbosa, and Aggleton, 165–90.

Robinson, P. 1976. *The modernization of sex: Havelock Ellis, Alfred Kinsey, William Masters, and Virginia Johnson*. Ithaca: Cornell University Press.

Rosaldo, M. Z. 1974. Woman, culture and society: A theoretical overview. In *Woman, culture and society*, ed. M. Z. Rosaldo and L. Lamphere, 17–42. Stanford: Stanford University Press.

Rosenthal, S. L., K. M. Von Fanson, S. Cotton, F. M. Biro, L. Mills, and P. A. Succop. 2001. Sexual initiation: Predictors and developmental trends. *Sexual Transmission of Disease* 28, no. 9: 527–32.

Rubin, G. 1984. Thinking sex: Notes for a radical theory of the politics of sexuality. In *Pleasure and danger: Exploring female sexuality*, ed. C. S. Vance, 267–319. New York: Routledge.

Said, E. 1978. *Orientalism*. New York: Pantheon.

Satcher, D. 2001. The surgeon general's call to action to promote sexual health and responsible sexual behavior. July 9. www.surgeongeneral.gov/library.

Scheper-Hughes, N. 1992. *Death without weeping*. Berkeley: University of California Press.

Setel, P. 1999. *A plague of paradoxes*. Chicago: University of Chicago Press.

Shweder, R. A. 1990. Cultural psychology: What is it? In Stigler, Shweder, and Herdt 1990, 1–46.

Singer, M. 1961. A survey of culture and personality theory and research. In *Studying personality cross-culturally*, ed. B. Kaplan, 9–90. New York: Harper and Row.

Spiro, M. E. 1979. Whatever happened to the id? *American Anthropologist* 81:5–13.

Stigler, J. W., R. A. Shweder, and G. Herdt, eds. 1990. *Cultural psychology: Essays on comparative human development.* New York: Cambridge University Press.

Stimpson, C. R. 1996. Women's studies and its discontents. *Dissent* 43:67–75.

Stocking, G. 1997. *Malinowski, Rivers, Benedict, and others.* Madison: University of Wisconsin Press.

Stoller, A. L. 1995. *Race and the education of desire.* Durham: Duke University Press.

Stoller, R. J. 1968. *Sex and gender, vol. 1: On the development of masculinity and femininity.* New York: Science House.

———. 1975. *Sex and gender, vol. 2: The transsexual experiement.* London: Hogarth.

———. 1985. *Observing the erotic imagination.* New Haven: Yale University Press.

Teunis, N., ed. n.d. Sexual inequalities. Unpublished manuscript.

Tiefer, L. 1991. Social constructionism and the study of human sexuality. In *Forms of desire: Sexual orientation and the social constructionist controversy,* ed. E. Stein, 295–324. New York: Garland Publishing.

———. 1995. *Sex is not a natural fact, and other essays.* Boulder: Westview Press.

———. 2000. Discussion paper——let's look at contexts. In Bancroft 2000, 46–50.

Tolman, D. 1994. Dating to desire: Culture and the bodies of adolescent girls. In *Sexual cultures and the construction of adolescent identities,* ed. Janice M. Irvine, 250–84. Philadelphia: Temple University Press.

Tolman, D. 1996. Adolescent girls' sexuality: Debunking the myth of the urban girl. In *Urban girls: Resisting stereotypes, creating identities,* ed. B. Leadbetter and N. Way, 255–71. New York: New York University Press.

———. 2003. *Dilemmas of desire.* Cambridge: Harvard University Press.

Tolman, D., M. Striepe, and T. Harmon. 2003. Gender matters: Constructing a model of adolescent sexual health. *Journal of Sex Research* 40:4–12.

Tuzin, D. F. 1994. The forgotten passion: Sexuality and anthropology in the ages of Victoria and Bronislaw. *Journal of the History of Behavioral Sciences* 30:114–37.

Vance, C. S. 1991. Anthropology rediscovers sexuality: A theoretical comment. *Social Science and Medicine* 33:875–884.

———. 2001. Social construction theory: Problems in the history of *sexuality.* In *Sexualities: Critical assessments,* ed. K. Plummer, 356–71. London: Routledge.

Wallace, A. F. C. 1969. *Culture and personality.* 2nd ed. New York: Random.

Weston, K. 1993. Lesbian/gay studies in the house of anthropology. *Annual Review of Anthropology,* 22:339–367.

Weeks, J. 1985. *Sexuality and its discontents.* London: Routledge.

Weeks, J., and J. Holland, eds. 1996. *Sexual cultures: Communities, values, and intimacy.* New York: St. Martin's Press.

Whiting, B., and C. Edwards. 1988. *Children and their worlds.* Cambridge: Harvard University Press.

Whiting, J. W. M., R. Kluckhohn, and A. Anthony 1958. The function of male initiation ceremonies at puberty. In *Readings in social psychology,* ed. E. E. Maccoby, E. Newcombe, and R. Harley, 359–70. New York: Holt.

Leonore Tiefer

14

Sexuopharmacology

A Fateful New Element in Sexual Scripts

Drugs are cultural entities as well as chemical compounds.
MONTAGNE (1996, 11)

It seems inescapable that a raft of new sexuality medicines, many still under development but some already available, will substantially alter cultural, interpersonal, and intrapsychic sexual scripts. We can deduce this from popular culture even before we have data about people's actual sexual lives.

The first sexuopharmaceutical, Viagra, was approved by the Federal Drug Administration (FDA) in 1998 for the treatment of erection problems. Almost immediately, it became a popular metaphor for vigor, stiffness, and uplift, used by writers and performers in all sorts of serious and comic media (Tiefer 1998). In a March 2001 cartoon in the *New York Times*, the U.S. secretary of the treasury holds a piece of paper with sorry-looking economic prognostications, and says to the president of the United States, "Frankly, sir, I'm not sure slipping Viagra into Greenspan's coffee will do the trick" [Greenspan being chairman of the Federal Reserve at the time]. All readers are expected to understand the reference.

Newspaper and magazine articles predicting, promoting, and reporting on the many Viagra-wannabe drugs and Viagra-for-women gels, suppositories, creams, patches, and inhalants indicate that sex drugs have become part of everyday sexual vernacular. Sexual script theory offers an excellent theoretical perspective to help us think about the types of impact sexuopharmaceuticals will have on sexual life.

The emergence of "plastic sexuality": The backdrop

In the twentieth century, improvements in public health and technology led to increased life expectancy, sanitation, leisure, education, travel, and exposure to new media for many in the industrialized world. Global political and economic relations shifted in response to industrialization and wars. Consequently, as many have concluded, the twentieth century witnessed huge value changes in work and family life, personal relationships, life goals, experiences of the body and health, gender-based roles and expectations, and "sexuality" (e.g., D'Emilio and Freedman 1988; McLaren 1999). Cultural analysts such as Anthony Giddens (1992) and Philip Cushman (1995) have examined at length the rise of a new psychological "self" and consequent new sexual values and experiences.

Here, Giddens coins the term "plastic sexuality" to summarize some of these changes:

> The emergence of what I term plastic sexuality is crucial to the emancipation implicit in the pure [love-based] relationship, as well as to women's claim to sexual pleasure. Plastic sexuality is . . . freed from the needs of reproduction . . . [and] it becomes further developed . . . as the result of the spread of modern contraception. . . . *Plastic sexuality can be moulded as a trait of personality and thus is intrinsically bound up with the self.* (Giddens 1992, 2, emphasis added)

The existence and promotion of sexuopharmacology will become part of that molding process. We see before our very eyes how cultural values about sex change and aspects of sexual life are medicalized by the huge media attention focused on new drugs. Individuals and couples, young and old, are bombarded with media accounts of new drugs, patches, and creams; what they are for; and who is using them and the (always) positive results; and thereby ordinary individuals and couples learn new expectations of what sexuality is, and should be, all about. They learn, perhaps for the first time, about the biology of genital blood flow and about the alleged importance of maintaining a high level of sex hormones throughout adulthood to stave off "deficiency" conditions. They hear about arousal and orgasm and G-spots and booty calls over and over again, and receive the market-driven message that lifelong sexual activity and sexiness are mandatory for personal and relationship happiness. This marketing/education focuses the public's understanding of sex on individual and biological perspectives and omits factors such as culture and politics, values and relationships, sensuality and relaxation. The rewards and costs of sexual activity are never compared with those from other forms of individual or dyadic activities or discussed in the context of lived existence.

At the same time as the public's expectations for sexual performance are inflated, health professionals are shaped as the new "experts" in sexuality. Industry-sponsored continuing education seminars stress that sexuality is a primary element of "quality of life." Healthcare providers are taught how to incorporate routine questions about patients' genital functions (though not where they got their expectation) into their practices. Advertisements for sexuopharmaceuticals instruct the public to "ask your doctor," placing physicians in the awkward position of being asked to provide sex education and prescriptions on demand.

In the language and conceptual framework of scripting theory, medicalization affects people because "cultural scenarios are the instructional guides that exist at the level of collective life." (Simon and Gagnon 1986, 98). Let us consider how sexuopharmacology has emerged as a key element in sexual life.

The emergence of sexuopharmacology

The FDA's approval of sildenafil citrate (brand name Viagra, Pfizer company's oral drug for "erectile dysfunction") in March 1998 capped a fifteen-year-long process of medicalizing men's sexuality through the creation of an official classification system, designated experts, and an extensive scientific literature all promoting a medical mindset towards men's sexual problems and downplaying nonmedical alternatives (Tiefer 1986, 1994; Luciano 2001; Loe 2004). An unprecedented global public relations campaign put the news about Viagra in every media outlet.

The approval of Viagra was then followed by an aggressive phase of medicalizing women's sexual problems through marketing "female sexual dysfunction" (FSD) as a condition comparable to "erectile dysfunction" (Moynihan 2003, 2005). As of 2006, although FSD has been successfully branded, as a result of years of public relations efforts largely funded by megacorporations Pfizer and Procter & Gamble (P&G), there is as yet no approved sexuopharmaceutical treatment.

"Medicalization" is a term favored by sociologists to denote the process of social control whereby areas of behavior are brought within a medical framework both conceptually and institutionally (Conrad 1992; Riessman 1983). Medicalizing sexuality means that in the name of "health," certain sexual interests and activities are prescribed and others proscribed (Rubin 1984; Giami 2000). Of course, sexual prescriptions and proscriptions are hardly new; they exist in all societies. What is new is how the prescriptions and proscriptions—indeed, how sex itself—have all been sucked into the discourse of *health* (rather than, say, viewed as matters of individual habits or hobbies, as expressions fundamentally athletic or spiritual, or as a sign of moral strength or weakness). A central theme of the medicalization of sex is how medical authorities have become the culturally approved guardians and arbiters of sexual knowledge and advice (Irvine 2005, Cushman 1995).

A new medical area of "male sexual dysfunction" grew within the surgical subspecialty of urology throughout the 1980s and 1990s, as evolving technologies of erection (implants and injections) were widely publicized. At first, like earlier instances of medicalization (e.g., pregnancy or drunkenness), this was largely driven by the professional entrepreneurialism of physicians. Later, profitable industries got involved, as they had with the medicalization of children's hyperactivity or of social anxiety disorder (Moynihan and Cassels 2005).

The development of men's sexual health and dysfunction clinics was supported by many urological publications and conferences as well as evangelical statements proclaiming "the emergence of the urologist as the primary coordinator of care for the patient with sexual dysfunction, whether the cause of that dysfunction is an organic, a psychogenic, or as sometimes [sic] occurs, a combined one" (Krane, Siroky, and Goldstein 1983, xiii). When FSD emerged after 1998, it was again spearheaded by urologists who capitalized on their relationships with the pharmaceutical industry. Former urological organizations became sexual medicine organizations, and conferences and publications that had featured papers on ED began to include papers on FSD, with the authors still primarily urologists.

Socioeconomic and political events beginning around 1980 with the purpose of bringing academia and business closer together created opportunities for medicalization

(Tiefer 2000; Kennedy 1997; Marsa 1997; Slaughter and Leslie 1997; Teitelman 1994; Krimsky 2003; Bok 2003; Washburn 2005). A new ideological climate of economic conservatism resulted in patent law changes that led to partnerships between academics and various industries in the development of commercial products. Universities began to privatize many of their activities. Declining government support for research and training programs gradually made commercial funding for university-based science a necessity (Kennedy 1997). Overall, what had been previously seen as "applied" science came to occupy the center ring of scientific activity, with "pure" or theory-driven scientific work relegated to the margins. In sexology, this can clearly be seen in the shift to industry-supported surveys and questionnaire development in the late 1990s.

A second background element to consider is change within the huge pharmaceutical industry, now the most profitable business in the United States (Payer 1992; Greider 2003; Angell 2004). Its growth had to do with demographic and scientific factors such as the increasing age of the population and the effectiveness of drugs, but also with upward trends in pharmaceutical use as well as drug profitability. Greg Critser (2005) points out that the average number of prescriptions per person has been steadily increasing. In 2004 it was up to twelve, and "in 2004, almost half of all Americans used at least one prescription drug on a daily basis," representing "a substantial rise from the early 1980s, when Americans seemed more leery about using new drugs" (2). Drugs to enhance everyday function as well as treat medical complaints are now routinely advertised, prescribed, and used (Elliott 2003). P&G, the Fortune 500 manufacturer of soaps, shampoos, and snacks, has come only recently to pharmaceuticals, and to date only makes five drugs.[1] Yet, P&G's 2004 annual report states that its drug Actonel (approved in 1998 for Paget's disease and in 2000 for osteoporosis), "became a billion dollar brand faster than any other brand in P&G history."[2]

It is really only because Viagra proved so successful that pharmaceutical companies have been willing to get involved with as controversial and political a subject as sex. Indeed, Pfizer sent a committee to the Vatican before the drug was approved to make sure there would be no opposition (Luciano 2001), and its first few advertising campaigns were very decorous. The lack of substantial public criticism around Viagra paved the way for the rest of the industry to come to the party.

Because there is so much money to be made, the pharmaceutical industry is hugely competitive, always looking for new products, new markets, and new ways to link the two through branding and public relations. Challenges from managed care have been compensated for by increased marketing and speeded-up FDA approval processes for new drugs (Ballance 1996; Eichenwald and Kolata 1999). Viagra, for example, was a beneficiary of the new "fast-tracking" process approved by Congress in 1997, moving from new drug application to FDA approval in a mere six months. No outside advisory committee met; the press had no opportunity to assess the research; the public had no opportunity for input.

In addition to fast-tracking, the 1997 regulatory changes (called FDAMA, or the FDA Modernization Act) removed the prohibition on advertising drugs directly to the public on television and in print media (Morrow 1998). This represented an enormous change for the industry and for popular culture, and pharmaceutical industry analysts rightly predicted it would multiply sales and increase companies' reliance on "blockbuster" drugs (Langreth 1998). No other industrialized country except New Zealand (not Canada, not the United Kingdom, not any country in Europe) permits advertising of prescription medicines to the public. The pharmaceutical industry spends billions of dollars annually on consumer ads (Greider 2003; Angell 2004; Hall 2001; Norsigian 2001).

Other crucial regulatory changes occurring during the 1990s made disease awareness campaigns and off-label prescription practices far more acceptable (Buist, Muhtadie, and Walters 2005). For example, Viagra can be prescribed to women despite the fact that the FDA has not approved the drug for women or that published research to date suggests it is ineffective in women. Years before it even applied for FDA approval, Procter & Gamble promoted its testosterone patch for women (Intrinsa) through continuing medical education courses to physicians of every specialty and, even more, through press releases announcing every step forward in clinical trials. Those press releases always made it into the science and health news of the day, sounding as if the drug was already safe and effective as opposed to merely being tested in small selected groups. By the time the FDA turned thumbs down on Intrinsa in December 2004, the product was already branded in the public mind and women were asking their doctors for it. A Knight-Ridder exposé in 2003 revealed that off-label prescribing was growing far more rapidly than on-label prescribing, up about 96% between 1997 and 2002 (Young and Adams 2003). Pharmaceutical industry developments are no longer obscure matters affecting only chemical manufacture and doctors' thinking. These are developments that affect popular culture and social life.

Sexual scripts and sexuopharmacology research

Sexual script theory offers some explanation of how medicalization and pharmaceutical industry activity affect people's thinking and behavior. Sexuality drugs affect sexual scripts via obvious routes, including the imagery in drug advertisements and the implied messages in television and movie jokes, and also via covert routes such as the peculiar requirements of clinical trials research. Clinical trials research for sexuopharmacological drug products must focus on quantifiable and operationalizable aspects of sexual experience and satisfaction in order to satisfy industry and FDA requirements for objective methods with high reliability. However, since the outcome of a sexuopharmaceutical drug trial cannot be measured in the laboratory or office, questionnaires and self-report measures are required. But what do clinical trial researchers ask to see if a drug is effective?

In drug trials for ED, the most important questions are simply about erections: how hard does the penis get? How long does the erection last? In both ED and FSD drug trials, the vast plain of sex is narrowed to frequencies of "sexual activity" (despite lack of consensus over what exactly study subjects should count), extent of genital arousal and orgasm (despite ambiguity over how people subjectively assess arousal and orgasm), and yes/no responses to questions about sexual satisfaction (with no opportunity for answers like "partly" or "in some respects"). Questionnaire language is assumed to be straightforward and to have universal meaning (e.g., "is your erection sufficient for intercourse?"). No opportunity is given to acknowledge or explore variations in sexual conduct, goals, or satisfactions because of different partners or circumstances.

The result is a narrowing and freezing of acceptable sexual performance into a sexual function script of frequent sexual activity, regular erections "sufficient for intercourse," no delayed or premature orgasm/ejaculation, regular vaginal lubrication, absence of pain, and reliable orgasm. Such a function script becomes the standardized norm for successful sexuality and is treated as if it were universal, built-in, involuntary, and necessary for health, like breathing or urination. The language of pleasure, emotional intimacy, sensuality, playfulness or self-expression is completely absent. No inquiry is made about expectations or education. Sexual function is assumed to be hard-wired.

Canadian rhetoric professor Judy Segal recently reviewed the proceedings of the 17th World Congress of Sexology conference in Montreal, Canada (2005). She found that, of over 400 presentations, only eight were concerned with women's pleasure. Moreover, she found that the word "pleasure" in reference to both men and women occurred only 20 times in 2759 keywords indexed in the program. The vast majority of presentations were concerned, by contrast, with elements of sexual function.

Participants are enrolled in clinical trials for sexuopharmacological drug products only if their medical and psychosocial history is judged to offer no potential interference with proper sexual function from psychological or relationship problems, medical conditions, or any other medications they might be taking. Sex partners are not involved in the clinical trial research, either to verify the problem, corroborate the drug effects (or side effects), or discuss their feelings about the couple's sexual life together. The FDA's guidelines on clinical trials for "female sexual dysfunction" drugs, for example, suggest excluding all women taking oral contraceptives, all who have relationship or medical problems, all who are depressed, etc. (Tiefer et al. 2000).

Drugs thus tested on highly selected populations are then marketed to the largest possible audience using time-worn strategies of encouraging identification with suggestive or idealized role models, such as an attractive couple gazing at each other in a "natural" outdoor setting, a well-dressed couple romantically dancing together, a muscular man throwing a football cleanly through a hanging tire while a woman smilingly watches, or a man grinning "devilishly" with horns sprouting from his head. The copy in such ads promotes the drug as helpful and effective for all, and the companies defend such practice because "postapproval" research supposedly will correct any mismatch between clinical trial conditions and real-world use. Of course, no extensive research is usually undertaken.

The heterocentrism of the sexuopharmacology industry is shown not only by the heterosexual images and messages of the drug ads, but by the exclusion of gay men from the international Viagra clinical trials. Nevertheless, small studies of recreational Viagra usage among gay men consistently show higher use than in the general population, up to even one-third of gay men (Breslau 2002). Confident performance of penis-in-vagina intercourse is promoted in mainstream media as necessary to sexual self-esteem and successful intimate relationships. From a cultural point of view, erection, briefly dethroned by the feminist revolution, is now restored to its central location by biomedical fiat. The sexuopharmacological industry actively promotes the importance of lifelong sexual function in order to keep the demand for drug products high. The rhetoric of sexuality as "central to the quality of life" shapes marketing to both professionals and the public. Even nondrug sex experts are invested in "fixing" any deviation from this script. Just as the alcohol industry needs heavy drinkers,[3] a vigorous sexuopharmacology industry requires scripts promoting high levels of intercourse.

In their clinical trials for Intrinsa, the testosterone patch for women, P&G had to use a combination of measures and messages that would satisfy the FDA requirements for objectivity (i.e., measure the frequency of sexual events) as well as signify respect for both traditional heterosexual norms and emancipatory feminist rhetoric. They did this by repeatedly indicating respect for the medical seriousness of hypoactive sexual desire disorder (HSDD), the condition Intrinsa was supposed to treat.[4] Having women's complaints taken seriously has been a hard-won result of the feminist health activism movement.

But now, just as men have long been encouraged to view genital virility as the centerpiece of masculinity, so women are reading and hearing that vaginal lubrication and endogenous desire are central features of sexual vitality (Marshall 2002). A high prevalence of FSD is predicated on having women believe that changes in sexual desire not only threaten their marriages and indicate a loss in the quality of life, but signify loss of femininity. No industry goes broke banking on the need for women in an aging individualistic culture to look for ways to preserve their femininity.

Conclusion: Sexual scripts in a world with sex-enhancing drugs

There are many ways in which the contemporary individual in consumer society is encouraged to view his or her body as an object in need of fixing, and even of perfecting. Some of these encouragements are more obvious consumer appeals than others, and increasing numbers have to do with sexuality. Drugs play a role in many of these opportunities: prescription medications when the "imperfection" can be medicalized, nonprescription medications (including illegal psychoactive drugs, "nutraceuticals," and "cosmeceuticals") when the theme is enhancement. In each case, advertising and public relations increasingly hold out the promise of transformation through chemistry.

Has the ordinary person's experience of recreational sport activity been affected by the type of sports-performance-enhancing prescription drugs that seem to be widely used at the Olympics and professional levels? Probably not. The weekend golfer, the volleyball player on a company team, and the aerobics class enthusiast are probably not asking their doctors for stimulants for extra practice energy or steroids for greater muscle mass. Individual and cultural scripts for recreational athletics seem able to resist the blandishments of pharmathletic enhancements. Why is this? Lifelong athletic training opportunities offer people a variety of cultural and interpersonal (and, then, intrapsychic) scripts for athletic life. People can identify with world-class athletes at an inspirational level, not as guides for everyday behavior choices. Widespread publicity about athletes' strenuous training regimes and about the dangers of stimulants and steroids also serve to disabuse people from seeing pharmaceutical drugs as magical quick-fixes to transform the ordinary person. All of these corrective aspects are missing with regard to sexuopharmaceuticals, since we still live in an era where the topic of sex produces embarrassment and laughter rather than rational discussion and where the ideas of training or talent are unfamiliar.

The promises of sex drugs are part of the growing industry in cosmetic surgery and collagen injections that promise individuals world-class beauty and eternal youth. "Makeovers" and "shapeovers," filling pages of both men's and women's magazines are part of huge "beauty project" and "body project" trends (Giddens 1991; Brumberg 1997). The sexuopharmaceutical industry seems poised to shift its emphasis from medical necessity and "dysfunction" to a more consumerist discourse of enhancement. Viagra is already widely used for sexual enhancement among gay and straight club-going urban young adults (Trebay 1999). Sex drugs will become normalized in a dating world where high (i.e., "normal") standards of genital performance are expected with unfamiliar partners in unfamiliar settings. In a society still lacking sexual coaching, training, or comprehensive sex education, sexuopharmaceuticals take advantage of an insecure public that has been fed high expectations for both the rewards of sexual success and the punishments of sexual failure.

I expect that the way the new sexuopharmaceuticals have been developed and marketed will affect sexual script elements as follows:

1) increased emphasis on genital performance of routine, rapid arousal and orgasm as the measure of sexual success and satisfaction in both men and women;

2) increased insecurity among young people or people newly returned to dating about the adequacy of their sexual performance and subjective experience;

3) further growth of a black (internet) market for sexuopharmaceuticals;

4) self-monitoring of genital arousal and orgasm during sex (with a consequent anxiety-related rise in performance difficulties);

5) reduced attention to nonphysical definitions of sexual satisfaction such as romance or playfulness, as well as less attention to aspects of sexual enhancement such as better communication or sensuality; and

6) reduced visibility for women's sexual discontents arising from social inequalities such as greater childcare and eldercare responsibilities. Fatigue and lack of time to "get into" the mood will be less respected when anyone can get "into the mood" through drugs.

The commodification of sexuality is part of larger transformations of personal and interpersonal experience. Scripts for sexual experience and satisfaction are constantly shifting in response to cultural trends, including massive pharmaceutical industry marketing. The language and theory of sexual scripting offer us a demystified and denaturalized perspective on sexual conduct with which to see how socially produced expectations affect meaning and satisfaction.

Notes

1. www.pg.com/product_card/prod_card_rx_drugs.jhtml
2. www.pg.com/annualreports/2004/pdf/pg2004annualreport.pdf
3. Ten percent of drinkers consume over 60 percent of all alcohol sold (Kilbourne 1999, 156).
4. Details about the Intrinsa clinical trials are best found in the "briefing document" that P&G submitted to the FDA Advisory Committee. www.fda.gov/ohrms/dockets/ac/04/briefing/2004–4082b1.htm

References

Angell, M. 2004 *The truth about the drug companies: How they deceive us and what to do about it.* New York: Random House.

Ballance, R. H. 1996. Market and industrial structure. In Davis 1996, 95–108.

Bok, D. 2003. *Universities in the marketplace: The commercialization of higher education.* Princeton: Princeton University Press.

Breslau, K. 2002. The "Sextasy" craze: Clubland's dangerous party mix: Viagra and Ecstasy. *Newsweek,* June 3: 30.

Brumberg, J. J. 1997. *The body project: An intimate history of American girls.* New York: Random House.

Buist, S., L. Muhtadie, and J. Walters. 2005. Blind faith: Worry grows as MDs prescribe drugs for unapproved uses. *Hamilton Spectator,* June 29.

Conrad, P. 1992. Medicalization and social control. *Annual Review of Sociology* 18:209–32.

Critser, G. 2005. *Generation Rx: How prescription drugs are altering American lives, minds, and bodies.* Boston: Houghton Mifflin.

Cushman, P. 1995. *Constructing the self, Constructing America: A cultural history of Psychotherapy.* Reading, MA: Addison-Wesley.

Davis, P., ed. 1996. *Contested ground: Public purpose and private interest in the regulation of prescription drugs.* New York: Oxford University Press.

D'Emilio, J., and E. B. Freedman. 1988. *Intimate matters: A history of sexuality in America.* New York: Harper and Row.

Eichenwald, K., and G. Kolata. 1999. Drug trials hide conflicts for doctors. *New York Times,* May 16.

Elliott, C. 2003. *Better than well: American medicine meets the American dream.* New York: Norton.

Giami, A. 2000. Changing relations between medicine, psychology, and sexuality: The case of male impotence. *Journal of Social Medicine* (Finland), 4:263–72.

Giddens, A. 1991. *Modernity and self-identity.* Oxford: Polity.

Giddens, A. 1992. *The transformation of intimacy: Sexuality, love, and eroticism in modern societies.* Stanford: Stanford University Press.

Greider, K. 2003. *The big fix: How the pharmaceutical industry rips off American consumers.* New York: Public Affairs.

Hall, S. 2001. Prescription for profit. *New York Times Magazine,* March 11.

Irvine, J. M. 2005. *Disorders of desire: Sexuality and gender in modern American sexology.* Rev. and expanded ed. Philadelphia: Temple University Press.

Kennedy, D. 1997. *Academic duty.* Cambridge: Harvard University Press.

Kilbourne, J. 1999. *Can't buy my love: How advertising changes the way we think and feel.* New York: Simon and Schuster.

Krane, R. J., M. B. Siroky, and I. Goldstein, eds. 1983. *Male sexual dysfunction.* Boston: Little, Brown.

Krimsky, S. 2003. *Science in the private interest: Has the lure of profits corrupted biomedical research.* Lanham, MD: Rowman and Littlefield.

Langreth, R. 1998. Prescriptions and hot products aid drug firms. *Wall Street Journal,* January 28.

Loe, M. 2004. *The rise of Viagra: How the little blue pill changed sex in America.* New York: New York University Press.

Luciano, L. 2001. *Looking good: Male body image in modern America.* New York: Hill and Wang.

Marsa, L. 1997 *Prescription for profits: How the pharmaceutical industry bankrolled the unholy marriage between science and business.* New York: Scribner's.

Marshall, B. 2002. "Hard science": Gendered constructions of sexual dysfunction in the "Viagra age." *Sexualities* 5:131–58

Montagne, M. 1996. The Pharmakon phenomenon: Cultural conceptions of drugs and drug use. In Davis 1996, 11–23.

Morrow, D. J. 1998. From lab to patient, by way of your den. *New York Times*, June 7.

Moynihan, R. 2003. The making of a disease: female sexual dysfunction. *British Medical Journal* 326:45–7

———. 2005. The marketing of a disease: female sexual dysfunction. *British Medical Journal* 330:192–94.

Moynihan, R., and A. Cassels. 2005. *Selling sickness: How the world's biggest pharmaceutical companies are turning us all into patients.* New York: Nation Books.

McLaren, A. 1999. *Twentieth-century sexuality.* Oxford: Blackwell Publishers.

Norsigian, J. 2001. Feminists challenge unethical marketing by prescription drug companies. *Sojourner*, March 8–9: 12.

Payer, L. 1992. *Disease-mongers: How doctors, drug companies, and insurers are making you feel sick.* New York: Wiley and Sons.

Riessman, C. K. 1983. Women and medicalization: A new perspective. *Social Policy* 14:3–18.

Rubin, G. 1984. Thinking sex: Notes for a radical theory of the politics of sexuality. In *Pleasure and danger: Exploring female sexuality*, ed. C. S. Vance, 267–319. Boston: Routledge.

Segal, J. 2005. Values and the rhetoric of pleasure. Presentation for *Women and the new sexual politics: Profits vs. pleasures*, the 2005 New View Conference, Montreal. www.fsd-alert.org/connewviewconf2005.html.

Simon, W., and J. H. Gagnon. 1986. Sexual scripts: Permanence and change. *Archives of Sexual Behavior* 15:97–120.

Slaughter, S., and L. L. Leslie. 1997. *Academic capitalism: Politics, policies, and the entrepreneurial university* . Baltimore: Johns Hopkins University Press.

Teitelman, R. 1994. *Profits of science: The American marriage of business and technology.* New York: Basic Books.

Tiefer, L. 1986. In pursuit of the perfect penis: The medicalization of male sexuality. *American Behavioral Scientist* 29:579–99.

———. 1994. The medicalization of impotence: Normalizing phallocentrism. *Gender and Society* 8:363–77.

———. 1998. Doing the Viagra tango: Sex pill as symbol and substance. *Radical Philosophy* 92: 2–5.

———. 2000. Sexology and the pharmaceutical industry: The threat of co-optation. *Journal of Sex Research* 37:273–83.

Tiefer, L., and 21 others. 2000. Letter to FDA regarding Docket No. 00D-1278, draft guidance for industry on female sexual dysfunction: Clinical development of drug products for treatment; availability. Mailed in two parts, June 19 (12 co-signers), and July 10 (9 co-signers).

Trebay, G. 1999. Longer harder faster: From sex parties to raves, for both men and women, it's not Bob Dole's Viagra anymore. *Village Voice*, November 2.

Washburn, J. 2005. *University, Inc.: The corporate corruption of higher education.* New York: Basic Books.

Young, A., and S. Adams. 2003. "Off-label" drugs take their toll. *Miami Herald*, November 2.

Steven Epstein

15

"The Badlands of Desire"

Sex Research, Cultural Scenarios, and the Politics of Knowledge Production

*The estrangement of the erotic from the domain of everyday life, so fundamental
a part of the modern Western tradition, made it available to fulfill the beliefs of
those who sought its expulsion in the first place. The erotic became the badlands of
desire. . . .*

SIMON AND GAGNON (1984, 55)

In July 2003, the U.S. House of Representatives came within two votes of revoking the
funding previously granted by the National Institutes of Health (NIH) to four research
projects on topics related to sexuality and health. "I ask my colleagues, who thinks this
stuff up?" remarked Rep. Pat Toomey, a Republican from Pennsylvania and the author of
the amendment, referring to studies of San Francisco sex workers and masseuses, American Indian and Alaskan transgendered individuals, the sexuality of older men, and the
relation of mood arousal to sexual risk-taking (Fram 2003). Within a few months, a
"hit list" of 157 sexuality researchers—compiled by the Traditional Values Coalition
(TVC), a self-described "grassroots church lobby" renowned for its attacks on "the gay
agenda"—was winding its way through Congress and the NIH. "There needs to be some
adult supervision at NIH," said Andrea Lafferty, the executive director of the coalition
and daughter of its founder, the Reverend Lou Sheldon. "Nameless, faceless bureaucrats
[are] doling out money like a federal ATM" on "smarmy projects" that don't "pass the
straight-face test," Lafferty told the press (Weiss 2003). Researchers on the list were contacted by their NIH program officers and asked to come up with language justifying
their funded grants and explaining the contributions of their research to the promotion
of the public health.[1] This scrutiny sparked a range of protests by professional associations and liberal politicians; it even proved sufficiently newsworthy to generate an episode of the NBC hit television show *West Wing*.[2]

Because the attack on sexuality research appeared to garner support from within
both Congress and the executive branch, it seemed of a piece with a number of inci-

An earlier version of this chapter appeared as "The new attack on sexuality research: Morality and
the politics of knowledge production." *Sexuality Research and Social Policy* 3, no. 1 (2006): 1–12.

dents that unfolded during the first term of President George W. Bush. These incidents concerned the work of various agencies within the U.S. Department of Health and Human Services (DHHS), which also contains the NIH. They have included a crackdown by the Centers for Disease Control and Prevention (CDC) on the use of federal funds by community-based AIDS prevention organizations perceived to be "promoting" sexuality (Block 2003; Smith 2003); an unwillingness on the part of the CDC to endorse the efficacy of condoms in preventing the spread of HIV (Cocco 2002); a decision by the Food and Drug Administration (FDA) to overrule its expert advisory panel and ban a morning-after contraceptive pill (Harris 2004); the institution of a DHHS policy limiting attendance by government scientists at international AIDS conferences (Reuters 2004; Walgate 2004); and attempts by the DHHS to impose ideological "litmus tests" when appointing experts to scientific advisory panels (Zitner 2002; Steinbrook 2004). Strikingly, several of these efforts seemed to target for elimination not only sexual ideas and practices deemed dangerously liberal, but also the scientific practices responsible for generating and disseminating knowledge about sexuality in the first place.

Like other contests over knowledge-making, these can be studied as "credibility struggles" (Epstein 1996)—the competition to establish knowledge claims as believable and their claimants as authoritative. More specifically still, these political developments have implications for what sociologist of science Stephen Hilgartner has called the "production of the unknowable"—the social processes through which things are rendered unavailable to our understanding (2003). Or, as the historian of science Robert Proctor has asked, in another context:

> Why do we know what we know, and why don't we know what we don't know? If the politics of science consists (among other things) in the structure of research priorities, then it is important to understand what gets studied and why, but also what does *not* get studied and why not. One has, in other words, to study the social construction of ignorance. Ignorance has a distinct and changing political geography that is often an excellent indicator of the politics of knowledge. (1995, 8)[3]

I will argue that an examination of the present political climate of sexual knowledge-making and "non-knowledge making" is instructive for thinking about the sociology of knowledge as well as the sociology of sexuality. However, the current moment is not without precedent, and that history is particularly relevant to sociological scholarship. For example, in 1992, the U.S. Senate voted 51–46 to bar federal funding for two planned surveys of sexuality, including one headed by sociologists; and conservatives in Congress singled out pioneer sociologist of sexuality John Gagnon, an investigator on one of the studies, as emblematic of the evils of sex research (di Mauro 1995, 8–12; Ericksen 1999, 80–89; Hunt 1999, 185–91). The ultraconservative congressman William Dannemeyer, warning (in a curious anatomical metaphor) that "the heart of the study will rest on the shoulders of John Gagnon," went on to associate Gagnon (inaccurately) with organizations promoting the legalization of illicit drugs (Ericksen 1999, 158), while the hard-right senator Jesse Helms raised questions on the floor about Gagnon's "normality" (Hunt 1999, 187) and portrayed Gagnon as an advocate of sex between children and adults (Ericksen 1999, 205).

In this essay, I hope to exact symbolic revenge on Gagnon's behalf by invoking his conceptual apparatus as part of an analysis of the political scrutiny of sex research. In a foundational move, Gagnon and long-time collaborator William Simon developed the metaphor of "sexual scripts" to describe the complex orchestrations of physical activities and social meanings that make up human sexual behavior (Gagnon and Simon 1973; Simon and Gagnon 1984). The concept of sexual scripts has proven an analytically rich way of approaching and analyzing how people go about "learning the meaning of internal states, organizing the sequences of specifically sexual acts, decoding novel situations, setting the limits on sexual responses, and linking meanings from nonsexual aspects of life to specifically sexual experience" (Gagnon and Simon 1973, 19). However, sexual scripting has been studied primarily on a microsociological level—not inappropriately so, given Gagnon and Simon's interactionist emphases. Though some analysts have described the sexual scripts that exist on a broadly cultural level (Parker 1991, 1999; Carrillo 2002), most invocations are concerned with the scripted behavior of the sexual dyad.

I argue for the importance of examining the "macro" structuring of sexual scripts— a project that directs attention to the constitution of knowledge about sex through political contest. I proceed by building on suggestions provided by Gagnon and Simon themselves. In their 1984 theoretical elaboration, Gagnon and Simon described three dimensions of scripting, which they termed "intrapsychic scripts," "interactional scripts," and "cultural scenarios" (53–60). The last of these, cultural scenarios, are "the instructional guides that exist at the level of collective life." Individuals absorb ideas about how to behave sexually from a wide array of cultural sources, and in the writing of their own intrapsychic scripts, they adapt, rework, or reject these messages. Here Gagnon and Simon focused attention on key social institutions that are in the business of providing instruction on sexuality—the family, schools, churches, the military, medicine, and law, among others—proposing that these institutions could be read as "systems of signs and symbols through which the requirements and the practice of specific roles are given" (53; see also Gagnon 2004, 138–42). Importantly, they also observed that, in modernity, these cultural scenarios are neither static, nor uncontested, nor universally binding on social actors. Indeed, as Gagnon has commented more recently:

> In complex societies . . . cultural scenarios for sexuality are not monolithic or hegemonic, even within institutions. Instead there is a constant struggle between groups and individuals to foster their own scenarios. Some groups and individuals are more powerful than others, but no individual or group or institution is in entire control of the sexual scenarios . . . (2004, 140)

My strategy, then, will be to leave behind the "micro" interactional ordering of sexuality for purposes of this article, and to use the underutilized concept of cultural scenarios to discuss the "macro" politics of sexual knowledge-making. My claim is that cultural scenarios help to structure policy debates regarding sexual practices and our knowledge about them—and, inevitably, that the prominence and viability of those cultural scenarios are themselves at stake in those same debates.

Historical precedents

When attending to the particularities of present-day debates about sexuality and sexual knowledge, it is important to consider the stigmatized character of research on human sexuality throughout the twentieth century in the United States. In an assessment of sexuality research, Diane di Mauro observed that, as early as 1921, the National Research Council complained of difficulties in obtaining support for such studies (di Mauro 1995, 8). In the 1950s and 1960s, according to Janice Irvine,

> Sexologists were routinely attacked for studying sexuality. The Rockefeller Foundation terminated the funding of Alfred Kinsey in 1954 after a congressional investigation prompted by public outrage over the publication of *Sexual Behavior in the Human Female*. . . . Mary Calderone, who founded the Sex Information and Education Council of the United States in 1964 to advocate for objective sexuality research and education, was denounced as a communist and a pervert as a result of her efforts (2003, 451).

I already have alluded to similar dynamics in the hostile targeting of Gagnon's past research. In 1987, Gagnon, along with sociologists Edward Laumann and Robert Michael, responded to an NIH request for research proposals on the topic of "Social and Behavioral Aspects of Health and Fertility-Related Behaviors." The investigators won a contract to design a comprehensive national survey of adults on sexual attitudes and behaviors related to reproductive health and sexually transmitted infections, including HIV/AIDS. At a time when the AIDS epidemic was finally being recognized as a substantial threat to the U.S. population, the study proposed to use sophisticated techniques of data collection and analysis to fill in the yawning gaps in knowledge about sexual beliefs and practices and their relation to the risk of HIV transmission. In 1989, after extensive pre-testing of their survey instrument, the researchers submitted it to the federal Office of Management and Budget (OMB) for review—normally a formality (Laumann, Michael, and Gagnon 1994, 34–35).

This time, however, a well-orchestrated attack was unleashed after word got out that the OMB was reviewing a "sex questionnaire." One published account of these events, by Morton Hunt, quotes Gagnon's surmise that "we and our plans were being tracked by the Right." In Hunt's analysis, after the 1988 election, conservatives were "well represented within [the DHHS] and other government agencies." Indeed, "it might have been an inside source at OMB that tipped off *Science* that it was reviewing a federally funded sex questionnaire . . ." (1999, 186). *Science* magazine trivialized the news by reporting it alongside a picture (from the film *Bob and Carol and Ted and Alice*) of two couples in a king-size bed. This depiction caught the attention of the mass media, which publicized the proposed study (Laumann, Michael, and Gagnon 1994, 35).

Conservatives in Congress, including Helms and Dannemeyer, denounced the study as an unwarranted intrusion into private matters as well as an attempt to promote the agenda of the gay movement. In response to mobilization by a Christian radio station, the OMB was bombarded with phone calls from opponents of the research (Laumann, Michael, and Gagnon 1994, 35). Ultimately, Helms introduced an amendment to a budget bill that took the money targeted both for the survey and for a large study of adolescent fertility and sexuality, and reallocated it to abstinence education (Ericksen 1999, 205). This transfer of $10 million in federal funding passed the Senate with the support of two thirds of its members but was deleted by a House-Senate conference committee. However, a provision backed by Helms that permanently banned federal funding of these two studies was passed by both houses and was signed into law in 1993 (Hunt 1999, 190–91). Meanwhile, Laumann, Gagnon, and Michael had managed to piece together partial funding from a number of private foundations and were then able to complete a scaled-down version of their original proposal, which became the National Health and Social Life Study, published in 1994 as *The Social Organization of Sexuality*.[4]

As is typical of "moral panics," entrepreneurial individuals here sought to advance their agendas through the designation of scapegoats (Rubin 1984; Freedman 1989; Nathan and Snedeker 1995; Judith Irvine 2002), and there can be little doubt that the attack on these studies was in some measure opportunistic, as opponents sought to make political hay of various kinds. For example, in her account of these events in her book analyzing the history of sex research in the United States, Julia Ericksen has noted that "many conservatives opposed all federally funded research"—not just research on sexuality—"and saw this survey as a chance to garner support for their views" (Ericksen 1999, 182). Despite the diversity of targets, certainly a large part of what was at stake was the competition to say which cultural scenarios should orient sexual practice. For example, in a letter to Assistant Secretary for Health Louis Sullivan, Rep. Dannemeyer expressed the clear concern that detailed knowledge about the demographics of homosexuality might legitimate gay sexuality in the United States: "Imagine the political landscape if any one demographic grouping were to increase their rank from 10% of the population to 15% or 20%," wrote Dannemeyer: "This is the exact reason why the purveyors of laissez-faire sexual attitudes want to use tax dollars and the federal cloak of scientific legitimacy to produce this work" (Ericksen 1999, 188). In addition, the contention that sex research was an improper intrusion into the private lives of Americans sought to shore up a cultural scenario in which sexuality is conceived of as something shameful or dangerous that must be kept as well hidden as possible. These and other themes resurfaced a decade later in the debates over sexuality research in the George W. Bush administration.

The "hit list"

In their own analysis of their experience with the DHHS and Congress, Laumann, Gagnon, and Michael (1994) described the unwritten rules of censorship in federal funding. Calls for proposals routinely avoided use of "the plain English word 'sex,'" substituting such convoluted euphemisms as "proximate determinants of fertility" or "fertility-related behavior." The researchers noted, "We, too, have played by these rules" (37). Nearly a decade later, in April 2003—in a harbinger of what was to come—program officers at the NIH began advising their grant applicants to avoid an extended list of terms in the titles and abstracts of their grants, lest their research come under special scrutiny either by Congress or by administrators within the DHHS. Terms to be shunned included "sex worker," "men who have sex with men," "anal sex," and "needle exchange." For example, a researcher at the University of California reported being told by his program officer that the abstract of the grant he intended to submit "should be 'cleansed' and should not contain any contentious wording like 'gay' or 'homosexual' or 'transgender'" (Goode 2003). The attention here specifically to titles and abstracts of grants is revealing, for those are the portions of NIH grants that appear in a publicly accessible database called CRISP (Computer Retrieval of Information on Scientific Research). One NIH official who spoke with a *New York Times* reporter on condition of anonymity acknowledged that the advice to avoid controversial terms was not new, but that the amount of scrutiny directed at NIH grants under the George W. Bush administration was "much worse and more intense" (Goode 2003).

The program officers' concerns proved well-founded. A few months later, Rep. Toomey's amendment to de-fund four approved studies on sexuality failed by a vote of 210–212, with 177 Republicans and 33 Democrats voting in favor (Agres 2003). Meanwhile, a staff member working for another Republican member of Congress, Mark Souder from Indiana, sent an email message to the NIH complaining about the funding of research on prostitutes. Souder's office requested detailed information about who had reviewed these studies and what scores they received (Kaiser 2003b, 403). Then, in October 2003, at a meeting with NIH director Elias Zerhouni, several members of Congress grilled him about "provocative" NIH research projects and demanded explanations. Zerhouni followed up by asking for a list of precisely which studies were at issue. Apparently by mistake, a staff member in the office of Rep. Billy Tauzin, a Republican from Louisiana and the chair of the House Energy and Commerce Committee, supplied Zerhouni not with the ten specific studies under discussion but with a much more extensive list of 157 researchers and their funded research projects—the list that had been provided to Congress by the TVC (Associated Press 2003; Kaiser 2003a, 758; Shane 2003).

The "hit list," as it was quickly dubbed by Democratic member of Congress Henry Waxman, showed studies funded since 1997 that were being conducted by researchers from prominent institutions across the United States (Brainard 2003). It appeared to reflect an organized effort to document federal funding going to sexuality researchers. Indeed, some senior luminaries in the field, such as John Gagnon, were listed alongside the commentary "Nothing found on HHS search," suggesting that the TVC had combed the CRISP database not only for keywords but also for the names of eminent individuals. (Gagnon's collaborator, William Simon, was one of several on the list for whom a null finding was not surprising, given that they were deceased.)[5]

The TVC, along with the broader Christian fundamentalist movement that it represents, must certainly be seen as an important player in the struggle to shore up or establish hegemonic cultural scenarios regarding sexuality. The descriptions appearing alongside investigators' names on the list made clear which messages about sex it wanted to target. "Promotes a 'sex-positive' attitude among teens" was the TVC's characterization of one study; "queries 9th graders on their 'current and past sexual behavior'" was their description of a second one. In yet another case, they observed, "Study reads, 'Cohabitation is recognized as an important feature of family formation and children's well being.'" Just as pointedly, the TVC's notations made clear which sorts of sexual topics it considered it better simply not to know about: the sex and drug networks of U.S. truckers; sexual identity formation among young gay male Puerto Ricans; sexual activity in sex clubs and bathhouses; commercial sex work; the sexuality of immigrants; the demographics of gay and lesbian households; experiences of homophobia as a predictor of unprotected sex. Thus, the TVC's ideological project linked the politics of knowledge-making (or non-knowledge making) with the fierce protection of what it perceived as traditional cultural scenarios about sex. At the same time, as its list of suspect objects of scientific scrutiny makes evident, the issue was never just sexuality, but its complex articulation with the broader politics of difference and inequality in the United States, including question of gender, race, ethnicity, and nation. In a favorable political climate and given the right conjuncture of political circumstances, the influence of these conservatives proved to be considerable.

In response to the query from Congress, NIH program officers contacted the scientists on the hit list with active grants and asked them to craft short statements explaining the public health significance of their work. Though the NIH probably hoped thereby to defuse the crisis, the very act of contacting so many researchers around the country launched a blitz of media reports and editorials. Concerned about the prospect of an expanded assault on peer-reviewed science, professional organizations soon rallied in defense of the NIH. The Association of American Medical Colleges was one of many such organizations that objected to "efforts to subject the NIH research portfolio and individual research grants to ideological litmus tests" (AAMC 2003). Alan Leshner, the head of the American Association for the Advancement of Science (AAAS), published a strongly worded editorial in the organization's flagship publication, *Science,* warning that "the moralizers are trying to muck with U. S. science again" (2003). The Consortium of Social Science Associations, a national advocacy organization, created the Coalition to Protect Research, consisting of dozens of professional associations and public health groups. Along with the AAAS and others, the Coalition organized a Congressional briefing "to educate and inform Members of the important public health significance of sexual health research" (CPR 2004b).

Defenders of the NIH in Congress also mobilized. Rep. Waxman, in an angry letter to DHHS Secretary Tommy Thompson, accused government insiders of working in conjunction with conservatives in Congress to sabotage scientific research (2003). However, Lafferty, the director of the TVC, sent Waxman a letter in response, telling him: "Congressman, if you think you are mad wait until you see how angry the American people get when they discover that you and your allies at NIH have been using federal tax dollars to study 'lot lizards'—prostitutes who service truckers in parking lots" (2003). Lafferty sought to generate as much publicity as possible from the brouhaha, telling the Associated Press, "We know for a fact that millions and millions of dollars have been flushed down the toilet over years on this HIV/AIDS scam and sham" (Russell 2003).

In the end, the NIH—institutionally committed to the preservation of its own decision-making autonomy, if not to sexuality research per se—came to the defense of the researchers under attack. In January 2004, NIH director Zerhouni responded to Congress describing the results of a "comprehensive review of the human sexuality research that we support." Standing behind the research, Zerhouni noted, "The constant battle against illness and disease . . . cannot be limited to biological factors but has to include behavioral and social factors as well." An appended summary described the public health relevance of particular studies that had been featured in the public debate, beginning with the Emory University study of HIV risk among long-haul truckers that had earned Lafferty's scornful condemnation (Zerhouni 2004; see also Grady 2004; Kaiser

2004). However, those who may have thought the matter settled were caught off guard the following September, when Rep. Randy Neugebauer, a Republican from Texas, sponsored an amendment to the annual DHHS appropriations bill to de-fund two NIH studies he deemed frivolous (neither of them, however, on topics related to sexuality—and, ironically, both of them already completed). This time the amendment passed the House on a voice vote of members present, but it then failed to gain comparable support in the Senate (CPR 2004a, 2004c; Keiger 2004).

Sex and science

Waxman was by no means alone in suspecting that congressional critics of NIH funding had their allies within the DHHS and the Bush administration generally. A number of analysts have tended to interpret the NIH episode as consistent with a broader, recent pattern: a war on science and truth by an ideologically driven administration more concerned with its pre-given beliefs than with any inconvenient facts that threaten them (*Scientific American* 2004). At his website, Rep. Waxman documented dozens of examples, from global warming to contaminated drinking water to missile defense. In February 2004, the Union of Concerned Scientists issued a statement claiming that the Bush administration has disregarded the principle that scientific evidence "should always be weighed from an objective and impartial perspective to avoid perilous consequences" (UCS 2004; Borrego 2004). Since then, more than 5,000 scientists, including 48 Nobel laureates, have endorsed the organization's statement.[6] Scientists have taken particular exception to attempts by administration officials to pack governmental advisory committees with right-leaning experts: potential appointees have complained of being interrogated about their views on topics such as abortion, stem-cell research, and human cloning, and being asked to reveal whether they voted for George W. Bush (Steinbrook 2004). "I don't think any administration has penetrated so deeply into the advisory committee structure as this one," said Donald Kennedy, a past president of Stanford University and editor-in-chief of *Science* (Zitner 2002). The topic of appointments to advisory committees so galvanized the scientific community that the National Academy of Sciences took it up in a report. "It is inappropriate to ask [nominees] to provide nonrelevant information, such as voting record, political-party affiliation, or position on particular policies," the report declared (2005, 10).

It does make sense to locate the attack on sexuality research in relation to a broader disdain by some conservatives for "inconvenient" science. And perhaps some in the present administration have (in the memorable words of a senior advisor to the president) rejected the worldview of the "reality-based community," in favor of the metaphysical presumption that "we're an empire now, and when we act, we create our own reality" (Suskind 2004). But is a casual—or motivated—disregard of science the best or the only frame for understanding the events I have recounted? It is worth noting just how many instances of interference by the administration and Congress with the conduct of science have been related specifically to the topic of sexuality:

Condoms: In July 2001, a fact sheet on condoms mysteriously disappeared from a CDC website. Eventually it was replaced by one that stressed that condoms may not be reliable (Cocco 2002). In December 2002, U. S. officials at an international conference in Bangkok argued against a recommendation for "consistent condom use" to fight AIDS and other diseases—prompting *New York Times* columnist Nicholas Kristof to wonder if the administration supported only "inconsistent condom use" (2003).

Abortion: In 2002, the National Cancer Institute (one of the NIH institutes) removed information from its website documenting the absence of evidence for an association between abortion and breast cancer. In the face of protest, the institute convened a conference on the topic and later updated its website to reflect the scientific consensus (*Detroit Free Press* 2003; NCI 2003).

Abstinence-only: A report commissioned by Rep. Waxman ("The content of federally funded abstinence-only education programs"), presented to Congress in December 2004, documented errors and distortions in federally-funded abstinence-only curricula, including false and misleading information about the efficacy of contraception and the safety of abortion. Waxman has also charged that "HHS has changed performance measures for abstinence-only education to make the programs appear successful . . ." (Committee n.d.).

Community-based HIV education: At least fifteen of the most prominent community-based AIDS organizations in the U.S. were audited by the DHHS, following a protest targeted at DHHS Secretary Tommy Thompson at an international AIDS conference (Kaplan 2004, 21). The San Francisco-based Stop AIDS Project was investigated repeatedly over 14 months, receiving special scrutiny after Rep. Souder accused them of obscenity (Smith 2003). Each time the agency was cleared of any wrongdoing, but when Souder persisted, the CDC informed the organization in July 2003 that their workshops were in violation of the Public Health Service Act, which prohibits federal funding of any materials that "promote or encourage, directly, homosexual or heterosexual activity" (Block 2003). More recently, the CDC has proposed a stiffening of the procedures for approval of any written or visual materials related to HIV produced with federal funding (2004).

AIDS conferences: In 2004, DHHS announced that only 50 of the 90 government scientists whose presentations had been accepted for the International AIDS Society conference in Bangkok would be permitted to attend (Reuters 2004; Walgate 2004).

Morning-after pill: In May 2004, the acting director of the FDA's Center for Drug Evaluation Research rejected not only the advice of the agency's expert advisory committee but also that of his own staff when he refused to permit over-the-counter sales of an emergency birth control medicine designed to prevent the implantation of a fertilized egg. Former FDA employees said it was "unheard of" for a high FDA official to overrule the recommendations of both an advisory committee and agency staff (Harris 2004).

Cultural scenarios and the politics of knowledge about sex

This list of flashpoints concerning the production and dissemination of knowledge about sexuality suggests the tight intertwining of two sorts of political struggles: those over the meanings and uses of science, and those over the cultural scenarios that tell people what sort of sexuality is right, proper, and desirable. Here a set of actors—some located within government and other in the ranks of advocacy organizations, often drawing on conservative Christian doctrine—sought to shore up traditional cultural scenarios that they saw as embattled. These actors found it both sensible and strategic to advance their cause by attacking a knowledge-production enterprise that seemed, through its emphases, to take for granted and even endow with legitimacy the kinds of cultural transformations that they abhorred. It mattered little that researchers were not endorsing gay bathhouses, truck-stop prostitution, adolescent sexuality, or any of the other topics whose social consequences the researchers on the "hit list" wanted to track. The simple idea that anyone could describe such activities with dispassion was enough to set off opponents. That researchers proposed to expand the fount of knowledge about these activities—and thereby place alternative sexualities more squarely in public view—made the research agenda anathema.

While the defenders of cultural conservatism have emphasized the linkage between the politics of knowledge and the politics of sexuality, the defenders of sex research mostly have shied away from this intertwining of concerns. They have done little to counter the relative absence, in mainstream political discourse, of well-articulated alternatives to the conservative and religious representations of sexuality. Instead, the primary official response to the recent round of attacks on sexual freedoms and sexuality research has been a vigorous defense of the autonomy of science. Over and over again, liberal politicians, scientists, and columnists have decried the intrusion of politicians and other "outsiders" into the process by which the scientific community decides which research has merit.

This framing plays well in the U. S. political context, making it nearly irresistible to beleaguered defenders of sex research. Yet it is not without its own difficulties, especially when presented without nuance. The notion that the domains of science and politics can or should exist entirely separate from one another, with the former "uncontaminated" by the latter, bears little if any relation to what science studies scholars describe as the normal workings of science, now or in the past (Shapin and Schaffer 1985; Latour 1987; Jasanoff 1990; Gieryn 1995).[7] Nor are right-wing critics such as Lafferty wrong to propose that, in a democratic polity, citizens should have a say in how tax dollars are spent and in how public agencies go about their business. Indeed, though Lafferty would be unlikely to raise these examples, the noisy but sometimes quite productive contributions of AIDS and breast cancer activists to the research process stand as refutations to the notion that biomedical science magically functions best when left to its own devices (Epstein 1996). Thus, adopters of the "autonomy of science" frame potentially find themselves on politically and epistemologically shaky ground, even as they leave quite to one side the question of how to think about sexuality itself.

A secondary, and certainly important, line of defense is the insistence on the public health significance of research such as that targeted by Congress and the TVC. While this argument is important and entirely appropriate in the case of NIH-funded research, one consequence of the near-exclusive reliance upon it is that the rationale for sexuality research tends then to center on the link between sexuality and disease, especially sexually transmitted infections. This argument then sidesteps the question of whether sexual health might be conceived of in broader terms that extend beyond the medical model— or of whether such conceptions merit study. Moreover, the justification of sexuality studies on the grounds of health impact alone does little to counter the cultural scenarios invoked and reinforced by social conservatives, or to put forward alternative imaginings of how diverse sexual experiences might bring pleasure and meaning to people's lives.[8] Neither does it open up space to imagine the possibility that a society might choose to invest funds in studying sexuality *for its own sake.*

My goal is not to trumpet the virtues of utopianism over pragmatism in difficult political circumstances, but rather to do two things. First, I seek to promote serious study of the complex politics of producing knowledge and producing the unknowable (Proctor 1995; Hilgartner 2003). Here the "unknowability" of sex should be understood not as simple repression but as the outcome of a multitude of practices and a cacophony of competing discourses (Foucault 1978). Second, I hope to encourage a more fine-grained empirical analysis of the battles around the cultural scenarios that inform individuals' interpersonal and intrapsychic sexual scripts. The questions are multiple: Within diverse and multicultural societies, how widespread is any specific cultural scenario, and to what degree does its penetrance vary from one subculture to another? What determines the likelihood that particular cultural scenarios regarding sexuality will retain their cultural salience? Under what circumstances do counter-hegemonic scenarios become serious contenders? At any given moment, which social institutions are the most important sites of struggle over cultural scenarios, and which social actors are their principal enunciators? In what ways are these struggles shaped by, and implicated in the shaping of, social debates around gender norms, racial inequality, immigration patterns, globalization, and other salient concerns? What are the primary markers of historical shifts in cultural scenarios?

While the history of debates over sex research may rightly suggest continuities in attempts to police cultural scenarios, it is important not to exaggerate the stability of the scenarios themselves. Upon the release of the film *Kinsey*, an essay in the "Arts and Entertainment" section of the *New York Times* invoked the recent NIH "hit list" episode to suggest that little has changed since Kinsey's day: "Long After Kinsey," the headline declared, "Only the Brave Study Sex" (Carey 2004). Yet the comments of John Gagnon, as quoted in the *Times'* essay, challenge this conception of overwhelming cultural stasis. "Back then, white small-town Protestants' morality was American morality, and it spoke with one voice," said Gagnon, referring to Kinsey's time. Nowadays, "they no longer solely define the conversation; there are competing secular voices talking about sexual health, about pleasure, feminism, the gay movement and so on." And in response to these changes, Gagnon added, "the critics of sex research have become more organized and politically connected," in an important alteration of the political landscape. Gagnon's reflections suggest the importance of engaging in detailed historical reconstructions of how the cultural "instructional guides" that inform sexual practice have themselves been rewritten over time.

The foundational work of Gagnon and Simon did more than just put forward the suggestive concept of cultural scenarios: it also rejected the essentialisms on which most of the dominant cultural scenarios in our society have themselves been built. Gagnon and Simon challenged the notion of a clear-cut division between "natural" and "unnatural" expressions of sexuality, and they called into question the image of sexuality as a dangerous force that society must contain in order to preserve social order. (In that sense, and not for the reasons articulated by Jesse Helms, conservatives might indeed be correct to see Gagnon and Simon's work as inimical to their agenda.) What Gagnon and Simon did not do, however, was systematically analyze the production, circulation, contestation, or transformation of cultural scenarios. And although they insisted, as a programmatic matter, on the "dynamically interactive" relation among the three levels of scripting (Gagnon 2004, 141), they did not have much to say, concretely, about the links between the "macro" and the "micro." There is still much work to be done to show, precisely and empirically, how cultural scenarios—or the battles between competing ones—work their way into the interpersonal and intrapsychic scripts of individuals, and how the everyday script-writing of individuals may contribute to the transformation of those scenarios or the outcomes of those battles (Parker 1991, 1999; Carrillo 2002). By developing a more thoroughgoing empirical analysis of connections among the different levels of sexual scripting, while uniting that analysis with other intellectual approaches to the study of knowledge, science, culture, and politics, we can begin to gain a clearer understanding of the broader processes by which states, social movements, scholars, and activists compete to say what sexuality means and what places it might hold in our lives.

Acknowledgments

I am grateful to Michael Kimmel for his support of this work; Diane di Mauro for pointing me to relevant materials; Héctor Carrillo for helpful comments on a previous draft; Daniel Wolfe and Richard Elovich for discussion of these issues; and John Gagnon for intellectual inspiration.

Notes

1. I should note that although I am not named on the "hit list," I am a co-investigator on a study included on it. I also have personal ties to individuals named on the list.
2. While borrowing many details from the actual events, the television script enhanced the quotient of prime-time drama by supposing that one of the labs whose funding was threatened just happened to employ the president's own daughter, a researcher on sexually transmitted infections.
3. Of course, as Foucault (1980) reminds us, non-knowing about sex typically is accompanied not by silence but by a voluble proliferation of discourses, and that was certainly the case in the heated episodes described here.
4. This is an abbreviated account of the events. For more extended discussions, see di Mauro 1995, 8–12; Ericksen 1999, 80–89; and Hunt 1999, 185–91.
5. The list ended up circulating among academic researchers, and I was able to obtain a copy. It is entitled only "HHS Grant Projects," and it appears to be the printout of a computer spreadsheet program.
6. www.ucsusa.org/scientific_integrity/interference/prominent-statement-signatories.html.

7. To be sure, constructivist studies of knowledge and science run up against their own difficulties when deployed in public debates over the adequacy of scientific claims. For a recent and provocative discussion of this problem with reference to the climate change controversy and other issues, see Latour 2004.

8. For a related analysis of the tension between pursuing public health goals and advancing sexual freedoms, see Epstein 2003.

References

AAMC (American Association of Medical Colleges). 2003. AAMC statement in support of the NIH peer review system. October 29. www.aamc.org/newsroom.

Associated Press. 2003. NIH questions researchers on AIDS grants. October 28

Agres, T. 2003. Politicizing research or responsible oversight? *Scientist,* July 14.

Block, J. 2003. Science gets sacked. *Nation* (September 1/8): 5–6.

Borrego, A. M. 2004. Scientists say White House manipulates and distorts research data to meet its policy goals. *Chronicle of Higher Education,* February 19.

Brainard, J. 2003. Congress asks NIH to justify more than 160 research projects. *Chronicle of Higher Education,* October 27.

Carey, B. 2004. Long after Kinsey, only the brave study sex. *New York Times,* November 9.

Carrillo, H. 2002. *The night is young: Sexuality in Mexico in the time of AIDS.* Chicago: University of Chicago Press.

CDC (Centers for Disease Control and Prevention). 2004. Proposed revision of interim HIV content guidelines for AIDS-related materials, pictorials, audiovisuals, questionnaires, survey instruments, marketing, advertising and web site materials, and educational sessions in CDC regional, state, territorial, local, and community assistance programs. *Federal Register* 69, no. 115: 33824–26.

Committee on Government Reform. n.d. The effectiveness of abstinence-only education. democrats.reform.house.gov/features/politics_and_science/example_abstinence.htm (accessed December 8, 2004).

Cocco, M. 2002. White House wages stealth war on condoms. *Newsday,* November 14.

CPR (Coalition to Protect Research). 2004a. House approves symbolic attack on NIH grants. www.cossa.org/CPR/symbolic_attack.html (accessed May 2, 2005).

———. 2004b. Lost in translation: Public health implications of sexual health research. www.cossa.org/CPR/congbriefing.htm (accessed May 2, 2005).

———. 2004c. Omnibus does not include Neugebauer Amendment. www.cossa.org/CPR/omnibus.html (accessed May 2, 2005).

Detroit Free Press. 2003. Research grants: Health science takes back seat to politics, religion. Editorial. November 14.

di Mauro, Diane. 1995. *Sexuality research in the United States: An assessment of the social and behavioral Sciences.* New York: Sexuality Research Assessment Project.

Epstein, S. 1996. *Impure science: AIDS, activism, and the politics of knowledge.* Berkeley: University of California Press.

———. 2003. Sexualizing governance and medicalizing identities: The emergence of "state-centered" LGBT health politics in the United States. *Sexualities* 6, no. 2:131–71.

Ericksen, J A. (with S. A. Steffen). 1999. *Kiss and tell: Surveying sex in the twentieth century.* Cambridge: Harvard University Press.

Foucault, M. 1978. *The history of sexuality,* vol. 1. Trans. R. Hurley. New York: Vintage Books.

Fram, A. 2003. House rejects conservative bid to block four federal grants for sex research. *Associated Press,* July 10.

Freedman, E. B. 1989. "Uncontrolled desires": The response to the sexual psychopath, 1920–1960. In *Passion and power: Sexuality in history,* ed. by K. Peiss and C. Simmons, 199–225. Philadelphia: Temple University Press.

Gagnon, J. H. 2004. *An interpretation of desire: Essays in the study of sexuality.* Chicago: University of Chicago Press.

Gagnon, J. H., and W. Simon. 1973. *Sexual conduct: The social sources of human sexuality.* Chicago: Aldine.

Gieryn, T. F. 1995. Boundaries of science. In *Handbook of science and technology studies,* ed. S. Jasanoff, G. Markle, J. C. Petersen and T. Pinch, 393–443. Thousand Oaks, CA: Sage.

Goode, E. 2003. Certain words can trip up AIDS grants, scientists say. *New York Times,* April 18.

Grady, D. 2004. Federal health official defends sex studies. *New York Times,* January 30.

Harris, G. 2004. Morning-after-pill ruling defies norm. *New York Times,* May 8.

Hilgartner, S. 2003. Expertise and the production of the unknowable. Talk given at the annual meeting of the Society for Social Studies of Science, Atlanta, October 17.

Hunt, M. 1999. *The new Know-Nothings: The political foes of the scientific study of human nature.* New Brunswick, NJ: Transaction.

Irvine, Janice M. 2003. "The sociologist as voyeur": Social theory and sexuality research, 1910–1978. *Qualitative Sociology* 26, no. 4: 429–56.

Irvine, Judith. 2002. *Harmful to minors: The perils of protecting children from sex.* Minneapolis: University of Minnesota Press.

Jasanoff, S. 1990. *The fifth branch: Science advisers as policymakers.* Cambridge: Harvard University Press.

Kaiser, J. 2003a. NIH roiled by inquiries over grants hit list. *Science* 302, no. 5646: 758.

———. 2003b. Studies of gay men, prostitutes come under scrutiny." *Science* 300:403.

———. 2004. Sex studies "properly" approved. *Science* 303, no. 5659: 741.

Kaplan, E. 2004. Follow the money. *Nation* (November 1): 20–23.

Keiger, D. 2004. Political science. *Johns Hopkins Magazine,* November.

Kristof, N. D. 2003. The secret war on condoms. *New York Times,* January 10.

Lafferty, A. 2003. TVC response letter to Congressman Waxman on NIH grants. www.traditionalvalues.org. October 29.

Latour, B. 1987. *Science in action: How to follow scientists and engineers through society.* Cambridge: Harvard University Press.

———. 2004. Why has critique run out of steam? From matters of fact to matters of concern. *Critical Inquiry* 30:225–48.

Laumann, E. O., J. H. Gagnon, R. T. Michael, and S. Michaels. 1994. *The social organization of sexuality: Sexual practices in the United States.* Chicago: University of Chicago Press.

Laumann, E. O., R. T. Michael, and J. H. Gagnon. 1994. A political history of the national sex survey of adults." *Family Planning Perspectives* 26, no. 1: 34–38.

Leshner, A. I. 2003. Don't let ideology trump science." *Science* 302, no.5650: 1479.

Nathan, D., and M. Snedeker. 1995. *Satan's silence: Ritual abuse and the making of a modern American witch hunt.* New York: Basic Books.

National Academy of Sciences. 2005. *Science and technology in the national interest: Ensuring the best presidential and federal advisory committee science and technology appointments.* Washington, DC: National Academies Press.

NCI (National Cancer Institute). 2003. Abortion, miscarriage, and breast cancer risk. www.cancer.gov/cancertopics/factsheet/Risk/abortion-miscarriage.

Parker, R. G. 1991. *Bodies, pleasures, and passions: Sexual culture in contemporary Brazil.* Boston: Beacon Press.

———. 1999. *Beneath the equator: Cultures of desire, male homosexuality, and emerging gay communities in Brazil.* New York: Routledge.

Proctor, R. N. 1995. *Cancer wars: How politics shapes what we know and don't know about cancer.* New York: Basic Books.

UCS (Union of Concerned Scientists). 2004. Restoring scientific integrity in policymaking. www.ucsusa.org/scientific_integrity (accessed December 8, 2004).

Reuters Health Information. 2004. U.S. charged with silencing scientists.

Rubin, G. 1984. Thinking sex: Notes for a radical theory of the politics of sexuality. In *Pleasure and danger: Exploring female sexuality,* ed. C. S. Vance, 267–318. New York: Routledge.

Russell, S. 2003. AIDS, sex scientists on federal list fear their research is in jeopardy. *San Francisco Chronicle,* October 28.

Scientific American. 2004. Bush-League Lysenkoism. Editorial. 291, no. 5 (May): 10.

Shane, S. 2003. NIH notifies scientists on grant "hit list." *Baltimore Sun,* October 28.

Shapin, S., and S. Schaffer. 1985. *Leviathan and the air-pump: Hobbes, Boyle and the experimental life.* Princeton: Princeton University Press.

Simon, W., and J. H. Gagnon. 1984. Sexual scripts. *Society* 22, no. 1: 53–60.

Smith, M. 2003. Vicious cycle: Federal investigators clear AIDS prevention programs of wrongdoing—and then reinvestigate them. *SF Weekly,* May 7.

Steinbrook, R. 2004. Science, politics, and federal advisory committees. *New England Journal of Medicine* 350, no. 14: 1454–60.

Suskind, R. 2004. Without a doubt. *New York Times Sunday Magazine,* October 17.

Walgate, R. 2004. Why no Americans at AIDS event? *Scientist,* July 13.

Waxman, H. A. 2003. Letter to Secretary of Health and Human Services Tommy G. Thompson. October 27. democrats.reform.house.gov.

Weiss, R. 2003. NIH faces criticism on grants. *Washington Post,* October 30.

Zerhouni, E. L. 2004. Letter and summary of Institute directors' findings. democrats.reform.house.gov/features/politics_and_science/pdfs/pdf_politics_and_science_nih_hit_list_jan_29_let.pdf.

Zitner, A. 2002. Advisors put under a microscope. *Los Angeles Times,* December 23.

Postscript:
The Never-Ending Conversation

Two Interviews

Desire is a fuzzy matrix:
An interview with William Simon

Schmidt: A few days ago, I happened to read a review you wrote of Alan Bell's book [*The Mind and Heart of Human Sexual Behavior*, 1997]. The review has the title "In search of the deeper truth." This sounds a little bit sarcastic, I have to say. Is there no deeper truth to sexuality?

Simon: That may be, I think, the deeper truth about sexuality. After all these years, the one conclusion I have come to is that there are no permanent significant truths about sexuality. That which is permanent is rarely significant and that which appears to be most significant rarely turns out to be permanent.

Schmidt: What then is the task of the sex researcher if there are no greater truths to be found?

Simon: I think our task is what it's always been. Not unlike poets and dramatists, our task is to give voice to those who have no voice; to hold up mirrors through which people can recognize themselves. For me, the offense that we who engage in public talk regarding sexuality commit is to hold up images of the self and of the "normal" that alienate people from their experience of themselves. For example, there is the prevalent view that mature and healthy sex, in addition to [being] heterosexual,

Gunter Schmidt interviewed William Simon on June 24, 1999, at the 25th annual meeting of the International Academy of Sex Research (Stony Brook, New York). He interviewed John Gagnon at the 21st annual meeting of the IASR in Sermione, Italy in 1995, in a hotel room on the shores of Lake Garda. The Gagnon interview was first published in German, in *Zeitschrift für Sexualforschung* 11 (1998):353–66. © John Gagnon.

must be deeply imbued with sentiments of love. That may sound very attractive, but I don't think that describes very many people's experience. Montaigne, in his essay on experience, describes a critical interplay between knowledge and experience. With the rapid growth in recent years in research and scholarship focused on sexuality, we have become proficient in producing impressive quantities of "knowledge." However, too often in our enthusiasm for the persuasive generalization or the "validated" hypothesis, we've banished from visibility the full range of current experiences.

Schmidt: In the absence of greater truths, do you have visions or utopian ideals with regard to sexuality?

Simon: No, but I have fantasies. For many of us, the present appears bereft of attractive utopian visions. Not since the Renaissance have we been as lacking in a vision of a more attractive tomorrow than we are currently. However, one of the things I have learned is that as a species our capacity for prediction is not very great. Alfred Schutz, the great phenomenologist, was absolutely convinced in 1939 that the National Socialists would ultimately rule the world. And I am amazed that somebody as bright as Schutz could not have seen beyond, that there'd be an alternative world after Hitler. One of my favorite quotes comes from Schutz: "Nevertheless," he said, "we will die as we have lived, trying to find order in 'our' world that we find lacking in our 'world.'" And I think that's true for many of us almost all of the time. Namely that we are out there scrambling to find order in our world that is frequently lacking it, which is what makes a social scientist in the first place. Theorizing, however primitive, is inseparable from autobiography. The danger, I think, is not to recognize this and to impose our image of the future on our children by describing the local and temporarily significant as if they constitute a universal imperative. That's the great source of conflict between generations. Such intergenerational conflict perhaps is inevitable in a social context with a pervasive sense of liminality. Which is why my own children are semi-Martians to me.

Schmidt: You place a great deal of focus on changes in sexuality. Can you discuss such changes without having an idea—maybe a less than scientific idea—about how you would like things to be?

Simon: At the end of his lectures on biology at MIT, the Nobel laureate Salvador Luria observed that any one mode of perception or digestion—or mode of organizing sexual behavior, we might add—is only one of an infinite number of ways in which that could have been organized. Whatever occurs in nature or social life is really something of a miracle and ought to be treated with all the respect and curiosity that miracles deserve. Yes, I remain enormously optimistic. I think these are very, very exciting times. They will be different. For example, we have a generation, at least in North America's upper middle class—and I suspect Western Europe and Germany [are] not vastly different—that'll now have many more years of premarital sexual experience—in many cases cohabitation—than any prior generation we know. Moreover, this generation comes of age in the context of a more explicit erotic landscape than any of us could have predicted less than a third of a century ago and in the context of widely held beliefs regarding the virtual universality of the sexual as a compelling human interest.

Schmidt: What is exciting for you with regard to these developments?

Simon: I don't mean to romanticize; much of this change can be terribly disordering and self-alienating. But I have the feeling something new is being born every day, including new visions of the future.

Schmidt: You are a bit envious?

Simon: Of course—the swiftness with which technology transforms itself creates the near permanent illusion of some dazzling new experience waiting just beyond to-day's horizon line. As Buckminster Fuller used to remind us, it took humanity millennia to invent the vacuum tube and anything you might want to use the vacuum tube for. From the vacuum tube to the transistor it took approximately half a century. To go from the transistor to microminiaturization to the chip took less than ten years. With these shifts of technology have come pervasive changes that alter our very sense of time and space. Persons whose age differences are relatively small, sharing the same culture, may in fact represent a different response to the world. As the layers of cultural stratigraphy become increasingly narrow, the pluralization of the world increases. The very possibility of learning to live with a tolerance for ambiguity and differences strikes me as being extremely exciting.

Schmidt: You are quite enthusiastic!

Simon: Yes. Though current ethnic strife around the world does little to encourage optimism. Such instances, however, may represent a symptom of change rather than a resolute obstacle. "Globalization" inevitably brings with it largely unmeasured amounts of cultural globalization.

Schmidt: Is this part of what you have termed the "postmodernization of sex"?

Simon: Yes. I think the critical element is increasing pluralization within what previously appeared to be homogeneous defining and constraining identities, mainly involving gender. Initially I was very hostile to the emergence of queer theory. I now take the queer theorists much more seriously. The conceptual deconstruction of both sexuality and gender tends to follow the disassembly of both in experience. Both gender and sexual orientation come to lose the illusion of a homogeneous unity, fragmenting into a mosaic of meanings and gestures that the self struggles to coordinate. Sexual identity, sexual preference, and sexual behavior are more loosely correlated than ever before and will become more so in the near future.

Let me put it this way: I think each generation seems to have its characteristic or signature mental disorder. The early part of this past century could property be called an "age of anxiety." And our most commonly recognized neuroses were anxiety neuroses. By midcentury, with the beginnings of affluence, the signature disorder became narcissistic disorders. And now it's the multiple personality that seems to be very fashionable. Or the borderline case—typically individuals with so little structure that therapies designed to repair damaged psychic structures will not help. This shift points to what might be termed a shift in the politics of the self.

Schmidt: Do you think this development of disorders is a mere construction or does it reflect real personality changes over time?

Simon: It's a real change in the architecture of personality—or, perhaps more accurately, there has been a dramatic shift in the distribution of configurations of personality and, of critical significance, the goodness of fit between specific types of personality and the surrounding social world. Those who become clinical cases are often not as different from everybody else as most of us would like to think.

Schmidt: So all of us are borderline, but only a few realize it?

Simon: Many of our inherited theories of personality tended to privilege characterological stability as preparation for life in a stable social order. Flexibility, a kind of characterological opportunism, might be seen as more suitable where change becomes a continuing aspect of social life. The borderline phenomenon as it was initially described in the psychoanalytic or psychiatric literature was largely a disorder of successful people. People that previously managed well who then began experiencing significant psychic distress. People with many of the same symptoms who more effectively struggle to manage the pervasive liminality of persistent change without visibly failing apart remain invisible, so they never become part of the clinical statistic.

A world that increasingly trains us to bargain with it for what we want to be must first train us to bargain with ourselves; it's the flexibility and uncertainty of alternatives that are enormously frightening or unnerving for many. During much of the modern age, virtually everyone negotiated with themselves for their destinies, but we learned to do it behind our own back. For many, that process of self-negotiation ceases to be hidden. Some call it the emergence of an executive self.

Schmidt: Does that mean that the intrapsychic scripts become more and more relevant?

Simon: Yes. And this has several dimensions. One, that the varied and sometimes incompatible components that enter intrapsychic life now will become much more manifest. And we may move from a kind of monosexuality toward a more polysexuality and not necessarily in the sense of bisexuality, but rather in different ways of experiencing yourself and others as being sexual. Gender identity, sexual identity, and sexual behavior are less commonly experienced as being cut from a single cloth.

Schmidt: Which means for one and the same person there are many ways to be heterosexual or homosexual.

Simon: Yes, or bisexual. There are times I may desperately want to possess the desired object. There are times I want to be the desired object. Now what happens conventionally is that we assign these two roles: You'll be the object of desire, I'll be the subject of desire, to use those clichés. And we end up sort of performing. But which one of these I am in my head cannot be determined from observation. I am currently beginning some research on sadomasochism—consensual sadomasochism. And one of the things that becomes increasingly clear to me is that for many people their manifest role in this form of sex play is the price for entry into the behavior. For example, one characteristic of being a masochist or the submissive, presumably, is that you don't appear to have to take responsibility for what's going to happen. For men to enter that role is often exceedingly difficult. So they may enter the role being the dominant. But that may not tell us a great deal about who they are in their heads during the performance. The difference between that which gets you into the scene and that which triggers excitement may not be the same as that which you experience yourself as being in the performance or even that which sustains excitement.

Schmidt: How do the intrapsychic scripts develop? And when do they develop?

Simon: Individually; really sort of accidentally.

Schmidt: Accidentally?

Simon: Yes. I don't think there will be a general theory. I think there are some general principles that we ought to learn to observe, but the specifics of desire invariably involve an ultimate mystery. The word that postmodernists perhaps have overused is terribly valid here: that term is *contingency*. And when my students ask, "What do you mean when you say 'contingency'?" I say what it means is: Any particular behavioral outcome just as easily could have been something else— something seemingly quite different. So the moment at which something becomes eroticized is really something magical about the human experience. One of the major deceptive palliatives that social science provides is obscuring what is essentially the accidental nature of our personal and social destinies. Or, as Norbert Elias cautioned us, it may be an error to think of a process as if it were a system.

Schmidt: That is, we don't know for certain what it is.

Simon: Yes. And I think we at least begin to open a lid and take a look at some of the variability. Where it comes from, how it comes about. We may look at it, we may try to explain it, but it would be a mistake to anticipate reducing it to a formula, even a complex formula. In the work on the sexual scripts of gay men I'm currently doing with David Whittier, we found ourselves describing sexual desire as a fuzzy matrix.

Schmidt: Does that mean that intrapsychic scripts can develop and redevelop over the whole lifespan? Or do you think childhood and adolescence are especially important?

Simon: For the vast majority, I think adolescence is the time in which we learn to eroticize desire. We never come to sexual desire innocently. It is not the desire that is new, but the attachment of that desire to sexual possibilities. Desire is like Velcro; it attaches very easily. And like Velcro, it invariably carries residues of earlier attachments. Freud observes in an early essay—unfortunately describing himself as well—that we'll make little progress in understanding our sexuality until we have a generation of doctors who can remember their own youths. It is significant that even for those of us who spent our lives studying adolescence as a subject, it remains among the most abstract yet most obsessively preoccupied with the sexual of all lifecycle studies. All of us went through it. Why are we so silent? You have the notion of finding links so that the really satisfying sexual act somehow manages to touch many of the layers of change and adaptation that ultimately connect to early constructions of desire. I think that's what my friend the late Robert Stoller meant with his wonderful concept of microdots: the current partner doesn't have to be a teenager, as it were, but there ought to be a lot about her or him, as it were, that allows me to recognize desires formulated during earlier ages.

Schmidt: Stoller's microdots, however, are mostly formed in early childhood.

Simon: That's because of Stoller's training as a psychoanalyst. In my view, we are born desiring organisms and, as a result, we come to sexuality with an existing history of desire. That, however, does not mean, that any desire is inherently sexual.

Schmidt: Is the microdot for you a synonym for intrapsychic script?

Simon: No, microdots might be defined as the raw material out of which intrapsychic scripts and interpersonal scripts are fashioned—they are complex metaphors that condense histories of meanings and uses. They are what I call the desire of the dream that is hidden by the dreamer in the dream of desire.

Schmidt: Microdots in Stoller's thinking are mainly developed unconsciously. When I listen to you I get the impression that the intrapsychic scripts are actively constructed by the individual—they don't just happen.

Simon: We certainly may be more authorial than earlier generations, if only because we have more alternatives. Traditional societies only require that we learn to be actors in scripts that the world has prepared for us. And there is a middle stage, the age of anxiety, where we learned to be critics; we are constantly watching the performance with fully social idealizations in mind. And now increasingly we have to add taking responsibility as the authors of our own scripts. And if not authors of our own scripts in terms of what our bodies are doing in engagement with other bodies, then at least as authors of the scripts of what's going through our heads.

Schmidt: We have been socialized in a quite different period of social history. How do men and women of our age adapt to all the sudden change we are experiencing? Do we reconstruct our intrapsychic scripts, too?

Simon: Many manage it by becoming gradually de-eroticized. Roland Barthes made a useful distinction between what he called the "text of bliss" versus the "text of comfort." I would translate this in sexual terms as the "orgasm of excitement" versus the "orgasm of reassurance." Individual and interpersonal viability is affirmed by sex, and that too is a source of pleasure, a form of gratification. Orgasm becomes an articulate witness; it affirms, "Yes, I am still potent; yes, you are still attractive." For others, a crisis of aging—particularly in a youth-obsessed culture—often occasions previously unexpected experiments.

Schmidt: So sexuality acquires quite a different meaning.

Simon: Yes. So we remain sexual, but it becomes problematic, less urgent, and the memory of the historically cumulated idealizations attached to the sexual continue to resonate. I have a niece who is about forty; two of her female friends recently unnerved her by leaving what appeared to be very successful marriages. And when asked why did they leave, they replied almost identically: "This may be the last time I will ever know being in love again." The sexual, that once was scripted almost entirely as rituals of social solidarity, must increasingly be scripted as rituals of self-solidarity that allow the actor to reconfigure identity themes that often differ from the less intimate, more public of our presentations of self.

Schmidt: In the paper you gave this morning ["Human sexuality: the future of an illusion"], you raised a very interesting issue: What are the resources of desire? Perhaps you could summarize here what they are.

Simon: In terms of the significance of the experience, the nineteenth and the twentieth centuries may have created the most overeroticized worlds that humanity has ever known. I think for most of humanity the sexual really wasn't a measure of central preoccupation or a measure of moral worth. The modern world conflated the sexual with so many forms of significance that many experience it as an intimidating hyperreality. The generation that now is coming of age, those who initiated sex experience at relatively early ages may in fact be much more pragmatic about their uses of the sexual.

Schmidt: A sort of "de-dramatizing" sex?

Simon: Yes, and not seeing it as quite as important or compelling. For my generation, to find somebody to have sex with, if you were heterosexual, you frequently had to marry. And for the honeymoon you allegedly went away and spent four days having sex. Today's young people seem to drift into cohabitation. In many cases their peers and parents are aware of it. And they move in with each other. I have the feeling, that if somebody said, "Let's go to the movies tonight," they would just as soon go to the movies as stay home and have sex.

Schmidt: And the movies would be as much fun as going to bed with each other.

Simon: Yes. There may be a deflation of the sexual. Deflation may not be the correct word. Perhaps, pedestrianization might be more apt. A shift over a relatively few generations from a sexual anomie of deprivation to a sexual anomie of affluence.

Schmidt: Does that make sex more serene?

Simon: Perhaps duller for some, but also less painful and perhaps less costly. We've mischaracterized the cohorts that followed the sexual revolution. There has been much public talk about unintended pregnancies, we talk about epidemics of STDs, but we forget that millions more shared that postrevolutionary history than experienced either of these unfortunate outcomes. I think they may have been better equipped to handle their own lives, as well as handle the lives of their parents. Recently, for example, Arthur Miller wrote a play about a woman [*Broken Glass*] who so thoroughly loathed her husband that she couldn't stand being touched by him. However, she can only express her feelings by a hysteria that leaves her partially paralyzed. And in the aftermath of televising the play, the host turned to Miller and asked why such a woman would have continued to endure such a marriage. Miller replied, "You know, I was twenty-seven years old before I met my first divorced person." There are very few who grow up in your country and my country who by age fifteen haven't experienced divorce in their own family or one fairly close to them. Many of the young occasionally engage in shocking behavior and social critics are prone to say, "See what loosening of moral standards has done." We don't see that the vast majority of them may have been liberated, in part, by watching their parents' generation go through a second adolescence.

Schmidt: So it's not just an evil that happens to them when their parents are separating. There is an opportunity for them in the process, as well.

Simon: Freud again—with age I think I have learned to respect him more and more—noted at the end of *Civilization and Its Discontents* that we commit two sins against our children: The first one, that we wait too long to tell them about sex, is surely irrelevant for much of today's world. The second one is still very relevant. He said we wait too long to let them know that people's emotions are complex—that you can love and hate at the same time—leaving the young children feeling that they are the only ones who are weird or strange because sometimes they love us and sometimes they hate us. Today early sophistication in regard to the complexity of human relationships may be a better training school than any form of formal sex education. It's obviously better if parents learn to continue to talk to each other and not use their children as a battleground. But overall I am not sure that children have been really hurt by divorce as much as those who grow up in households that remained intact where people didn't speak to each other, where the anger was felt but never expressed. Hopefully this may be a generation that is kinder in expecting less of their parents and may learn to be as kind in what they expect of themselves.

Schmidt: Let's stick to the topic "sex as drama." Many Western intellectuals—sex researchers included—have been very attracted to this notion. Susan Sontag explored this idea in an exemplary way in her famous essay on the pornographic imagination, saying that sex will forever be something beyond good and evil, beyond rationality, beyond love, beyond everything. Do you think this idea makes sense?

Simon: Unfortunately no. I actually lived in a commune during the sixties.

Schmidt: You did?

Simon: Oh yes. And it was a very complex relationship with eleven or twelve of us. It was also among the happiest and most productive periods of my life. By the way, we saw these communes naïvely in the late sixties and early seventies as what the future was going to be like. But, at best, it really was a resocializing setting, affording new sexual capacities, values and styles. I learned, for example, to be much more casual about my own body. But I also realized how quickly conventionalized this seemingly exotic situation became. This is one of the major implications of Stoller's later nonclinical work on S&M clubs and on the porn industry. Part of what he was then saying is that any reality, as exotic it appears, when translated into a seven-day-week, twenty-four-hours-a-day setting, ultimately becomes pedestrian. What we have done, of course, is unrealistically create pornographic phantasmagoric worlds which inspire as they frustrate. The future indeed may have less need for these elements of fantasy; it may balance out in the sense that the emotion may be less intense but the experience more frequent and less commonly requiring a fragile balance of conflicted emotions—particularly the conflict between personal desire and social expectations.

Schmidt: Let's come back to adolescence. You mentioned before that this time in life is so important because we then learn to eroticize desire. Can you explain this more?

Simon: Yes. We can talk about two distinct but overlapping dimensions. One is the experience of the desire for sex and the other is experiencing sexual desire. They are not really the same. For many boys of my generation, at least in North America, sex was an obsession. You could describe most of our early experiences as experiences where having done "it" was significantly more pleasuring than the actual doing. The same may have been true for many women, as a matter of fact, who having done it . . .

Schmidt: Having done "it" for other reasons?

Simon: Yes. As a confirmation of gender competence, to approximate a romantic relationship, other things like that. That's what I would call the desire for sex. But it's not sexual desire or that which is associated with the beginnings of sexual excitement.

Schmidt: This term "eroticizing of desire" sounds like it has been taken from the French. What is your relationship to the French philosophers—for example, Foucault or Baudrillard?

Simon: I think I was to varying degrees influenced by both. It may be irrelevant for this, but again it's speaking of contingency. In the late seventies, early eighties as a sex researcher I could truly describe myself as being thoroughly burned out, really bored. And at the time two of my three children were in college. One was at Berkeley, who as an undergraduate was allowed into Foucault's seminar. And the other, who is a filmmaker, did his junior year at the Sorbonne, where he attended lectures by Christian Metz, Kristeva, and others. And they began talking with me about these people—and these were people I had never heard of. And so for the next few years I partially retired from the field; it was like going back to graduate school. I think we all ought to do that several times in our lives. It was pure pleasure. I think many of us forget that we had much more fun being students than we have being teachers. Foucault, despite substantial differences, hit me like a case of diarrhea. His social-constructionist view of sexuality was not unlike the view that Gagnon and I had developed somewhat earlier. However, he placed the conceptions in a much richer intellectual context. It was his influence that moved me from a fairly conventional social learning position to that of a radical social constructionist.

Schmidt: Did you meet him?

Simon: No, but I did meet Baudrillard, who I found wonderfully unpretentious and thoroughly likable—despite his somewhat hyperbolic prose. In general, I was influenced by the French rediscovery of the Germans, which is really what we are talking about: a Heideggerian return to Nietzsche. As a graduate student I attended a seminar led by Max Horkheimer who came to visit one quarter at the University of Chicago. And there were about sixty of us attendant at the first meeting of the seminar. It was called "Society and Values" and he announced that there would be only one text for the quarter's work; it would be Nietzsche's *Genealogy of Morals*. The next time the seminar met there were nine of us. I fortunately was one of them. However, even with Horkheimer's guidance, the *Genealogy of Morals* wasn't the same book I read twenty-five years later. The French texts had prepared me. And so in that sense I think at least I personally owe the French at this point an enormous debt. Roland Barthes obviously has played a great influence on my thinking. Foucault, Baudrillard, Barthes, and Castoriades would be the four most important.

Schmidt: Among French thinkers.

Simon: French, yes. And I must confess I have found less among contemporary German social theory. Luhmann had become the resurrected Talcott Parsons. I already suffered that as a graduate student; I don't need to do it again. Habermas bores me. He persists in creating grand theory with very little by a way of direct contact with ongoing social life. I noticed that in recent years he rediscovered George Herbert Mead and the importance of the exchange of symbols in social interaction. Mead assumes that there is a community of consensus—what I call a paradigmatic society, a world with a predominance of shared meaning that allows the regulatory "generalized other" to emerge so easily because training in each household sufficiently approximated training and meaning in all other households. So that consensus produces civility. Unfortunately the need for civility does not by itself produce consensus. In highly individuated social orders, where individuals living virtually identical lives have difficulty recognizing each other or experiencing a common bond, this becomes a critical question. One not easily resolved by any theoretical formulation.

Schmidt: In your lecture today you mentioned two metaphors: postmodern "pulp" and "skin." I think these are very central to your concept of the postmodern. Can you explain?

Simon: Yes, sure. "Pulp" is literally the interior of a piece of fruit. One of the things that the postmodern world does is make us very pulpy. While we incorporate many inconsistent and changing elements, we increasingly find ourselves lacking a kind of coherent, comfortably constraining "skin." That's what traditional society really provided. Now increasingly we have to self-consciously fashion our skin: we have to tailor it, we have to suture it, or find some basis for integrating the multiple roles into a single, coherent identity. Sometimes there are master identities that are so powerful that, failing all else, make you plausible to yourself by giving you a way of explaining your current existence. This is why I believe—though I have no evidence for it, it's an intuition—that "coming out" in the gay world all at once seemed to be progressively easier and easier during the seventies until the eighties. As problematic as being gay was—and it was and is in a homophobic society—it allowed to you to understand yourself: you became plausible to yourself. Now casually people tell me at cocktail parties: "You know, I am a child of alcoholic parents" or "I was victim of child sex abuse." And I must wonder why are these people telling me these things?

Schmidt: And this is "skin"?

Simon: This is skin, the interface between the interpersonal and the intrapsychic, the basis for maintaining or refashioning a coherent identity; one that somehow accounts for and makes plausible the narratives of the self. For some, it appears seamless, as if derived from a single cloth. For others, it may take the form of a patchwork garment that is manifestly the object of continuing revision. There is so much of this in the resurrection of ethnicities and religious fundamentalisms that we previously thought would quietly fade away. We can see it in Yugoslavia today. We can see it in most Western countries, with the appearance of passionate religious fundamentalists—individuals who manage the pulp, the confusions of the inner self, by making some social code an absolute imperative. The politics of the self are changing and in their resolution may rest the future of the politics of society.

Schmidt: This is quite a superficial form of identity, isn't it?

Simon: Yes, it is superficial in the sense of describing our appearance in the world. But something more than that is social context where identity frequently must adapt to changing contexts, changing audiences, and changing opportunities. That is what the passionate religious fundamentalist can do that the rest of us find increasingly problematic: find expressions of their fundamentalist belief and place every faith over the totality of their life. Patriarchy didn't merely describe the household; it described the relation between the king and the subject, the teacher and the student, the healer and the patient, the employer and the employee. Wherever you went, patriarchy gave you a sense of all was right with the world and you were right in the world. Now one is so uncertain. That's what I mean by a postparadigmatic society: that the shared master identities of the world, ones that fashioned a sense of who you were, have diminished.

One of the things that define the postmodern condition, again, is the increasingly temporary quality of our lives. The changes surround us. And not only is there change, but also pervasive pluralization; almost everything comes in multiple forms. Charles H. Cooley put it in a wonderful phrase: "Choice broadens as it moves through history, like a river." To which he adds, by the way: "Requiring much stronger swimmers, because otherwise more will drown." And what he is really talking about is having to pick and choose without the world picking and choosing for you. And again, many learn to do it easily—many more than we think, I hope. And for others, the ambiguities of the temporary, the fact that again we may all be temporary—our employment, our relationships, our expectations—learning to live with the provisional for many of us who are conditioned to worlds of stability can be enormously painful and unnerving. But I think there are others for whom the absence of such conditions would simply be boring.

Schmidt: Today you talked about "Sexuality: The future of an illusion." Why is sex an illusion and what is its future?

Simon: It's an illusion, again, very much in the same way Freud meant religion is an illusion. Namely, that its meaning and significance is metaphysical and is produced by the variable world of human uses, rather than being a natural continent dark in mysterious ways waiting for heroic biologists to fully explore and return having captured its absolute essence. I think we are going to find that humanity, down to some very fundamental levels, is beginning to exhibit the capacity to change and to adapt to change much more quickly than our history up until now has prepared us for. At this point, again, history becomes far less of a guide. We really are reinventing the world consistently. So sex as illusions, as concepts, both personal and shared, becomes the more important truth than the actual organs. So I really mean it as being an illusion, in that sense. We have to begin to respect it as such. These metaphysical beliefs are not to be taken lightly because they are not rooted in some organ or somehow encoded in our DNA.

Schmidt: And the future of sex?

Simon: Otis Dudley Duncan, a very wise person, once described social forecasting as logically impossible, morally dubious, and esthetically unattractive. The only aspect I can affirm with any confidence is that the human uses of the sexual will surely continue to frustrate any simple or overarching generalizations.

Schmidt: That's a good ending. Thanks a lot, Bill Simon.

Simon: Thank you.

Revisiting the text:
An interview with John Gagnon

Schmidt: Twenty-five years ago, you and William Simon published *Sexual Conduct*, a "pathbreaking study," as Ken Plummer put it recently, "constituting the approach which now is commonly known as the 'social-constructionist approach.'" Do you share this evaluation?

Gagnon: My answer has two parts. The first part is to agree that the book that we wrote offered an original alternative to prior ways of thinking about sexuality. So in that sense it can be described as "pathbreaking." I am not sure that's exactly the right word; perhaps we only remapped what was thought to be a well-understood terrain. The second part is to say I don't think we have viewed ourselves as social constructionists. We have never had any sense of ourselves being directly influenced by the German constructionist tradition exemplified by Alfred Schutz, Peter Berger, or Thomas Luckman. That tradition had no direct connection to us. Our thinking was much more rooted in the tradition of pragmatism in the United States, an intellectual orientation that is very, very American, especially in terms of its attempt to declare independence from its European origins.

Schmidt: What persons are you thinking of?

Gagnon: Simon and I had been trained in sociology at the University of Chicago, but the Chicago department was changing dramatically when we there in the 1950s. George Herbert Mead, Robert Park, and Herbert Blumer were no longer heroes of Chicago sociology. Young people who were influenced by the Chicago school, primarily in the person of Everett Hughes—students like Erving Goffman and Howard Becker and others who would continue some aspects of the Chicago tradition—had all left. The old faculty had been replaced by a new generation trained at Columbia University. The Chicago tradition was replaced by the middle-range sociology of Robert Merton and Paul Lazarsfeld, a perspective which dominated the intellectual climate at the end of our careers at the University of Chicago. Actually, there are two other intellectual threads which connected the two of us. First is the work of a man named Kenneth Burke who was a profound influence on Bill and me. Burke is not widely known either internationally or even in American sociology anymore, though there has been a revival of interest since his death two years ago.

Schmidt: He was a sociologist?

Gagnon: No, he was a music critic, a book reviewer, a literary critic and scholar, an intellectual. He belongs to the tradition of American eccentrics: people who are outside the mainstream, who are not academics, but who are public intellectuals. Bill and I were influenced independently by Burke. He began reading Burke when he was in literary studies at the University of Michigan. Before that Bill was an activist in the far left of the American labor movement. I started reading Burke in college because I was interested in his ideas about interpretation. We actually used fragments of Burke's work, but these were critical elements in our shared perspective.

Schmidt: We will come back to Burke. But which was the second thread of connection between Gagnon and Simon?

Gagnon: The second connection was and is that tradition in the Chicago school of thinking about nonoccupational aspects of social life metaphorically as a "career." The career model offered a processual and contingent perspective on how people assimilated new ways of living, how they enacted them, and how life choices changed the self. This perspective goes back to the roots of Chicago criminology, when Clifford Shaw and Henry McKay began to write about criminal careers in the same way that others wrote about conventional occupational careers. The metaphor could then be extended to marijuana smoking, pregnancies out of wedlock, homosexuality. Also thinking about alternate life paths as careers allowed a certain moral neutrality while thinking about deviance. The careers of a banker and a gangster could be analyzed in exactly the same way: learning how to do a job, acquiring skills and insider knowledge, learning how to deal with all of the other social actors in a particular social milieu. By emphasizing the common features of learning and performing, the usual moral differences between occupational and life style categories could disappear. The concept of social careers was an important idea in conceiving certain parts of *Sexual Conduct*.

Schmidt: Let's come back to Kenneth Burke and read a few sentences from your book.

Part of the legacy of Freud is that we had all become adept at seeking out the sexual ingredient in many forms of nonsexual behavior and symbolism. We are suggesting what is in essence the insight of Kenneth Burke: it is just as plausible to examine sexual behavior for its capacity to express and serve nonsexual motives as the reverse. Is this one of the central messages of *Sexual Conduct*?

Gagnon: Yes, absolutely. Following Burke we began to think about the way in which sex—both symbolically and physically—could be expressive of other interests—work, politics, religion—and that the sexual did not have a priority in causal explanation. If there is a network of different influencing factors, Freud always chose the sexual to explain all the others. By this simplification you often eliminate what is most interesting, which is that the sexual is one element in a dynamic network of forces, including gender, class, race/ethnicity, nationality. You may do something sexually dramatic for quite mundane other reasons. That came directly out of the Burkean texts.

Schmidt: What makes the difference between sexual behavior and sexual conduct?

Gagnon: The sexual conduct phrase actually came from Ernest W. Burgess, who worked with Robert Park. Park and Burgess were two of the great figures of the second Chicago school. What Burgess was arguing—this was in a critique of Kinsey—was that behavior is always morally evaluated. There is no human behavior without moral—hence social—evaluation. So you don't have biologically naked sex behavior, you have socially clothed sexual conduct. And so we took the phrase "conduct," because we wanted to say we are not talking about socially unevaluated behavior. The crucial issue is, sexual behavior is socially constituted so that it becomes sexual conduct.

Actually this formulation is backwards and wrong. It probably should be said that thinking about sex as behavior is one aspect of the way we conduct ourselves sexually. Sex becomes behavior when we decide to take off the cultural clothing of sexuality which is its socially "natural" condition to reveal the unnatural condition of sex as naked behavior.

Schmidt: Three years after the publication of *Sexual Conduct*, the psychoanalyst Robert Stoller developed similar thoughts in his theory of perversion and in his theory of sexual excitement, stressing the sexualizing effect of meanings. Did you know something about Stoller, when you were writing *Sexual Conduct*?

Gagnon: No. And I don't think Bill did either. Bill and Stoller developed a very close relationship later on. And I recall that an interesting correspondence then resulted, in which Stoller indicated the importance of the ideas of *Sexual Conduct* for his own work. He had read the book and he had used some of the ideas in it. I am less persuaded by Stoller's notion of the microdot. Stoller's microdots have their origins too early in childhood for me and remain influential far later in life than I give them credit for. We did however take a critical microdot-like example from the novelist Jerzy Kosinski in a discussion of the independent role of the intrapsychic in arousal.

Schmidt: I remember this story—where a man is attracted by his female colleague and it doesn't work if she was accessible?

Gagnon: Yes. So he fantasizes about an airline stewardess raising her arms above her head to put away a bag in an overhead bin. Her breasts are pulled up by her brassiere and this becomes an erotic provocation in a way that is similar to the microdot. However, we preferred a less restrictive source of erotic symbols—a more general menu of arousing symbols—than Stoller.

Schmidt: However, similar ideas developed in quite different places, in quite different disciplines, in quite different schools of thinking in those years. You and Stoller get rid of traditional approaches of sexuality—the naturalization of sex and the concept of sex drive.

Gagnon: Stoller began in the context of psychoanalysis as a practitioner and theorist. Consequently, he has had a more difficult intellectual task in revising Freud—given the centrality of libido theory to psychoanalytic practice—than we did. We resisted Freud in general.

Schmidt: And admired him at the same time.

Gagnon: Freud was one of the great men we had to push aside in order to establish our own point of view. And so we may have simplified him more than we should have. But we were young and he was in the way. I don't think we were as generous as we should have been, or even as thoughtful about what he could have given us. Stoller's position was much more complicated than ours because he had to keep Freud, and had to selectively retain and honor those elements that still worked for him as a practicing psychoanalyst. And so his reading of Freud is much more nuanced than ours was, at least in that first version. I think that Bill in his own work has reconstituted his relationship to Freud in important ways. I think I have done that less than he has.

Schmidt: So one hero you tried to put aside as a young man was Freud; the second was Kinsey. Is there a connection of Freud and Kinsey?

Gagnon: Well, I think that I resist the label "sexology" because it has at its core the theory of sexual naturalization; that idea that stretches from Krafft-Ebing to Masters and Johnson that sex is a natural phenomenon. Kinsey's naturalism is very different than Freud's. Freud's notion is that nature must be resisted to create civilization. Kinsey's view of nature is much more beneficent. In his view, nature produces a variety of opportunities to be sexual. For Kinsey the problem of civilized sexual culture is that it's like agriculture. It produces only one sexual product, one sexual crop. The only approved crop is heterosexuality.

Schmidt: Destroying variability . . .

Gagnon: That's right. Kinsey—and I think this is why he is so badly misunderstood—really was a taxonomist of evolution. He believed in the beauty of diversity in nature. Nature provided you with all these variations. And what culture did, was to place limits on nature. This turns Freud upside down. However, nature remains for Kinsey the origin of desire. And so we had to get rid of both of them in order to get a completely socially determined sexuality. We had to eliminate nature.

Schmidt: And you did it by creating what you call the script theory?

Gagnon: We created script theory in an attempt to have a device to describe how people go about doing sex socially, and to demonstrate the importance of social elements in the doing of the sexual.

Schmidt: What would you say, what is script theory in your sense today?

Gagnon: Where did it go? I think we lost control of it. You know, one loses control of every idea. When I hear people say the word "script" at a meeting, I often don't recognize what they are talking about. But that's inevitable. I think that at this moment neither Bill nor I have made a fully coherent argument about scripts.

Schmidt: In your recent book *The Social Organization of Sexuality* there is a small and very comprehensive description of script theory. In its shortness it's quite informing. Can you respond to this?

Gagnon: I am actually quite labile in my intellectual relationship to people I respect intellectually. When I talk to them I am always actively influenced or resistant to what they are saying and I often revise my own ideas as they talk. In a way, there is sort of a Gagnon–Laumann script theory in the book you mentioned, and there is a Gagnon-Simon script theory and there is a Gagnon script theory and there is a Simon script theory without Gagnon. As I listened to Ed Laumann talking about social networks and the importance of networks, scripting linked into those ideas. One can think about a sequence of events—such as all the separable events that make up a wedding as a sequence of scripts, and then think about who is present or absent at various moments in the unfolding of the larger set of events. The key ideas are the co–presence or absence of actors and the ordering of the scripts. And so you get a matrix which is "scripted events" on one axis and "actors" on the other and the social arrangement then becomes the matrix of actors and events. In the work which I did with Bill there was a much greater concern with what went on inside people's heads—with the intrapsychic and the social origins of mental life.

Schmidt: Do you still stick to the three levels of scripting: the cultural scripts, the interpersonal scripts and the just mentioned intrapsychic scripts?

Gagnon: The reason that we invented the three levels of scripting was to deal with the quasi-independent relation between the agentive individual, the interactional situation, and the surrounding sociocultural order. This was always the weakness of traditional culture-personality theory in anthropology. The individual often appeared to be a simple replicate of the sociocultural order. The same simplification appeared in robust sociological theories which emphasized the dominance of the social order in the production of social life. The problem for such theories is that they could not account for variations in individual conduct in what appeared to be the same socially structured situation.

We formulated the concept of cultural scenarios somewhat later than the intrapsychic and the interpersonal levels of scripting, though this idea was implicit in *Sexual Conduct*. "Cultural scenarios" was the name we gave to the instructional semiotic system that is the intersubjective space of the sociocultural. All social institutions have instructions of how to behave built into them, and these instructions are not internal properties of individuals, they are the property of the organized collection of individuals who were enacting that institution or situation. In between these two levels was the interpersonal, social conduct in the presence of other individuals. I think that *Sexual Conduct* was good on dyads—perhaps guided by the dyadic nature of much of sexuality—but less good on complex social situations or complex sequences of events. This is what Ed Laumann was good at: understanding the contribution of audiences to ongoing social action. My work with Laumann made me more sensitive to the role of "stakeholders"—both individual and institutional—in what appear to be purely interpersonal interactions.

Finally, to preserve the independently acting individual—this has some connection to Meade's "I"—we needed intrapsychic scripting, a socially based form of mental life. What went on in people's heads was critically important since it embodied planning, remembering, fantasy. I actually think at the time we wrote *Sexual Conduct*, Bill was better at theorizing about mental life than I was—better at thinking about the intrapsychic.

Schmidt: More interested, I think. Is that the connection to Stoller?

Gagnon: That's the connection to Stoller. It is also the connection to poetry.

Schmidt: To poetry?

Gagnon: Yes, he had read a lot of poetry, and in our discussion of the intrapsychic he was always arguing that thought processes are not always linear, but there are always masses of unrelated associations. So creating the poem, particularly the modern poem, means disrupting conventional prose/speech, calling on private images and experiences. Essentially, everyday thought is noisy, messy, chaotic. I think it was this conception of the symbolic that brought him back to Freud.

And from my point of view, it is abnormal to think scientifically. Most thought processes, as you go through the world, are impressions and fragments and pieces. You have to create an environment in which linear and highly coherent thought can go forward: you find a quiet room, you close the doors, you turn on the computer, you look at the screen, you type, you pretend like there is nothing else going on in the world or in your head. But that describes a specialized environment for a very specialized form of thinking.

Schmidt: Is the differentiation of cultural scripts, interpersonal scripts, and intrapsychic scripts still reasonable for you?

Gagnon: It remains an analytic device for me. In my new thinking, the critical tension in the individual is managing the relationship between the public and the private. The private is the domain of the intrapsychic. Both cultural scenarios and interpersonal scripts are enacted in the public domain. It's not that the intrapsychic does not depend on these other two domains. It's that you can manipulate mental life more freely than you can manipulate either other people or the culture at large.

Schmidt: It gives way to more variance?

Gagnon: That's right. You can allow fantasy to flourish. And the flourishing of fantasy is not only sexual. Political and social fantasies abound. For instance, in order to make a better world we must first fantasize, "How can we make this a better world?" Marxist communalism was first of all a fantasy in a burgeoning capitalist world about how to create a post-capitalist world. Certain social orders create a need for this more complicated mental world. And as modern social orders get more complicated, there is actually an increase in the density and significance of intrapsychic life. As concrete situations get more various, psychic life has to get even more various. Dealing with a concrete social situation requires a concomitant mental effort. And as we come in contact with an increasingly sexually complex world, we have to bring more mental resources to bear to understand that the person you are going to deal with is not only a man, but a man of a certain culture and history and biography. We can deal with that by narrowing and simplifying the other to their body or their organs. However, if we want to have a shared social relationship, we have to take account of the variousness of this sexual situation from all the other sexual situations we have been in. And that requires a great deal of mental agility in private matters.

Schmidt: Is that what other sociologists call "reflexivity"?

Gagnon: I think so: it's a version of reflexivity, but hopefully a more highly elaborated version than the usual version. Again, it is closer to Burke and perhaps Freud. Sometimes when social scientists talk about reflexivity, it's too automatic, too simple. It is as if reflexivity did not cost anything. Being reflexive is enormously complex because the actor has to think of many possibilities and many consequences, not only for others, but for the constitution of the self. The pressure to select, to choose one of many lines of action, increases the more you get into the public world, but at the same time the integrity of the fantasy must be maintained. This relationship between mental life and other levels of scripting is the aspect of scripting about which I have been thinking. The other part is the ways in which the cultural and interpersonal order are connected in mental life. Culture has no direct relationship to interpersonal relations. It must go through the heads of the actors. The task of the actor is to continually link and adjust and transform and stabilize the interpersonal and the cultural while maintaining the plausibility of the self. At the same time, the interpersonal and cultural worlds the actor inhabits are not passive, for other individuals and social institutions are always trying to either constrain or change the individual. The levels now become interactive. I think in our first version it was a bit more static. There was culture, the interpersonal, the intrapsychic, all sort of freestanding.

Schmidt: In *Sexual Conduct*, your first version of script theory, you don't have the cultural scripts.

Gagnon: It's largely implicit and it's actually more visible in the chapter on pornography than in other places. *Sexual Conduct* as a book is enormously uneven. It's trying out a lot of different ideas.

Schmidt: It convenes a number of essays on quite different areas.

Gagnon: Yes, I think that's a real difficulty. But, on the other hand, approaching each topic separately allowed us to try out our theoretical perspectives deductively. When we wrote about homosexuality among men, we emphasized the concept of careers. It is in that essay where the idea of career is very visible. When we wrote about lesbianism, our concern was the relationship between gender differences and sexuality. In both of those essays, we also addressed what we called the specious problem of etiology. When we wrote about pornography, we were interested in how culture offered people sexual stories which they then bring into their own lives. Pornography was also a textual testing ground for the script concept.

Schmidt: And then you were talking about childhood and adolescence, a very broad chapter in this book.

Gagnon: Yes, it's a rich chapter full of underdeveloped ideas. For instance it's where we invent the concept "homosocial." As a concept, it is now absolutely ubiquitous, and nobody knows where it came from. But it's first used there, though perhaps in a different spirit. We were looking for a word to substitute for "homosexual." At the time, when thinking of the affiliative behavior of boys in adolescence, the available language of psychoanalysis was "these are homosexual groups" or "this is a homosexual period." We invented the word "homosocial" exactly to get rid of the idea of the casual centrality of sexuality; first the social, we argued, then the sexual, second.

Schmidt: It could include sexual acts, too?

Gagnon: Yes, but it subordinated the sexual acts to social processes. These are groups of boys in whose social practices the sexual is embedded, but it is performed for other social purposes. It doesn't give priority to the sexual. The sex is interesting to the boys, but not nearly as important as the approval of other young men. And once again this was the concrete version of the Burkean notion, that you do sexual things for other social purposes.

Schmidt: Let's come back to the intrapsychic scripts. Was Stoller a specialist in this?

Gagnon: I don't want to psychoanalyze Stoller. But I think that his situation was different, the kinds of people he saw were different. He sought out more dramatic instances of sexuality to analyze.

Schmidt: And around you?

Gagnon: We were working primarily in the world of the mundane, and Stoller remained, as a psychoanalyst must, in the world of the drama, of powerful emotions, of events filled with affective intensity. If there was a weakness in Stoller, it was his belief in the intensity of the sexual. He still believed that the sexual was powerful.

Schmidt: But only because it took over emotions and energy from nonsexual sources.

Gagnon: Right. But essentially it was still powerful. It was still a drama. And for Bill and I, at that time, we saw the sexual at a much lower level of emotional intensity. The script for us was not *Faust*. And I think that Stoller and psychoanalysis in general invites dramatic stories, important stories. We were interested in ordinary people and everyday tasks: How did people get home from work, have dinner, turn on the television, watch the television, have sex together, then go to sleep? And in a way we were the voice of the common man and woman, which is what sociology pretends to be. It's the story of everyday life. We were in fact the enemies of the traditions that stressed the power of the sexual for purposes of social change or appealing to sexuality as a source of personal or political redemption, or as the primary terrain of social meaning. We said that sexuality was routine, and that it was produced by routine social causes.

Schmidt: Quite unromantic!

Gagnon: Quite unromantic. But I think both Bill and I are romantics as individuals! But being in this crazy discipline of the everyday and of the unremarkable and the nonmiraculous, we worked against our own personal interests. For many people, sex remains the only place where there are miracles. Sex and love remain the world of the miracle. You cross a crowded room, you fall in love, you change your life—something transformative happens. And what we were saying was, the feeling of transformation is socially orchestrated: you feel transformed, but you are enacting the script of transformation. My work with Laumann went somewhat further: The argument is, of course you can fall in love across a crowded room. The question to ask is, how did the two of you get into the same crowded room? And the answer is, everyone in the room has the appropriate social characteristics to be in the same crowded room. The emotions are real, but arranged by social structure and enacted through sexual scripts.

Schmidt: Coming back to the cultural scripts, do you think that Foucault is some expert on cultural scripts? Are discourses cultural script?

Gagnon: I have lots of ambivalence about Foucault. I think he was a poor historian, but I also think that he asked more general questions than we did. He tried to grasp other, perhaps larger issues. And I think he is wrong in a number of ways. For instance, I think that the impulse to reduce things to texts—discourses—is an error. Because what social life is really about is performances. It's really people performing in social spaces. Scripts are closer to the performative than is discourse. I think what Foucault does is too texty—it's too parochially French, within its interest in discourse and the power of discourse.

Schmidt: You said ambivalence, so there must be something that you could take from Foucault?

Gagnon: I am not sure. In many cases I don't understand his arguments and I don't know where they take me intellectually—what these ideas do for my thinking. If we interpret what he says as meaning that people have power over other people and they use discourses to do so, well, I would suggest a reading of Marx. Often I think much of Foucault is not very new except to folks who are not well-read in history and the other social sciences. Other people have made his arguments better, or at least more clearly and less infused with the local intellectual circumstances of Paris in the 1970s. Foucault is sort of an intellectual figure who I worry about and push against largely because of his importance to others, but I don't think I actually have ever really been engaged by him.

Schmidt: Looking at American social constructionists, be they feminist or gay theoreticians, they much more refer to Foucault, as I see, than to Simon and Gagnon. Is that embarrassing for you, disappointing?

Gagnon: Well, disappointing. I think we were there first. And at least some people think that we said it better. Most of the non-social-science people who do gay and lesbian studies and cultural studies have not read very much in the relevant social sciences. What they have read is their business, but, for instance, they don't know anything about the American pragmatist tradition. They don't realize that the notion that the meaning is in the response, which is at the core of Derrida, was said by George Herbert Mead and Kenneth Burke decades ago. Only Richard Rorty seems to have recognized the common roots of these ideas in Hegel. It's the usual American provincialism: that if they say it in France, it must be so. There is a deference to French intellectual life by Americans that in fact I don't think it always deserves. Being knowledgeable about France and French ideas is a way American intellectuals separate themselves from the common herd.

Schmidt: You say it as a person who really loves France.

Gagnon: Oh, yes, absolutely. I think the French probably more than anybody else in the Western world are resisting being Americanized. They value their language; they think that speaking French is better than speaking English. It is admirable—a way to avoid being Coca Cola-ed to death. But at the same time French intellectuals don't read anybody else either. And they don't read anybody who writes in Lyon either. If you don't write from inside Paris, you aren't anybody. The deference which contemporary Americans show to French intellectuals is similar to the deference Americans showed to European culture in general at the end of the nineteenth century. Members of a colonial society showing deference to its intellectual superiors. If you say "Foucault," you don't have to make any more arguments.

Schmidt: Your rejection of the naturalism in the Freudian and Kinseyan sense offered quite new perspective on social change in sexuality.

Gagnon: Well, I think what we were trying to do is actually in the last line of the book.

Schmidt: We have to cite it.

Gagnon: [*reads*] "The critical posture to maintain is that the future will not be better or worse, only different." This sentence was our attempt to say that the future of sexuality was not a matter of "progress" or moral improvement or utopia or dystopia. We are always involved in the human struggle to make the future, but the future that is being created is just going to be different than the present, not better or worse. This phrase also signaled our belief in the historical/cultural constitution of mental life, which we alluded to in the beginning of the book. When the future comes, who and what we are now will be lost. Each generation is always the dinosaurs to the future. We have lost the nineteenth century; the twenty-first century will lose us. The past is always the worlds we have lost.

Schmidt: In contrast to some Freudians—for example, Wilhelm Reich or Herbert Marcuse—or in contrast to Kinsey, you then cannot have a positive utopia of sexual change.

Gagnon: Yes, that's the root theme that ran through all of this work: the antiutopian, the antidramatic, the antimagical, the antiromantic.

Schmidt: De-dramatizing sexuality?

Gagnon: That's right. I think perhaps that was really the key idea. The fact that there was no magic in the world. We were really searching for disenchantment. The world is no longer enchanted, and it cannot be enchanted again. And the search for enchantment in sexuality must end in failure.

Schmidt: This means, too, that you have no sympathy for the cultural pessimistic attitude many social philosophers present?

Gagnon: The notion that culture is declining or so? No, it's just going to be different. If you asked me how I would like the world to be, I could only repeat to you the standard democratic platitudes: equality, democracy, justice. I would repeat all those catchphrases, like everybody would. What else would you say?

But the world is not going to be like that.

Schmidt: What should it be sexually?

Gagnon: I think the only way that you can make the world sexually the way you want it to be is to have ambition for your ideals, as the psychoanalyst Heinz Kohut put it. This is what Marx was: he was ambitious for his ideals. I don't see anyone, or any movement, which has new ambitions for sexuality. And particularly given the posture I took, how can you have ambitions for the mundane? It doesn't go together, to be ambitious for the commonplace. The desire to make orgasm better, to help men to have more erections, that is like improving cooking. You have to construct something interesting out of the sexual. That something has to be richer than the behavioral; sexuality has to be transformed. But then, into what? Into better communication, into Habermas's just communication?

Schmidt: Sociological research shows that many people are looking for authentic emotions, passion, exciting thrills coming from sexuality. So they are ambitious.

Gagnon: Well, I think that in the everyday world the belief in the romantic is still very powerful. And I think it's not just the sexual, I think it's about love. I think we underestimate the importance of the intensity of love. People are looking for intensity, spontaneity. Our argument was that spontaneity is scripted. We had already undermined ourselves. It wasn't that life was not variable; it was only scripted variously. Spontaneity is always bounded, even in fantasy. You are always enacting a script, even when you are playing with it; trying to make it anew, you are making up a system of scripted action. And in a way there is only the social. It's actually a much darker vision than the notion of decline, because the notion is that at one time sexuality was something important and now there is decline, and our argument was, there never was anything wonderful. And it's not going to get better or worse. We simply say: In 1940 they did it that way; in the year 2040 they're going to do it this other way. That's what the creature does. It's a cultural animal. A gloomy perspective, I must say.

Schmidt: In what respect gloomy?

Gagnon: Because there was never anything special. Or if there was something special, it was only because we as cultural/historical creatures made it special in the ways the culture dictated. So many social theories begin with the notion that from out of nowhere we will eventually be blessed. Perhaps this is the source of the current alien craze. Or that there is some larger purpose to human life. I think that our book is a celebration of purposelessness. That the only purpose to sexuality is the one we create in a given time and place. God, evolution, the state, patriotism, progress, communism, capitalism—those are all collectivist notions which we have imposed on ourselves to avoid purposelessness.

Schmidt: You have made a lot of predictions in your book, or speculations about the future. Please imagine for a minute that you are a sleeping beauty, falling asleep in 1973, and awake being kissed by a princess or a prince in these days. What would you be astonished about and what would you be not astonished about, seeing today's sexual landscapes?

Gagnon: Starting now, I think I would have been struck by the transformation of gay and lesbian life and feminism in the West. The intellectual bravura of the gay and lesbian movements and feminism is deeply surprising, if you start in 1973. In *Sexual Conduct* we had a sentence that said, "The homosexual community . . . serves simply as a sexual marketplace." And I don't think that anyone can now make the claim today. The gay world is an immensely rich and complicated social world—a community created and creating an identity. It is a fascinating set of options. And the amount of original thought which is going on—it is really a very rich intellectual world. I am not sure I agree with all of it, but it's clearly an interesting place.

We probably overestimated the sexual originality of American culture at the behavioral level. I don't think that I would have been surprised by the amount of pornography. The erotic landscape seemed to me already on its way to current development in 1973.

Schmidt: What about the heterosexuals?

Gagnon: I don't think they changed very much; that's really been kind of remarkably stable. What does happen actually? Well, they have intercourse a little bit sooner. They have a few more partners.

Schmidt: Not only sex partners but love partners.

Gagnon: Love partners. Basically serial monogamy now begins at fifteen or sixteen and proceeds through life.

Schmidt: That's a difference. If you look at their grandparents . . .

Gagnon: That is a difference. But, in a sense, even if it is not the same couple over the life course, but many couples, the Durkheimian effects may remain the same. The opposite-gender couple remains the primary way of organizing emotional and psychic life, children, houses, cars, ownership. Actually, maybe the triumph of capitalism is its capacity to maintain at the individual level large numbers of satisfied consuming and reproducing couples. I think what's most interesting is the remarkable disconnection between the cultural erotic life of the society—the amount of erotica—and the absolute conventionality of the people.

Schmidt: A discrepancy between . . .

Gagnon: . . . this level of the production of erotic cultural scenarios and this level of what people in fact do.

Schmidt: Do you have an explanation for it?

Gagnon: I do, but it will sound a little crazy.

Schmidt: That sounds interesting!

Gagnon: I think there are really two arenas of sexual action which don't have anything to do with each other most of the time. There is the domain of the symbolic and the domain of the behavioral. People go to the domain of the symbolic not because it compensates for how dull things are; people in fact are perfectly happy with their dull sexual lives. It's because what the symbolic domain offers you—and now this is a much more general argument about capitalism—is a world without social friction, a world without cost. You can play, you can have contact with beautiful bodies, you can look at lovely things without investment. That's the difference between owning an automobile and looking at an advertisement for an automobile.

Schmidt: Different worlds, but both are important.

Gagnon: But they are independent in many ways. They come together every once in a while when there are in moments of cultural crises. You may have people saying, "My fantasies are not the same as my behavior." But otherwise people do not compare the world of fantasy and the world of what they do everyday and neither has a natural priority. The most important thing is that it is very pleasant.

We have to move outside the sexual and we can see it everywhere: fantasy consumption, fantasy celebrity. If you want to know that you are watching a movie and you are not sure—you think you may be hallucinating, but you won't know—you know it's a movie when the car pulls up to park in New York City and there is no other car parked on the block. Well, fantasy copulation has the same quality. You don't have to pull next to other cars, look and see how big the parking space is, block traffic and listen to the horns blowing, go through all the maneuvers of parking—there is always a space available in fantasy.

Why are you satisfied emotionally from an advertisement in which a beautiful person drives a fancy car up in front of a fancy building and stops—an advertisement that calls the BMW the ultimate driving machine? In reality, everyone in New York knows that the ultimate driving machine will only go fifteen miles an hour in city traffic, if they are lucky. It's the psychic independence that exists between real-world driving and the fantasy of driving. One does not criticize the other. Similarly there is real-world sexuality and the fantasy of sexuality. And they are simply separate. Fantasy is a world without friction. No one denies you, and you can turn it off. I think that's how people live in the postmodern world.

Schmidt: In what respect?

Gagnon: There is an increase in the importance of intrapsychic life which is absolutely crucial. To survive the modern world requires more mental activity rather than less.

Schmidt: Are you going to reprint *Sexual Conduct*?

Gagnon: We have made an agreement with the original publisher. The new version, we think at this moment, will have an introduction about the origins of the key ideas, the circumstances of invention. What were the biographical, cultural, historical circumstances of writing the book, including the fact it was written during the sixties. It was written during a period of crisis, by two people who had a tangential relationship to that crisis. At the end of each chapter, we will put a few comments, trying to not destroy the original structure. And then at the end there will be a discussion of where the central ideas of the book have gone. We will leave the original text the same, only making it nonsexist in its language.

Schmidt: It is sexist?

Gagnon: Yes, it was the 1960s, so we were not yet aware of gender-neutral language.

Schmidt: More than twenty-five years ago, I met you and Bill Simon in a New York Hotel. And by chatting around you said, "We have just one problem: to know who is Marx and who is Engels." Did you decide upon this question?

Gagnon: [*laughs*] A revolutionary remark!

Schmidt: I was deeply impressed!

Gagnon: I think that I had the wrong people in mind. The better choice would have been "Who is Freud and who is Durkheim?"

Schmidt: Thank you very much, John, for this talk.

Notes

The title of this postscript comes from Kenneth Burke, who describes an individual's experience of intellectual life in the following fashion:

> Where does the drama get its materials? From the "unending conversation" that is going on at the point in history when we are born. Imagine that you enter a parlor. You come late. When you arrive, others have long preceded you, and they are engaged in a heated discussion, a discussion too heated for them to pause and tell you exactly what it is about. In fact, the discussion had already begun long before any of them got there, so that no one present is qualified to retrace for you all the steps

that had gone before. You listen for a while, until you decide that you have caught the tenor of the argument; then you put in your oar. Someone answers; you answer him; another comes to your defense; another aligns himself against you, to either the embarrassment or gratification of your opponent, depending upon the quality of your ally's assistance. However, the discussion is interminable. The hour grows late, you must depart. And you do depart, with the discussion still vigorously in progress. (*Philosophy of Literary Form* (1957), 110–11)

Burke does not discuss power here, though he understands that getting (as opposed to putting) one's oar "in" is always a matter of that. His foci are the social conversation in which one is only a temporary participant and a reflection on individual mortality.

John H. Gagnon

Selected Publications

Books and Pamphlets

2004 *An interpretation of desire: Essays in the study of sexuality.* Chicago: University of Chicago Press.

1997 (editor) With Martin P. Levine and Peter M. Nardi. *In changing times: gay men and lesbians encounter AIDS/HIV.* Chicago: University of Chicago Press.

1995 (editor) With Richard G. Parker. *Conceiving sexuality: Approaches to sex research in a postmodern world.* New York: Routledge.

1994 With Edward O. Laumann, Robert T. Michael, and Stuart Michaels. *The social organization of sexuality: Sexual practices in the United States.* Chicago: University of Chicago Press. Gordon J. Laing Award, 1995 (presented to University of Chicago faculty authors of books that add the greatest distinction to the list of the Press).

1994 With Robert T. Michael, Edward O. Laumann, and Gina Kolata. *Sex in America: A definitive survey.* New York: Little Brown.

1978 With Cathy Stein Greenblat. *Life designs: Individuals, marriages, and families.* Glenview: Scott Foresman.

1977 *Sexuality in today's world: A reader.* Boston: Little Brown.

1977 *Human sexualities.* Glenview, IL: Scott Foresman.

1976 With Cathy Stein Greenblat. *Blood money: A gaming simulation.* DHEW Publication No. (NIH) 76-1082. Washington, DC: National Heart and Lung Institute.

1975 With Bruce Henderson. *Human sexuality: An age of ambiguity.* Boston: Educational Associates and Time, Inc.

1973 (editor) With William Simon. *Sexual conduct: The social sources of human sexuality.* Chicago: Aldine Books. Second edition, 2005.

1973 (editor) With William Simon. *The sexual scene* (Second Edition). Trans-Action Society Books, Number 5. New York: E. P. Dutton. First edition, 1970.

1967 (editor) *Sexual deviance: A reader.* Introduction written with William Simon. New York: Harper and Row.

1965 With Paul H. Gebhard, Cornelia V. Christenson, and Wardell B. Pomeroy. *Sex offenders: An analysis of types.* New York: Harper and Row.

1957 With Joseph D. Lohman. *Crime and community* [a syllabus for Sociology 176, University of Chicago]. Chicago: University of Chicago Press.

1956 With Joseph D. Lohman, Hans W. Mattick, Hyman Frankel, and Richard Boone. *Juvenile delinquency.* Cook County, Illinois: Office of the Sheriff.

Articles and Chapters

1999 Les usages explicites and implicites de la perspective des scripts dans les recherches sur la sexualité. With a commentary by Michel Bozon and Alain Giami. *Actes de la Recherche en sciences sociales* 128 (Juin): 73–79.

1999 Virtuous actions in the absence of a compelling dogma: Reproductive health in a socially constructed world. In *Reflexiones: Sexualidad, Salud y Reproduccion* 2, no. 12 (September): 9–11.

1999 Who was that girl? In *The obscure subject of desire: Freud's female homosexual revisited,* ed. Erica Schoenberg and Ronnie Lesser, 76–86. New York: Routledge.

1999 Sexual conduct: As today's memory serves. In *Sexualities* 2, No. 1 (February): 115–26.

1998 Totem in the land of taboo. *Sexualities* 1, no. 1: 91–94.

1998 Sexual conduct revisited. Interview by Gunter Schmidt. *Zeitschift für Sexualforschung* 11:353–66. [In German.]

1997 Others having sex with others: Captain Cook and the penetration of the Pacific. In *sexual cultures, migration and AIDS: Anthropological and demographic perspectives,* ed. Gilbert Herdt, 23–38. New York: Oxford University Press.

1997 Introduction. In *Encounters with AIDS.*

1996 Interventions inside of interventions. [Solicited comment on Douglas Heckathorn and Robert Broadhead, "Rational choice, public policy and AIDS."] *Rationality and Society* 8, no. 4 (November): 503–8.

1995 With D. Binson, S. Michaels, R. Stall, T. J. Coates, and J. A. Catania. Prevalence and social distribution of men who have sex with men: United States and its urban centers. *Journal of Sex Research,* 32, no. 3: 245–54. Hugo Biegel Award for best article published in the journal in 1995.

1994 Having sex with both women and men: Ideologies and practices. In *Bisexualitan. Ideologie und Praxis des Sexualkontaktes zu beiden Geschlechtern,* ed. Erwin J. Haeberle and Rolf Gindorf. Stuttgart: Gustav Fischer. [In German.]

1994 Conceiving sexuality. In *Conceiving Sexuality.*

1994 With Edward Laumann. A sociological perspective on sexual action. In *Conceiving Sexuality.*

1994 With Heather Miller and Joseph A. Catania. The prevalence of informal care-giving to persons with AIDS in the United States: Caregiver characteristics and their implications. *Social Science and Medicine* 38, no. 11: 1543–52.

1994 With Edward O. Laumann and Robert T. Michael. A political history of the adult sex survey. *Family Planning Perspectives* 26, no. 1 (January/February): 34–38.

1993 With M. Margaret Dolcini, Joseph A. Catania, Thomas J. Coates, Ron Stall, Esther S. Hudes, John H. Gagnon, and Lance M. Pollack. Demographic characteristics of heterosexuals with multiple partners: The national AIDS behavioral surveys. *Family Planning Perspectives.* 25, no. 5 (September/October).

1993 With Edward Laumann, Stuart Michaels, Robert Michael, and L. Philip Schum. Monitoring the AIDS epidemic using a network approach. *Journal of Health and Social Behavior* 44, no. 1 (March): 7–32.

1993 With Albert Jonson, James Trussell, and Shirley Lindenbaum. Introduction and summary. In *The social impact of AIDS*, ed. Albert Jonson and Jeffrey Stryker, 1–22. Washington, DC: National Academy Press.

1993 With Shirley Lindenbaum, Albert Jonson, Jeff Stryker, and James Trussell. The HIV/AIDS epidemic in New York City. In *The social impact of AIDS*, 243–304.

1992 With Joseph A. Catania, Thomas J. Coates, Ron Stall, Heather Turner, John Peterson, Norman Hearst, M. Margaret Dolcini, Estie Hudes, James Wiley, and Robert Groves. The prevalence of AIDS-related risk factors and condom use in the United States. *Science* 258 (November 13): 1101–6.

1992 The self, its voices and their discord. In *The sociology of subjectivity*, ed. Carolyn Ellis and Dennis Flaherty, 221–43. Newbury Park, CA: Sage.

1992 Epidemics and researchers: AIDS and the practice of social studies. In *Social analysis in the time of AIDS,* ed. Gilbert Herdt and Shirley Lindenbaum, 27–40. Newbury Park, CA: Sage.

1991 Comments on Virginia Goldner: Radical approaches to gender. In *Psychoanalytic dialogues* 1, no. 3: 273–76.

1991 Sex and science. *Entre Nous: The European Family Planning Magazine* no. 18 (August): 7.

1991 The implicit and explicit use of scripts in sex research. *Annual Review of Sex Research* 1.

1990 An unlikely story. In *Authors of their own lives: Intellectual autobiographies of twenty American sociologists,* ed. Bennett Berger, 213–34. Berkeley: University of California Press. Reprinted in *An Interpretation of Desire.*

1990 Gender preference in erotic relations, the Kinsey scale and sexual scripts. In *Heterosexuality, homosexuality and the Kinsey scale*, ed. David McWhirter, Stephanie Sanders, and June Reinisch, 177–207. New York: Oxford University Press.

1989 With E. O. Laumann and R. T. Michael. Life course and network considerations in the design of the health and sexual behavior survey. In *Proceedings of the Fifth Annual Conference on Health Survey Research Methods,* ed. Floyd J. Fowler, 227–34. DHHS Publication No. (PHS) 89–3447. Washington, DC: Department of Health and Human Services, National Heart & Lung Institute.

1989 Disease and desire. *Daedalus* 118, no. 3 (Summer): 47–77.

1989 With Edward O. Laumann, Stuart Michaels, Robert T. Michael, and James S. Coleman. Monitoring the AIDS epidemic in the United States: A network approach. *Science* 244 (June 9): 1186–89.

1989 Sex research and sexual conduct in the era of AIDS. *Journal of Acquired Immunodeficiency Syndromes* 1:593–601.

1989 With Cathy Stein Greenblat, Susan Katz, and Diana Shannon. An innovative program of counseling family and friends of hemophiliacs about HIV and AIDS. *AIDS Care* 1, no. 1 (March): 67–75.

1989 With Robert E. Fay, Charles F. Turner, and Alfred D. Klassen. Prevalence and patterns of same gender sexual contact among men. *Science* 243 (January 20): 338–48.

1989 Sexual conduct and the life course. In *AIDS, sexual behavior and IV drug use,* ed. Charles F. Turner et al., 500–33. Washington, DC: National Academy Press.

1989 Understanding human sexual behavior. In *AIDS, sexual behavior and IV drug use,* 73–185.

1988 With Robert T. Michael, Edward O. Laumann, and T. W. Smith. Number of sex partners and potential risk of sexual exposure to human immunodeficiency virus. *Centers for Disease Control and Prevention Morbidity and Mortality Weekly Report* 37, no. 37 (September 23): 565–67.

1987 Dr. Mary Birschstein: The mother of Soviet simulation gaming. *Simulation and Games* 18, no. 1 (March): 3–12.

1987 With Joan Atwood. Masturbatory behavior in college youth. *Journal of Sex Education and Therapy* 7:35–42.

1987 With William Simon. Sexual theory: A sexual scripts approach. In *Theories and Paradigms of Human Sexuality*, ed. James H. Geer and William T. O'Donohue, 363–83. New York: Plenum Press.

1987 With William Simon. Sexual scripts: Permanence and change. *Archives of Sexual Behavior* 15, no. 2: 97–120.

1987 With William Simon. The scripting of oral genital sexual conduct. *Archives of Sexual Behavior* 16, no.1: 1–25.

1987 Science and the politics of pathology. *Journal of Sex Research* 23, no.1 (February): 120–23.

1985 Attitudes and responses of parents to pre-adolescent "nasturbation." *Archives of Sexual Behavior* 14, no. 5: 451–66.

1984 With William Simon. Sexual scripts. *Society* 22, no.1 (November/December): 53–60.

1984 Notes toward the understanding of the transformation of sexual conduct. *Concilium, Sociology of Religion: The Sexual Revolution, Sexuality and Society.* No. 193: 11–19.

1984 Success = Failure/Failure = Success: The co-optation of the romantic program in the nineteenth century. In *Romanticism and culture,* ed. H. W. Matalene, 97–108. Columbia, SC: Camden House.

1983 On the sources of sexual change. In *Fostering mature sexuality and preventing sexual problems: The seventh annual Vermont symposium on the prevention of primary psychopathology,* ed. G. Albee and H. Leitenberg, 157–70. Burlington: University Press of New England.

1983 With Cathy Stein Greenblat. Temporary strangers: A sociological perspective on travel and tourism. *Sociological Perspective* 1, no. 1 (Spring).

1983 Sex research and social change. In *Challenges in sexual science,* ed. C. M. Davis, 32–41. Philadelphia: Society for the Scientific Study of Sex.

1983 Age at menarche and sexual conduct in adolescence and young adulthood. In *Menarche,* ed. Sharon Golub, 175–86. Lexington, MA: D. C. Heath.

1982 With Raymond C. Rosen and Sandra Leiblum. Cognitive and social aspects of sexual dysfunction: Sexual scripts in sex therapy. *Journal of Sex and Marital Therapy* 8, no. 1 (Summer): 44–56.

1982 With Elizabeth J. Roberts. Men versus fathers: Images and ideals. In *Television and Children* 5, no. 2 (Spring): 9–15.

1981 Selections from the gay male and lesbian bookshelf: Essay review of ten volumes on homosexuality. *American Journal of Orthopsychiatry* 51, no. 3 (July): 560–68.

1980 With Elizabeth J. Roberts. Parents' messages to pre-adolescent children about sexuality. In *Childhood and sexuality: Proceedings of the international symposium,* ed. J. M. Samson, 276–86. Montreal: Editions Etudes Vivants.

1979 With Cathy Stein Greenblat. Further explorations on the multiple reality games. *Simulation and Games* 10, no. 1 (March): 41–56.

1979 The interaction of gender roles and sexual conduct. In *Human sexuality: A comparative and developmental approach,* ed. H. Katchadourian, 225–45. Berkeley: University of California Press.

1978 Reconsiderations. [Review of Kinsey, et al., *Sexual behavior in the human male* and (1948) and *Sexual behavior in the human female* (1953).] *Human Nature* 1, no. 10 (October): 92–95.

1977 Sexual dimorphism in erotic function: A psychosocial approach. In *Progress in sexology,* ed. R. Gemme and C. C. Wheeler, 11–19. New York: Plenum.

1977   Environment and self-control in substance abuse. In Appendix C of *Proceedings: Conference on commonalities in substance abuse and habitual behavior*, 223–35. Washinton, DC: National Research Council.

1977   With Cathy Stein Greenblat. Health care planning and education via gaming simulation. *Health Education Monographs* 5, Supplement 1: 42–57.

1976   With Cathy Stein Greenblat. Hemophilia health care planning and education: A gaming approach. In *The hemophilia games: An experiment in health care planning*, 1–6. Washington, DC: National Heart and Lung Institute, DHEW Publications (NIH) 76–977.

1976   With Gerald C. Davison. Asylums, the token economy, and the metrics of mental life. *Behavior Therapy* 7:528–34.

1976   With William Simon. The anomie of affluence: A post-Mertonian conception. *American Journal of Sociology* 82, no. 2 (September): 356–78.

1975   Sex research and social change. *Archives of Sexual Behavior* 4, no. 2 (March): 111–41.

1974   Scripts and the coordination of sexual conduct. In *1973 Nebraska symposium on motivation*, ed. James K. Cole and Richard Deinstbier, 27–59. Lincoln: University of Nebraska Press.

1973   With William Simon and Alan Berger. Youth and pornography in social context. *The Archives of Sexual Behavior* 1, no. 4: 279–308.

1973   With William Simon. Sex, youth and the future. In *Youth and contemporary society*, ed. David Gottlieb, 11–25. Beverly Hills: Sage.

1972   With William Simon and Stephen A. Buff. Son of Joe: Continuity and change among white working class adolescents. *Journal of Youth and Adolescence* 1, no.1: 13–34.

1972   The creation of the sexual in early adolescence. In *Twelve to sixteen: Early adolescence*, ed. Jerome Kagan and Robert Coles, 231–57. New York: Norton.

1972   With William Simon and Alan Berger. Beyond fantasy and anxiety: The coital experiences of college youth. *Journal of Youth and Adolescence* 1, no. 3: 203–22.

1971   Physical strength, once of significance. *Impact of Science on Society* 21, no. 1: 31–42.

1971   Ambition in the two cultures. *Quarterly Review of Biology* 46, no. 1 (March): 58–65.

1970   Some aspects of sexual adjustment in early and later adolescence. In *Psychopathology of adolescence*, ed. Joseph Zubin and Alfred M. Freedman, 275–95. New York: Grune and Stratton.

1970   With William Simon. Perspectives on the sexual scene. In *The sexual scene*, 1–21.

1969   The uses of failure. *Change* 1, no. 3 (May/June): 27–31.

1969   Prospects for change in American sexual patterns. In *VD: The Challenge to Man*, Social Health Papers, No. 4. New York: The American Social Health Association, January.

1969   With William Simon. On psychosexual development. In *Handbook of socialization theory and research*, ed. David A. Goslin, 733–52. New York: Rand McNally. Reprinted in *Transaction* 6, no. 5 (March).

1969   With William Simon and Donald Carns. Working class youth, alienation without image. *New Generation* 51, no. 2 (Spring): 15–21.

1969   With William Simon. Sex education and human development. In *Human sexual function and dysfunction*, ed. Paul J. Fink, 113–26. Philadelphia: F. A. Davis.

1968   With Arnold Abrams and Joseph J. Levin. Psychosocial aspects of addiction. *American Journal of Public Health* 58, no. 11 (November): 214–55.

1968   With William Simon. The social meaning of prison homosexuality. *Federal Probation* 32 (March): 23–29.

1968   Prostitution. In *The International Encyclopedia of the Social Sciences*, 12:592–98. New York: Crowell-Collier.

1968   Sexual deviation: social aspects. *The International Encyclopedia of the Social Sciences*, 14:209–15.

1968 With William Simon. Sexual deviance and the contemporary American scene. *Annals of the American Academy of Political and Social Science* 375 (March): 106–22.

1967 With William Simon. Femininity in the lesbian community. *Social Problems* 152, no. 2 (Fall): 212–21.

1967 With William Simon. Homosexuality: The formulation of a sociological perspective. *Journal of Health and Social Behavior* 8, no. 3 (September): 177–85.

1967 The sociological perspective on homosexuality. *Dublin Review,* No. 512 (Summer): 96–114.

1967 Beyond Freud. *Partisan Review* 34, no. 3 (Summer): 400–14.

1967 With William Simon. The lesbians: A preliminary overview. In *Sexual Deviance: A Reader,* 247–82.

1967 With William Simon. Pornography: Raging menace or paper tiger? *Trans-action* 4, no. 8 (July/August): 41–48.

1967 With William Simon. The decline and fall of the small town. *Trans-action* 4, no. 5 (April): 42–51.

1965 Female child victims of sex offenses. *Social Problems* 13, no. 2 (Fall).

1965 Sexuality and sexual learning in the child. [A revised and expanded English version of "Sessualita e apprentimento sessuale del bambino."] *Psychiatry* 28, no. 3 (August): 212–28.

1965 With Cornelia V. Christenson. Sexual behavior in a group of older women. *Journal of Gerontology* 20, no. 3 (July): 251–56.

1964 With Paul H. Gebhard. Sex offenders against very young children. *American Journal of Psychiatry* 121, no. 6 (December): 576–79.

1964 With Alfred Lindesmith. Anomie and drug addiction. In *Anomie and deviant behavior,* ed. Marshall Clinard, 158–68. New York: Free Press of Glencoe.

1964 Sessualita e apprentimento sessuale del bambino. *Scuola e Citta* 15, no. 4 (April): 249–58.

1962 Wonder drugs, fear of venereal disease, infection, and sexual contacts. In *Proceedings of the World Forum on Syphilis and the Other Trepanomatoses* (PHS Publication 997), 424–30. Washington, DC: U. S. Government Printing Office, September 4–12.

1960 Longshoe-ology. *Key Issues: A Journal of Controversial Issues in Criminology* 1, no. 1 (November): 21–25.

Contributors

BARRY D. ADAM is University Professor of Sociology at the University of Windsor (Ontario), author of *The Survival of Domination* and *The Rise of a Gay and Lesbian Movement*, and co-author of *Experiencing HIV* and *The Global Emergence of Gay and Lesbian Politics*. He has also done extensive community-based research on gay male sexuality and HIV risk-taking.

SHARI L. DWORKIN is Assistant Professor of Behavioral Medicine in the Department of Psychiatry at Columbia University and Research Scientist at the HIV Center for Clinical and Behavioral Studies. Her areas of research are gender inequality, HIV/AIDS, and medical sociology. Dworkin's articles have appeared in the *American Journal of Public Health, Journal of Sex Research, AIDS and Behavior,* and more. She has a forthcoming book titled *Size Matters: Body Panic, Health, and Consumer Culture.* She currently serves on the editorial boards of *Social Problems* and *Gender and Society* and remains an active reviewer for several gender, sexuality, health, media, sport, and HIV/AIDS-related journals.

ANKE A. EHRHARDT has been, since 1987, Director of the HIV Center for Clinical and Behavioral Studies at the New York State Psychiatric Institute. She is also Professor of Medical Psychology in the Department of Psychiatry at Columbia University. Ehrhardt is an internationally known researcher in the field of sexual and gender development of children, adolescents, and adults. For the past 15 years, her research has included studies on sexual risk behavior among children, adolescents, heterosexual women and men, and the gay population, and on comprehensive approaches to preventing HIV and STD infection.

JEFFREY ESCOFFIER writes on sexuality, gay politics, and dance. He is the author of *American Homo: Perversity and Community, John Maynard Keynes*, and a book on the choreography of Mark Morris. His most recent book is *Sexual Revolution,* an anthology of writings from the 1960s and 1970s. He is currently working on a book about the gay porn industry.

STEVEN EPSTEIN is Associate Professor of Sociology at the University of California, San Diego. He teaches classes on the sociology of science, medicine, sexuality, and social movements, and much of his research has focused on the politics of biomedical research. His book *Impure Science: AIDS, Activism, and the Politics of Knowledge* received three awards from professional societies.

GILBERT HERDT, an anthropologist, is Professor and Director of Human Sexuality Studies at San Francisco State University. Recently, he was appointed director of the new National Sexuality Resource Center in San Francisco. The author and editor of 30 books and some 100 scientific papers, Herdt is the recipient of a Fulbright Scholarship, an NIMH Fellowship, and a Guggenheim Fellowship. He has most recently written *Secrecy and Cultural Reality*.

STEVI JACKSON is Professor of Women's Studies and Director of the Centre for Women's Studies at the University of York (UK). She is the author of *Childhood and Sexuality*, *Christine Delphy*, and *Heterosexuality in Question*. She has co-edited *Contemporary Feminist Theories*, *Feminism and Sexuality*, and *Gender: A Sociological Reader*. She has also published numerous articles on family and gender relations and on sexuality.

MICHAEL KIMMEL is Professor of Sociology at SUNY–Stony Brook. His books include *Changing Men*; *Men Confront Pornography*; *Men's Lives*; *Against the Tide: Profeminist Men in the United States, 1776–1990*; *The Politics of Manhood*; *Manhood: A Cultural History*; and *The Gendered Society*. He co-edited *The Encyclopedia on Men and Masculinities* and *Handbook of Studies on Men and Masculinities*. He is the founder and editor of *Men and Masculinities* (the field's premier scholarly journal) and a book series on gender and sexuality, and edited the Sage Series on Men and Masculinities. He is the spokesperson for the National Organization for Men Against Sexism (NOMAS) and lectures extensively to corporations and on campuses in the United States and abroad.

EDWARD O. LAUMANN is the George Herbert Mead Distinguished Service Professor of Sociology at the University of Chicago. Since joining the University in 1973, Laumann has acted as the editor of the *American Journal of Sociology*, chair of the Department of Sociology, dean of the Division of Social Sciences, and provost. He is currently the director of the Ogburn Stouffer Center for Population and Social Organization. Laumann's many research interests include research on human sexuality among older Americans, sexuality in urban places, the spread of sexually transmitted infections via sexual networks, subjective well-being, quality of life and health status, social networks in various social contexts, and the urban legal profession.

JENNA MAHAY is Assistant Professor of Sociology at Concordia University, Chicago. Mahay received her PhD in Sociology from the University of Chicago, where she worked extensively with the Chicago Health and Social Life Survey and the National Health and Social Life Survey. Mahay was a co-editor of *The Sexual Organization of the City* and has published research on sexual scripts in *Sex, Love, and Health in America* and the *Handbook of Women's Sexual and Reproductive Health*. Mahay's current research interests include marriage and family, human sexuality, and aging.

RITA M. MELENDEZ is Research Associate at the Center for Research in Gender and [297]
Sexuality and an Assistant Professor in Human Sexuality Studies at San Francisco State
University. She received her PhD in Sociology from Yale University and earned a Master's Degree in Biostatistics from the Mailman School of Public Health at Columbia University. Melendez was a postdoctoral research fellow at the HIV Center for Clinical and
Behavioral Studies at Columbia University, where she combined quantitative and qualitative methods in researching HIV issues. She has published in numerous journals on
issues relating to gay men, gender, and domestic violence in relation to HIV.

PETER M. NARDI is Professor of Sociology at Pitzer College. He is the author of *Doing
Survey Research: A Guide to Quantitative*; *Interpreting Data: A Guide to Understanding
Research* and *Gay Men's Friendships: Invincible Communities*. He has edited or co-edited
five other books and published over thirty articles in journals and books. He is a past
president of the Pacific Sociological Association (the largest regional sociology group in
the country) and former editor of the journal *Sociological Perspectives*.

LUCIA F. O'SULLIVAN is Associate Professor in the Department of Psychology at the
University of New Brunswick and Canada Research Chair in Adolescents' Sexual Health
Behavior. Her research addresses affective and cognitive components of sexual risk decision-making as well as communication in heterosexual interactions of young adults and
adolescents. She also has worked extensively on developing health-related studies relevant to impoverished communities, including a study of reproductive health care among
adolescents in the Bronx, the impact of gender on sexual risk among young South Afri-
cans, and the implementation of an HIV partner notification program in Guatemala.

REBECCA F. PLANTE is Assistant Professor of Sociology at Ithaca College. Plante has
written *Sexualities in Context: A Social Perspective* and co-edited (with Michael Kimmel)
Sexualities: Identities, Behaviors, and Society. Her primary interests include gender and
sexualities, with special interests in masculinities, pop culture, the body, and the sexual
self. With extensive training and certification as a sexuality educator and HIV/AIDS
evaluator, Plante has worked in diverse communities, educating adolescents, teens, and
adults. *Latex & Vinyl*, a radio call-in show about sex, featured Plante (as "Dr. Victoria
Monk") answering questions about everything from best sexual positions to having better orgasms.

KEN PLUMMER has been Professor of Sociology at the University of Essex and is now
partly retired. He came to Essex in 1975 and has taught, researched, and written widely
on sexuality (especially lesbian and gay studies); is interested in the development of a
humanistic method and theory (especially through narrative, life story and the postmodern turn); and has a long standing interest in the teaching of introductory sociology. He has published around 15 books and some 100 articles. His main books include
*Sexual Stigma, Telling Sexual Stories, Documents of Life 2: An Invitation to a Critical Hu-
manism*, and *Intimate Citizenship*. He also edited *The Making of the Modern Homosexual*
and *Modern Homosexualities*. His most recent articles include "Intimate citizenship in
an unjust world" (in the *Blackwell Companion to Social Inequalities*), and "Rights work:
Constructing lesbian, gay and sexual rights in modern times" (in *Rights*). He is editor of
the journal *Sexualities*.

PEPPER SCHWARTZ is Professor of Sociology at the University of Washington in Seattle. She is past president of the Society for the Scientific Study of Sexuality and president-elect of the Pacific Sociological Association. She is the winner of the Matrix Award in Education and the International Women's Forum Award in Education. She is a fellow of the International Academy of Sex Research.

DAVID WYATT SEAL is Associate Professor and Qualitative Methods Core Director at the Center for AIDS Intervention Research in the Department of Psychiatry and Behavioral Medicine at the Medical College of Wisconsin. He is a social psychologist whose primary program of research has utilized qualitative and quantitative methodologies to explore individual, interpersonal, and contextual influences on emotionally and sexually intimate communication, decision-making, negotiation, and behavior. He also has been involved in the development and implementation of HIV and STD prevention intervention research with incarcerated populations, couples, young men who have sex with men, and at-risk heterosexuals.

ARLENE STEIN teaches Sociology and Women's and Gender Studies at Rutgers University. A collection of her essays, *Shameless: Sexual Dissidence in American Culture,* was recently published. Her 2001 book *The Stranger Next Door: The Story of a Small Community's Battle Over Sex, Faith, and Civil Rights* won the Ruth Benedict Prize. Her first book, *Sex and Sensibility: Stories of a Lesbian Generation,* is a study of sexual identity practices. In 2006, she was the recipient of the Simon-Gagnon Award, given by the American Sociological Association.

LEONORE TIEFER began her career with a Berkeley PhD specializing in animal mating research, but switched to clinical, critical, and theoretical analyses of sexuality in response to feminism in the 1970s. She has written or co-edited four books and scores of papers, including *Sex is Not a Natural Act.* In 2000, Tiefer initiated the Campaign for a New View of Women's Sexual Problems (www.fsd-alert.org) to challenge the medicalization of women's sexual problems. Its success defies John Gagnon's taunt in 1998 that "the [medicalization] train has already left the station."

DAVID KNAPP WHITTIER is a Research Behavioral Scientist at the Centers for Disease Control and Prevention. He received his PhD in Sociology from the State University of New York at Stony Brook. Whittier has held postdoctoral fellowships at the Centers for Disease Control and Prevention, the HIV Center for Clinical and Behavioral Studies at Columbia University, and at the University of Houston with the Sexuality Research Fellowship Program of the Social Science Research Council. Whittier has published in numerous journals on issues relating to gay men, sexuality, and STI/HIV prevention.

YOOSIK YOUM is Assistant Professor of Sociology at Yonsei University (South Korea). He is also Research Specialist at the Institute for Health Research and Affiliated Professor of Sociology at University of Illinois at Chicago. Youm's research interests include health, sexuality, and network analysis.